The Turkishness Contract

In the series *Critical Race, Indigeneity, and Relationality*, edited by
ANTONIO T. TIONGSON JR., DANIKA MEDAK-SALTZMAN, IYKO DAY,
AND SHANTÉ PARADIGM SMALLS

ALSO IN THIS SERIES:

Ofelia Ortiz Cuevas, *Visuality of Violence: Witnessing the Policing of Race*
Pacharee Sudhinaraset, *Worlds at the End: Los Angeles, Infrastructure, and
the Apocalyptic Imagination*
Wendi Yamashita, *Carceral Entanglements: Gendered Public Memories of Japanese
American World War II Incarceration*
Joo Ok Kim, *Warring Genealogies: Race, Kinship, and the Korean War*
Maryam S. Griffin, *Vehicles of Decolonization: Public Transit in the Palestinian
West Bank*
Erin Suzuki, *Ocean Passages: Navigating Pacific Islander and Asian American Literatures*
Quynh Nhu Le, *Unsettled Solidarities: Asian and Indigenous Cross-Representations in
the Américas*

BARIŞ ÜNLÜ

Translated by John William Day

The Turkishness Contract

TEMPLE UNIVERSITY PRESS
Philadelphia • *Rome* • *Tokyo*

TEMPLE UNIVERSITY PRESS
Philadelphia, Pennsylvania 19122
tupress.temple.edu

Originally published in Turkey in the Turkish language under the title
Türklük Sözleşmesi by Dipnot Yayinlari, Ankara, Turkey.

Library of Congress Cataloging-in-Publication Data

Names: Ünlü, Barış, 1975– author. | Day, John William, translator.
Title: The Turkishness contract / Barış Ünlü ; translated by John
William Day.
Other titles: Türklük Sözleşmesi. English | Critical race, indigeneity,
and relationality.
Description: Philadelphia : Temple University Press, 2025. | Series:
Critical race, indigeneity, and relationality | Originally published in
Turkey in the Turkish language under the title Türklük Sözleşmesi by
Dipnot Yayinlari, Ankara, Turkey in 2018. | Includes bibliographical
references and index. | Summary: "This book analyzes the historical
formation, institutional operations, and embodiment (as habitus) of
Turkishness, approached as a set of certain schemas for seeing,
thinking, feeling, and acting, and certain privileges, real or
potential"— Provided by publisher.
Identifiers: LCCN 2025012697 (print) | LCCN 2025012698 (ebook) | ISBN
9781439924723 (cloth) | ISBN 9781439924730 (paperback) | ISBN
9781439924747 (pdf)
Subjects: LCSH: Social structure—Turkey. | National characteristics,
Turkish. | Turks—Ethnic identity. | Turkey—Social conditions.
Classification: LCC HN656.5.Z9 S67213 (print) | LCC HN656.5.Z9 (ebook)
LC record available at https://lccn.loc.gov/2025012697
LC ebook record available at https://lccn.loc.gov/2025012698

The manufacturer's authorized representative in the EU for product safety is
Temple University Rome, Via di San Sebastianello, 16, 00187 Rome RM, Italy
(https://rome.temple.edu/).
tempress@temple.edu

9 8 7 6 5 4 3 2 1

Contents

Preface to the English Edition   vii

Preface to the Turkish Edition   xi

Introduction   1

1. The Muslimness Contract   32

2. The Transition to the Turkishness Contract   83

3. The Privileges, Performances, and States of Turkishness   110

4. The Crisis of Turkishness   155

Conclusion   201

Bibliography   209

Index   229

Preface to the English Edition

This is the English edition of *Türklük Sözleşmesi*, a book I published in Turkish in 2018 with Dipnot Press. But it is not the same book. I made a number of rather comprehensive changes in the English edition. I entirely did away with the first chapter of the original. That chapter was a general overview of Whiteness Studies and was written with readers in Turkey in mind, who, in 2018 at least, were largely foreign to such discussions. Having that as a separate chapter struck me as unnecessary in the English edition. The other main change is to the Introduction, which is now, relative to the original, more sweeping and more theoretical. Since 2018, critical race theory (CRT) has come to occupy more space, both in the social sciences more broadly and, personally, in my own mind. These intellectual and political developments have made CRT more central to this study, compared to Whiteness Studies. Similarly, the new Introduction also reflects the growing importance, for my thinking, of the concept of intersectionality, which, to a significant extent, overlaps with the intellectual history of CRT. And the third basic change is to the Conclusion, which is newly written and largely parallels new ideas I have developed since 2018. Its basic theme is about how two parallel and relational logics of power—what I term contractual power and colonial power—have shaped modern history, more generally, and the moment of crisis we are now experiencing. This new Conclusion is also something of an introduction to future work in progress. Aside from these three major changes, I also made countless minor changes and abridgments throughout.

This book analyzes the historical formation, institutional operations, and embodiment (as habitus) of what I have termed "Turkishness," approached here as a set of certain schemas for seeing, thinking, feeling, and acting and certain privileges, real or potential. My debt to the insights and concepts about whiteness and structural racism developed, in particular, by Black thinkers is evident throughout. This was one of the ostensible reasons for the negative reactions that the original book attracted among certain Turkish readers from within the political left. Briefly, I was accused of having imported insights and theories from the United States that do not really suit Turkish realities (in the Turkish preface, the brief history of this book was written, in part, in anticipation of such criticisms). Yet, the reactions of Kurds and Armenians from Turkey—that is, the reactions of non-Turkish readers—have been generally positive. In abbreviated form, many said that they found here, in the form of insights and concepts, many things they had always felt but somehow could not quite conceptualize and that this had an empowering effect. At any rate, the book has been both widely read in Turkey and widely discussed, with its fifteenth edition in press at the time of this writing. Such popularity, rather rare for a book in the social sciences, is likely tied to the strong feelings, whether positive or negative, aroused by the new perspective the book tries to develop on Turkish history, society, and the individual. That said, my aim was not only to say something about Turkey; I tried to show that the theories, perspectives, and concepts developed on whiteness and Blackness—at least a significant number, if not all—could be valid and meaningful beyond a Black/white binary. I also tried to, in a sense, globalize (theoretically, historically) CRT debates. In doing so, I got much of my inspiration from the late Charles W. Mills's influential book, *The Racial Contract*.

In preparing the English edition, I relied on the assistance of a number of institutions and individuals. Funding for the book's translation came from a scholarship provided by the Alexander von Humboldt Stiftung's Philipp Schwartz Initiative. Eugenia Dahl, Çağan Duran, Bülent Eken, Kader Konuk, Egemen Özbek, Elif Sönmez, and Kadir Yıldırım from the University of Duisburg-Essen, where I was a guest researcher between 2019 and 2022, were helpful in many ways. Neriman Ceylan, Ercan Coşkun, Ahmet Güven, Sadık Mermeroğlu, Filiz Öncel, Gilda Schönberg, Jens Umlauf, and Metin Yılmaz, thanks to their generosity, made my Berlin years more beautiful and comfortable.

From the Department of Sociology at the University of Virginia, where I began working recently as General Faculty, Raven Custer, Fiona Greenland, Ian Mullins, Simone Polillo, Gökhan Şensönmez, and Katherine Shiflett greatly eased the transition. Simone, in particular, made everything more pleasant, both as the department head and as a friend. John William Day translated the book with enthusiasm and care. Since my doctoral years at Binghamton University, the support of my dear Professor Michael O. West and my dear friends Kaan Ağartan, Tuba Ağartan, Zeynep Gönen, and Jeffrey D. Howison has been constant. The mentorship and friendship of Carla Freeman and Robert Goddard from Emory University were invaluable at critical moments. The staff at Temple University Press, especially my editor, Shaun Vigil, consistently addressed all my questions and problems quickly and delicately. The advice of the book's anonymous reviewers improved the book.

Esra Sarıoğlu's role was instrumental, both in the formation of ideas central to the Turkish edition and in spurring, through her labor and encouragement, the English edition. Without Esra, there would be no Turkish book and no English translation.

My thanks to everyone.

Barış Ünlü
İstanbul, July 2024

Preface to the Turkish Edition

Behind this book is a personal turning point. Some ten years ago, I took a road trip with a few friends from Turkey who, like me, were doing their doctorates at Binghamton University. We drove to Providence—about a five-hour trip—to listen to a speech by Sebahat Tuncel, a member of Parliament from the Democratic Society Party who was on a speaking tour at the time. On the night of the talk, members of the Kurdish diaspora welcomed us into their home. They were quite excited by Tuncel's arrival and by having successfully organized the talk. The home was as full as can be, with someone always offering tea or a snack as the conversation flowed, both in Turkish and Kurdish. As I do not speak Kurdish, I imagine I missed important parts of what was said. But I also struggled to follow some exchanges in Turkish, as I was simply unfamiliar with so much of what was being discussed. I could neither share their enthusiasm nor grasp the significance, in their eyes, of the events, people, and subjects they so passionately discussed. And when I entered the room of the son of the family with whom I was staying, my sense of dissociation only grew. The walls were decorated with posters of symbolic figures from Kurdistan's political history. There was a Kurdish flag hanging on the wall and a picture of Abdullah Öcalan on the desktop background of his computer. This was not so unfamiliar to me. In my younger days, in high school or university, the walls of my rooms were covered with pictures of socialist thinkers and revolutionaries. Nevertheless, the symbols in this room were quite foreign to me. I felt out of place and, if I'm honest, found the son's choices odd. I looked down on them, in fact.

The conversations I could not understand that evening, the enthusiasm shared by those around me, their heroes unfamiliar to me—all filled me with a nebulous sense of alienation, as though this was no longer a small city in the United States I had come to know, but a small Kurdistan. For years in Turkey, I had voted for parties identifying as pro-Kurdish and had myself identified as a socialist. Further, I was even "open-minded" enough—so to speak, at least, looking back from today—to drive for hours to hear a controversial Kurdish MP speak. Yet none of this prevented me from feeling estranged that evening. This feeling had nothing to do with how the Kurds I met and stayed with behaved toward me. They were nothing but extremely warm and, perhaps because they saw in me a Turk who might be able to understand them, particularly sympathetic. Behind this estrangement was, rather, the experience of meeting people who, though they came from the same country as I did, nevertheless thought and felt very differently than what I knew. For the first time, I guess, I had realized how different Kurds are from me. My discomfort that day came down to this: they were Kurds, and I was not.

The next morning, I awoke estranged not so much from my surroundings as from myself. It is a bit difficult to explain this feeling, but there I was, as someone who did not really see himself as Turkish or feel any sort of pride in Turkishness, realizing how Turkish I, in fact, am. I not only saw them as Kurds, just as I had the night before; I felt more distinctly aware of myself as a Turk. Over breakfast, I tried, clumsily, to explain myself to a friend I had come to Providence with: "I really felt like a Turk." When she pushed me to explain what I meant, I started to think more seriously about this feeling. I tried to make sense of what I felt, of what this feeling meant.

Those preliminary reflections on Turkishness, which came to occupy my thoughts, were based on some basic observations of myself and other Turks around me. My circle at the time was mostly made up of socialists, of people who did not actively identify as Turks, or who at least felt no particular pride in Turkishness, and who very likely believed their thoughts and emotions to have little to do with Turkishness. Yet, after this turning point, I began to think more and more about such self-images. Increasingly, it seemed to me that, like fish in water, they were unaware that what they knew and did not know, what they paid attention to and what they ignored, and what moved them and what did not—all were shaped by an unrecognized investment in Turkishness. At first, I struggled to give conceptual shape to these thoughts, these intuitions. I could only recognize that certain behaviors or reflexes were tied to Turkishness. Whenever I voiced these initial ideas, meanwhile, the reactions of those around me were generally negative, sometimes severely so.

At an impasse, I wondered whether much had been written about white-ness. It was a simple Google search that first brought the field of Whiteness Studies to my attention. I found a literature exploring whiteness (a phenom-enon seen even in the "best" of white people) as ways of seeing, thinking, know-ing, feeling, and sensing; strategies of ignorance, indifference, and apathy they have fostered against nonwhite people; and myriad forms of white privilege from which white people often benefit in largely unconscious ways. As I was reading the Wikipedia page, I came to discover, with great pleasure, that much of what this literature discussed in relation to whiteness resembled what I had been thinking about in relation to Turkishness. Seeing so many points of simi-larity, it seemed to me that comparing whiteness and Turkishness might gen-erate new and important insights. I then read all I could find on whiteness and wrote a few preliminary pieces examining Turkishness—approached as a world of thought and feeling, a set of privileges, a habitus—through this lit-erature's concepts.[1]

What I mean to say here is that the perspective presented in this book was arrived at not through a simple desire to survey a slice of current literature, or from some external pressure to publish, but from an impulse tied to per-sonal experiences and perceptions, from a sort of natural spontaneity. I did not arrive at my thoughts on Turkishness as a result of delving into Whiteness Studies; rather, I came to Whiteness Studies through my initial thoughts on Turkishness. The path toward the historical and sociological model that I have tried to develop here began not from theory or a body of literature but from personal insights. Behind this book, then, is a nearly ten-year journey from insights to observations, from accumulated observations to conceptual pur-suits, and from new concepts to a rethinking of Turkish history and society.

This book was written at a moment when the academy in Turkey was under attack from many sides and academics had to contend with law-suits, criminal investigations, dismissals, and threats. To Kaan Ağartan, Özkan

---

1. For a chronological list of articles in which I analyze and conceptualize Turkishness through Whiteness Studies, see "Türklüğün Kısa Tarihi," *Birikim*, no. 274 (February 2012): 23–34; "Türklük ve Beyazlık Krizleri: Türkiye ve Güney Afrika Üzerine Karşılaştırmalı Notlar," *Birikim*, nos. 289–290 (May–June 2013): 103–111; "Türklük Sözleşmesi ve Türk Solu," *Perspec-tives*, no. 3 (2013): 23–27; "Türklük Sözleşmesi'nin İmzalanışı (1915–1925)," *Mülkiye Dergisi* 38, no. 3 (2014): 47–81; "The Kurdish Struggle and the Crisis of the Turkishness Contract," *Philosophy and Social Criticism* 42, nos. 4–5 (May–June 2016): 397–405. There are, naturally, many similarities between these articles and this book. Yet the book was written anew from a perspective allowed to mature over a number of years and contains many thoughts and positions not found in the articles.

Ağtaş, Yaman Akdeniz, Elçin Aktoprak, Ayça Alemdaroğlu, Kerem Altıparmak, Ahmet Murat Aytaç, Eren Barış, Nazan Bedirhanoğlu, Efe Beşler, Coşku Çelik, Onur Demir, Ali Dinçer, Yağmur Dönmez, Candan Dumrul, Evin Elçi, Zeynep Gönen, Jeffrey D. Howison, Aslı Iğsız, Zeri İnanç, Çağlar Keyder, Kader Konuk, Nisan Kuyucu, Nil Mutluer, Aydın Ördek, Ümit Özger, Yasemin Özgün, Türkan Yalçın Sancar, Murat Sevinç, Bahar Şimşek, Emir Ali Türkmen, Michael O. West, Pınar Yıldız, and Deniz Yonucu: if it were not for their different kinds of assistance, encouragement, and support, this process would have been far more difficult for me.

Melissa Steyn arranged for me to spend a summer at Witwatersrand University as a visiting researcher, which created the conditions I needed to develop certain ideas central to this book. The very existence of Eğitim-Sen (the Education and Science Workers' Union), to which I belong, was a source of institutional security at a moment when so many institutions were collapsing. The Ankara Solidarity Academy cultivated an alternative academy beyond the university, allowing us to remain engaged with students.

Thanks to my interlocutors, whom I interviewed to enrich the fourth chapter (the third in the English edition), I came to better understand what I was working on. Faruk Alpkaya, Bülent Batuman, Dinçer Demirkent, Levent Kanat, Utku Özmakas, and Ayşe Serdar read early drafts of this book, and it was through their recommendations and criticisms that I was able to address a number of errors, deficiencies, and ambiguities. Utku's editorial work, executed with the utmost professionalism, but with the warmth and approachability of an amateur, made the text far more flowing and far more readable.

Esra Sarıoğlu has been my companion for years, from the first germ of an idea I had for this book to its final sentence. Many of the ideas in this book developed in conversation with her. Through the questions she asked, through both the contributions and the criticisms she brought to what I wrote, she ensured that I saw better, thought better, and wrote better.

My gratitude to all.

Barış Ünlü
Ankara, November 2017

The Turkishness Contract

Introduction

This book seeks to understand and analyze Turkishness, approached here as a world of privileges and certain ways or schemas of seeing, hearing, knowing, thinking, feeling, and behaving. Turkishness has taken shape within historical and ongoing relations, entangling non-Muslim[1] communities (Armenians, Greeks, Jews, and Assyrians, whose religious differences preclude them from becoming or being considered real Turks) and Muslim Kurds, who, as Muslims, are able but refuse to Turkify.[2] In one sense, schemas of Turkishness are products of hierarchical power relations that tie various religious and ethnic groups that are not, cannot, and/or do not want to be Turkish to a regime of domination. In another, these schemas produce everyday political, economic, legal, cultural, and ethical relations and inequalities between Turkish and non-Turkish individuals, reproducing power hierarchies and regimes of domination.

---

1. Translator's note: non-Muslim (*gayrimüslim*, in Turkish) is a discriminatory term used to describe Ottoman and Turkish Christians and Jews. The term's discriminatory force in Turkish is not really captured in the English "non-Muslim." The reader is asked to keep this force in mind, especially since the Turkish-language version of this book uses *gayrimüslim* throughout, deliberately and advisedly, as a means of keeping our attention on the structural discrimination against Christians and Jews (a central topic of this study) that is carved into the very foundations of the Turkishness Contract.

2. Translator's note: the terms "Turkify" and "Turkification" are used throughout this book. While perhaps not stylistically graceful, these terms are widely used, in the relevant historical and social-scientific literature, as translations of different derivations of the root verbs *Türkleşmek* and *Türkleştirmek*. On the political and phenomenological significance of the difference made by the causative suffix "*-tir*" between the two verbs (roughly, the difference between "becoming Turkish [oneself]" and "causing someone to become Turkish"), see Chapter 3, n. 22.

Turkishness is a relational category, and, in what follows, I analyze its historical formation and everyday functioning as a contractual phenomenon. Specifically, through the concepts of the *Muslimness Contract* and the *Turkishness Contract*, I analyze the ways in which historical contingency is naturalized in the Turkish subject. It is my sense that these successive contracts (the latter emerging from the former) provide a conceptual framework for better understanding the concomitant formation, evolution, functioning, and performance of the Turkish state, Turkish nation, and Turkish individual. The concept or metaphor of "contract" allows us to better discern the ways in which structural Turkism and Turkish supremacy render Turks privileged and advantaged in all areas of life relative to non-Turks. Approaching Turkishness as a contract also sheds light on the lines, strategies, and performances of knowledge, thought, and emotion that Turkish subjects develop within these structures.

I am indebted, in the concepts and perspectives I draw on throughout this book, to the thinking and sensibilities about white supremacy and states of whiteness that have been developed and inspired by a number of Black thinkers. The application of analyses on whiteness beyond the United States has been met with many loud objections, even when applied to historical contexts shaped by slavery, racism, and colonialism (e.g., the United Kingdom, France, the Netherlands). Generally, such objections hold that the use of such perspectives as critical race theory (CRT) for countries and contexts not defined by the Black/white binary peculiar to the United States is inapt, if not impossible. In light of such objections, my use here of the conceptual tools drawn from perspectives on whiteness for a context like Turkey, where differences in skin color are, historically, relatively insignificant, and where there is no history of capitalist slavery, may seem, at first glance, controversial. Yet, as I show, these conceptual tools, developed for the critical examination of white supremacy and structural racism and their attendant states of whiteness, speak to a global phenomenon, even if they typically have no such claim: namely, that racial and ethnic hierarchies, the historical products of modernity, have become institutionalized in nation-states and that these hierarchies operate in various fields and institutions, working on and through minds and bodies.

One reason for the similarities between whiteness and Turkishness is that regimes of domination (due to the very nature of domination and inequality) broadly resemble each other, engendering similar psychologies and dispositions in those occupying both the highs and the lows of hierarchies.[3] For example, Simone de Beauvoir, who draws an analogy between racism and sex-

---

3. See, e.g., Allen ("Whiteness and Critical Pedagogy," 121–136), whose work draws on Paulo Freire's analysis of oppressors, in general (which does not mention racism), to understand whiteness.

ism, detects, in a famous passage, "deep similarities between the situation of woman and that of the Negro. . . . One of the benefits that oppression confers upon the oppressors is that the most humble among them is made to *feel* superior; thus, a 'poor white' in the South can console himself with the thought that he is not a 'dirty nigger'—and the more prosperous whites cleverly exploit this pride. Similarly, the most mediocre of males feels himself a demigod as compared with women."[4] Such similarities mean that a perspective or concept developed to understand, say, racism may be useful for the analysis of sexism, or vice versa. But the similarities between whiteness and Turkishness go beyond analogy. Whiteness and Turkishness result from the same kind of regime of domination, not different ones. The organization of modern nation-states around racial and ethnic hierarchies—structural racism and structural Turkishness—produced both whiteness and Turkishness.

Of course, Turkishness, like whiteness, is not a monolithic category. It takes different forms in different contexts of social class, gender, ethnicity, and religious belief or sect. There are significant differences in privileges, thoughts, feelings, performances, and strategies between the Turkishness of a Turkish capitalist and that of a Turkish worker, or that of a man and that of a woman, or that of a Sunni and that of an Alevi. Similarly, as with race and whiteness, Turkishness as a form of ethnic supremacy intersects with categories of experience marked by class, sexual, and religious inequalities. In other words, in modern Turkey, ethnic, class, sexual, and religious inequalities both interlock with and are interdependent on each other, in tangled and intricate ways. This knowledge and awareness of intersectionality, similar to the importance of intersectionality in analyses on whiteness, served as the essential background that made this book possible. That said, this book does not focus on the differences between Turkishnesses or on how Turkishness intersects with separate but related categories. Rather, as with early work on whiteness, I show that there is a supraclass, supragender, supraethnic, supraideological category called Turkishness—that is, there are certain ways of seeing, hearing, knowing, thinking, feeling, and behaving that are common to and that unite different social, sexual, ethnic, and ideological groups. Such an approach may appear, when read from the context of critical discussions of whiteness in the contemporary United States (where it is now largely accepted, even axiomatic, that there is such a category as whiteness), as overgeneralizing and simplistic. However, in the contemporary intellectual life of Turkey as well as in the academic subfield of Turkish Studies, there is no analogous axiom for Turkishness. Turkishness has begun only recently to enter into the world of thought and research as a

---

4. Beauvoir, *Second Sex*, 22–23.

subject and object of analysis and has been met with strong resistance from different ideological positions (nationalist, Kemalist, Islamist, liberal, Marxist).[5] Thus, one of the most important aims of this book is to underscore the very existence of Turkishness and then to encourage further debate. Another important aim is to present readers who are not from Turkey (or those unfamiliar with Turkish Studies) with a compelling case through which to consider that much of what we identify with whiteness is, in fact, not specific to whiteness but occurs in other contexts as well, thus expanding the discussion on whiteness conceptually, contextually, and geographically. Accordingly, this analysis of Turkishness by way of perspectives on whiteness can also be seen as an attempt to contribute to moving CRT beyond its genesis within a Black/ white binary.

The rest of this Introduction is devoted to giving conceptual substance to the basic claims and aims of this book. I begin with a general overview of the relevance of the analysis of whiteness and its historical trajectory to the critical analysis of Turkishness. Then, through the concept of the social contract, I examine the shared modern historical context that gave rise to whiteness and Turkishness and makes them comparable. I conclude with a brief plan for the rest of the book.

Black Thought, Intersectionality, and Whiteness

Black people know all too well how centuries of global white supremacy and structural racism have shaped not only their own lives but also white worlds of thought, emotion, and action. Insofar as knowledge of white supremacy, structural racism, and whiteness is necessary for surviving and getting on in a white world, it is a knowledge that Black people have gained throughout their lived experience. We also know that the same knowledge is quite rare among white people themselves. Consider the fact that Whiteness Studies, which scrutinizes the relationalities that make up whiteness, white supremacy, and structural racism and is largely carried out by white social scientists, only truly emerged around the 1980s. This late arrival points to how difficult and rare it is for those at the top of the racial hierarchy to be able to reflect on themselves, as a consequence of the structural, psychocognitive, and epistemic barriers (or, rather, privileges) that I discuss throughout this book. A similar difficulty and delay apply to the analysis of Turks and Turkishness, for similar reasons. Kurds and Armenians, for instance, know how and why Turks think, know, hear, feel, and behave in certain ways, whereas the overwhelming ma-

---

5. See Chapters 3 and 4 for more on this.

jority of Turks have no such knowledge and awareness. Even the most educated and leftist of Turks can be quite clueless about the operations—even
the existence—of Turkishness.

The roots of radical Black thought about global white supremacy and its
political, economic, cultural, psychological, and physical effects on the lives
of Black and white people run deep. While any starting date is somewhat
symbolic, a compelling case can be made for the Haitian Revolution, when
Black people, displaced by slavery, racism, and colonialism across the world,
began to develop a global consciousness of Blackness and global Africa.[6] The
same revolution is, through its absence, also crucial to the emergence of Eu-
rocentric or white-centric thought, insofar as the white world ignored, silenced,
and erased this world-historical event.[7] Emerging from the political contexts
of abolitionism, Garveyism, anti-colonialism, pan-Africanism, and the civil
rights movement in the Caribbean, North and South America, Europe, and
Africa, Black radical intellectuals—or "heretics,"[8] in Anthony Bogues's term,
on account of their subversion of white normativity by refusing to think like
a white person in a white world—developed concepts and perspectives on the
workings of white supremacy and how it has shaped the ways in which white
people feel, think, and behave.[9] For example, W.E.B. Du Bois's concept of psychological wage is still widely used in works on whiteness, especially in analyses
of the white working class. According to Du Bois, not only do rich and proper-
ty-owning white people enjoy privilege; the same is true for poor and proper-
tyless white people over Black people of the same class. Financially, the former
hold jobs that are relatively safer, more respectable, and better paid than their
Black counterparts, and to this relative material privilege is added an immaterial privilege: a psychological wage able to morally compensate for material
poverty by supplying a sense of superiority over Black people.[10] These material and immaterial hierarchies are responsible both for preventing the formation of a supraracial working-class consciousness and for the extraordinary
efforts of poor European immigrants to become white, through a range of
strategies and performances, as they struggle for acceptance into U.S. whiteness. The historical reality to which the concept of psychological wage refers
is, of course, not only limited to whiteness or U.S. history; it can be applied
to all countries where ethnic and racial hierarchies are built into the nation-

---

6. See West, "Global Africa," 85–108.
7. See, e.g., Trouillot, *Silencing the Past*, 72–103; Buck-Morss, "Hegel and Haiti," 821–865.
8. Bogues, *Black Heretics, Black Prophets*.
9. See Roediger, *Black on White*.
10. Du Bois, *Black Reconstruction in America*, 700–701.

state and experienced as structural phenomena—which, of course, includes Turkey and Turkishness.

The observations of such Black literary figures as Richard Wright and James Baldwin on whiteness coincide with a broader shift in attention in discussions of racism, particularly since the mid-twentieth century, from Black people to white people—that is, from those at the bottom to those at the top. Take Wright's response to a journalist: "There isn't any Negro problem; there is only a white problem."[11] This marks an important moment in shifting the critical gaze to whiteness, to those above as the problem, rather than to those below. When an intellectual or Kurdish politician in Turkey states, "There is no Kurdish problem, there is a Turkish problem"—increasingly common in recent years—the echoes are clear.

To Baldwin's eye, whiteness was never simply a problem of the uneducated. Among the educated, liberals, and leftists, he detected whiteness in even more striking forms: "Negroes want to be treated like men: a perfectly straight-forward statement, containing only seven words. People who have mastered Kant, Hegel, Shakespeare, Marx, Freud, and the Bible find this statement utterly impenetrable. The idea seems to threaten profound, barely conscious assumptions. A kind of panic paralyzes their features, as though they found themselves on the edge of a steep place."[12] Baldwin saw, in white America's unwillingness to accept the reality of the problems of Black America, a refusal of white people to face certain disconcerting truths about themselves and their country that such recognition would entail. So while white people believed insistently in myths about American history, took pride in them, and waxed nostalgic about lost values, Black people had no such belief, pride, or nostalgia.[13] Baldwin offers, for the analysis of whiteness, a forensics of the often unconscious intellectual, emotional, and epistemic strategies developed to maintain white power and privilege. Equally vital are his observations on the feelings of panic, set in motion as Black people began to develop their own definitions and concepts, about a perceived threat to a white monopoly over defining reality.[14]

Indeed, the horror that the Black Power generation—in some ways a continuation of the Civil Rights Movement, in others a departure—engendered in white people had less to do with any advocacy of violence as a potential tool and more to do with the radical criticisms introduced to the white pow-

11. Quoted in Lipsitz, *Possessive Investment in Whiteness*, 1.
12. Baldwin, "Fifth Avenue, Uptown: A Letter from Harlem," in *Collected Essays*, 177.
13. Baldwin, *Fire Next Time*, 101; Baldwin, "Nobody Knows My Name: A Letter from the South," in *Collected Essays*, 200–208.
14. Baldwin, *Fire Next Time*, 69, 77.

er structure and with the ideas and attitudes developed against this structure's various monopolies (over defining, over the use of violence, and over economic life). The influence on the Black Power generation of Frantz Fanon's structural, psychological, and phenomenological analyses (of racism in *Black Skin, White Masks* and of colonialism in *The Wretched of the Earth*) of the making of Black/colonized and white/colonizer souls and bodies is well known. For example, Stokely Carmichael (a.k.a. Kwame Ture), inspired by *The Wretched of the Earth*, argued that the Black/white relationship in the United States constitutes a colonial situation, on the idea that the main factor defining colonization is not geographic distance but objective relations of domination and exploitation. Carmichael further described racism as a structural, rather than an individual, phenomenon. Racism is a structure organized to keep one race above and the other race(s) below through the constant reproduction of political, economic, cultural, and psychological inequalities. Seeing racism as structural entails seeing white people who may not individually harbor racist views as, nevertheless, beneficiaries of structural racism and, thus, as part of the structure.[15] According to Carmichael, although some white people had begun, at the time of his writing, to think about racism in earnest, they were hesitant to take the radical steps needed to dismantle the structure. They found it more agreeable to feel good and freed of guilt by joining the same organizations as Black people and were unable to let go of their internalized entitlement and paternalism, which materialized in the form of constantly offering advice to Black people.[16] Steve Biko, leader of the Black Consciousness movement,[17] the South African equivalent of the Black Power movement, made similar observations about white progressives: "A number of whites in this country adopt the class analysis, primarily because they want to detach us from anything relating to race. In case it has a rebound effect on them because they are white. This is the problem. So a lot of them adopt the class analysis as a defense mechanism and are persuaded of it because they find it more comfortable. And of course a number of them are terribly puritanical, dogmatic, and very, very arrogant. They don't quite know to what extent they have to give up a part of themselves in order to be a true Marxist."[18]

Baldwin, Carmichael, and Biko's critical observations on the forms of blindness, nostalgia, paternalism, dogmatism, and arrogance delimiting white progressives are very similar to those of Kurdish and Armenian intellectuals

---

15. Carmichael and Hamilton, *Black Power*, 3–6, 47.

16. Carmichael and Hamilton, 28, 31, 81–83.

17. For a comparative analysis of the Black movements in the two countries, see Fredrickson, *Black Liberation*.

18. Gerhart, "Interview with Steve Biko," 34.

in Turkey about Turkish progressives; it is enough to change a few names and references in the Baldwin and Biko quotes. Their overlap stems from the broad similarities in the psychological mechanisms, forms of cognitive blindness, and epistemic escape strategies of dominant groups across different ethnic and racial hierarchies. Just as the concept of psychological wage sheds light on certain attitudes of the Turkish working classes, the criticisms and concepts developed against white intellectuals offer much for analyses of the predilections and practices of educated Turkish progressives.

The Black Power movement posed a dual challenge to white people. First, white people now faced a far more self-confident, uncompromising, radical, and exacting generation. Second, by putting structural inequalities, the privileges of whiteness, and the ways of being white that stem from these privileges at the center of racism debates, Black Power exposed to critical scrutiny the countless white people who considered themselves free from racism and began to analyze them as a part of the problem of racism. Liberalism, which personalizes issues and solutions, was replaced by radicalism, which structuralizes issues and solutions. This radicalism, born of the anti-colonial and anti-racist struggles and ideas of the Third World (as well as the Third World within the First World), was a key driving force behind the worldwide cultural revolution of 1968.

If we look at the spirit rather than the letter of the 1968 world revolution—at its cultural impact in the medium and long terms rather than its political defeat in the short term—we see a permanent cultural revolution that continues to this day.[19] The revolution left us with the idea that no regime of domination and exploitation is primary; therefore, no regime of domination can be made light of as secondary, nor can their solutions be postponed (after elections, after the revolution). It introduced a radical critique and rejection of the Old Left's identification of certain contradictions as primary (e.g., the class contradictions and inequalities or the national contradictions and inequalities) and others as secondary (racial, ethnic, and sexual contradictions and inequalities), resulting, initially, in a division and fragmentation of the left. I have already mentioned the critique of whiteness motivating the separate organizational logic of Black Power and Black Consciousness. Similarly, feminists began to break away from the male-dominated Old Left and New Left movements after the 1968 revolution, rejecting both the downplaying by male leftists of sexism as secondary to anti-capitalism and anti-imperialism and the repro-

---

19. For an analysis of 1968 as a geocultural revolution, see Wallerstein, *End of the World*; Wallerstein, *World-Systems Analysis*; Arrighi, Hopkins, and Wallerstein, *Anti-Systemic Movements*.

duction of gendered divisions of labor within leftist organizations, where men were assigned roles as thinkers and leaders and women as secretaries and cooks.

Feminists created separate and autonomous organizations to overcome the gender blindness of Marxism and Marxists by bringing Marxism into conversation with feminism. Feminists presented both compelling frameworks for the analysis of capitalism and patriarchy as intertwined structures of domination, supporting and producing each other, and interpretations, variously inspired by Marxist, socialist, radical, and anarchist thought, of the nature of this intertwining.[20] But the problems did not end with the separation of leftist women from leftist men. Just as white feminists diagnosed gender blindness in leftist men, Black feminists diagnosed race blindness in white feminists. White women were not only women, in other words, but also white, and this whiteness blinded them to matters of race. The Black feminist Gloria Joseph, for example, argued that one cannot speak of a single generalized category of oppressed women, or, if so, this should be immediately qualified by race and class. According to Joseph, though white women were oppressed because of their womanhood, their whiteness was a position of domination. Crucially, Joseph also called attention to different logics of solidarity: the racial solidarity between white women and white men was stronger, she said, than the gender solidarity between white men and Black men. For these reasons, Joseph held that Black women could not trust white women to liberate them in or after the revolution, just as women could not trust men. Consequently, any analysis or politics focused on the intricate interplay of capitalism and patriarchy must necessarily include racism as a system of domination, on par with capitalism and patriarchy. For this to happen, leftist white women first had to recognize their whiteness to understand that their attitudes, thoughts, and positions were shaped as much by their whiteness (racism, white supremacy) as by their womanhood (sexism, male supremacy).[21]

The idea of intersectionality was introduced and developed by Black feminists in the context of these divisions and in the spirit of 1968. For Black feminists, single-axis analyses and politics (whether based in class, gender, or race) made it theoretically and politically impossible to understand and change the nature and functioning of intertwined and coproductive regimes of domination. Consider the Combahee River Collective Statement of 1977, one of the first texts to develop the idea (if not the concept) of intersectionality as a theoretical and political framework: "The most general statement of our politics at the present time would be that we are actively committed to struggling

20. See, e.g., Sargent, *Women and Revolution.*
21. Joseph, "Marxism, Feminism, and Racism," 91–107.

against racial, sexual, heterosexual, and class oppression, and see as our particular task the development of integrated analysis and practice based upon the fact that the major systems of oppression are interlocking. The synthesis of these oppressions creates the conditions of our lives."[22] The interlocking, manifold, and simultaneous nature of the regimes of domination is one of the reasons why the signatories of the declaration, who were lesbian Black feminists, simultaneously identified themselves as anti-racist, anti-sexist, anti-capitalist, and anti-imperialist. Similarly, the theoretical and political sensibility of Deborah King's "Multiple Jeopardy" perspective developed Frances M. Beal's concept of "Double Jeopardy" to underscore that systems of repression and control are interdependent and interactive, not merely additive, as in a mathematical equation: "To the extent that any politics is monistic, the actual victims of racism, sexism, or classism may be absent from, invisible within, or seen as antagonistic to that politics. . . . That is, black and/or poor women may be marginal to monistic feminism, women's concerns may be excluded from nationalistic activism, and indifference to race and gender may pervade class politics. . . . A black feminist ideology fundamentally challenges the interstructure of the oppressions of racism, sexism, and classism both in the dominant society and within movements for liberation."[23]

The term "intersectionality" was introduced by Kimberlé Crenshaw. Through intersectionality, Crenshaw describes how dominant feminist perspectives and judicial decisions on gender discrimination are based on white women's experiences, which overlook the ways in which Black women face dual discrimination (as women, as Black). Thus, for Crenshaw, to think and act beyond whiteness, feminism had to stop speaking as though it occupied a space of nonracial objectivity.[24] That Crenshaw also helped pioneer CRT underscores the reciprocity of intersectionality and the structural analysis of racism. Liberal discourse on and criticism of racism—mainstream after the civil rights reforms of the 1960s—framed racism as a set of irrational prejudices, a deviation from the dominant myth of meritocracy in the United States. Accordingly, the problem of racism could be overcome (so went the supposition) by a return to rational meritocracy and the individual color blindness of judges, politicians, professors, or policemen. Against this liberal discourse of racism, CRT emerged as an empirical and theoretical field of study examining how racial power is constructed and operates in the legal system, and in American society more generally, analyzing racism not as a problem rooted in individual prejudices or racist judges but as the very system that creates

22. "Combahee River Collective Statement," *Black Past*.
23. King, "Multiple Jeopardy, Multiple Consciousness," 52–53, 72.
24. Crenshaw, "Demarginalizing the Intersection of Race and Sex," 139–167.

individual prejudices and racist judges.[25] The coexistence of intersectionality theory and CRT, as embodied in the person of Crenshaw, was the natural outcome of a parallel dual development, stretching back at least to the 1960s: (1) the analysis of racism and sexism as structural regimes of domination and (2) new ideas, sensibilities, and politics that saw no regime of domination as primary or secondary, focusing instead on the interlocking, interdependent, and co-constitutive nature of regimes of domination.

Identity politics also grew out of this process, initially with a leftist and radical meaning quite unlike its negative connotations in leftist circles today.[26] Crenshaw summarizes the impact of identity politics on groups organizing around their own concerns: "The process of recognizing as social and systemic what was formerly perceived as isolated and individual has also characterized the identity politics of African Americans, other people of color, and gays and lesbians, among others. For all these groups, identity-based politics has been a source of strength, community, and intellectual development."[27] Nor were these positive effects limited to individual identity groups; through coalitions, different groups came to better appreciate and understand one another's concerns. Mari Matsuda explains how coalitions reveal intersections: "The way I try to understand the interconnection of all forms of subordination is through a method I call 'ask the other question.' When I see something that looks racist, I ask, 'Where is the patriarchy in this?' When I see something that looks sexist, I ask, 'Where is the heterosexism in this?' When I see something that looks homophobic, I ask, 'Where are the class interests in this?' Working in coalition forces us to look for both the obvious and non-obvious relationships of domination, helping us to realize that no form of subordination ever stands alone."[28]

Three interrelated accomplishments of the concept and metaphor of intersectionality, as developed by Black feminists, stand out.[29] First, using intersectionality's tools, it is possible to analyze modern structures of domination (capitalism, colonialism, racism, sexism, heteronormativity) without reducing one to another or positing one as derivative of another. At the same time, intersectionality demonstrated the historical relationality of these structures, that is, how they overlap and create multiple hierarchies and inequalities. Second, intersectionality exposed the forms of blindness that structures of domination

---

25. See Crenshaw et al., *Critical Race Theory.*

26. The term "identity politics" was first used in 1977 in the Combahee River Collective Statement.

27. Crenshaw, "Mapping the Margins," 1241–1242.

28. Matsuda, "Beside My Sister," 1189.

29. For an overview of the didactic and transformative capacities of intersectionality, see Collins, *Intersectionality as Critical Social Theory.*

can create in groups and individuals. One who enjoys the privileges of (or, at least, is not oppressed by) a certain structure of domination may not be able to see how that structure of domination functions—or, more importantly, may not want to see it and may develop various mechanisms of defense and escape in order not to see it (or not to take it seriously). Indeed, it was this world of multiple blindnesses that led to divisions after 1968: gender blindness, race blindness, class blindness. Third, it taught leftists in the broadest sense (socialists, anarchists, feminists, anti-racists, environmentalists, etc.) to reflect on multidimensional and intersectional interests, inequalities, relationalities, and connections, to look within themselves, and to see their own blind spots; white people learned to see their whiteness, men their masculinity, heterosexuals their heteronormativity, Marxists their race and gender blindness, and feminists their race and class blindness.

In an essay on the history of CRT, Crenshaw summarizes the negative reception of critical race theorists' critiques of white leftist legal scholars: "'What is it about the whiteness of [Critical Legal Studies] that keeps people of color at bay?' This was long before 'Whiteness Studies' came on the scene, so the challenge posed by the question—to think about race not within the traditional terms of uplifting the 'Other,' but through interrogating racial power from inside out—was to some a discordant, uncomfortable and even shocking experience."[30] The traces of this intersectional critique and history of thought are evident in the works of both Peggy McIntosh and Ruth Frankenberg, considered groundbreaking for Whiteness Studies. McIntosh, for example, describes how she came to recognize her own privileges of whiteness through reflecting on the privileges of masculinity and men's resistance to thinking about these privileges: "Thinking through unacknowledged male privilege as a phenomenon with a life of its own, I realized that since hierarchies in our society are interlocking, there was most likely a phenomenon of white privilege which was similarly denied and protected, but alive and real in its effects. As a white person, I realized I had been taught about racism as something which puts others at a disadvantage, but had been taught not to see one of its corollary aspects, white privilege, which puts me at an advantage."[31]

For Frankenberg, the framework for her pioneering book grew, she relays, out of the intellectual and political environment of the United States in the 1980s, when white feminists like herself could no longer ignore the criticisms of whiteness, white centrism, and false universalism. Many in the movement had long turned a deaf ear to these criticisms because they saw racism as

---

30. Crenshaw, "Twenty Years of Critical Race Theory," 1290.
31. McIntosh, "White Privilege and Male Privilege," 1. McIntosh refers to the Combahee River Collective Statement on p. 17 of the same text.

something external to them: "Because we were basically well-meaning individuals, the idea of being part of the problem of racism (something I had associated with extremists or institutions but not with myself) was genuinely shocking to us."[32] Two factors—(1) assuming that racism is something that illiberal others do and (2) writing and thinking from a structural position of whiteness within the system—made it difficult for many to understand racism as a system that shapes the lives, everyday experiences, and sense of self of not only Black people but also white people. Therefore, the moment of realization of this deep and sheltered ignorance of racism, and of their own selves, shook many highly educated, well-meaning, leftist white people profoundly.[33]

This moment of self-discovery, closely related to the emergence of Black people with power and concepts of their own (a turning point after which Black movements and intellectuals could no longer be ignored or overlooked), engendered not just a reactionary backlash but also a productive crisis of whiteness—a crisis not limited to the intellectual space in which Whiteness Studies emerged. The transformation of countless white people—the fact that they now see, think, and behave in other ways—is also part of this crisis, as has become especially clear in recent years. As I discuss in detail in Chapter 4 of this book, there exists now a crisis of Turkishness similar to the crisis of whiteness. The criticism of Turkish history and Turkishness by the Kurdish movement(s), which broke away from the Turkish left after 1968 and became autonomous, as well as by Kurdish feminism, which became autonomous in time within the Kurdish movement, has transformed countless Turks. Just as practices embodied in the idea of intersectionality exposed to white people their own blind spots, there is an increasing number of Turks who are now able to see their own blind spots.

The basic findings and aims of Frankenberg's book, itself a product of the crisis of whiteness, are something of a general blueprint for the analysis of whiteness, as increasingly institutionalized in the 1990s: "First, Whiteness is a location of structural advantage, of race privilege. Second, it is a 'standpoint,' a place from which White people look at ourselves, at others, and at society. Third, 'whiteness' refers to a set of cultural practices that are usually unmarked and unnamed. This book seeks to begin exploring, mapping, and examining the terrain of Whiteness."[34] Privilege is a favorite theme of researchers working on whiteness. The historian David Roediger, for example, sees the material advantages of the white working class relative to the Black working class as the main reason for whitening, for efforts to be accepted as

---

32. Frankenberg, *White Women, Race Matters*, 3.
33. Frankenberg, "Mirage of an Unmarked Whiteness," 77.
34. Frankenberg, *White Women, Race Matters*, 1.

white, as well as for the insistence on remaining white.[35] The sociologist George Lipsitz describes whiteness as a field of investment providing white people with resources, wealth, opportunities, and power.[36] The legal scholar Cheryl Harris conceptualizes whiteness as a form of property that endows white people with a lifetime of material wealth, advantages, and expectations, guaranteed by law. It is because of these material advantages and the related sense of security, for instance, that Harris's light-skinned grandmother passed as white while at work during the day and, returning home in the evening, took off her white mask and reverted to her Blackness.[37] Some Black people who are white enough to pass are known to prefer passing as a permanent exile from Blackness, never to return.[38] Toni Morrison, meanwhile, writing on the material and psychological advantages of whiteness, pointed out the reasons why Europeans who immigrated to North America fled Europe (powerlessness, poverty), and how they felt free and powerful in their new lands by comparing themselves to and dominating Black people: "Power—control of one's own destiny—would replace the powerlessness felt before the gates of class, caste, and cunning persecution. One could move from discipline and punishment to disciplining and punishing; from social ostracism to social rank."[39] All of these insights and concepts, developed specifically to analyze American whiteness, offer much to the analysis of Turkishness, as I aim to show in the following pages.

As those who study the relationship between whiteness and privilege often emphasize, while discrimination is typically obvious to the disadvantaged, privilege is often invisible to the privileged. One reason for this invisibility or inability to see is that privilege falls into the lap of the white person, she swims with the current or at least does not swim against the current, and her whiteness does not present various obstacles and closed doors. Another reason is an unwillingness to see; the privileged want to think that their advantages, wealth, or status are the result of personal achievements through hard work (that they are deserved), as constantly affirmed by the dominant myth of meritocracy. Insofar as invoking racial privilege offends this sense of entitlement, it generates anger and resolute denial of any relationship between race and status.[40]

Ignorance of white privilege is part of a much more general and comprehensive white ignorance of how white supremacy and racism have shaped the American state, society, and the individual. Ignorance is itself a privilege: the

35. Roediger, *Working toward Whiteness*; Roediger, *Wages of Whiteness*.
36. Lipsitz, *Possessive Investment in Whiteness*.
37. Harris, "Whiteness as Property," 1707–1791.
38. See Hobbs, *Chosen Exile*.
39. Morrison, *Playing in the Dark*, 35.
40. See Kimmel and Ferber, *Privilege*; Twine and Gardener, *Geographies of Privilege*.

privilege to not know. Unlike the oppressed, the colonized, or the victimized (who have no choice but to know), there are no risks or losses for the powerful in not knowing, not caring, or not listening. In other words, ignorance comes from the power to ignore. For white people, knowledge itself, rather than ignorance, is threatening, because knowing how others see themselves and the world can disrupt a white person's material and emotional comfort. As long as ignorance and indifference are allowed to persist undisturbed, a narrative of white innocence, free from guilt and responsibility, can be maintained.[41] Such are the boons of ignorance.

White ignorance, which Charles W. Mills proposes to analyze the concept of the "epistemology of ignorance," results not from the absence of knowledge but from a strong, determined, and active resistance to knowing: "White ignorance. . . . Imagine an ignorance that resists. Imagine an ignorance that fights back. Imagine an ignorance militant, aggressive, not to be intimidated, an ignorance that is active, dynamic, that refuses to go quietly—not at all confined to the illiterate and uneducated but propagated at the highest levels of the land, indeed presenting itself unblushingly as knowledge."[42] Ignorance is able to present itself as knowledge because epistemic authorities devalue nonwhite knowledge as emotional, subjective, ideological, one-sided, nonscientific—thereby providing seemingly respectable and ethical intellectual escape routes from knowing. The liberal discourse of color blindness (skin color does not matter, is not even seen) is one such "noble" escape route to perpetuate structures of ignorance and indifference. Thus, the problem of race is blamed on those who suffer from racism; they are said to be obsessed with race or even reverse-racist. Color blindness is a strategy not for not seeing the other person's Blackness but for not seeing one's own whiteness.[43]

But these forms of blindness and strategies of ignorance are not always conscious; they are not experienced at the level of consciousness. Whiteness, rather, refers to certain ways of looking at one's self, one's environment, history, society, and the world and to the tendencies and habits of understanding and perceiving self, history, society, and so on, in certain ways. Whiteness denotes certain lines of thinking, feeling, and behaving that are learned, internalized, and, insofar as they come to seem normal and natural, not thought about. In other words, whiteness is a racialized habitus and normativity.[44] Therefore, not only are the privileges of whiteness and white ignorance invis-

---

41. See Wekker, *White Innocence*; Steyn, "Feeling White," 3–8.
42. Charles W. Mills, "White Ignorance," 13.
43. See Bonilla-Silva, *Racism without Racists*; Ansell, "Casting a Blind Eye," 333–356.
44. See Bonilla-Silva, Goar, and Embrick, "When Whites Flock Together," 229–253; Sullivan, *Revealing Whiteness*.

ible to white people; so is whiteness itself. Whiteness is an unmarked and invisible category. This, in part, explains the shock, panic, and anger elicited when whiteness is seen and pointed out by others. The crises of whiteness prompted by the political and intellectual empowerment of Black people and the loss of white control over Black people's critical, knowing, and judging gaze are partly related to this shock of visibility.

As with the other conceptual perspectives I have touched on here, the correlations between power and privilege, and their further correlation with the ignorance of dominant groups and the strategies developed to maintain this ignorance, are not limited to whiteness. Fundamentally, they are about the racial/ethnic hierarchies and the maintenance of these hierarchies by power structures. As such, these conceptual perspectives can be applied to the analysis of Turkishness, or, for that matter, Frenchness, Hinduness, or Russianness.

The study of whiteness has long attracted criticism from different angles. For example, whiteness is said by some to be an essentialist, reductionist, homogenizing, and generalizing category. As such, it renders invisible the heterogeneity of white people and white identity as well as geographic and class-based specificities of and transformations to whiteness. The category of whiteness is also said to encourage identity analysis and identity politics rather than class analysis and class politics.[45] Further, in light of the fact that research and approaches in the field of Whiteness Studies are mostly carried out and developed by white researchers, the field is criticized either as a means for white people to escape responsibility by confessing privilege or as a means to again assume a white and masculine heroic role as "race traitors,"[46] thus attributing a key role to white agency and recentering the very whiteness they aim to destroy.[47] (Similar criticisms have been voiced about the colonization, degeneration, and appropriation of intersectionality theory by white feminists and the white power structure.[48]) Taking these critiques seriously, new research agendas, which some call second- or third-wave Whiteness Studies,[49] focus

---

45. See Hartigan, "Establishing the Fact of Whiteness," 495–505; Arnesen, "Whiteness and the Historians' Imagination," 3–32; Hartman, "Rise and Fall of Whiteness Studies," 22–38. For an important critique that appeared in Turkish, see Ağartan, "Beyazlık Çalışmaları Aynasında Türklüğe Bakmak," 67–75.

46. On "race treason," see Ignatiev, "Treason to Whiteness," 607–612; Delgado, "Rodrigo's Eleventh Chronicle," 614–618.

47. Wiegman, "Whiteness Studies and Paradox of Particularity," 115–150; Chen, "Contentious Field of Whiteness Studies," 15–27.

48. For a discussion of this issue, see Nash, *Black Feminism Reimagined*.

49. Twine and Gallagher, "Future of Whiteness," 4–24; Jupp and Badenhorst, "Second-Wave Critical Whiteness Studies," 596–608.

more on the intersectional and relational complexities of whiteness and the ways in which class, gender, religion, and locality inflect whiteness.

As I have tried to outline here, and as I expand later, this book owes much to the perspectives and conceptual tools developed by Black radicals/feminists, CRT, and Whiteness Studies, particularly on white supremacy and structural racism as well as the relationalities between these structuralities and the material privileges, internalized and embodied modes of habitus, psychological dispositions, and the cognitive, emotional, and epistemic habits of those at the top of the racial hierarchy. Among these perspectives, Charles W. Mills and his work *The Racial Contract*, which inspired the title of this book, occupy a particularly prominent place. The social contract, as a concept and logic, provides a useful method for analyzing the ways in which nation-states take shape around racial, ethnic, and religious inclusions and exclusions and the political, economic, cognitive, and psychological effects this transformation has on the lives of the included and excluded. Thinking through the notion of contract, I contend, allows for the development of a more inclusive theoretical and comparative framework for understanding racism, nationalism, and racial and ethnic supremacy in the modern world—one that goes beyond whiteness and Blackness. But this, I argue, requires a certain extension of Mills's theoretical framework.

The Racial Contract, National Contracts, and the Turkishness Contract

Mills begins his book by pointing out that, although white supremacy has been the dominant political system transforming the world for hundreds of years, this global system is never mentioned in philosophy courses taught by white people nor in philosophy or political science books written by white people. White supremacy is a form of domination that goes unnamed and unmarked by even the most educated white people; it is taken for granted, insofar as white people cannot see or understand their own racial privilege. White philosophers, for example, see racism or colonial violence as a deviation from the ideals of equality, democracy, and freedom that gave the Western world its original color. However, nonwhite people, the victims of white supremacy, have "a perspectival cognitive advantage that is grounded in the phenomenological experience of the disjuncture between official (white) reality and actual (nonwhite) experience" and, therefore, know that racism is not a stain or defect on a white surface; it is constitutive of supposedly universalist and color-blind modern concepts and systems such as democracy, republic, and liberalism.[50]

---

50. Charles W. Mills, *Racial Contract*, 109.

Mills's book is an attempt to bridge the great gap between the abstract/ mythical/ideal (white) and the concrete/real/historical (nonwhite) by showing how white supremacy as a political system is established and operates through a racial contract between white people. For Mills, the social contract is not only a useful normative concept for thinking about what is just, democratic, and popular but also a descriptive tool for understanding "the actual genesis of the society and the state, the way society is structured, the way the government functions, and people's moral psychology."[51] But this is only possible by replacing, or at least qualifying, the fictions of social contract theory (which explains the establishment of society and the state in terms of the consent of and agreement among equal individuals) with the actual and real racial contract. The racial contract, Mills summarizes, "is not a contract between everybody ('we the people'), but between just the people who count, the people who really are people ('we the white people')."[52] In other words, while the social contract theoretically includes everyone, the racial contract divides the world into white people and nonwhite people and, in real terms, only includes white people.

Rather than some sort of contract "signed" in one single act, the racial contract, as a set of formal/informal agreements, designates the active and tacit participation, the support and consent, of white people to the different forms that global white supremacy has taken at different times, gradually dominating the world over the past five centuries. An important feature of the racial contract is that a white person does not have to be individually racist (e.g., endorsing slavery, colonialism, and segregation) to benefit from the contract. Mills puts it pithily: "All whites are *beneficiaries* of the Contract, though some whites are not *signatories* to it."[53] Critical to being party to the contract is not being actively racist but rather not actively opposing and resisting white supremacy and the privileges it entails. Fulfilling this latter condition—the complicity of silence—implies consent to the contract.

The racial contract is simultaneously an economic, political, ethical, and epistemological contract. Consider, for instance, the field of morality. Moral feelings, rules, and concerns are directed toward white people, whereas nonwhite people are excluded from this circle of morality. Epistemologically, "one has an agreement to misinterpret the world. One has to learn to see the world wrongly, but with the assurance that this set of mistaken perceptions will be validated by white epistemic authority, whether religious or secular."[54] Cogni-

---

51. Charles W. Mills, *Racial Contract*, 5.
52. Charles W. Mills, *Racial Contract*, 3.
53. Charles W. Mills, *Racial Contract*, 11.
54. Charles W. Mills, *Racial Contract*, 18.

tive dysfunctions and structured blindness (which are socially and psychologically functional) generate "the ironic outcome that whites will in general be unable to understand the world they themselves have made."[55] In sum, the moral, cognitive, and epistemological worlds of white people are shaped by misunderstandings, misinterpretations, misrepresentations, evasions, self-deceptions, and bad faith that enable one to believe wrong is right.

Mills's conceptual framework, presented here in broad strokes, also applies to the Turkishness Contract that has shaped the formation of the Turkish state, Turkish nation, and Turkish individual but with necessary contextual adaptations and modifications. Mills himself limits his theoretical framework to racialized whiteness and white supremacy: "What is needed is a global theoretical framework for situating discussions of race and white racism, and thereby challenging the assumptions of white political philosophy, which would correspond to feminist theorists' articulation of the centrality of gender, patriarchy, and sexism to traditional moral and political theory."[56] If, then, Mills limits himself to the analysis of white supremacy and whiteness, how can the theoretical framework he develops be useful for analyzing Turkishness, a category historically outside of whiteness? The answer, in my view, is that the race-based (say, white) nation and the ethnicity-based (say, Turkish) nation as analytical categories and historical constructions are variations of the same modern phenomenon in different spaces. This phenomenon is the construction of a nation and nation-state around certain racial/ethnic characteristics: that is, the rules that unite, divide, and classify a given population; the construction of borders determining who is in and who is out and who can and cannot enter; the hierarchies and relations of power that distribute varying degrees of privilege to those inside the border and systematically disadvantage those outside; and the cognitive and emotive schemas that shape the ways in which individuals see, know, think, interpret, and feel.[57]

Viewed in this way, it is not surprising that Mills's work on whiteness also offers lessons for understanding Turkishness. Thus, what if instead of trying to develop a global theoretical framework for the analysis of *white racism*, which is not necessarily relevant either to the countless racially and ethnically oppressed peoples or to the historical and everyday experience of many peoples

---

55. Charles W. Mills, *Racial Contract*, 18–19.

56. Charles W. Mills, *Racial Contract*, 2–3.

57. For a number of important studies that conceptualize ethnicity as a constructed cognitive structure and describe it as an ensemble of shared forms of perception, classification, thought, and emotion, and, in this sense, see race as a subcategory of ethnicity, see Loveman, "Is 'Race' Essential?" 891–898; Brubaker, Loveman, and Stamatov, "Ethnicity as Cognition," 31–64; Wimmer, "Strategies of Ethnic Boundary Making," 1025–1055; Wimmer, "Making and Unmaking of Ethnic Boundaries," 970–1022; Brubaker, "Ethnicity, Race, and Nationalism," 21–42.

around the world, we develop a global perspective on *racism*? Examining white-ness and Turkishness from such a global perspective and comparing their operations (their divergences, their overlaps), what new insights might result? The concept of the social contract, Mills's point of departure, seems to me an exceptionally useful vantage point from which to develop this kind of global theoretical framework about race, ethnicity, nation, racism, and nationalism.

The idea of the sovereignty of the people is directly related to the forma-tion of modern nation-states. To think of sovereignty as something belonging to the people—and not to God or his representative on Earth, the monarch—was a revolutionary idea from the outset. It transformed the source of legiti-macy and foundations of the state (divine right, nobility, charisma, violence), making the real owner of the state the people. This idea of popular sover-eignty, which developed gradually and perhaps found its strongest expression in Jean-Jacques Rousseau, was the source of a set of overlapping questions that preoccupied all the social contract theorists (notwithstanding the significant differences between them). Setting out from the principle that all legitimate governments are constituted by the governed, contract theorists put forward a range of (largely fictitious) assumptions about the hows and whys of the emergence of the original contracts. Their main aim, though, was to establish a normative model of the contract for the future. What does popular sover-eignty entail, and how should it be embodied? What kind of mutual rights, duties, agreements, and promises should be established between equal indi-viduals and between the society or people made up of individuals and the state, and what should be the basic rules and principles of this unity? The contract, as metaphor and concept, provided many with a means by which to examine these questions.[58]

But the categories of people and society proved to be too abstract, obdurate, and vague, and, as such, potentially too inclusive and democratic. This ambigu-ity and radical potentiality began to recede as the concept of nation came to replace that of people and society, imposed, in some cases, from above, and in others through an alignment of interests, feelings, and expectations from above and below. Unlike people or society, nation is a concept suffused with and evocative of emotion, arousing almost immediate loyalty. Another function (and advantage) is its capacity to determine the boundaries of people and society: who is included in these terms, who could be included in time, and who would never be. Nation signified a shared history (the present and future of a par-ticular race or ethnicity, full of suffering and triumphs); a common language,

---

58. For a useful compilation focusing on the differences and overlaps of social contract theo-rists, see Boucher and Kelly, *Social Contract from Hobbes to Rawls*.

religion, and culture (held to be superior and unique); and a common world of emotions, thoughts, and solidarity (transecting different classes and status groups). As people and society, which in theory included everyone, were replaced by the nation, which in practice included only people with certain characteristics, social contracts became national (that is, racial and ethnic) contracts. In some historical contexts, the primary condition for inclusion in national contracts has been race, in others ethnicity or religion. Whatever the primary condition, though, in most historical cases, national contracts were formed by a combination of race, ethnicity, and religion. Consequently, the institutions, structures, and ideals that social contract theorists envisioned for the society and state of the future (democracy, the republic, the constitution, morality, justice) came to belong solely to a particular nation and to function for that nation within the historicity of national contracts.

The idea of a national contract developed gradually through impositions from above and the demands and struggles arising from below. It, perhaps, reached its most elaborate form after World War II. The basic logic of the national contract is as follows: (1) the state belonged to a nation with specific racial, ethnic, and religious characteristics and with clear borders, and worked only in the interest of that nation; and (2) members enjoyed the right to vote and be elected (democracy) and/or to be promoted based on their skills and labor (meritocracy), equality before the law and fair trial (rule of law), a range of social rights and guarantees (the welfare state), and physical security (police and army). Loyalty, obedience, labor, taxes, and military service were expected in return. The immaterial cement holding together the material bases and benefits of these national contracts were such worldviews and ideologies as racism, nationalism, and civilizationism. Such ideologies were capable of smoothing out intracontractual class differences of interest through emotions. They compensated the material poverty of the intracontractual poor on the immaterial plane (feelings of superiority to the noncontractual poor, even to the rich) and enabled the exploitation of the noncontractual poor under even worse conditions. And they naturalized forms of violent rule over peoples other than those from the acceptable, legitimate, respectable, and superior nation.

To make a conceptual distinction that I find salutary for the analysis of modern logics of power and sovereignty, we can distinguish between the logic of contractualism and its opposite, the logic of colonialism, which complement one another and often operate in tandem within the same state. While the contractual logic of power is a form of sovereignty based on consent, violence forms the basis of the colonial logic of power. The contracting state operates in the interests of the contracting nation, within a certain democracy, legality, normality, and predictability, and has the explicit or implicit consent of the nation to which it offers various guarantees and privileges. Those out-side the contract, meanwhile, are governed by cultural and physical violence, threats, oppression, and states of emergency; therefore, the state does not have their consent. In other words, while the contractual logic of power rules al-most invisibly over the supposedly superior and singular nation, the colonial logic rules over those outside this nation in open and bare ways (in formal colonies, in the ghettos of the metropoles, in minority geographies of nation-states, in prisons, etc.). Putting aside, for the moment, the matter of whether colonial logics are, indeed, theoretically opposed to contractual logics (some-thing I take up in more detail in the Conclusion), what is clear is that the critical difference between being inside or outside the contract is at the heart of many contemporary economic, political, cultural, and psychological inequalities.

My argument that national contracts offer a compelling comparative frame-work for thinking about racial and ethnic inequalities and the similarities in their effects does not, of course, negate the existence of crucial differences be-tween race and ethnicity—between, say, white racism/supremacy and Turkish racism/supremacy. For example, capitalist slavery and its ongoing material effects, which are directly related to the formation of whiteness, are simply not an issue in Ottoman-Turkish history. In the same way, through this capitalist history, whiteness came to global supremacy, whereas Turkishness, as I ana-lyze it, is a form of supremacy largely limited to national borders (though it is useful for understanding states of Turkishness in countries like Germany, where millions of immigrants of Turkish origin live). The difference here is conse-quential. A white person of European origin, for example, can enjoy a privi-leged position beyond his or her national borders and feel at home in many parts of the world, whereas a Turk can experience such a position and feeling only in her own country. Sara Ahmed, as a feminist and woman of color, admi-rably describes this global privilege of whiteness: "If the world is made white then the body at home is one that can inhabit whiteness. As Fanon's work shows, after all, bodies are shaped by histories of colonialism, which makes the world 'white' as a world that is inherited or already given. This is the familiar world, the world of whiteness, as a world we know implicitly. Colonialism makes the world 'white,' which is of course a world 'ready' for certain kinds of bodies, as a world that puts certain objects within their reach. Bodies remember such histories, even when we forget them."[59]

The phenomenology of Blackness, as much as the phenomenology of white-ness, corresponds to lived experiences that are in some ways unique. As many thinkers have emphasized, the fact that Blackness is visible from the outside

---

59. Ahmed, *Queer Phenomenology*, 111.

is by no means trivial.[60] While the body is of little importance in social contract theory, little else is as important as the body in the reality of the racial contract. In Stuart Hall's words, the visibility of women and Black people facilitates racism and sexism's naturalization of difference: "Use the evidence of your eyes, don't you see they are different?"[61] Black people's permanent difference results in their inability, if they choose, to become permanently white or to pass for short periods of time. According to Mills, unlike religious differences, which conversion might bridge, "The new secular category of race . . . had the virtue of permanency over any given individual's lifetime."[62] Precisely for this reason, the lighter skinned a Black person is, the more likely he or she is to pass as white, to be comfortable around white people, and to be accepted by white people. Whereas, for example, a Jew, an Irish, or an Italian can become almost completely white over time. Fanon explains: "The Jewishness of the Jew . . . can go unnoticed. . . . He is a White man, and apart from some debatable features, he can pass undetected. . . . The Jew is not liked as soon as he has been detected. But with me things take on a *new* face. I'm not given a second chance. I am overdetermined from the outside. I am slave not to the 'idea' others have of me, but to my appearance. . . . The White gaze, the only valid one, is already dissecting me. I am *fixed*."[63]

The opportunity to pass that Fanon speaks of also applies to Armenians and Kurds in everyday interactions in Turkey. Their religious and ethnic differences, and the intellectual and emotional differences that arise from them, are generally not visible from the outside and can thus be hidden. Therefore, if they so choose, Armenians and Kurds can be invisible, unnoticeable. However, even if it is not outwardly obvious that an Armenian is not a Turk, this does not make her a Turk; it only enables her to pass momentarily, for an Armenian, as a non-Muslim, can never truly become or be accepted as a Turk. Even if she converts to Islam, the state never forgets her non-Muslim birth and lineage. Contrary to what Mills says, in other words, in certain types of national contracts, religious differences may not be bridged by conversion. Kurds, on the other hand, can (as Muslims) make a definitive transition to

---

60. In her controversial essay on segregation ("Reflections on Little Rock," 233), Hannah Arendt remarks, "The Negroes stand out because of their 'visibility.' They are not the only 'visible minority,' but they are the most visible one. In this respect, they somewhat resemble new immigrants, who invariably constitute the most 'audible' of all minorities and therefore are always the most likely to arouse xenophobic sentiments. But while audibility is a temporary phenomenon, rarely persisting beyond one generation, the Negroes' visibility is unalterable and permanent. This is not a trivial matter."

61. Hall, "Teaching Race," 129.

62. Charles W. Mills, *Racial Contract*, 54.

63. Fanon, *Black Skin, White Masks*, 95.

Turkishness in a way not limited to daily passing, but this requires a great deal of effort and investment and can leave great wounds on their souls and the souls of their families, which may not heal for generations. Moreover, bodily invisibility may also add both to the broader intellectual invisibility of problems faced by, say, Armenians and Kurds and to a more determined denial of the very existence of these problems by Turks. The inability of minorities from Turkey to accept that their problems are real requires a rephrasing of the racist logic outlined by Hall: "Use the evidence of your eyes, don't you see that we are the same?"

My point is that the capacity for invisibility does not necessarily make ethnic and religious differences less important than racial differences. Indeed, two of the biggest genocides of the past century were committed against religious minorities: Jews and Armenians. To be sure, the differences between whiteness and Turkishness, or between Blackness and Kurdishness, are important. But these differences make their comparison more interesting and instructive, I believe, rather than rendering them incomparable (which is the dominant tendency of thought in the Turkish intellectual world, for example, with very few exceptions to this de facto rule of incomparability). The concept of contract and the specific contractual histories of different countries can provide a comparative framework for the simultaneous analysis of overlaps and divergences. How do various national contracts, whatever the bases (racial, ethnic, religious) of their logic of nation-building, mark and shape bodies, minds, and institutions? What forms of unity and division do they engender between people and peoples? What sorts of historical conditions determine the flexibility or rigidity of contracts—that is, who can be included in due course, and whose inclusion is opposed? Considering such questions through the concept of contract can draw attention both to the universality of modern forms of racism and to the specific forms that racism takes in different political geographies.

There are more advantages to the concept of contract. The contract is a useful metaphor for thinking about the implicit rules in a system of inequality that distribute privilege and disadvantage and about the mechanisms of compliance to these implicit rules. It is not surprising, therefore, that Mills was inspired by Carol Pateman's *The Sexual Contract*—not surprising, that is, that Pateman's work, in calling attention to the sexual dimensions of the social contract, provides conceptual tools for the analysis of the racial dimensions of the social contract.[64] Moreover, the social contract, or, more pre-

---

64. See Pateman, *Sexual Contract*. For a dialogue between two social scientists on the metaphor of contract, see Pateman and Mills, *Contract and Domination*. Monique Wittig, meanwhile, describes the social contract as a heterosexual contract ("On the Social Contract," 33–45).

cisely, the national contract, allows for a nuanced analysis of power, insofar as it allows us to see the mutual agreements through which the lower classes of the dominant racial or ethnic group safeguard their interests through a range of strategies and performances, benefiting from power relations in different ways. The advantages of thinking through the contract are particularly clear when compared to the concept of (dominant) ideology, with its associations of "false consciousness" as a totality of shared ideas and perceptions imposed and transmitted in a top-down manner by the ruling classes to the exploited, which, ultimately, render the underclasses incapable of apprehending power relations in their full reality. It further seems to me that thinking through the concept and metaphor of the contract contributes to what C. Wright Mills famously called the sociological imagination:[65] the ability to move between different disciplines and perspectives within the social sciences and to grasp the relational ties between the social, the institutional, and the individual; between history and biography; between general political and social history and the history of ideas and emotions; and between what is seen as the most intimate and specific and the most public and general.

At this point, to concretize what I have said so far regarding the logic of the contract and to provide a general introduction to the rest of the book, it may be useful to outline the process that I call the Turkishness Contract—the process that brought forth the Turkish state, nation, and individual. The Turkishness Contract emerged gradually through a zigzagging historical process and comprises certain basic agreements and rules (some written but mostly implicit) between state and society and within society itself. Three main unwritten articles make up the contract. According to the first, to be able to enjoy a privileged and secure life in Turkey, to enjoy social mobility, and to ensure future potential mobility, one must be Muslim[66] and Turkish. As a basic condition of one's birth, Islam functions, in a way, like whiteness (race) in the United States. Those who are Muslim by birth—for the purposes of the contract, being Muslim by birth means that one's ancestors were Muslim—can later become Turkish even if not Turkish by birth (e.g., if they are ethnically Kurdish, Circassian, Bosnian, or Albanian), whereas non-Muslims have no such right or potential. According to the second article, it is strictly forbidden to speak

---

65. C. Wright Mills, *Sociological Imagination*.

66. In Ottoman and Turkish history, Islam has mainly meant Sunnism, starting from the early sixteenth century. Therefore, the first condition of the Turkishness Contract could have been Sunnism instead of Islam. However, the Turkishness Contract, especially after 1923 with secularism, developed some mechanisms to include Alevis and did not consider Alevis as non-Muslims, that is, did not categorically exclude them from the contract. Therefore, although Sunnism is a much more privileged and powerful sociological category than Alevism, I think it is more accurate to call it Islam instead of Sunnism.

the truth about what happened to non-Muslims in the Ottoman Empire and Turkey (political histories of deportation, massacre, genocide, extortion, racism, and discrimination), to sympathize with these groups, and to politically and intellectually engage in their favor. Along similar lines, according to the third article, it is strictly forbidden to speak the truth about what happened to Muslims, especially the Kurds, who resisted Turkification, to sympathize with them, and to politically and intellectually engage on their behalf.

The Turkishness Contract is secured primarily through mechanisms of reward and punishment. One who complies with the contract is able to benefit from real and potential privileges, such as finding work and making use of different means of social mobility (consolidating one's position in various social fields, ascending or gaining in status, moving up in class). In addition to these material privileges, there are such psychological privileges as the senses of superiority, righteousness, and normality that come with Turkishness. Failure to comply is punished with severity: one can be fired, not hired, imprisoned, killed, or, at the very least (but for some, the worst), ostracized. In addition to these material disadvantages, there are such psychological disadvantages as the senses of worthlessness, wrongness, and abnormality that come with not being Turkish. These mechanisms of reward and punishment further impact not only the discrete individuals but often their families as well. Therefore, in accepting or rejecting the Turkishness Contract, one has to think about not only oneself but also one's family. This may explain why millions of Muslims who are not ethnically Turkish—including many Kurds—have assimilated to Turkishness, as well as why countless Turks who are ethnically Turkish, but who are, by worldview, not inclined to attach importance to being Turkish (who do not consciously do so) nevertheless comply with the contract.

As I see it, the Turkishness Contract, though (or perhaps because) unwritten, is a more influential constitution for modern Turkey than any formal written constitution. For both Turks and the Turkified, the historical formation and social functioning of the contract shape not only their ways of seeing, hearing, knowing, caring, and feeling but also their ways of not seeing, not hearing, not knowing, not caring, and not feeling. States of Turkishness are experienced almost automatically and reflexively by the vast majority of Turks. This automaticity or spontaneity is the result of individuals having internalized states of Turkishness through socialization within the environments and institutions of one's birth, upbringing, and professional life, particularly through what I later discuss as the *performances of Turkishness* expected of actors in specific environments and institutions. Turkishness is experienced as *habitus*, as history and society become the nature of individuals—what Pierre Bourdieu termed "history turned into nature"[67]—and seep into the unconscious. Anyone not subjected to a similar socialization process (one born and raised in social environments where Turkishness is not dominant, such as certain Kurds or Armenians) performs Turkishness more consciously. When they enter Turkish-dominated circles or institutions, they can speak, behave, or dress like a Turk—that is, they can pass. Unlike in the United States, non-Muslims and non-Turks are often not obvious from the outside, such that casual and spontaneous passing is relatively common and easy. And when non-Muslims or non-Turks enter fields and spaces dominated by Kurds or Armenians (their homes or churches), in a sense, they take off their Turkish clothes and mask and return both to Kurdishness and Armenianness and to their true selves. For non-Turks, the ability to execute performances of Turkishness and to enter the world of Turkishness are necessary strategies for getting on and for survival. In James C. Scott's words, "The more menacing the power, the thicker the mask."[68]

The contract further determines the mentality and functioning of public and private institutions and fields. It determines who is to be favored and who is to be punished as well as the mechanisms of social inclusion and exclusion. To maintain one's place in the social structure or to rise in the ranks, then, anyone who reaches working age must know the explicit and implicit rules of the institutions and fields of work and must meet these expectations. For example, a judge in the justice system is expected to rule as a Turk, a journalist in the media is expected to report as a Turk, an academic at a university is expected to write as a Turk, and, at the end of the day, most perform accordingly. These expectations and the roles that take shape in response practically become one's character. In other words, these roles are so internalized that one does not realize that she sees, knows, and behaves in such a way; he does not realize what he does not see, does not know, and does not attend to. This is, in part, what I mean by describing Turkishness as certain (often unconscious) states of seeing, hearing, knowing, caring, and feeling as well as not seeing, not hearing, not knowing, not caring, and not feeling.

The states of not seeing, not hearing, not knowing, not caring, and not feeling, which I describe as the negative states of Turkishness, may appear, at first glance, as deficiencies. In fact, though, the negative states of Turkishness are, as with whiteness, privileges. Because, in any country, only the dominant group has the right—more importantly, the power—not to see, not to hear, not to

---

67. Bourdieu, *Outline of a Theory*, 78–79.
68. Scott, *Domination and the Arts of Resistance*, 3.

know, not to care, not to be interested, and not to feel. There is a close correlation between one's ethnic and class position within a power hierarchy and the forms of seeing and not seeing, hearing and not hearing, knowing and not knowing, caring and not caring, and feeling and not feeling. Specifically, a member of the dominant ethnic group may not care about those at the bottom of the ethnic hierarchy, may not care about their opinions, and may not listen to them, because he or she has the power to do so, and nothing is lost or risked thereby. The people at the bottom, meanwhile, must know what the people at the top think, and must listen to what they say, because such knowledge is the basic condition for getting on and surviving. Correspondingly, only the dominant ethnic/racial group in a country can believe and claim that there is no ethnic or racial problem. One believes because he does not know, and one does not know because of one's power. This suggests that, just as those at the bottom have an interest in knowing, caring, and feeling, those at the top have an interest in not knowing, not caring, not feeling.

The negative states of Turkishness are secured by such institutions as politics, religion, the judiciary, the media, the university, and the family—all part of the Turkishness Contract. These institutions are organized either around *not* producing knowledge about the subordinate and the marginalized and the realities in which they live, or else around framing such knowledge as worthless, false, a lie, or a sin. Not knowing is, in a sense, guaranteed. However, the ignorance, indifference, and callousness of educated and literate Turkish intellectuals, particularly those with universalist ideological affiliations (Marxism and internationalism, Islamism and ummahism, Kemalism and enlightenmentism), is arguably less passive. That is, it is not for a lack of knowledge that they do not know. Their ignorance stems from refusing to take such knowledge seriously, rejecting its veracity, or assuming something is "fishy." Yet these strategies of ignorance and mechanisms of escape from knowledge must necessarily be unconscious for intellectuals to maintain their self-esteem. Universalist ideologies can thus be thought of as respectable and noble escape routes. For example, a Marxist may not take the Kurdish or Armenian issue seriously enough on the assumption that Armenians and Kurds are "playing into the hands of imperialism" or "practicing identity politics, not class politics." An Islamist may accuse Kurds of "tribalism" or "dividing the ummah." A Kemalist may think of Kurds as "feudal, reactionary and religious." So long as they are not seen as intellectual strategies of Turkishness, such objections, criticisms, and frames function as escape mechanisms. To the extent that they are (or appear to be) universalist, the escape they offer seems respectable. By shifting the blame and externalizing, they make it possible to remain apathetic and righteous. Moreover, they can only be sustained through profound self-ignorance. That is, they perpetuate the illusion that one's thoughts and feelings are determined solely by one's ideology or worldview, independent of Turkishness. And there is, of course, an interest in maintaining this self-delusion or self-deception. Perhaps more importantly, in the hands of universalist intellectuals, this particular interest is able to appear as disinterested.

My aim here is not to equate socialists, Islamists, and Kemalists in the crucible of Turkishness. Nor is it to blur their differences or present them as insignificant. On the contrary, as I discuss in Chapter 4, the overwhelming majority of Turks who have exited the Turkishness Contract and paid a range of prices for doing so have been socialists, even if they make up a small minority within Turkey. However, this reality should not blind us to another: many socialists have not exited the contract; they have developed a range of strategies to avoid doing so, allowing their thoughts and feelings to remain shaped by Turkishness and the blind spots that they fail to recognize. Reflecting on these blind spots may make it possible to recognize and thus remove some of the often invisible obstacles before such leftist ideals as equality and freedom. This is, after all, what the 1968 world cultural revolution, in general, and ideas like intersectionality, in particular, teach us.

A General Map of the Book

Chapter 1 begins with what I call the Ottomanness Contract, a political, legal, and institutional project through which the nineteenth-century Ottoman Empire, beset by a range of problems and struggling to survive, attempted to keep its heterogeneous population together. The main subject of the chapter, however, is the Muslimness Contract, which replaced the Ottomanness Contract, as the latter proved, for reasons I discuss, unsuccessful and unpopular. This contract came to define the past fifty years of the Ottoman Empire and gave rise to the formation of a new state and nation around Islam. Islam became the basic innate condition of the social contract—that is, of the nation and the state. And non-Muslims were eliminated from Anatolia through the practices and policies of massacre, deportation, economic boycott, wealth transfer, genocide, and population exchange. That horizontality—the shared feelings, interests, and expectations of both Muslim elites and the ordinary Muslims, and between the center and the provinces—defined the Muslimness Contract is one of the main claims of this chapter.

Chapter 2 focuses on the new nation-state, the Republic of Turkey, the establishment of which, in 1923, owed much to the Muslimness Contract, yet narrowed and Turkified this contract in a vertical move from top to bottom. With the transition to the Turkishness Contract, being Muslim was no longer sufficient in itself to benefit from the contract in a meaningful sense. A Muslim was now also expected to be Turkish, or to Turkify. Such a narrowing of the contract further ushered in the now-long-standing Kurdish issue. The Kurdish uprisings that began in 1925 continue to this day by different means, and the state has ruled over Kurdistan through states of emergency, lawlessness, and physical and cultural violence—in short, as though it were administering a colony.

In Chapter 3, I analyze how and why certain forms of seeing and not seeing, knowing and not knowing, hearing and not hearing, and caring and not caring have taken shape and examine how these forms are connected to the strategies, performances, and privileges of Turkishness. How has the Turkishness Contract shaped the characters, bodies, and ways of presenting/hiding oneself in interactions with Turks, not only for those who grew up within the contract but also for non-Muslims and Kurds who remained outside of it. In this chapter, I draw on in-depth interviews I conducted with Kurds as well as on interviews by other researchers with non-Muslims working in different fields and exposed to different aspects of Turkishness. It may perhaps seem odd, at first glance, for a book on Turkishness to make use of field studies conducted with non-Muslims and Kurds. The reason for this choice is simple. Whereas Turks' knowledge of and insights into the Turkishness Contract and their own Turkishness is acutely limited, that of non-Muslims and Kurds is necessarily highly developed and aware.

In Chapter 4, I examine the relative loss of power and privilege of Turks, which I describe as a "crisis of Turkishness." This loss is largely due to the resistance of Kurds to the Turkishness Contract across the past forty years and to forms of Kurdish power of their own making. Through their empowerment, Kurds have both eroded the Turkish privileges of not seeing, not hearing, not knowing, not caring, and not feeling and chipped away at the Turkish monopoly over definition. As important as it is to understand the Turkishness Contract's hierarchy of power and privilege in order to grasp Turkishness, it is equally important to understand how this hierarchy of power and privilege has changed in order to grasp how Turkishness has changed, even transformed. This reminds us that contracts, as historical agreements, are not stable but perpetually changing (expanding, contracting, stretching, hardening, being born, and dying). In this chapter, by examining the personal transformation of the Turkish intellectual İsmail Beşikçi, I analyze the crisis of Turkish ignorance and explore how this gives rise to new subjectivities and new ways of knowing. I approach Beşikçi, who was severely punished by the state for his writings on the Kurdish issue, purged from academia, and imprisoned for more than seventeen years, as a singular phenomenon whose life and trajectory demonstrate the strategies that sustain ignorance as well as the transformations and new ways of knowing born of the failure of these strategies. That said, the crisis and transformation of Turkishness in academia are today more encompassing, as evidenced by the fact that, in 2016, more than two thousand academics, known as Academics for Peace (Barış Akademisyenleri), signed a radical text criticizing the state's Kurdish policy, for which hundreds paid a serious price. Chapter 4 includes a brief analysis of the Academics for Peace affair.

1

The Muslimness Contract

In this chapter, I explore the Islamization of Anatolia and the process of its "cleansing" of non-Muslims through the concept of the Muslimness Contract. I focus on such large-scale historical incidents as the Armenian Genocide, the War of Independence, and the foundation of the Turkish state. Nothing that I draw on here is strictly new, nor is anything presented here for the first time. What I have rather tried to do is to reevaluate the existing knowledge and literature through a new concept, from a new perspective.

The Muslimness Contract is of critical importance for making sense of the historical and contemporary nature of the Turkishness Contract. After all, the Muslim state and nation that came to form the basis of the Turkishness Contract took shape within the context of a Muslimness Contract, which involved the purging, by various means, of Ottoman non-Muslims by Ottoman Muslims. Another characteristic of the Muslimness Contract that I find important for the analysis of twentieth-century Turkey is this: the Muslimness Contract grew out of a parallelism and horizontality both between the center and the provinces and between different social classes—in short, it emerged from a set of common interests and feelings shared by Muslims. I aim to show later how this contract, forged of the common interests, sentiments, and wills of Muslims, constitutes a historical example of the concretization of certain abstract and normative concepts put forward by seventeenth- and eighteenth-century philosophers under the idea of a social contract.

The idea of a social contract is tied to efforts to create a new state and society, in an age of great change in Europe, around new principles arrived at through consensus. Old orders were toppled and new ones established. Aristocracies were on the decline, replaced by an ascendant bourgeoisie. The idea of the individual came to replace that of communities. And the idea of a people or nation composed of equal citizens came to replace God as the source of sovereignty. In this general context, the nineteenth century saw Ottoman attempts to ensure the unity of its heterogeneous population through a modern consensus between state and society, based on new principles and institutions: equality, secularism, freedom, rule of law, human rights, consent, and parliamentary forms of rule. This attempt, which I describe as the Ottomanness Contract, failed for reasons to be discussed later. Yet, it was, if nothing else, an attempt to construct—if in the abstract—a true social contract, claiming to include the whole of society (Muslims, Christians, Jews, etc.). This distinguishes the Ottomanness Contract from what came to be the triumphant Muslimness and Turkishness Contracts, which were never *social* contracts, as they favored only Muslims and Turks and penalized non-Muslims and non-Turks. They were, in short—and as their names clearly attest—contracts of *Muslimness* and *Turkishness*.

In this chapter, I describe the transition from the Ottomanness Contract to the Muslimness Contract. In Chapter 2, I describe the transition to the Turkishness Contract as emerging from the Muslimness Contract. Yet, one should not picture this transition as something linear, smooth, or preplanned. It zigzagged, developing in relation to domestic dynamics, conflicts, contradictions, alliances, and the various interventions of the Great Powers (Britain, France, and Russia). At times, the Ottomanness Contract was at the forefront, at others, the Muslimness Contract, and, at still others, the Turkishness Contract. This politics of contracts, for instance, was such that the Ottomanness Contract, thought to have been consigned to history, occasionally resurfaced and became, once again, the dominant politics. Or, in another instance of such a politics, when Unionists ousted Abdülhamid II, they reinstated a form of his Muslimness Contract. The analysis that follows reflects, then, this oscillation between the different conceptualizations and different politics of contracts.

The Ottomanness Contract

In the late eighteenth and early nineteenth centuries, the Ottoman Empire faced a range of external and internal threats of a magnitude that jeopardized its very existence. Militarily, it was losing power and territory to its historical rivals, Russia and Austria. It was exposed to the increasing aggression of the Great Powers (Britain, France). And the Ottoman economy, largely based on agriculture and artisanship, was increasingly unable to compete with the productivity and speed of the Industrial Revolution. The empire struggled, more and more, to hold together its multireligious and multilingual cosmopolitan population. And the centrifugal tendencies of notables (*ayan*) in the provinces and principalities (*mirlik*) or tribes along the borders, in addition to the efforts of Mehmet Ali Pasha of Egypt to take over the center, posed a vital threat to the very existence of the empire.[1] To be able to counter such challenges, the Ottoman Empire set in motion a series of modernization and centralization reforms in the military, diplomatic, administrative, legal, educational, financial, and economic fields—reforms that began during the reign of Sultan Selim III but truly accelerated under Mahmud II. Through these reforms, the state sought to prevent territorial fragmentation or retraction, chiefly through the elimination or weakening of internal obstacles. It also aimed to be able to catch up rapidly with Europe in the fields of power and civilization (bureaucracy, science, technology, industrialization, urbanization, etc.).

That said, material reforms were necessarily accompanied by what we might call ideological reforms. The traditional idea of empire, which not only tolerated and prided itself on cultural diversity but also included a rigid hierarchy inherent in the logic of tolerance,[2] was no longer sufficient to hold together what was perhaps the most cosmopolitan population in the early nineteenth-century world. Particularly with the French Revolution, the ideas of freedom and equality, spreading rapidly across the globe, also touched down in the Ottoman Empire, as non-Muslim populations began to demand equality and freedom. Yet, such demands, especially in the Balkans, often involved not individual but collective and national forms of equality and liberty. In other words, increasingly, non-Muslim peoples sought to cast off the "Ottoman yoke" and establish their own national states. To curb this trend, Mahmud II was willing to abandon a certain hierarchical notion of being Ottoman, advancing in its place a concept of Ottomanism promising equality among Ottoman subjects, regardless of religion or language. This corresponded, in some sense, to the modern ideal of the equal citizen and included a certain notion of secularism. Mahmud II's purported statement toward the end of his life—"I recognize, of my sub-

---

1. For a summary, see Hanioğlu, *A Brief History of the Late Ottoman Empire*, 6–41.

2. This phenomenon of diversity as well as pride in diversity, present in nearly all traditional or premodern empires, was, in the Ottoman Empire, further fostered by Islamic law. Under Islamic law, members of the Abrahamic religions were under the protection of the Islamic state and society, as long as they recognized and did not rebel against the sovereignty of Islam. These so-called *zimme* were, in a sense, indebted to (*zimmetli*) Islamic state and society. Claude Cahen ("Zimme," 566) describes the concept of *zimmet* through that of contract: "[Zimmet] refers to a type of contract, in force indefinitely, whereby the Muslim community provides hospitality and protection to members of other Abrahamic religions, on the condition that they recognize Islamic sovereignty."

jects, the Muslims in the mosque, the Christians in the church, and the Jews in the synagogue; there is no other [kind of] difference between them"³—is representative of this new understanding. A further reflection of this new understanding of equality and secularism was the abolition of traditional laws requiring different *millets*⁴ to wear different clothing, which were replaced in 1829, under Mahmud II's reign, by equality in dress.⁵

Such ideas were first articulated in a coherent manner in the Tanzimat Edict of 1839 (Edict of Reorganization), announced after Sultan Abdülmecid took the oath of allegiance. Equality before the state and the law was envisaged between Muslims and non-Muslims. The security of life, honor, and property of every individual was to be protected by the state. And there could be no punishment, it was declared, without law or trial. The edict promised to limit the power of the sultan and the state and to transform the state into a state of law. After touching on rights and immunities, it went on to detail the duties of subjects (military service, taxation), promising equality and justice in such duties as well. State officials were tasked with reading the edict aloud in the provinces, taking an oath while doing so. Another edict, sent to the provinces alongside the Tanzimat Edict, emphasized the equality of all before the law, from viziers to shepherds.⁶

To my mind, the ideas, principles, and promises embodied in the Tanzimat Edict can be seen as a form of Ottomanness Contract. Though Yavuz Abadan does not employ a metaphor of contract, he explains the "first and considerable task" of the edict as follows: "To gather the masses, on whom the Empire rests, and who are exposed to the danger of disintegration, around new principles, and, basing state activity on these principles, to establish, among various elements, restraint and unity, order and regularity among the various elements—the fundamental conditions for unity and security—as well as to establish the foundations for disciplined work for the achievement of common goals."⁷ In terms of its legal form, Bülent Tanör notes, "It is not bilateral (a covenant or contract), it is unilateral, it is a decree."⁸ Though this may be the

3. Quoted in Kaynar, *Mustafa Reşit Paşa ve Tanzimat*, 100.

4. Translator's note: broadly speaking, the Ottoman millet (literally, nation) system divided the social world into different communities based on religion—e.g., the Rum millet, the Armenian millet, etc. Each millet enjoyed a certain degree of decentralized autonomy, even if this degree shifted in practice across historical and political contexts. Yet all millets were ultimately subsumed within a hierarchical order, wherein Ottoman Muslims enjoyed the status of *millet-i hakime*—literally, the dominant nation.

5. On transformations in Ottoman dress codes, see Quataert, "Clothing Laws, State, and Society," 403–425.

6. On this additional edict, see Kaynar, *Mustafa Reşit Paşa ve Tanzimat*, 180–182.

7. Abadan, "Tanzimat Fermanı'nin Tahlili," 40.

8. Tanör, *Osmanlı-Türk Anayasa Gelişmeleri*, 92.

case from a technical and legal standpoint, the edict was nevertheless essentially a contract; it was a call and a "promise" made on behalf of the state to Ottoman subjects, read by the sultan, viziers, and sworn state officials: a call and promise of a common and equal life based on new principles. The state promised to protect the rights of individuals in exchange for taxes, military service, and, most important, loyalty—that is, a shared sense of Ottomanism and patriotism. It was a liberal contract, consonant with the spirit of the nineteenth century, that sought a consensus between state, society, and the individual, through an emphasis on individual rights and freedoms and limitations to state power.[9] Thereby, it was hoped, the Ottoman Empire would survive as a unified whole and catch up rapidly with Europe.

The call to Ottomanization in the Tanzimat Edict was not solely theoretical. Between 1839 and 1876—what we might call the period of the Ottomanness Contract—modern schools were opened, secular laws (including criminal, commercial, civil, and land laws) were enacted, courts were established, and non-Muslims were able to work in central and provincial advisory councils and in the rapidly growing bureaucracy, all while preserving their religion. The Islahat Edict (Edict of Reform) of 1856 underscored even more strongly the equality of Muslims and non-Muslims. It ensured the continuation of the rights and privileges of non-Muslims and banned the use of negative or insulting terms directed at such groups. Meanwhile, when the first Ottoman constitution, the *Kanun-u Esasi*, was announced in 1876 (through the acts of a number of constitutionalist Ottoman bureaucrats and intellectuals, chiefly Midhat Pasha), this represented in many ways the nineteenth-century culmination of the Ottomanness Contract. The constitution guaranteed a range of rights, freedoms, and immunities, declaring, "All citizens of the Ottoman Empire, regardless of their religion and sect, are called Ottomans, without exception" (Article Eight). Further, all Ottomans were deemed equal before the law, in both rights and duties (Article Seventeen).[10] Indeed, in accordance with the spirit of the constitution, non-Muslims were represented in the first Ottoman parliament in proportion to—even higher than—their population (around 30 percent).[11]

These and similar developments underscore, again, the practical and concrete, and not merely theoretical, nature of the Ottomanness Contract. But the contract was not sufficiently embraced, either by the state or the people,

---

9. Abadan and Enver Ziya Karal call attention to the liberal-philosophical tint of the edict: Abadan, "Tanzimat Fermanı'nin Tahlili," 57; Karal, "Gülhane Hatt-ı Hümayunu nda Batı'nın Etkisi," 79.

10. Kili and Gözübüyük, *Türk Anayasa Metinleri*, 44.

11. Ortaylı, "İlk Osmanlı Parlamentosu," 169–183.

and eventually failed. A number of reasons can be offered for this failure, in no particular order of importance, as follows. First, the state—due to internal intellectual divisions and divergent interests—failed to fulfill its promises of legality, equality, and secularism. A religious/secular dichotomy persisted in both education and law. Sharia law was consistently referenced alongside secular laws, and Islam was emphasized as the state religion. Sharia courts continued alongside secular courts, and religious instruction continued alongside secular instruction.[12] Second, a significant proportion of the non-Muslim population demanded self-governance—autonomy or independence—rather than individual equality; this represented, in a sense, the claim and the will of traditional Ottoman millets to become modern nations. Thus, the Ottomanness Contract was in line with the liberalism of the nineteenth-century spirit but at odds with another critical component of the same spirit: nationalism.[13] Third, while the international Great Powers were unable to find a solution to the "Eastern Question"—that is, they could not agree on how to divide the Ottoman Empire among themselves—they were nonetheless able to support non-Muslim peoples striving for autonomy or independence from the Ottoman Empire. The interest of foreign states and missionaries in non-Muslim Ottomans led to much fear among Muslims about the loss of the lands they inhabited. Such details underscore the extent to which not only domestic but also international factors influenced this and subsequent contracts. Indeed, critical steps such as the Tanzimat Edict, the Islahat Edict, and the constitution were all taken in an environment of international crisis engulfing the Ottoman Empire. Fourth, there was a growing sense of resentment against non-Muslims among the Muslim populations of the empire. Many of the latter simply could not stomach being equal to—or being characterized as equal to—non-Muslims, whom they were accustomed to being superior to. Many were further upset by the economic and legal privileges granted to non-Muslims by foreign states, or else granted by some degree of force by the Ottoman Empire. A sense of economic and cultural inferiority vis-à-vis non-Muslims also bred jealousy. In other words, many Muslims were told they were equal to those they did not want to be equal to and felt they could not be equal in ways they wanted to be.[14]

---

12. Ortaylı, *İmparatorluğun en Uzun Yüzyılı*, 185–186.

13. Further, the community leaders of non-Muslim millets thought that ideas such as Ottomanism, citizenship, and equality, which would entail giving up the millet system, would reduce their power, and thus did not favor it. Hanioğlu, *History of the Late Ottoman Empire*, 75. Şükrü Hanioğlu reports that some Ottoman Greeks also disliked the idea of being equal to Ottoman Jews.

14. On the reasons for the failure of the Tanzimat ideal of equality, see Davison, "Attitudes Concerning Christian-Muslim Equality," 844–864.

It is perhaps something near universal for those who see themselves as superior and who are accustomed to seeing the world in this way to balk at and resist policies of equality. After all, equality spells the end of superiority. Not only the policies of equality but even the very idea of equality threatens supremacy. Were the idea of equality to become widespread and legitimized, those who claim superiority would lose the power either to emphasize the inferior status of the other or to call the other what they want to call them— potentially a source of great anger and resentment for those who see themselves as superior. For instance, in the context of the Edict of Reform, we can interpret a common lament—"will we not be able to call a *gâvur*[15] a *gâvur*?"— as encapsulating, in pithy form, a more universal lament of groups whose superiority within racial, ethnic, class, and sexual hierarchies is jeopardized, and who can no longer address those below them as they wish. Not being able to call a *gâvur* a *gâvur* is an emotional wound for Ottoman-Turkey Islamists that has yet to heal. (And, in fact, it is this wound, I believe, that, in 2016, prompted then–Deputy Prime Minister Numan Kurtulmuş to say, 160 years after the edict, "One of the most fundamental characteristics of this great civilization, which we call Turkish Islam and which has survived to this day, is to be able to stand up against the *gâvur* by calling a *gâvur* a *gâvur*."[16]) The insistence on calling a Black person *zenci* (negro), a woman *bayan* (lady), or a Kurd an Easterner (*Doğulu*), an Eastern citizen (*Doğulu Vatandaş*) or of Kurdish origin (*Kürt kökenli*) is clearly related to the effort to maintain superiority through a monopoly over the power of definition. The spread of terms chosen and used by those at the bottom for themselves is, meanwhile, experienced by those at the top as a great loss of position.[17]

---

15. Translator's note: *gâvur* refers to non-Muslims, corresponding more or less to "infidel," and, in contexts of usage, is derogatory and injurious. Though, in an illustration of the author's point here, not all speakers would admit to or even recognize the injuriousness in the term's pragmatics.

16. Following these remarks, Kurtulmuş said that *gâvur* means not non-Muslim but despot and imperialist. "Bağımsızlık Gâvura Gâvur Diyebilmektir," Hürriyet, December 3, 2016, available at http://www.hurriyet.com.tr/bagimsizlik-gavura-gavur-diyebilmektir-40296043.

17. Translator's note: the italicized terms are well-chosen examples of terms whose pragmatic injuriousness (as with *gâvur*) users or speakers may very well deny: *zenci*, corresponding to something like negro (at best); *bayan*, being a rather invented derivative of a term for men, corresponding to something like "lady," and with many activists and scholars mindful of the linguistic pragmatics of gender politics calling for *kadın* ("woman") instead; *Doğulu* and *Doğulu vatandaş*, being ways of avoiding having to actually refer to a person's Kurdishness by simply vaguely referring to a geographic space that is largely Kurdish; and *Kürt kökenli*, a means of avoiding calling someone Kurdish by saying she may be Kurdish in origin or may speak Kurdish but is nevertheless allied with Turkishness.

The Ottoman State in the Tanzimat period, and the Ottomanness Contract in particular, also had to take Ottoman intellectuals into account in the
emerging debates around the concept of equality. When the Tanzimat Edict
was issued, the figure of an Ottoman intellectual independent or relatively
independent from the state did not yet exist. In the coming decades, however, the emergence of an Ottoman press and Ottoman public opinion, the
opening of modern secular schools, and the growing influence of ideas ema-
nating from Europe gave birth to the Ottoman intellectual, who was partially independent of the state and spoke to a readership and audience beyond
state rulers, with the Young Ottomans as the first representatives of this new
figure. Emerging in the 1860s, the Young Ottomans grew concerned with
how to rescue and advance the empire and in which direction to steer the
inevitable changes around them.

To be sure, significant differences of opinion and emphasis existed across
such Young Ottomans as Şinasi, Ziya Pasha, Ali Suavi, and Namık Kemal.
Yet, significant overlaps—opposition to the dictatorship of the Sublime Porte,
constitutionalism, advocating freedom, and an indigenous modernization free
of mimicry—also make it possible to speak of them as a coherent group. More
central to our topic was the fierce opposition such figures cultivated in their
newspapers against the Tanzimat Edict, especially the Islahat Edict, which
they labeled the Edict of Privilege, on the grounds that it abolished the dominant status of Muslims, privileging non-Muslims (whose subordinate status,
they emphasized, was clear in Sharia). In this sense, the Young Ottomans
assumed the role of the voice of the disgruntled Muslim majority. For example, Ali Suavi said of Muslims, "Short of being unable to tolerate the privileged state of subordinate people, [they] can never accept that [non-Muslims]
are dominant. . . . They dare to do anything, and they shall spill so much
blood." And in Ziya Pasha's words, "Although the Nation of Islam has been
tolerant until now, because things have reached levels that cannot be tolerated and forborne, and that the honor and zeal of Islam cannot stomach, the
day will come when push comes to shove and things will get out of control."[18]

The Young Ottomans embraced the ideas of modernization, progress, and
freedom thought to be represented by the West in the nineteenth century. But
they also gave them an Islamic spin, Islamizing the concepts and demanding
a modern constitutional monarchy and order based on Islam. Islam was held
to be capable of providing an important unifying force and sense of solidarity among Muslims for the survival of the empire. They envisioned a unity *of*
Muslims—a Union of Islam (*İttihad-ı İslam*)—and largely *for* Muslims with-

---

18. Quoted in Türköne, *Siyasi İdeoloji Olarak İslamcılığın Doğuşu*, 68–70.

in the Ottoman Empire. They were also aware that with Europeans colonizing Muslim lands across the globe, the Ottoman caliphate had the potential
to lead the Muslims of the world. The Young Ottomans were thus the first
Islamists of the Ottoman Empire. Or, in the language of this book, by arguing that Islam has a tradition of democracy (*meşveret*) and contract (*biat*) at
its core—in other words, by considering the participation and consent of
people in governance as indispensable for Islam[19]—they were proposing a
modern Muslimness Contract. To be sure, in the country they envisioned, it
was Muslims who would be superior and privileged and would enjoy safety
and dignity. They also declared this, with great self-confidence, to be the
aspiration of the majority, of the dominant element (that is to say, Muslims);
they were merely its spokespersons. In other words, the Young Ottomans saw
themselves as addressing the state on behalf of the people, proposing a new
contract to the state. But, in the 1860s and 1870s (and unlike the 1920s), the
non-Muslim population was still of sufficiently significant size, perhaps too
large even, to be termed a minority. For this reason, Young Ottomans could
not simply dismiss this population, leading them to sometimes resort to a
more inclusive Ottomanist language. For instance, in the parliament they advocated non-Muslim and Muslim parliamentarians sitting side by side, thereby abolishing the practice of spatial segregation. Yet, examining Young Ottoman
intellectuals more generally, any emphasis on Ottomanism appears to be rather
weak and inconsistent. The central emphasis was instead on Islam and, at
times, Turkishness therein.[20] It is in this sense that we can think of the Young
Ottomans as the intellectual pioneers of the Muslimness Contract.

Abdülhamid II and the Muslimness Contract

It was Abdülhamid II who transformed both Islamic reactions and emotions
from below (among Muslim Ottomans) and the rising political Islamism of
the middle class into a state project—namely, into the Muslimness Contract.
In contrast to what Young Ottomanist thinkers proposed, however, he did so
through authoritarian rather than constitutional and liberal means. The exile
of the Ottomanist Midhat Pasha, the architect of the constitution, and the
dissolution of the parliament and suspension of the constitution on the pre-

---

19. Türköne, *Siyasi İdeoloji Olarak İslamcılığın Doğuşu*, 102–124. Şerif Mardin argues that
the Ottoman state and social structure harbored the idea of an implicit contract. Revolts broke
out when the contract was not respected by the state, he says, and died down when the contract
was reestablished. According to Mardin, we see the effects of this tradition of social contract even
in Republican history. See Mardin, "Osmanlı Bakış Açısından Hürriyet," 103–122.
20. Mardin, *Yeni Osmanlı Düşüncesinin Doğuşu*, 362–367.

text of the Ottoman-Russian War of 1877–1878, all pointed to the end of the Tanzimat Period and the Ottomanness Contract and allowed for Abdülhamid to establish his regime of tyranny. Yet, the war also symbolized the fact that Ottomanism no longer made sense in the eyes of Muslims.

Taken together, the persistent revolts in the Balkans, Russia's overwhelming victory in the war, and the Ottoman loss of large territories in the Balkans and Caucasus definitively spelled, for many, the failure of Ottomanism. As a consequence of territorial losses, the relative proportion of the Ottoman Christian population decreased while that of Muslims increased. Perhaps the most important factor behind this shift was the migration of Muslims from lost territories to Anatolia. In fact, Muslim migration had begun much earlier and was rooted in two main factors: migration from territories lost by the Ottomans to Christian nations through wars or uprisings, and migration from the conquests and massacres of Russia. From the 1820s to the 1920s, millions of Muslim immigrants irreversibly lost their lands, employment, and family, and their relocation came to play a critical role in the implementation and success of both the Muslimness and the Turkishness Contracts—indeed, in the very construction of contemporary Turkey.[21] Immigrant Muslims harbored great anger and resentment toward Christians. Among their greatest fears, as landless and homeless strangers in a new country, was to experience the same thing again in their new home. It was this, arguably, that rendered them far more vulnerable to state manipulations and threats. Of course, it was not only immigrant Muslims who were angry with Christians; local Muslims also feared losing their land at any moment. In short, the Ottoman-Russian War of 1877–1878 brought tremendous territorial losses and demonstrated Russia's power to invade Anatolia from both west and east. It thus constitutes one of the most critical moments in the making of key Muslim emotions: anger, resentment, and fear. Abdülhamid II was the first Ottoman-Turkish ruler to deliberately make use of such historically formed sentiments for a political project; therein lies much of his significance.

The historian Kemal Karpat describes the growing significance of this Muslim emotional consciousness after the Ottoman-Russian War of 1877–1878

---

21. E.g., the historian Nedim Pek notes: "On the other hand, Turkish migration from Rumelia gave the Turkish element, already in the majority in Anatolia, an overwhelming numerical superiority . . . [and] the mass of immigrants would constitute a resource of soldiers for the Balkan War, the First World War and the War of Independence, alongside the native population of Anatolia. . . . The successful integration of the masses of immigrants into Ottoman society strengthened the social structure of Anatolia and paved the way for the establishment of the national Turkish State" (*Rumeli'den Anadolu'ya Türk Göçmenleri*, 228, 239).

(a consciousness that he himself participates in and reflects in his academic work) as follows:

> Although the war was disastrous for the Ottoman state in every possible way, it helped transform overnight the Muslims' sense of religious brotherhood into a political consciousness, and thus it opened the way for a new sense of solidarity and development of the idea of a new type of political community. . . . This was a mental and psychological transformation that made the Muslims in even the remotest corners of the Empire aware of their position in society and in the world at large. . . . Awareness of the significance of the Ottoman defeat and of the possibly imminent collapse of the Empire also seeped into the consciousness of the Muslim-Ottoman masses and brought about a degree of self-awareness and popular self-defensive mobilization. The Ottomans lost the war on the battlefield and, together with it, the delusion that they were a *devlet-i muazzama* (great power) and the illusion of *devlet-i ebed müddet* (eternal state); but they won the war of the mind by learning how to think realistically and, if necessary, to take concrete action of their own volition without the prodding of a higher authority.[22]

The condition of the Kurds at the time offers an apt example through which to explore this Muslim emotional consciousness and how Abdülhamid transformed this consciousness into state policy. Many Kurds feared expulsion from the lands they had inhabited for centuries at the hands of Armenians, who had also been living in more or less the same lands for centuries. This was the era of the emergence of Armenian nationalism, and the fear was that Russia, in particular, and the Christian Great Powers, more generally, would support the Armenian cause. This fear was, indeed, not unfounded; the powers in question largely viewed matters solely in terms of an Armenian issue, largely ignoring Kurds living in the same geography. Another factor that particularly worried Sunni Kurds was the growing influence of missionary activities in Kurdistan/Armenia.[23] The well-known sixty-first article of the Treaty of Berlin, signed in the wake of the Ottoman-Russian War, summarized the relationship between migrant Muslim Circassians and indigenous Muslim Kurds, on the one hand, and indigenous Christian Armenians on the other; the growing ten-

---

22. Karpat, *Politicization of Islam*, 125, 149.

23. For an important work tracing tensions in the region of Armenia and Kurdistan through missionary activities, see Kieser, *Iskanlanmış Barış*.

sions especially during the war;[24] and how the Great Powers viewed these relations: "The Sublime Porte undertakes to carry out, without further delay, the improvements and reforms demanded by local requirements in the provinces inhabited by the Armenians, and to guarantee their security against the Circassians and Kurds. It will periodically make known the steps taken to this effect to the Powers, who will superintend their application."[25]

Though there were reforms, or at least pretenses to reform, during the reign of Abdülhamid and the later Young Turk period (e.g., during such internationally challenging periods for the Ottoman Empire as 1895 and 1914), these were not carried out. Nor was it only the Ottomans who failed to comply with Article Sixty-One. The Great Powers also failed to follow up on the necessary reforms, largely due to power struggles and disagreements among them. There was also considerable uncertainty about how and where reforms were to take place. Most important was the dual fact that Armenians and Kurds lived side by side in many parts of Armenian lands and in Kurdistan and that Kurds were the majority in most places. Population ratios were important, for they would determine the shape and location of reforms, and this set off a number of statistical wars. Armenian communities attempted to overestimate the Armenian population, while the state attempted to overestimate the Muslim population.[26] The left-nationalist Armenian organizations Hunchak and Dashnak, founded in the 1880s and advocating for autonomy or independence, further alarmed the Kurds.[27]

Indeed, the 1879 Kurdish Revolt of Sheikh Ubeydullah was as much against the Armenian threat embodied in the Treaty of Berlin as it was against the Ottoman and Iranian states.[28] Abdülhamid suppressed the rebellion in 1881 and, accurately diagnosing the Kurds' fear of Armenians, established the Hamidiye regiments in 1890, consisting of about sixty units. According to Janet Klein, Abdülhamid's aims here were threefold: (1) to create a force capable of fighting alongside regular armies in the event of a Russian attack, and thus to ensure border security; (2) to suppress Armenian rebellions and uprisings; and (3) to prevent any possible Kurdish separatism by ruling Kurd-

24. For a fine summary of theseis relations and the surrounding tensions, see Fikret Adanır, "'Ermeni Meselesi'nin Doğuşu," in *1915: Siyaset, Tehcir, Soykırım*, eds. Fikret Adanır and Oktay Özel (İstanbul: Tarih Vakfı Yurt Yayınlan, 2015), 3–43.

25. Karal, *Osmanlı Tarihi*, 132.

26. For a study devoted strictly to this matter, see Dündar, *Kahir Ekseriyet*.

27. Bloxham, *Great Game of Genocide*, 36–50.

28. The sheikh is said to have remarked in 1880: "And what are these things that I have heard, that Armenians are going to set up an independent state in Van, and Nestorians are going to declare themselves British subjects and raise the British flag? I will never allow this to happen, even if I have to arm women." Quoted in Jwaideh, *Kürt Milliyetçiliğinin Tarihi*, 167.

istan with the help of such regiments. The regiments, numbering around sixty thousand men, provided both their leaders and ordinary Kurds with significant material and immaterial privileges (exemption from various taxes and military service, various Ottoman titles, clothing, weapons). It was also at this time, around the 1890s, that the issue of the confiscation of Armenian property (cascading after 1915) first emerged with the Hamidiye regiments, primarily in the form of land grabs. The composition of the regiments, which were made up solely of Sunni Kurds, to the exclusion of Alevis,[29] further sheds light on Abdülhamid's understanding of the Muslimness Contract.

If we think of alternative contracts as, in a sense, alternative politics of privilege—that is, a politics determining who will and will not be included—then we can better understand the significance of the exclusion of Alevis from the Hamidiye regiments. Under the Muslimness Contract, which subjected non-Muslims to constant insecurity and threat, not all Muslims were to be rewarded. Only those true Muslims in the eyes of the state, Sunni Muslims, could be trusted and thus favored. For, according to Abdülhamid, the main force capable of sustaining the empire was Islamic solidarity, and solidarity could only be built around Sunnism, the official sect of the state. With this in mind, attempts were made (through schools, mosques, violence, or Sunni migration and re-settlement) to assimilate "deviant" groups that, though not Sunni, were nevertheless considered to be somehow tied to Islam: Alevis, Caferis, Zeydis, and Yazidis.[30] Emergent forms of Arab, Kurdish, and Albanian nationalisms were also cause for concern, leading to efforts to bind these Sunni Muslims to a form of Muslim-Ottoman patriotism overseen by Turks, through both the distribution of privileges and assimilation-cum-education institutions such as the Tribal School.

It is worth underscoring, to better get at the focus of this study, that Abdülhamid and the center of the empire did not create out of thin air the feelings of resentment, anger, and fear that Muslims harbored toward Christians. In other words, such sentiments were not imposed in some artificial or forced manner; they were not dictated from above by the empire. Rather, these were authentic sentiments, historically and socially forged from within the lived relations, conflicts, and rivalries of the nineteenth century, among Muslim and Christian peoples and populations. Abdülhamid's contribution, as noted, was to make use of these existing sentiments and divisions to craft state policy. To again offer an example from the Kurdish/Armenian conflict, according to some recent studies, the Armenian massacres of 1895–1896 in Eastern Ana-

---

29. See Klein, *Margins of Empire*. See also Gölbaşı, "Hamidiye Alayları," 164–175.
30. Deringil, *İktidarın Sembolleri ve İdeoloji*.

tolia took place largely on the initiative of local Muslims, not the central state. Kurds broadly feared that Kurdistan would become Armenia. Muslim Kurdish notables (local rulers, notables, clergy), in particular, feared that Armenian reforms would limit their power. Such was the emotional context for the main actors behind the massacres, wherein tens of thousands of Armenians were killed, perhaps as many more were forced to emigrate, and tremendous transfers of wealth occurred. That the massacres took place after Friday prayers in many cities, with clergymen issuing fatwas (such as those stating, "Armenian blood can be spilled; it is sanctioned that their honor be violated and their property seized)" confirms this thesis. Further, consonant with a classical requirement of the Muslimness Contract, the central state did not punish the Muslim mass murderers and perpetrators of the extermination of Christians.[31] In 1896, in the streets of İstanbul, thousands of Armenians were killed in plain sight as the state looked on—even, according to some strong allegations, encouraging pogroms by the Muslim population.[32]

Herein lies, then, the real success of the Muslimness Contract, in contrast to the Ottomanness Contract: it was based on a true commonality of feeling, a unity of interests, and a set of agreements between the state and Muslims. Recall, the state put forward the Ottomanness Contract based on an ideal of equality; yet this ideal remained largely artificial and did not resonate with society. The Muslimness Contract, meanwhile, based on the superiority of Muslims, was truly bipartite, spontaneous, and authentic. The Muslim center found its echo in the Muslim provinces, and the Muslim provinces found theirs in the center, all united around a common goal and interest: to "cleanse" the country of Christians. In this sense, the Muslimness Contract indicated complicity in crimes committed, past and future, against Christian peoples—though a unique form of complicity. The crimes in question were not classed as such, since Christians were thought to deserve what came or was to come to them: this was a form of complicity without guilt. The shared goals, interests, and feelings of Muslims would keep the Muslimness Contract going, except for a few years, until the early 1920s and would eventually result in the formation of a new state based on, and by way of, Islam.[33]

31. See Gölbaşı, "1895–1896 Katliamları," 140–163.
32. Eldem, "'Banka Vakası' ve 1896 İstanbul Katliamı," 176–198.
33. The origins of the ultimate success of the Muslimness Contract can also be traced to the Ottoman millet system (described earlier in the book), which, as noted in footnote 4 of this chapter, hierarchically classified and separated religious communities, positioning Muslims as the dominant group within this structure.

The Rise of the Young Turks and
the Search for a Contract

Those who would ultimately build the new state came from the generation generally known as the Young Turks or the Unionists. If we consider as a whole the period from 1889 (when the Committee of Union and Progress was established) until 1908 (when the constitutional monarchy was reproclaimed), it is rather difficult to identify common characteristics among the Young Turks. Still, at a very general level, we can point to some commonalities. First, Young Turks were intellectuals who struggled to air their ideas freely under Abdülhamid's tyranny and were bureaucrats who were not able to advance professionally in the way they felt they deserved, due to Abdülhamid's system of loyalty. Therefore, they harbored a great deal of hostility toward the sultan. They were also constitutionalists. They advocated the reopening of parliament and the reinstatement of the constitution—in other words, a form of parliamentarism capable of limiting the power of the sultan. Finally, the question of how to save the Ottoman Empire was as central for them as it was for their predecessors, the Young Ottomans. Such broad commonalities aside, though, the Young Turks were divided along political, ideological, and ethnic lines. For example, in 1889, the Committee of the Ottoman Union was founded by Muslim medical students who were not ethnically Turkish and who came from border regions where life and death struggles with Christians were taking place. Among them, İbrahim Temo was Albanian, Mehmed Reşid was Circassian, and İshak Sukuti and Abdullah Cevdet were Kurdish. Whatever their ethnic origins, though, uniting the organization was, as the name suggests, a strong Ottomanist vein.[34]

Around the same time that the committee was renamed the Ottoman Committee of Union and Progress (1894), Ahmet Rıza and Mizancı Murat came to the fore, representing in many ways two polar opposites. Rıza, the leader of the Paris center of the movement, was a secularist, even a "heathen," according to his opponents. He was an anti-imperialist completely opposed to the idea that the intervention of the Great Powers was necessary for the overthrow of Abdülhamid. Further, he was a positivist intellectual who, it was said, "couldn't be bought"; he refused to compromise with Abdülhamid's rule, in any manner, and recognized, in a sense, no other authority than his own. Murat, on the other hand, was a conservative intellectual who attached importance to the Islamic character of the state—a pragmatic politician who favored a coup to overthrow Abdülhamid, and a compromiser who, in one way or another, maintained his relationship with the Abdülhamid administration.[35] We know that Rıza

---

34. Hanioğlu, *Doktor Abdullah Cevdet ve Dönemi*, 9–28.
35. Mardin, *Jön Türklerin Siyasi Fikirleri*, 77–135.

was critical of Abdülhamid's Armenian policies at the time, while Murat approved of them.[36] Murat was active in the Geneva center and had risen to the leadership of the movement based on his activist stance on the subject of Abdülhamid's overthrow. Yet he lost both his leadership and his prestige when he reconciled with Abdülhamid and returned to İstanbul.[37]

Rıza's second major rival after Murat was Prince Sabahaddin, who had fled to Europe with his father and brother. The prince's financial power and his connections in high politics helped revitalize the Young Turk movement in Europe. Unlike Rıza, Sabahaddin held that foreign intervention was necessary to overthrow Abdülhamid and that, for this purpose, Ottoman non-Muslims who opposed Abdülhamid, especially Armenians, should be involved in the movement. In the first Young Turk Congress, which Sabahaddin convened in Paris in 1902, a decision was made in favor of foreign intervention. Further, it was declared that the reforms anticipated by Armenians would be carried out, but, rather than specific to Armenians, these reforms would be for all Ottomans across the empire.[38] Prince Sabahaddin conceived of this last point in terms of decentralization. He complained that Turks in the empire lived under greater persecution and poverty than Armenians, even if Europe was not aware of this. Indeed, it was not the Turks who persecuted Armenians, maintained Sabahaddin, but the "savage" Kurdish tribes, who were neither Turks nor true Muslims. If Europeans, or at least Armenians, appreciated this and demanded reforms not only for Christians but for the whole of the Ottoman Empire, then Turks would not overlook this gesture and would begin to trust Armenians. What was thus needed was for Turks and Armenians to join forces and overthrow the tyranny of Abdülhamid, replacing his rule with a decentralized government. The prince summarized decentralization as a system in which "everyone becomes the absolute master of his own home under the general direction of a common policy."[39] In fact, what Prince Sabahaddin strove for was the creation of an Ottomanness Contract in which all Ottoman elements could unite and participate. And, for this, he believed that non-Muslims had to be convinced first. This is what he meant when he said, "I have no doubt that the particular interests of the Armenians can be well reconciled with the general interests of the Ottoman Empire."[40]

Prince Sabahaddin was not alone in his emphasis on Ottomanism. Many of the Young Turks at the time, among them Rıza, were careful not to offend

---

36. Ramsaur, *Jön Türkler ve 1908 İhtilali*, 40, 53, 58.
37. Sönmez, *Ahmed Rıza*, 71–86.
38. Hanioğlu, *Young Turks in Opposition*, 190–194.
39. Sabahaddin, *Bütün Eserleri*, 119–121.
40. Sabahaddin, 88.

non-Muslim Ottomans, attempting rather to convince them of their cause.[41] For example, the Republican-era Turkish nationalist Tunalı Hilmi was a prominent Ottomanist earlier in the century and thus often reached out in Ottomanist terms to Armenians, Bulgarians, Albanians, and Assyrians: "Ottomanism is a spiritual garment, and does not constrict the national body it covers. On the contrary, it animates, nourishes, grows and vitalizes. Let us keep Turkishness, Arabness, Kurdishness, Armenianness in our hearts, such that there will be no place for transgressions, and thereby for the emergence of disputes and disunity. We should exist in such a way that we will have left Judaism in the synagogue, Christianity in the church and Islam in the mosque. Let us be Ottomans, let us work and think for Ottomanism." Tunalı Hilmi tried to allay concerns that Turks would again be the dominant nation in Ottomanism, noting, "Ottomanism does not mean Turkishness. It neither harms anyone nor tampers with any nationality. As such, who wouldn't want to be Ottoman?"[42]

Nonetheless, from the early 1900s onward, Turkism was increasingly the predominant inclination of the Young Turks. Yusuf Akçura's publication of *Üç Tarz-ı Siyaset (Three Types of Policies)* in 1904 can be seen as a milestone in the transformation of Turkism from a cultural initiative to a political project. In this work, noteworthy in its dispassion and its lack of blame for any Ottoman constituent, Akçura analyzes three possible political projects: an Ottoman Union based on equality, an Islamic Union based on Islam, and a Turkish Union based on Turkishness. What explains this dispassion, in my opinion, is that Akçura views the matter through the logic of a contract. He seeks an answer to this question: "Now, let us investigate which of the three policies is useful and capable of being implemented: We said useful, but useful to whom and useful for what?"[43] Through such a lens, he examines the various interests (material and immaterial) and emotions of these different elements, and asks whether these interests and emotions might be united, taking into account both Ottoman factors and the possible attitude of the Great Powers, as well as the internal and external balance of power. His conclusions are simple: no one, particularly not Turks or Muslims, would want an Ottoman Union; European empires with large Muslim populations would not allow an Islamic Union, even if Islam was a strong emotional glue; thus,

---

41. Rıza explained the matter as follows: "Since the people in our country do not belong to a single element, religion, or people, it is harmful to arouse feelings only in the name of Turkishness or Muslimness. We must seek the good of the homeland in the unity of all Ottomans, and try to ensure and achieve it with the strength that will bring about this unity." Quoted in Sönmez, *Ahmed Rıza*, 100.

42. Quoted in Ateş, *Tunalı Hilmi Bey*, 130–133, 176–177.

43. Akçura, *Üç Tarz-ı Siyaset*, 24.

a Turkish Union, despite its various difficulties, is the most realistic and correct option.

There was hardly a Young Turk who entirely rejected Ottomanism as a general principle. Both the desire to prevent the empire from further shrinking due to separatist nationalist movements and the necessity of non-Muslim support for the overthrow of Abdülhamid led to a continued emphasis on Ottomanism, albeit in a rather abstract way. The resultant form of Ottomanism was clearly centralist and Turkish-dominated in tone. As able activists like Dr. Bahaeddin Şakir and Dr. Nazım rose to prominence within the Committee of Union and Progress, Turkism, too, began to dominate the movement. For example, Dr. Bahaeddin Şakir claimed that Prince Sabahaddin's decentralization project would only help non-Muslims who sought to divide the homeland, such that no Turk, whether sultan or peasant, would allow it.[44] Diran Kelekian warned his friend Dr. Şakir that a liberalism of "individual equality" would mean Turkification, maintaining the dominance and hegemony of Turkishness while doing little to prevent the collapse of the country. According to Kelekian, the cement that would hold the Ottoman Empire together was a liberalism of "racial and social equality" based on the principles of autonomy, partnership, and fraternity.[45] Kelekian's proposal for an Ottomanness Contract based on decentralization and autonomy was rejected by Dr. Şakir. (Kelekian, meanwhile, was arrested on April 24, 1915, at his home in Beyoğlu and murdered on November 2, 1915, on the banks of the Kızılırmak River between Yozgat and Kayseri.[46]) And, to those Jews who found Prince Sabahaddin's decentralization appealing, Dr. Şakir replied: "Prince Sabahaddin is dead, he no longer exists; the program of decentralization and autonomous nationalities and states has been abandoned. The Committee of Union and Progress wants centralization and a Turkish monopoly on power. . . . It wants a Turkish nation-state in unity with a system of Turkish schools, Turkish administration, and a Turkish legal system."[47]

Known as resourceful and ruthless men of action, as proven time and again, Dr. Şakir and Dr. Nazım assumed de facto leadership of the movement, breaking the power of Rıza and Prince Sabahaddin, who had devoted a significant part of their time to the social sciences and to their personal intellectual development. Their ideas largely coincided with Rıza's, with whom they acted in concert. They were firmly convinced, however, that the over-

44. Hanioğlu, *Preparation for a Revolution*, 88–89.
45. Hanioğlu, *Preparation for a Revolution*, 135–136.
46. On Kelekian's life and views, see İzrail, *24 Nisan 1915*, 189–190, 525–540.
47. Quoted in Hanioğlu, *Preparation for a Revolution*, 260.

throw of Abdülhamid was not possible under the leadership of Rıza, whose pacifism and evolutionism were well known.

The two doctors found in Macedonia a new group of activists and officers capable of following them in their revolutionary aspirations. Macedonia possessed a rather heterogeneous ethnic and religious structure and had become the site of conflict between Turkish, Greek, Slavic, and Bulgarian nationalisms and forms of banditry. In 1908, negotiations between Britain and Russia in Reval over the division of Macedonia panicked Muslims in the region, sparking the Young Turk Revolution. The activism of civilian Unionists like Talat Bey and the influence, within the army and the region, of young officers like Enver and Niyazi, who spoke both Turkish and Albanian, when combined with the support of the Muslim population, forced Abdülhamid to reinstate the constitution in July 1908 and to promise to open the parliament—in other words, he had little choice but to declare constitutional monarchy.

When we look at those Young Turks who remained influential across the various periods of the movement—from its emergence in 1889 to its revolution in 1908—perhaps their only common intellectual characteristic was that they were Social Darwinists. They strongly held, that is, a belief in the survival of the fittest, the determined, and the deserving in the struggle for existence, both between countries and within nations. As such, ideologies seeking social equality (Marxism, socialism) never appealed to this cadre. Yet, there were at least two important differences between the new leaders of the Committee of Union and Progress (Talat, Enver, Dr. Şakir, Dr. Nazım) and the old (say, İbrahim Temo, Abdullah Cevdet, Ahmet Rıza, Mizancı Murat, or Prince Sabahaddin). First, the former were far more skilled in realpolitik and were ruthless; they demonstrated on many occasions that there was nothing they would not do to save the homeland. Second, the new leaders, identifying as ethnically Turkish, were far more Turkist than their predecessors.[48]

Their Turkism aside, though, the official ideology of the Ottoman Empire between 1908 and 1912 was, again, Ottomanism. The Unionists felt that Ottomanism should be given a final chance to preserve the territorial integrity of the state, which was their main concern—a final chance, that is, to prevent the further shrinking of territory. Non-Muslim peoples, who still constituted a large part of the population, as well as Muslim groups such as Albanians could only be persuaded to abandon their separatist policies and remain a part of the empire within an Ottomanist framework, one in which all Ottoman citizens were equal, regardless of religion or language. Indeed, before the 1908

---

48. For work that focuses on the various differences between the two generations of the Young Turks, see Aydın, "İki İttihat-Terakki," 117–128.

revolution, Unionists were careful to address different ethnic groups in a language that would appeal to them. Unionists attached great importance to winning the support of the Armenians, who had suffered great atrocities under Abdülhamid's rule, and who had the experience of armed resistance against this rule. Thus, for instance, at the Young Turk Congress in 1907, Unionists were able to form an alliance, however flexible, with the Dashnaks (and with Prince Sabahaddin's Society for Private Initiative and Decentralization). A declaration jointly issued after the congress shows that, at least for the time being, agreement had been reached on a minimal Ottomanness Contract emphasizing the equality of Muslims and Christians, in contrast to the Muslimness Contract of Abdülhamid. The reign of Abdülhamid II "was the cause of ruin, not only for Christians, but also for all Muslims. He kept the Christians under constant pressure for the sake of his personal interest, and massacred them. . . . Muslims, meanwhile, were placed in captivity, exiled, slaughtered and killed. . . . The Armenian massacre, the horrifying feather in the cap to all these crimes, earned the titles of 'The Great Murderer' and 'The Red Sultan' for the perpetrator of the ongoing massacre in Arabistan." Without the overthrow of the Abdülhamid regime and its replacement by Ottomanism, disintegration was inevitable: "If this infamous method of administration . . . continues any longer, Albania, Macedonia, Arabia and Armenia will undoubtedly secede from the state."[49] Unionists were also able to win the vital support of Albanians and Jews in Macedonia, where the revolution took place. The hope was that this broad-based alliance could be maintained after 1908. The Unionists, therefore, temporarily suspended their Turkism, at least publicly.

Of course, there were serious differences between what the Turks, as the dominant group, and other ethnic groups understood about and expected from Ottomanism. For Unionists, a general Ottomanist discourse advocating the equality of individuals, the reinstatement of the constitution, and the representation of different ethnic groups in parliament was largely sufficient. Anything beyond this, such as demands for collective cultural and political rights, they equated with treason and separatism. Both the Hunchak and Dashnak Armenian revolutionaries knew from the outset, based on personal experiences with these individuals, that the approach of the new generation of Unionists would go no further than proclaiming the "Constitution of Mithat" and that each Unionist represented a dangerous form of Turkish nationalism.[50] It was, therefore, clear early on just how difficult it would be to bridge the gap between a purely constitutionalist Ottomanism, as imagined by

---

49. Quoted in Kuran, *İnkılap Tarihimiz ve Jön Türkler*, 291–295.
50. Kévorkian, *Ermeni Soykırımı*, 45, 64, 71, 74.

Unionists, and an Ottomanism based on collective rights and local autonomy imagined by both non-Muslim peoples (Armenians) and Muslims (Albanians) alike.

That said, despite these vital differences and mutual distrust, the first years of the constitutional monarchy passed with a minimal agreement on an Ottomanness Contract. On July 23, 1908, when, inspired by the French Revolution's slogans of liberty, fraternity, and equality, the constitutional monarchy was proclaimed, Vehip Bey of Yanya announced that all Ottoman constituents would "defend and protect each other's lives and honor with the same intensity and spirit of unity as they would their own lives."[51] Unionists were pleased, enthusiastic even, to be liberated from the absolutism of Abdülhamid II. So were non-Muslims, particularly Armenians, who had been systematically oppressed and persecuted under Abdülhamid II. Indeed, Dashnaks saw themselves as partial owners of the revolution, as confirmed by certain public gestures of the Unionists.[52] Even the Revolutionary Hunchak Party, which had always maintained its distance from the Young Turks, changed its name to the Social Democratic Hunchak Party, in a sign, possibly, of their openness to giving the new Ottomanness Contract a chance. In January 1909, the Sivas office of Hunchaks made the following public statement:

Comrades of the Ottoman Empire, after the proclamation of the constitution in our beloved homeland, the Hunchak Party ceased its revolutionary activities and became a legal party. It preferred a legal, peaceful parliamentary system to realize its goals of economic and moral development of the country. It will voice its complaints and demands through legal and parliamentary methods. The Hunchak Party rejects any separatist aims against the constitutional regime of Turkey. It will stand shoulder to shoulder with its liberty-loving Turkish brothers against both the internal enemies of the constitution and the attacks of foreigners. . . . Dear comrades, we are all children of the Ottoman homeland; solidarity between us will turn our country into a paradise. . . . We, Turks and Armenians, will stand shoulder to shoulder against all external attacks. We will join hands to democratize the Constitution and make it permanent.[53]

---

51. Quoted in Tunaya, *Türkiye'de Siyasal Gelişmeler*, 122.

52. For examples of this shared enthusiasm, see Der Matossian, *Parçalanmış Devrim Düşleri*, 55–90.

53. Quoted in Kılıçdağı, "Ermeni Toplumu ve Meşrutiyet," 266.

The period between 1908 and 1911 was a period of hope not only for non-Muslims but also for dissidents, in general, as well as for other non-Turkish Muslim peoples demanding certain collective rights. One by one, Muslim and Christian dissidents returned from exile. Illegal revolutionary organizations of the past were legalized. Turkish and Armenian revolutionaries organized commemorative ceremonies together for the victims of the massacres of Armenians during the reign of Abdülhamid II. The world of publishing grew more colorful, with the emergence of new newspapers and magazines. And new political parties were established, including a number of new Ottomanist organizations advocating for varying degrees of cultural rights (e.g., education in the mother tongue) and self-government (e.g., decentralization): the Ottoman Ahrar Party founded by followers of Prince Sabahaddin; the Ottoman Democratic Party founded by Temo, who was Albanian, and Cevdet, who was Kurdish, and both of whom were among the first founders of the Committee of Union and Progress; and the Freedom and Accord Party, which attracted non-Muslims.[54] Numerous political movements led by Turks, Armenians, Albanians, and Kurds proposed their own versions of the Ottomanness Contract during these years, declaring their ideas both the most just and the most feasible means of keeping Ottoman constituents together.

However, these proposals for various Ottomanness Contracts, advocating, albeit timidly, for the equality of Muslims and Christians, simply did not resonate with the Muslim middle and lower classes or in the Muslim provinces more generally. Many Muslims simply felt that they were superior to Christians and witnessed how non-Muslims had benefited economically and culturally from the Ottoman integration with capitalism and modernization. At the same time, these same non-Muslims, with the support of foreign states, posed a vital threat to Muslims' lives and homeland. In other words, there was a dangerous combination of the Muslim emotions and expectations I mentioned earlier: superiority, jealousy, resentment, fear, and a desire to replace Christians.

Emotions have the potential to motivate and mobilize people to achieve certain aims. But when they are collective, in particular, they often require a favorable conjuncture for this potential to yield fruit. It was just such a favorable conjuncture that led to the massacre in Adana in April 1909, in which it is estimated that more than twenty thousand Armenians were killed. Since

---

54. For brief histories, programs, and declarations of these and other constitutionalist parties, see Tunaya, *Türkiye'de Siyasal Partiler*, vol. 1. For an article analyzing the Ottomanism of the aforementioned parties based on their programs and summarizing the history of Ottomanism in general from 1839 onward, see Somel, "Osmanlı Reform Çağında Osmanlıcılık Düşüncesi," 89–116.

the 1860s, the region of Çukurova (the hinterlands of Adana) had been integrated into the capitalist world economy through cotton production. The
Armenians of this region, also known as Cilicia, were at the forefront of cotton production and trade. It is thought that the 1908 revolution added a
political assurance to this economic advantage, or so it was perceived, at least,
by Armenians. The growing self-confidence of Armenians, meanwhile, was
viewed by many Muslims as a form of arrogance. Further, it is also known
that in April, the month of the massacre, many missionaries had arrived in
the region for celebrations, and thousands of seasonal workers had come to
find temporary work but were unable to do so, as supply exceeded demand.
It was likely the overlap of these region-specific factors with the March 31
uprising in the center of İstanbul (or mid-April, by the new calendar) and the
temporary fall of Unionists from power, leaving a power vacuum, together
that triggered the massacre in the Çukurova provinces.[55]

Debate over who was behind the Adana Massacre continues to this day.
At the time, Armenians generally blamed Abdülhamid II and the anticonsti-
tutional and Islamist March 31 uprising, which they believed he instigated.[56]
After 1915, Armenian intellectuals, in particular, began to see 1909 as a re-
hearsal for 1915 and thus blamed the central leadership of the Committee of
Union and Progress.[57] I tend to see these interpretations as unrealistic. During
the March 31 events, it is highly unlikely that either Unionist leaders (who
had largely lost power and some of whom were hiding in the homes of their
Armenian friends in İstanbul) or Abdülhamid II (who had also largely lost
power) could have initiated and directed, from the center, the massacre in the
provinces, particularly in such a chaotic atmosphere of rebellion. Indeed, no
credible evidence has been found for either charge. Often overlooked is the possibility that, behind the massacre, a conspiracy may have existed of local Muslims (rulers, notables, clergy, migrant workers) from different political and
social classes, encouraged and inspired by the Islamist uprising in İstanbul.

A few months before the massacre, French consular deputies in Mersin and
Adana wrote a report to the French foreign minister and to their embassy in
İstanbul, pointing to such a concurrence: "Young and Old Turks now seem
to be putting their differences behind them on the basis of patriotism and
Islamism. Already, in the mosques, the mullahs are summoning the faithful
to defend 'their rights' with vigor." An Ottoman document, blaming Arme-

---

55. For the socioeconomic dynamics behind the massacre, see Toksöz, "Çukurova'da Sosyoekonomik Dönüşüm ve 1909 Adana Katliamı," 244–255, and Dinçer, "Adana Katliamı ve
Göçmen İşçiler Meselesi," 256–263.
56. E.g., see Şekeryan, *1909 Adana Katliamı*.
57. E.g., see Dadrian, *Ermeni Soykırımı Tarihi*, 265–272.

nian provocateurs and newly arrived settlers in the region, noted: "However, the fact that they made such audacious use of the freedom and equality that they had just obtained was not all appreciated by the Muslims." And such were the observations of a foreign journalist arriving in the region some two months after the massacre: "The Turks, who have always been the dominant group, have the feeling that they are the losers in the newly established order. As a result of the constitution, they have, in some way, ceded the predominance that was once theirs, and they feel that, in these conditions, the future can only visit destruction on them; in this context, they have risen up to defend their privileges by means of bloodshed and pillage. The Turks sensed this in the changes in the Armenians' behavior at the level of their daily relations."[58]

In other words, perhaps the massacre in Adana took place due to a supra-ideological Muslimness Contract addressing the common interests and feelings of local Muslims. The massacre, which demonstrated that non-Muslims could no longer live with privilege and security in Adana, was likely shaped by political and socioeconomic dynamics in the provincial countryside and set in motion through the collaboration of local nobles and local administrators.[59] What brought about 1915 was the Muslim center renouncing the Ottomanness Contract and reaching an agreement regarding the Muslimness Contract with the Muslim countryside, in something of a complete harmony between the center and the provinces. This is, in part, why 1909 was experienced as a local pogrom, whereas 1915 took the form of a genocide that would spread across Anatolia.

This idea that the Adana massacre came about through local dynamics does not mean that Unionists in the center were not acting contrary to the ideals of Ottomanness. As I emphasized earlier, the Unionist understanding of Ottomanness was one in which Muslims and, within that category, Turks would prevail, while non-Muslims and non-Turks (not seen as true Ottomans by Unionists) would be assimilated, or if unassimilable, "tamed" by various means. The first victims of this centralist and assimilationist understanding were Albanian Muslims, once allies of the Unionists. The Committee of Union and Progress organized military operations against the Albanians, who they thought would be easily assimilated, yet who resisted. In 1909, the committee tried to disarm the Albanians on charges of separatism. According to Ahmet Bedevi Kuran, the "Committee of Union and Progress's Albanian oversight" irrevocably embittered the Albanians—perhaps the sole Muslim

---

58. Quotes are from Kévorkian, *Armenian Genocide*, 75, 80, 88.

59. There were also Muslim administrators who protected Armenians, for which Armenians were grateful. See Kırmızı, "Feelings of Gratitude," 643–660.

constituent in the Balkans capable of resisting local Christians.[60] Dr. Nazım is said to have justified this policy as follows:

> The pretentions of the various nationalities are a capital source of annoyance for us. We hold linguistic, historical and ethnic aspirations in abhorrence. This and that group will have to disappear. There should be only one nation on our soil, the Ottoman nation, and only one language, Turkish. All groups have to disappear. On our lands, there must be one nation, the Ottoman nation, and one language, the Turkish language. It will not be easy for the Greeks and Bulgarians to accept this, although it is a vital necessity for us. To bring them to swallow the pill, we shall start with the Albanians. Once we have gotten the better of these mountaineers, who think they are invincible, the rest will take care of itself. After we have turned our cannons on the Albanians, shedding Muslim blood, let the *gâvurs* beware. The first Christian to move a muscle will see his family, house and village smashed to smithereens. Europe will not dare raise its voice in protest or accuse us of torturing the Christians because our first bullets will have been expended on Muslim Albanians.[61]

Kurds, like Albanians, were seen as "mountainous, savage and warlike" by both Abdülhamid and the Young Turks. Yet, Kurds occupied a curious position. On the one hand, they had to be assimilated; on the other, they were entrusted with protecting the territorial integrity of the Ottoman Empire against Christians in their region. Despite sharing this perspective, however, there were important differences in how Abdülhamid and the Young Turks related to the Kurds. As noted earlier, Abdülhamid favored Sunni Kurdish tribes in the region as a force against Armenians, as required by the Muslimness Contract. This is why he worked to gain the support of Kurdish tribal leaders. The Young Turks, meanwhile, were allied with Armenians in both Europe and Eastern Anatolia, partly due to Ottomanism and partly to realpolitik. Additionally, the "modern," İstanbul-educated sons of a number of established Kurdish families such as the Bedirhans or the Babans—families that saw their power eroded by the destruction of principalities (*mirlik*) in the Tanzimat period and the establishment of Hamidiye regiments in the Abdülhamid period—were themselves opponents of Abdülhamid and the Ottomanists. They were also, like the Armenians, enemies of the Hamidiye. This group,

60. Kuran, *İnkılap Tarihimiz ve Jön Türkler*, 367.
61. Quoted in Kévorkian, *Armenian Genocide*, 120–121.

known as the Young Kurds, came to make up an important part of the Young Turk opposition prior to 1908. Their brand of Ottomanism, which staked out a way of being Ottoman by remaining Kurdish and taking pride in one's Kurdishness, is evident in the newspaper *Kürdistan*,[62] published in Kurdish by the Bedirhan family in 1898, and in the newspaper *Kürd Teavün ve Terakki*, which started up immediately after the 1908 revolution.[63]

An alliance with Armenians required the Young Turks to resolve not only the problem of Abdülhamid but also that of the Hamidiye regiments. One particularly important condition of an alliance with the Dashnaks concerned the punishment of Hamidiye heads and the return to their original owners of those Armenian lands that the regiments had seized—in other words, to solve the "land issue."[64] The Committee of Union and Progress had also taken a number of important steps in this direction. One significant and interesting example was the revocation of the privileges of Huseyin Pasha, chief of the Haydaran tribe and a Hamidiye commander, the launching of an investigation into his actions, and the recovery of the lands he had seized. A 1910 secret Russian report summarized the historical significance of this event: "For the last few years, the Armenians of the region, who were the Kurds' main and most intransigent enemies, while once deprived of all manner of rights, have suddenly become citizens with equal rights. The Armenians, allied with the Young Turks and feeling powerful, wanted to hold the Kurds to account for past old crimes. Kurds now face everything they have done for years now, up to the declaration of Constitution."[65]

However, these measures soon put the Committee of Union and Progress in a difficult position. Those Kurdish tribal leaders who had benefited significantly from Abdülhamid's Muslimness Contract were already deeply suspicious of the Ottomanist Young Turks. The fact that Unionists were attempting to resolve the land issue and had begun punishing Hamidiye commanders proved that their suspicions were justified, resulting in their further alienation from the Ottoman Empire. Fearing arrest, Hüseyin Pasha fled to Iran with

---

62. The modern children of traditional Kurdish *mirs* who had fallen from power looked upon the traditional Hamidiye tribes that had newly gained power with a certain aristocratic condescension. For instance, an article published in the newspaper *Kürdistan* in 1900 had this to say of the head of the Miran tribe and commander of the Hamidiye forces, Mustafa Pasha: "Before this man was brought to the leadership of the tribe, some ten or fifteen years earlier, he was a shepherd who went by the nickname 'Misto Keçelo.'" Quoted in Bajalan, *Jön Kürtler*, 92.

63. A piece published in December 1908 in *Kürd Teavün ve Terakki* noted that educating Albanians and Kurds in their native language would result in better educated people, which would, in turn, benefit the Ottoman Empire. Bajalan, *Jön Kürtler*, 112.

64. See Klein, *Margins of Empire*, 128–169.

65. Abak, "Kürt Politikasında Hamidiye Siyasetine Dönüş," 284.

his tribe and soldiers. This move seems to have made the Unionists very uneasy, fearing that the tribe would start a Kurdish revolt in alliance with Russia—an uneasiness evidenced by the amnesty granted to Pasha and his tribe
if they agreed to return to the Ottoman Empire. Pasha saw this step back and
decided to return, upon which he became a member of the Committee of
Union and Progress and, in 1912, was appointed commander of one of the
light cavalry regiments established to replace the Hamidiye regiments.[66] This
incident is instructive of how difficult it was to implement the Ottomanness
Contract in Muslim provinces, forcing the Committee of Union and Progress
to backtrack at the expense of angering its ally, the Dashnak.

Despite such problems, Ottomanism remained the official ideology of the
state until 1912. After the 1909 Adana Massacre, the Committee of Union
and Progress and the Dashnak renewed their alliance by agreeing on such matters as Ottomanism (as a joint struggle against reactionism) and the expansion
of the administrative powers of the provinces, echoing a similar alliance between
the Hunchak and Freedom and Accord Party. An article published in July
1909 in the Erzurum-based Dashnak magazine *Harach* proposed an American model for the Ottomanness Contract: "Armenians do not have separatist
goals and will not have them as long as the constitution is perfectly implemented and true brotherhood and equality prevail among the peoples of Turkey. There are many peoples in America today, including Armenians. Why
don't any of them think about leaving? [Because] it does not occur to the
American state to constrain the language and religion of its peoples. . . . If
Turkey wants to eliminate all separatist ambitions, it must practice equality,
fraternity and freedom."[67] Along similar lines, in 1911, Halil Bey, the minister of the interior, put forward his model of the "common homeland":

> The goal pursued by the government in its internal policy . . . is the
> political unity of all Ottomans. The aim of this policy of unity is for
> all Ottomans to recognize every part of the Ottoman homeland as
> their own homeland and the Ottoman State as their own state with
> the same love and affection. . . . The government considers it as an evil
> and a danger for this country to attempt and act in such a way as to
> turn the Ottomans into a single nationality by Turkifying them or in
> any other way making them forget their nationalities.[68]

66. Abak, 287–291.
67. Quoted in Kılıçdağı, "Ermeni Toplumu ve Meşrutiyet," 269, 273.
68. Quoted in Tunaya, *Türkiye'de Siyasal Partiler*, vol. 3, 373–374.

The Horizontality of the Muslimness Contract

With the Balkan Wars of 1912–1913, the Committee of Union and Progress abandoned wholesale its policy of Ottomanism. The Balkan Wars brought the loss of the final remnants of the empire's European territories, which had been of great material and emotional importance to the Ottoman Empire since the fourteenth century. But, perhaps more importantly, the lost territories included Macedonia and Western Thrace, which many Unionist leaders called home. The loss of Thessaloniki, in particular, was an emotionally irreparable one for many Unionists, who took a crucial lesson from these losses: Macedonia and Western Thrace were lost because of their heterogeneous demographic structure or, more precisely, because of the presence of Christian populations. Unionists vowed never to make the same mistake again.[69] In practice, this meant the abandonment of the Ottomanness Contract, the favoring of Muslims, and the elimination of non-Muslims from the country by various means. Losses in the Balkan Wars, in a manner similar to the Ottoman-Russian War of 1877–1878, reduced the Christian population within the borders of the Ottoman Empire and thus increased the Muslim population proportionally. This, when coupled with the emigration of hundreds of thousands of Muslims, facilitated a transition from the Ottomanness to the Muslimness Contract, both demographically and emotionally, as it rejuvenated existing negative sentiments toward Christians.

In a way, losses in the Balkan Wars were a victory for those Turkist intellectuals who, in order to give cultural, ideological, political, and economic strength to the project of Turkishness, gathered around such associations as Türk Derneği (1908), Türk Yurdu (1911), and Türk Ocağı (1912), or in such journals as Genç Kalemler (1910) and Türk Yurdu (1911). After all, the death of Ottomanism, long the object of their criticism, was final.[70] This effectively paved the way for Turkism, which such intellectuals thought would rescue the country.[71] The journal Türk Yurdu (Turkish Homeland), where prominent names in twentieth-century Turkish thought wrote—Yusuf Akçura, Ahmed Ağaoğlu, Hüseyinzade Ali, İsmail Gaspıralı, Fuad Köprülü, Ömer Seyfettin, Hamdullah Suphi, and Ziya Gökalp—was particularly important in the development of Turkism.[72]

---

69. Halaçoğlu, Balkan Harbi Sırasında, 5–7, 26–27.

70. Akçura ("İttihad-ı Anasır Meselesi," 156–157) wrote in 1911 that Ottoman constituents differed greatly in terms of religion, language, and civilizational levels and that it was impossible to assimilate, bring together, or harmonize these components.

71. See Akçura, Türkçülüğün Tarihi, 164–182; Arai, Jön Türk Dönemi Türk Milliyetçiliği.

72. Kurt, "Türk'ün Büyük, Biçare Irkı."

Nearly every Turkist of this period held two different conceptions of Turkism. The first is what we might call a maximalist conception of Turkism. This is the idea of a Turkish empire that would unite Ottoman, Russian, and Central Asian Turks—in other words, a pan-Turkist utopia. The second, perhaps more realist, notion—what we might call a minimalist conception of Turkism—aimed to unite Muslims, particularly those living in Anatolia, under the umbrella of Turkishness. Even the second goal was no easy feat, though, since, apart from a small number of intellectuals, bureaucrats, and politicians, there was no consciousness or sense of Turkishness at this time. As Turkist intellectuals so often pointed out, there was Turkish history and Turkish culture, but there was no Turkish nation proud of and ready to fight for them; this nation would have to be created. Tekin Alp, in a famous article, "Turks Are Looking for a National Spirit," translated from the French by Akçura and published in *Türk Yurdu*, noted: "It should be tirelessly repeated to the Turks that they are Turks, that they have a victorious past and a future full of hopes; that solely for this they must be united in everything and be mutually supportive. . . . What constitutes a nationality is not real resemblance . . . but the imagination of this resemblance." Following Émile Durkheim and Gökalp, Tekin Alp sought some form of collective or shared conscience, belief, and emotion capable of constituting a nation and was convinced that if this could be found, then non-Turkish Ottoman Muslims would also be assimilated to Turkishness: "The nomadic Kurds, the disobedient Laz, the Muslimized Vlachs, Greeks and Bulgarians of Ottoman Europe, whose religions are strong, will soon be made to resemble one another or assimilated, so long as a shared Turkish conscience continues to grow stronger."[73]

Another Turkist who oscillated between maximalist and minimalist modes of Turkism was Gökalp. On the one hand, he advocated a romantic pan-Turkism, especially in his poetry; on the other, in his articles and books, he proposed models of realist Turkism, first for the Ottoman Empire and later for Turkey. Between 1912 and 1913—that is, during the Balkan Wars, precisely when Ottomanism collapsed entirely—Gökalp published in *Türk Yurdu* a number of famous articles, "Türkleşmek, İslamlaşmak, Muasırlaşmak" ("Turkification, Islamization, Modernization"), which we can think of as the official text of the Muslimness Contract. This series of articles puts forward the claim that the three intellectual currents of Modernization, Islamization, and Turkification, which Gökalp states were born out of genuine needs, are not at odds with, but rather complement, one another. According to Gökalp,

---

73. P. Risal [Tekin Alp], "Türkler Bir Ruh-ı Milli Arıyorlar," in Landau, *Tekinalp*, 148, 154. When Alp wrote this piece, the Balkans had yet to be lost.

Turks had put forward the idea of Ottomanism to save a multinational empire that they were at the center of, but no one else had accepted this idea. For this reason, while Turks wasted time on the idea of Ottomanism, other peoples busily set about to develop a national consciousness, with Turkishness consequently the latest national ideal to develop from within the Ottoman Empire. As Gökalp complained, while Kurds were proud of their Kurdishness, Albanians of their Albanianness, and Arabs of their Arabness, it was difficult to find a single soul proud of his Turkishness. This collective conscience, a consciousness and feeling of Turkishness, had to be created, and the culture that would provide the basis for this was, according to Gökalp, Islam, of which Turks saw themselves as a part. In other words, the conscience of Turks was a Muslim conscience. Turkishness was thus to be fashioned from the cultural repository of Islam in Anatolia, which he thought would lead not only Turkish speakers but also other Muslim peoples to accept Turkishness. Meanwhile, Turkish Islam would both preserve and strengthen its own conscience and spiritual culture *and* embrace the science, welfare, and prosperity of the West—that is, its material culture or civilization. In a sense, a synthesis of Turkish-Islamic consciousness and sentiment with Western reason was required. Thereby, thought Gökalp, this tripartite formula could respond to and satisfy the common interests and expectations of Ottoman Muslims and unite the rulers and the ruled in a "modern Islam and Turkishness."[74]

For a number of reasons, the Committee of Union and Progress was not able to fully seize power between 1908 and 1912. This period, one of "supervisory power," also coincides with the committee's Ottomanism, marked by relative political pluralism and liberal economy. Yet, before the First Balkan War, Unionists had been removed from even a position of supervisory power. At the same time, though, this loss of power ensured that they not be held responsible for the loss of territory in the Balkans. With the January 23, 1913, coup d'état, which Unionists claimed to have carried out in order to recover losses and save Edirne, in particular, and with the assassination of Grand Vizier Mahmut Şevket Pasha on June 11, 1913 (whom they could not fully control), Unionists seized "total power."[75] Following the establishment of such power by the committee, relative political pluralism came to be replaced by a militarist one-party dictatorship, Ottomanism by Turkish-Islamism, and liberal economy by national economy (*milli iktisat*) aimed at creating a Turkish-Muslim bourgeoisie.

---

74. Gökalp, "Türkleşmek, İslamlaşmak, Muasırlaşmak," 45–88.
75. For the distinction between "supervisory power" and "total power," see Akşin, *Jön Türkler ve İttihat ve Terakki*, 120, 321–323, 338.

The significance of these displacements cannot be emphasized enough. Ottomanism, pluralism, and economic liberalism were policies that aimed to keep the empire together. On paper, they were supposed to benefit all Ottomans, though Muslims felt they really only benefited non-Muslims. One would thus expect the forms of Turkish-Islamism, dictatorship, and national economy that came in their stead to punish non-Muslims and reward Muslims—which is, indeed, precisely what they did. It is also worth underscoring that the Islamism of the Unionists did not entail the establishment of an Islamic state; it rather amounted to trusting, favoring, and uniting Muslims.[76] Between 1912 and 1922, when the state faced total annihilation—when it was waging, that is, a life-and-death struggle—the state simply was unable to place much emphasis on Turkishness (which was not yet a unifying force), since it could not afford to alienate non-Turkish Muslims. Indeed, until 1922, when the decade-long war was finally over, Unionists and Kemalists largely employed an Islamic rhetoric. As much as this language served to unify Muslims around a common religious belief, a common cause to strive to survive, and common interests, it also served to rally people around such common emotions as fear, resentment, and animosity.[77] War was waged, in short, around the Muslimness Contract.

The Turkish-Islamist policy of the Committee of Union and Progress envisioned the liquidation of non-Muslims and the assimilation of a number of Muslim groups deemed unreliable. In short, it was thought to be necessary, for the liberation of the country, to create a suitable Turkish and Muslim population composition. All of this was fully in line with the Unionist worldview, which saw both state and society as an organism; any tumors, so to speak, disrupting the harmony of the body were to be excised. In other words, the Unionists finally had the chance to implement a policy in line with their Social Darwinist and organicist worldview. They never decisively implemented the Ottomanist policies they previously paid lip service to. Their new outfit, though, suited them perfectly.

To implement this new policy of ethnic engineering, it was first necessary to acquire some sort of ethnic knowledge of Anatolia. If non-Muslim peoples were not to be trusted in any way and were to be liquidated or deported, one by one, when the time was right, one had to know where they lived and what

---

76. On this matter, Tunaya notes, "One face of the Committee of Union and Progress was as Turkist-nationalist as the other was Islamist. . . . The nationalist-Turkist drift was its real face. . . . The Islamist drift seemed to be a matter of politics . . . [for] whichever party it was, it had to be Islamist to succeed" (*Türkiye'de Siyasal Partiler*, vol. 3, 377).

77. For examples of the ways in which animosity was praised and incited in the journal *Türk Yurdu*, see Kurt, "*Türk'ün Büyük, Biçare Irkı*," 27, 174–175.

their population numbers were. Where would immigrant Muslims from the Balkans be settled? Which Kurdish tribes, though Muslim, refused to pay taxes and were possibly separatists? Where did they live, and where could they be resettled? What were the beliefs of Alevis, who were seen as not fully Muslim, and how could they be assimilated to Sunnism? To arrive at a systematic answer to such questions, the Committee of Union and Progress commissioned sociological and ethnographic studies across Anatolia. Ethnomaps, ethnostatistics, and more qualitative ethnographic studies of the culture of ethnic groups soon emerged. After 1913, the Committee of Union and Progress would rely mainly on these ethnographic studies to de-Bulgarianize, de-Greekize, and de-Armenianize the country.[78]

The Committee of Union and Progress lacked the power to carry out large-scale deportations and massacres in the one-year period spanning the summer of 1913 until World War I. Instead, it intimidated, harassed, and sometimes forced non-Muslims to emigrate through such methods as the resettlement of Muslim immigrants from the Balkans and mob terror. Indeed, the *Teşkilat-ı Mahsusa* (Special Organization), established in November 1913, counted among its aims not just the organization of rebellions across the border (outside the country) in the event of war, the mobilization of Muslims, or the gathering of intelligence; it also aimed to harass and occasionally massacre traitorous and unreliable elements within the country through mob violence.[79] By boycotting the businesses and products of foreigners, especially non-Muslims, they not only rid the geography of many non-Muslims, who, being overwhelmed, felt compelled to emigrate; they also effected their replacement by an emerging Muslim bourgeoisie. It should be emphasized here that neither boycott (as a tool of economic warfare) nor national economy (as a means of creating a Muslim bourgeoisie) were imposed from above. These were not invented by the state or the center of the Committee of Union and Progress. Rather, these policies coincided with the aspirations of a Muslim middle class, in gestation since the nineteenth century. After 1908, the boycott, for example, was a movement in which almost all Muslim social classes participated, including workers. These early movements had put the Committee of Union and Progress in a difficult situation, in both the capital and the provinces. It was only after Unionists fully abandoned Ottomanism and economic liberalism that they began to pursue policies in line with the demands and sentiments of the Muslim middle and

---

78. See Dündar, *Modern Türkiye'nin Şifresi.*
79. On the *Teşkilat-ı Mahsusa*, see Özel, "Tehcir ve Teşkilat-ı Mahsusa," 377–407.

lower classes.[80] Or, in the language of this book, Unionists accepted an invitation to the Muslimness Contract from the Muslim middle and lower classes after 1913, and, thereby, Muslim social groups gained the active support of the state. A good example of how the Muslimness Contract worked in the context of the boycott as well as how those who broke it for the sake of fine clothing were punished can be found in a pamphlet printed and distributed in 1913, titled *To Muslims and Turks*: "We will forbid every Muslim from entering a Christian shop. . . . Honest and conscientious men who understand and listen to these words are admirable. But those who do not listen, as we said above, we will ban them by all means, and we are absolutely determined to do so. Please, let us think with our conscience. Let us (Respected Muslims and Turks) take an oath: let's swear to God, to the homeland, to religion and say: I will never buy from Christians; if I do, I am dishonest and despicable; I am deserving of every curse and insult."[81]

The loss of the Balkans, and Macedonia in particular, rekindled fears—at the level of both the ruling intelligentsia and the Muslim populations, both native and immigrant—that Eastern Anatolia might also be lost in an Armenian revolt. Specifically, Armenians were thought to be encouraged by the Macedonian example, mobilizing again to enact the reforms anticipated since 1878. Indeed, starting in 1912, Armenian organizations began negotiating with the Great Powers (Russia, in particular) to develop reform packages.[82] Meanwhile, Dashnak announced the end of its alliance with the Committee of Union and Progress, even if de facto close relations between Unionists and Dashnaks would continue until 1915.

Parallel to these developments, hatred directed at Christians was again on the rise, with an increase in violence against Armenians in the Eastern provinces and against Greeks in Western Anatolia. Consider the Armenian patriarchate's letter to the Russian, French, and British embassies: "Your Excellency is not unaware that the Armenians' situation deteriorated suddenly in the aftermath of the Balkan War. The unfortunate outcome of this war added a thirst for revenge to a centuries-old hatred. From one end of Anatolia to the other, a threat of massacre gathered over their heads. They became hostages in the Muslims' hands . . . [and] do not even have the right to defend

---

80. For a good critique of the historiography that often attributes the various forms of Muslim-Turkish nationalist policies in the second constitutional monarchy to the state and to Unionists, and that sees the Muslim middle and lower classes as passive followers of state policies, as well as an alternative model to the existing historiography, see Çetinkaya, *Osmanlı'yı Müslümanlaştırmak*. For the English translation, see Çetinkaya, *Young Turks and the Boycott Movement*.

81. Quoted in Çetinkaya, *Osmanlı'yı Müslümanlaştırmak*, 183–184.

82. Ahmad, *İttihatçılıktan Kemalizme*, 119–123.

themselves. If they procure arms, they immediately find themselves accused of preparing a rebellion. . . . The government's action, which is such as to suggest that the Armenians are always ready to take up arms, only whips up the hatred of the fanatical masses."[83] The patriarchate reported similar complaints to Grand Vizier Mahmut Şevket Pasha, who dismissed the complaints as unjustified and noted that necessary measures had been taken. Another letter, this one written by the Armenian National Assembly to Ottoman ministries in August 1913, sheds light on the social basis of the Armenian issue. It is worth citing at length, as this passage offers clues as to how the events of 1915 unfolded and how perpetrators acted:

This privileged class [notables and large landowners in the provinces] has gradually acquired such power that it has proved capable of foiling the projects and actions of the central state's best-intentioned members. Local civil servants—from those of the highest to those of the lowest ranks—have unfortunately never been able to escape its influence. . . . Over the last thirty years, the absolutist government [i.e., Abdülhamid] developed a system of oppression and exactions brought to bear, in particular, on the Armenians living in Eastern Anatolia: it went so far as officially to instruct the provincial authorities that it was licit to make attempts on the life, honor and property of Armenians, or at least intimated that to them. . . . This policy of harassing the Armenians culminated in the organization of appalling massacres. . . . This barbarous persecution, to which Armenians were exposed for more than a quarter of a century, eventually acquired—especially in the *vilayets* [provinces] of Eastern Anatolia—the character of natural custom and, one might say, of a law superior to the civil and religious laws. The tragedy of Adana, which took place after the proclamation of the constitution, was one logical consequence of the transformation of this policy into natural law. . . . Most of these [low-ranking] officials are sincerely convinced that patriotism and the law make it their duty to conceal crimes committed by Muslims against non-Muslims. . . . They use all sorts of tricks in an attempt to deny or cover up undeniable realities.[84]

Although Armenian leaders are careful in this text to avoid blaming Unionists—thereby, perhaps, partially underestimating the force of the central po-

---

83. Quoted in Kévorkian, *Armenian Genocide*, 147.
84. Quoted in Kévorkian, 150–151.

litical power at the same—the letter nonetheless contains important observations that allow us to better understand the Muslimness Contract at the time. First, despite a tendency, common to many debates on genocide, to focus on centralized control, in fact, the provinces enjoyed relative autonomy from the center. Power relations and networks in the provinces possessed their own dynamics. Despite the Tanzimat reforms and Abdülhamid's tyranny, that is, the provinces were still largely self-governing in practice. Principalities (*mirlik*) in the eastern provinces may have been abolished, but these powerful structures were replaced not by the central state but, often, by local forces and coalitions. This is not to say that the center had no authority in the provinces but, rather, that relations were constantly negotiated between the center and the provinces. The center had to consider the expectations of the provinces and the provinces those of the center; relations between the state under Abdülhamid and the Hamidiye regiments are, to my thinking, a prime example of this. Second, the text offers important clues about the operations of the Muslimness Contract. Criticism of the state is largely reserved for the Abdülhamid period, but the text nevertheless emphasizes that local power relations, networks of interests, and injustices continued during the constitutional monarchy. Indeed, echoing what I argued earlier, it attributes the Adana Massacre to local dynamics, if implicitly. The difference between the Abdülhamid period and the constitutional monarchy thus comes down to this: in the former, there was harmony between the center and the provinces, whereas, in the latter, the center did not fully comply with provincial expectations. In terms of the concerns of this book, what we see here is the Muslimness Contract at work locally. It is a contract that benefits, rewards, and protects Muslims and punishes not only non-Muslims but also those Muslims who do not abide by the contract. The local expects the center to participate in this contract and even lead it, as in the Abdülhamid era. This is my understanding of what came to pass in 1915. And this contract between the Muslim center and the Muslim provinces was not limited to 1915 but continued until 1923. In the end, its "success" can be measured in its ability to have purged non-Muslims from the country, homogenized its human geography largely around Sunnism, and, if taken as a single war, won the war of 1912–1922.

The Muslimness Contract and the Armenian Genocide

The Committee of Union and Progress shelved the Ottomanness Contract after 1912–1913. The international conditions for the decisive implementation of the Muslimness Contract, meanwhile, had yet to emerge. The state exited the Balkan Wars both militarily and financially rather weak, and Unionists had only recently taken full power. Under these circumstances, little could be done to counter the support that the Great Powers offered to Armenian demands for reform. In the end, the state had little choice but to sign on to a program of reform for its Eastern provinces. Brokered between the Ottoman and the Russian states on February 8, 1914, and later ratified by the other Great Powers, the agreement stipulated the appointment of two European inspectors general: one for Erzurum, Trabzon, and Sivas, and the other for Van, Bitlis, Harput, and Diyarbakır. The inspectors were to "monitor the civil administration, judiciary, police, and gendarmerie" of the provinces. They could administer military units in the name of security, dismiss any civil servant who abused his office, and request the dismissal of governors. They could also ensure that a "definitive census" be carried out within at most one year, to determine the "actual proportions of the various sects, nationalities and languages in the two regions," as well as appoint equal numbers of Muslims and Christians to the police and gendarmerie, in accordance with the "rule of equality."[85]

With the outbreak of World War I in the summer of 1914, Unionists found appropriate grounds for their imperial and nationalist ambitions. There was, in fact, no consensus among Unionists on whether to enter the war, and, if so, on whose side. Yet, the preference of two of the most powerful names, Enver and Talat, prevailed, and the Ottoman Empire entered the war as Germany's ally. Germany, a rising power in world politics and economy, was expected to win the war; moreover, Germany, unlike Britain, France and, most important, Russia, had no overt interest in the Ottoman territories. The main expectations of Unionists from the war were, first, to retake the recently lost Ottoman territories and then, if possible, to return the Ottoman Empire to its former imperial glory in a new and modern form of imperialism—namely, to establish a modern Turkish-Islamic empire. If we call this imperialist objective Plan A, there was also a national objective, or Plan B. According to the latter, Anatolia, seen as the last stronghold of the Ottoman Empire, was to be protected at all costs. For Plan B to succeed, non-Muslims, the unreliable elements of Anatolia in the eyes of the Unionists—"ethnic tumors"—had to be excised.

For both plans, the Unionists relied mainly on the Muslim population. But the Muslim population simply was not interested in Plan A: regaining lost territories or building a stronger empire. They did, however, share the same ideas and, more importantly, the same feelings as the Unionists about Plan B—namely, the defense of Anatolia, the last land in which they could live safely. The defeat of the Sarıkamış Campaign in January 1915 and the

---

85. For the text of the agreement, see Uras, *Tarihte Ermeniler ve Ermeni Meselesi*, 398–401.

defeat of the Suez Canal Campaign in February 1915 meant the final collapse
of Plan A. Consequently, in early 1915, Plan B was immediately put into action. This would come to mean both the defense of Anatolia and İstanbul and
the ethnic cleansing of non-Muslims.

Shortly after the outbreak of World War I, the Committee of Union and
Progress canceled the Armenian reform plan and dismissed the two Dutch
and Norwegian inspectors general. Years later, the Unionist/Kemalist ideologue Hasan Reşit Tankut would write: "Thank God the First World War
broke out and the realization of that sinister project was prevented. Otherwise, the majority of Alevis would have voted in favor of Armenians."[86] Three
factors encouraged the Unionists to launch the ethnic cleansing project they
had long planned for: (1) the Ottoman loss in Sarıkamış to Russia, the Ottoman Empire's greatest enemy for centuries and the patron of Ottoman
Armenians (and Armenian reform plans) for the past fifty years; (2) the deser-
tion of several thousand Armenians to the Russian side, fighting with the
Russian army in the war; and (3) the suspicion that Russia's advance into
Anatolia would encourage Armenians to revolt. To be clear, it was not a paranoia
that Russia would start Armenian revolts and arm Armenians. Just as the Ottomans attempted to create a Muslim and an Armenian revolt in the Russian
Caucasus,[87] Russia was planning to foment Armenian and Kurdish revolts in
Anatolia. The Van Uprising that began in April 1915, which the Ottomans
saw as a Russian-backed rebellion and the Armenians as self-defense, confirmed Unionist suspicions.[88] When the loss of control of Van coincided with
the start of the Battle of Gallipoli in the West, Unionists issued a decree of
deportation.

Although April 24, 1915, when more than two hundred Armenian intellectuals and politicians were arrested in İstanbul—most were later executed
in different parts of Anatolia—is accepted as the beginning of deportation

86. See Kieser, *Iskalanmış Barış*, 581.

87. At the beginning of the war, the Unionists asked the Dashnak to begin an Armenian revolt
in the Caucasus but were turned down—a rather foregone conclusion. See Y. Türkyılmaz,
"Devrim İçinde Devrim," 324–353.

88. On Russia's plans in Ottoman lands as well as on its Armenian and Kurdish policy, see
Reynolds, *Shattering Empires*; McMeekin, *Russian Origins of the First World War*. These two works
draw attention to the often ignored role of Russia in the ethnic cleansing of Ottoman Armenians, but, in doing so, they end up trivializing the role of the Ottoman Empire and its rulers,
who were primarily responsible. They draw a picture of events as if the Ottoman Empire were
forced both to enter the war and to ethnically cleanse the Armenians; Russia and the Ottoman
Armenians who collaborated with Russia are primarily held responsible for the catastrophe. This
is especially true of McMeekin's book. For a review of this book, see Evans, "Road to Slaughter."

and genocide,[89] the deportation of Armenians had already begun in Zeytun and Dört Yol. In May and June, a broad policy of deportation began to be applied to all Armenians living in Anatolia, with some exceptions (İstanbul, İzmir). Relocating Armenians to the desert region of Zor in present-day Syria was in itself a death sentence. Talat Pasha knew as much, as evidenced by his response, in July 1914, to why Muslim immigrants who had been resettled in areas inhabited by Greeks were not sent to empty lands from İstanbul to Basra: "If we were to send these immigrants there and scatter them in the deserts, as they say, they would all starve to death."[90] This is, indeed, what happened to hundreds of thousands of Armenians who died of hunger, thirst, and disease on the roads and in the deserts. Hundreds of thousands were massacred by mobs formed by *Teşkilat-ı Mahsusa* and local centers of power. Common criminals released from prisons, immigrants, and Kurdish tribesmen were employed to form these mobs. Perhaps tens of thousands of women and children who survived or were rescued from death ended up in Muslim families, compelled to convert to Islam. Armenian men who wanted to convert to Islam to escape deportation were not spared, as it was believed that a non-Muslim could never be a reliable Muslim. Within a year, Anatolia was almost completely de-Armenianized (except for the Armenians of İstanbul, Edirne, and İzmir, as well as Catholic and Protestant Armenians—all totaling around three hundred thousand). This is what Talat Pasha meant when he claimed that, in solving the Armenian question, he achieved in three months what Abdülhamid could not accomplish in thirty years.[91] Prior to deportation, the number of Armenians in Anatolia was close to two million, according to the patriarchate census,[92] and around one and a half million according to Talat Pasha's notebook.[93] Disputes over the precise numbers persist to this day, but this much seems clear: Armenians, who constituted at least 10 percent of Anatolia in 1915, were cleansed from this geography.[94] The magnitude, dramatization, and impact of this, after 1915, can be better understood if one

---

89. The execution of twenty-two Hunchak socialists on June 15, 1915, arrested about a year earlier, can also be considered as part of the genocide. The Hunchaks were executed for "organizing assassinations in order to establish an independent and autonomous Armenian State and attempting to remove a part of the Ottoman State from the state administration by inciting foreign states against the Ottoman State and organizing secret and open congresses in various countries for this purpose, and inciting through the press." Akın, *Ermeni Devrimci Paramaz*, 220.
90. Quoted in Dündar, *Modern Türkiye'nin Şifresi*, 257.
91. Suny, "Writing Genocide," *Ottoman Empire*, 20.
92. Kévorkian, *Ermeni Soykırımı*, 389–393.
93. Bardakçı, *Talat Paşa'nın Evrak-ı Mekrukesi*, 109.
94. See this important work on the pre-1915 presence of Armenians in Anatolia and Thrace, down to the village level, with very rich use of visuals: Kévorkian and Paboudjian, *1915 Öncesinde Osmanlı İmparatorluğu'nda Ermeniler.*

imagines what would have happened if approximately eight million to ten million of Turkey's current population of around eighty million were rapidly exterminated.

A further crucial dimension of the Armenian Genocide, in terms of understanding the social structure of the Republic of Turkey, involves the massive transfers of wealth at the time. Muslims confiscated the movable and immovable properties of hundreds of thousands of Armenians. Armenian businessmen were forced to leave their fields of business (mining, agriculture, trade, crafts, etc.). Muslims took over; Muslims who owed money to Armenians had their debts canceled. The Ottoman Empire, meanwhile, euphemistically referred to this looting and usurpation as *emval-i metruke* (abandoned properties). The Republic of Turkey would later adopt the same terminology, thereby legitimizing—in other words, normalizing—crime through the *Emval-i Metruke* Laws.[95] The seized wealth and businesses of Armenians became, in a sense, the starting capital for an emerging Muslim bourgeoisie, to which the wealth and businesses of exchanged Greeks would later be added.[96] Consider Talat Pasha's testimony from a 1916 trip abroad: "On this trip, I was proud to see the sacrifices that Islam is making. Just how correct was the transfer of Armenians is evident from here. The inhabitants of the occupied areas have settled down completely and have taken over the shops and goods abandoned by the Armenians, and have initiated their own unprecedented trade and commerce."[97] The governor of Aleppo proudly wrote in his report to İstanbul in 1917: "I am pleased to report that, in accordance with the wishes of the government, we have succeeded in completely changing the conditions here and in Maraş. My province has been cleansed of Christian elements. Merchants and business owners who were 80 percent Christian just two years ago are now 95 percent Muslim and 5 percent Christian."[98] As a result, as Akçura summarized, the Committee of Union and Progress became *the* party, *the* representative, of the Muslim/Turkish bourgeoisie during the war years.[99]

Equally intriguing is a document from 1917 about governmental desires. On February 4, 1917, Talat Pasha, who had become the grand vizier, added two separate articles to the handwritten draft of his program of government: "to be included in the declaration" and "not to be included in the declaration."

---

95. On these laws, see Akçam and Kurt, *Kanunların Ruhu.*
96. For the most comprehensive work, to my knowledge, on this topic, see Onaran, *Osmanlı'da Ermeni,* vol. 1.
97. Quoted in Kieser, *Iskalanmış Barış,* 406.
98. Quoted in Akçam, *İnsan Hakları ve Ermeni Sorunu,* 440.
99. Akçura, "İttifak'a Dair," 175–176.

To be included in the declaration was that all Ottoman individuals were to enjoy constitutional rights; to not be included was that Turks, as the foundation of the Muslim state, were to be empowered economically and socially, though without any negative impact on other Islamic peoples.[100] It seems to me that these statements are hidden for two reasons. First, they explicitly exclude Ottoman non-Muslims; such explicit statements would contradict the discourse of legality of a state that still had more than a million Christian citizens. But, in 1917, this reason was arguably of little importance, since no one believed that all Ottomans were equal, and everyone knew that Christians were to be punished at every opportunity. Second, and most important, this article is hidden because it is a partial violation of the Muslimness Contract, which was often maintained through unwritten agreements between the center and the provinces. The Muslimness Contract was an implicit contract in which all Christians were excluded and all Muslims—not yet Turkified—were favored. In a sense, the government deceived the provinces in secretly stating that Turks were to be favored among other Muslims. Such deception, as it were, on the part of the central government regarding the equality of all Muslims would continue until 1923, with the end to wars fought on behalf of the Muslimness Contract.

It is misleading, however, to think that the seizure of Armenian wealth was carried out entirely under government control. The central government aimed simultaneously to create a Muslim bourgeoisie, to cover the costs of deportation, and to offer, with certainty, spaces to live for poor and landless immigrants. To this end, the redistribution of Armenian property had to be as organized and planned as possible. Nevertheless, looting did occur in the provinces, often in ways embedded in local power dynamics. Local rulers and notables, who dominated the provinces, seized wealth without the approval or permission of the central government, in a sense disrupting the central government's plans. Therefore, if one purpose of the *Emval-i Metruke* Law was to legalize looting, another was to create a structure of regulation capable of preventing such corruption and irregularities in the future. Moreover, it was not only the Muslim upper and middle classes who looted the property of Armenians; it was also quite common for Muslims from the lower classes to participate in small-scale looting, depending on their social power and position.[101] The government tried to impose some order and centralized control over the looting but was often helpless. After all, war and ethnic cleansing were carried out within the framework of the Muslimness Contract, and, if they

---

100. Bardakçı, *Talat Paşa'nın Evrak-ı Mekrukesi*, 172–173.
101. Üngör and Polatel, *Confiscation and Destruction*, 80, 87–88, 110.

were to continue, the expectations of Muslim social groups and the provinces had to be met.

At what level and by whom was genocide perpetrated? Reflecting on this question presents a number of important possibilities for understanding the mechanisms of denial, the feelings of justification, the strategies of indifference, and the alliances between different social groups and political movements that were ongoing since 1915. The regnant belief, shared by both radicals and liberals critical of the Armenian issue in Turkey, is that the state and/ or dominant groups should be held responsible for the genocide. This perspective is shaped, or so it seems to me, by a fundamental theoretical—though often implicit—presupposition shared by Marxism and liberalism, the two main competing worldviews.[102] This presupposition holds, in general, that all large-scale "evil" comes from above, that is, from the state and/or the ruling classes. Those above are said to benefit from these evils, while those below— even contrary to what their own self-interest requires—consent to these evils, compelled as they are by the ideological apparatus of the state and the ruling classes. Those at the bottom have, in a sense, been deceived. And not only do theories and worldviews shape this perspective; also, there is, I believe, a political and pragmatic reason. The proportion of the non-Muslim population in Turkey was around 3 percent, in 1924, down from nearly 30 percent in the Ottoman Empire in 1914, and has since fallen to around 0.1 percent. In such a demographic and ethnic structure, political and ideological movements trying to gain the support of the overwhelmingly Sunni Muslim masses could not afford to hold the masses responsible for the Armenian Genocide, even if they accepted it. Such movements have thus largely been content to hold a small number of Unionists and dominant social groups (the bourgeoisie, agas, sheikhs) responsible.

Yet, revisiting this perspective will, I believe, lead to a much better understanding of the history of Turkey. It may be helpful to explore some of the many recent comparative studies of genocide and ethnic conflict. For instance, Roger Petersen argues that in trying to understand genocides or ethnic/religious violence in general, the assumption that the masses are manipulated or deceived by elites is often not correct; rather, he says, we should also squarely examine the motivations of the masses. According to Petersen, one

---

102. Nearly all so-called left-liberal intellectuals see the Committee of Union and Progress leaders as the main perpetrators of genocide and largely limit their criticism to the committee's "mentality." Radical Marxists, in contrast, while acknowledging the role of Unionists, attribute the genocide primarily to the class interests of the emerging Muslim bourgeoisie. For a good example of the second group, including a critique of the first group, see Savran, "Sınıf Mücadelesi Olarak Ermeni Soykırımı," 40–101.

way of turning the camera not only on elites but also on the masses is to look at emotions and the sociology of emotions (rather than the leadership of elites). Three mass emotions are particularly prominent in outbursts of ethnic violence: fear, hatred, and resentment. Fear arises in the absence of a sense of security and seeks safety; hatred arises from historical conflicts and seeks revenge; resentment arises from the practical superiority of a group that should theoretically be at the bottom of the hierarchy of status and power and aims to bring that group down to its rightful place—that is, to the bottom. These three emotions can be satisfied through ethnic violence, and their purpose or function can be achieved as well. Yet, ethnic violence can often be implemented only on a mass scale during periods of upheaval, such as wars, state collapses, or state building—periods that both intensify these emotions and remove various constraints to violence.[103]

There is no doubt that the main culprits and main decision-makers in the ethnic cleansing of Armenians were such Unionist leaders as Talat, Enver, Dr. Şakir, and Dr. Nazım. If the telegrams attributed to Talat Pasha, also known as the Andonyan Papers, are authentic, it would be beyond doubt that a centralized decision was made regarding genocide.[104] But ethnic cleansing took place not just at this level—that is, at the top layer. Rather, is almost a logical necessity that a crime on such a massive scale, in which hundreds of thousands of people are killed or deported and their property redistributed, would involve different layers of society. As Norman M. Naimark suggests, it may be more accurate to think of genocide as taking place on at least three social levels: the top level, where frameworks were drawn up and decisions made; the middle level, where provincial administrators and notables implemented orders from the center and often made and implemented their own decisions;

---

103. Regarding the model he has established on the links between emotions and ethnic violence, see Petersen, *Understanding Ethnic Violence*, 1–59.

104. Akçam, *Naim Efendi'nin Hatıratı*, 19, 22, 183, 193. In some of the telegrams, dated to 1915, allegedly belonging to Talat Pasha (though claimed by the Turkish state to be forgeries), the following orders are given: "The rights of Armenians to live and work in the territory of Turkey have been completely abolished, and the government has accepted full responsibility in this respect, in that no Armenians should be left, down to their children in the cradle"; "It was previously reported that the Government, by the order of the Committee, has decided to completely destroy and exterminate all Armenians existing in Turkey. . . . No matter how disastrous the measures of extermination, no matter whether women, children or cripples, they will be exterminated without conscience"; "Although the intention to exterminate the Armenian element, which for centuries had desired to destroy the solid foundations of the state and constituted an important scourge for the government, had existed, the conditions had not been created and it had not been possible to realize this sacred intention. Now that all obstacles have been removed and the time has come to rid the homeland of these harmful elements; it is necessary, without any feelings of pity and compassion, to put an end to their existence and to strive with all one's might to ensure that there is no Armenian name left in Turkey."

and the lower level, where ordinary people participated in killing and loot-ing.[105] This distinction does not mean that everyone at all three levels is complicit in crime in the same way but that there is broad participation in crime across different social levels. There was broad participation in this crime because Muslims from different social backgrounds shared common feelings of fear, hatred, envy, and resentment against Christians. Nor were these feel-ings unprovoked or invented. As I emphasized earlier, millions of Muslim immigrants had migrated to Anatolia across the previous fifty years, losing their lands and relatives, while native Muslims of Anatolia feared the same would happen to them. They also watched with anger and jealousy as the Christians with whom they lived in the same areas were growing richer and better educated as well as enjoying the external support of the Great Powers. All these long-standing and, crucially, genuine feelings only intensified in the context of World War I—the threat of extinction only increased—and, com-bined with expectations of material gain, led to colossal crimes taking many forms. Behind the fires set in Christian neighborhoods across Anatolia during World War I, there was also a combination of such feelings and the expecta-tion of material gain.[106] In Christian Gerlach's terms, the ethnic cleansing of Armenians and the appropriation of wealth took place in a society prone to extreme violence.[107] Equally crucial is that those who participated in the crime did not see it as such. A strong sense both of self-entitlement and of the other party deserving it, so to speak, ensured that such acts were not perceived as criminal. Had the Muslim population not seen things this way, and had these feelings not remained fresh in the first decades of the republic, the state's policy of denial and the official narrative put into effect as early as 1915 might not have been so successful in the following years.

The widespread nature of participation in the genocide and the reasons for it are perhaps best seen in Eastern Anatolia, where Armenians coexisted with Kurds. Today, largely due to the influence of the contemporary Kurdish movement, Kurds have, relative to the rest of Turkey, made great strides in coming to terms with the Armenian Genocide. But even among Kurds who acknowledge the enormity of the crime, there is a tendency to attribute re-sponsibility to a few Hamidiye regiments and the leadership of the Commit-tee of Union and Progress, as implied by the widespread discourse of having

105. Naimark, "Preface," xvi.

106. For a study that focuses on Ankara but also provides a breakdown of fires in different parts of Anatolia and that sees a connection between these fires and emotions such as resentment, jealousy, feelings of inferiority, and fear (a "political economy of emotions"), see Esin and Etöz, *1916 Ankara Yangını*, 98–99, 212, 216, 219.

107. Gerlach, "İştirak ve Vurgun," 151–194.

been "deceived" or "used." That said, there has been a flourishing, in recent years, of critical studies on this matter, discussing the reasons for the participation of tribes, notables, clergy, and ordinary Kurds in the genocide and emphasizing the role of "ethnic resentment, religious resentment, and economic resentment"[108] and the fear that Armenians and Russians would massacre Kurds.[109] Moreover, the question (on the table for nearly forty years) of whether the region would be Armenia or Kurdistan seemed to have been answered in favor of Armenia in the course of World War I.

Hilmar Kaiser, in a comprehensive study of the genocide, with a special focus on the province of Diyarbakır, argues that the literature on the Armenian Genocide has generally focused on central power and its intentions, whereas it is the power relations in the provinces that deserve more attention. Such attention would, he claims, help disrupt many embedded ways, today, of thinking about the genocide, leading to novel conceptualizations.[110] For example, in the case of Diyarbakır, the thesis that it was the Hamidiye Pashas who massacred Christians loses its general applicability, as İbrahim Pasha—chief of the Milli tribe, Hamidiye commander, and a dominant power in the region until 1908—appears to have been the protector of non-Muslims. After 1908, the Pirinçcizade family (to which the aforementioned Gökalp belonged) assumed leadership among the notables of the city of Diyarbakır and the Committee of Union and Progress and brought an end to the local reign of the Milli clan.[111] The Armenian Reform project did not sit well with Diyarbakır notables, now led by the Pirinçcizades; they felt it would lead to a loss of control of the city and their property, which had been seized from the Armenians in the 1890s. Thus, after the outbreak of the war, they welcomed the dismissal of the inspectors general and the alliance with Germany and increased their threats against the Armenians of the city. In 1915, one can say that they got the governor that they had long sought in the person of Dr. Mehmed Reşid. Allied with the notables of the city, Reşid organized a militia of thousands of men, mainly Circassians. These forces killed thousands of Armenians—in the city, in the province, and among those who had been transported through the province. In doing so, Reşid often acted on his own initiative, though likely in consultation with the city's elite.[112] In the center, Talat Pasha approved of some of Reşid's demands and actions and disapproved of

---

108. Aydınkaya, "1880'den 1915'e Kürt-Ermeni Hinterlandındaki," 98.

109. See Çelik and Dinç, *Yüz Yıllık AH! 1915 Diyarbekir*; Dağlıoğlu, "Diyarbakır'da Soykırım Nasıl Örgütlendi?" 232–236.

110. Kaiser, *Extermination of Armenians*, 4–6.

111. On the power relations between the Pirinçcizade family and the Milli and on their differing views, see Jongerden, "Diyarbekir'de Seçkinlerin Şiddete Dayalı Karşılaşmaları," 57–85.

112. Kaiser, *Extermination of Armenians*, 29–30, 90–91, 103, 151, 165–168.

others.[113] Yet, when Talat Pasha ordered deportation caravans to pass through the province of Diyarbakır, he was certainly aware that he was signing the death sentences of Armenians.[114]

The war, the genocide, and the appropriation of Armenian wealth were carried out by Muslims of different social classes and between the center and the provinces, all within the framework of the Muslimness Contract. According to the first and most fundamental article of this tacit contract, one had to be a Muslim in order to live safely, and with real or potential privilege, in Anatolia. The second article held that no one would oppose what was done to non-Muslims, especially Armenians; no one would sympathize with victims; and no one would speak the truth about what was done. Direct participation in massacres was not required to comply with the second article, nor to benefit from the contract in general. Keeping silent, silently approving, or overlooking things was often enough. Both ordinary and prominent Muslims who did not comply with this second point—those who actively opposed what was being done to Armenians and those who tried to protect Armenians—were punished. Some lost their jobs, some their lives. For the Muslimness Contract, this was such a crime and treason that even the children and grandchildren of those involved either know very little about their grandparents or, if they know, say very little.[115] What it means to oppose the Muslimness Contract and the Turkishness Contract is, in a sense, passed on from grandfathers to grandchildren.

The Muslimness Contract was opposed not only by individuals but also by whole regions. Dersim is exemplary, where Alevis were (and continue to be) the majority. People in Dersim demonstrated their noncompliance with the contract by protecting many Armenians fleeing deportation and massacre. In June 1915, the Ministry of Interior sent a telegram to the governor of Mamuretülaziz, stating that the *Teşkilat-ı Mahsusa* would take the necessary measures in Dersim, upon request, regarding the escape of thousands of Armenians to Dersim—demonstrating how closely the state was monitoring what was happening in the mountains of Dersim.[116] This historical knowledge is at least partly behind the state's distrust of Dersim, from the Abdülhamid period to the violence of 1937–1938 and into the present.

---

113. E.g., Talat Pasha criticized the massacre of not only Armenians but also other Christian communities, who, he said, were "slaughter[ed] . . . like sheep"; he ordered Reşid to cease this immediately. For the relevant telegram, see Üngör, *Making of Modern Turkey*, 92.

114. Kaiser, *Extermination of Armenians*, 421.

115. On what happened to those Ottoman administrators who opposed the deportation and extermination of Armenians as well as on the memory (or rather lack or suppression of memory) of their relatives about this opposition, see Gerçek, *Akıntıya Karşı*.

116. Akçam, *Ermeni Meselesi Hallolunmuştur*, 180.

The Muslimness Contract and
the War of Independence

When the Ottomans and Germany found themselves on the losing side of World War I in 1918, it seemed that not only Plan A but also perhaps Plan B had failed. Signed on October 30, 1918, the Armistice of Mudros granted Britain and its allies "the right to occupy any strategic point in the event of any situation arising which threatens the security of the Allies" and "in case of disorder in the six Armenian vilayets . . . the right to occupy any part of them" (Articles Seven and Twenty-Four).[117] It seemed only a matter of time before Anatolia, the last remaining territory of the Ottoman Empire, would be fragmented and divided. This, of course, did not happen; in the end, Anatolia remained in Muslim hands, in one piece. The success of Anatolian Muslims is tied to their determination to continue with Plan B, put into effect in 1915, within the framework of the Muslimness Contract. And behind their determination lies the possibility and fear of losing everything. Of course, determination alone may not have been enough; the ethnic cleansing of Armenians in 1915 and its aftermath also played a crucial role in this success, significantly transforming the demographic structure of Anatolia in favor of Muslims. This is what the Unionist intellectual Hüseyin Cahit Yalçın meant when he said that "those who conceived of and carried out the Armenian deportation saved Turkey."[118]

What some writers have called the "state problem" came to define the period of 1918 to 1922 in Anatolia (before Turkey was established): namely, "here, which state or states would exist, and how they be structured? Such is the essence of the state problem."[119] The Entente states (except for Russia, whose aims of sharing the Ottoman Empire dissolved following the Bolshevik revolution) wished to create small states and spheres of influence by dividing Anatolia into parts; the Ottoman Empire wished to preserve its existence, although in a manner that was reduced, weakened, and under trusteeship; and Armenians wished to establish an Armenia ("Greater Armenia"), while Greeks wished to establish a Greek state (the "Megali Idea"). Anatolian Muslims were mainly afraid of the latter two "state theses." It was assumed that Britain, France, Italy, and, after a possible mandate, the United States would sooner or later

---

117. In Turkish, see Meray and Olcay, *Osmanlı İmparatorluğu Çöküş Belgeleri*, 1–5. In English, see Maurice, *Armistices of 1918*, 85–87.

118. Yalçın, *Tanıdıklarım*, 45. For Dr. Şakir, whom he sees as the main architect of deportation, he noted on p. 83: "If one day it becomes necessary to revive the memory of Bahattin Şakir, the eastern provinces will open their arms with gratitude to his statue."

119. Tanör, *Türkiye'de Kongre İktidarları*, 15.

leave Anatolia. If Greek and Armenian states were established, though, Anatolian Muslims knew that this would mean the irreversible loss of Anatolia for Muslims. In fact, in 1918, when a common struggle of Muslims had not yet begun (and possibly never would), local congresses began to convene spontaneously, especially in the regions where there was a danger of Greek and Armenian occupation. In other words, at a time when there was a power vacuum in Anatolia and a threat of occupation, provincial Muslims, under the leadership of Unionists, clergymen, landowners, and notables who had grown rich thanks to the Committee of Union and Progress, convened congresses to organize the resistance. And these congresses led to the formation of the *Kuvayı Milliye* (National Forces), composed of militias. The logic of organizing in the form of congresses was to emphasize the legitimacy and legality of these actions. Thus, the congress governments that resulted were able to function something like a state: they made decisions, levied taxes, recruited troops, acted as a judiciary, and even, in some cases, drafted constitutions.[120] The most important shortcoming of the local congress governments, founded on the basic principles of the Muslimness Contract, was that, as the name implies, they were local. As such, they were incapable of raising the necessary resources for resistance.

One possible critical obstacle to the unification of Anatolian Muslims were the Kurds. In the power vacuum after the Armistice of Mudros, a number of prominent Kurdish families had organized in the Society for the Rise of Kurdistan, established in İstanbul. Key names included Şemdinan, Bedirhan, and Baban, and the organization had its own "state theses." They believed that conditions were ripe for the establishment of an autonomous or independent state of Kurdistan. Yet, there were also significant divisions between these families, rooted in historical rivalries and differences in political views. For example, Seyyid Abdülkadir of Şemdinan was in favor of autonomy and a caliphate, while the Bedirhans were in favor of independence and secularism. Where they overlapped, though, was in their desire to extract an autonomous or independent Kurdistan from the Paris Peace Conference, where Anatolia was to be dismembered and redivided.[121] The Kurdistanist leanings of these influential Kurdish families posed a great danger to the Muslim resistance

---

120. Tanör, *Türkiye'de Kongre İktidarları*, 41–42, 133–136, 177, 184.
121. On rivalries and differences between these families, see Özoğlu, *Osmanlı Devleti ve Kürt Milliyetçiliği*, 107–152. Hanioğlu notes that, during the armistice period, Dr. Cevdet also seemed to be something of a Kurdish "ethnic separatist," but following the national struggle and its successes never expressed such thoughts again. See Hanioğlu, *Doktor Abdullah Cevdet ve Dönemi*, 315–321.

against the Armenian threat in Eastern Anatolia, where Muslim unity was key to the success of the Muslim resistance.

Here is where Mustafa Kemal's achievements become relevant: he was able to unite the local congresses that had emerged before he moved to Anatolia, following the Greek occupation of Western Anatolia. He gained the support of Kurdish agas, notables, and clergy.[122] Yet, for the Muslim provinces, unification was not synonymous with centralization and Turkification; no one wanted to surrender their entire will to a form of central despotism again, nor did anyone wish to give up their own language and culture. Therefore, until the War of Independence was won and confirmed by the Treaty of Lausanne, relative democracy and decentralization prevailed among Muslims. The common thought and feeling of the union was tied to Islam, and its aim was to expel Greeks and Armenians from Anatolia. Both that it was an Islamic discourse of unity until the establishment of the Republic of Turkey and that this unity was based on the idea of Islamic brotherhood and the equality of Muslim peoples are related to this common feeling and purpose. Concepts of the national or the nation, deployed often during these years, must be read as referring to an Islamic nation, not a Turkish nation. When Mustafa Kemal gathered local congresses under a national congress and assembly, what actually occurred was the unification of local Muslimness Contracts under a national and general Muslimness Contract.

Texts, documents, and speeches from the years when the "state problem" was central—when the main struggle was over who would create what kind of state or states—clearly show that inter-Muslim unity was achieved through negotiations, agreements, invitations, mutual promises, and concessions. The common language is Islam, and the common enemies are Armenians and Greeks. The closing declaration of the Congress of *Vilayat-ı Şarkiye*, or the Erzurum Congress, dated August 7, 1919, reads as follows: "All the descendants of Islam living in these domains are brothers and sisters who are filled with a shared sense of sacrifice towards one another, and who respect one another's racial and social aspects."[123] Article Three of the Declaration of the Sivas General Congress, dated September 11, 1919, reads as follows: "A principle has been adopted of united defense and resistance against the operations aimed at establishing an independent Greek and Armenian entity within our

---

122. It was not only Mustafa Kemal Pasha who aimed to create unity; the Karakol Society, founded by Unionist leadership before they fled İstanbul and led by prominent Unionists Kara Vasıf and Kara Kemal, also sought to build common and collective resistance in Anatolia. In the end, though, it was Mustafa Kemal and his circle who won out. See Zürcher, *Milli Mücadele İttihatçılık.*

123. Quoted in Gologlu, *Milli Mücadele Tarihi*, vol. 1, 227.

homeland, as in the national jihad in the Aydın, Manisa and Balıkesir fronts."[124] The statute of the Anadolu ve Rumeli Mudafaa-i Hukuk Cemiyeti (ARM-HC; Association for the Defense of Rights of Anatolia and Rumelia), established by a decision of the Sivas General Congress, expresses the same points of reconciliation in its first and second articles.[125] In the Amasya Protocols signed between the government and the ARMHC on October 20–22, 1919, it is stated, albeit implicitly, that Kurds might be granted autonomy (as a means of forestalling any pursuit of independence on their part).[126] The *Ahd-ı Milli* (national oath), commonly known as *Misak-ı Milli* (national pact or national oath) was adopted by the last Ottoman Parliament on January 28, 1920, influenced by the ARMHC. The oath held that the Muslim majority was an indivisible whole, respecting one another's rights and the conditions of their environs. As Sinan Hakan points out, congress and assembly decisions should be viewed as "a social contract for all Muslim components," as a model for common life.[127]

Mustafa Kemal played the greatest role in the unification of Anatolian Muslims under a general Muslimness Contract. He seems to have sensed the needs, expectations, and feelings of Muslims well and was able to instrumentalize these. Mustafa Kemal was the main architect of the decisions and agreements reached at the Erzurum and Sivas Congresses, the Parliamentary Assembly in İstanbul, and the Grand National Assembly in Ankara. In each, only representatives elected from among Muslims came together, in accordance with the logic of the contract. He always talked about the brotherhood of Islam and the common interests of Muslims in his speeches and telegrams; he had the congresses and the national assembly opened with basmalas and Friday prayers; he said that Kurds, Turks, Laz, Circassians, and other Muslim elements were "siblings who respect each other's racial, local, moral and all rights"; he invited all Muslims to unity against the efforts to establish Armenian, Greek, and Pontus states; and he called on Kurdish tribal leaders and sheikhs (whom he got to know closely through the relations he established during World War I) in the name of a common defense of the homeland so

---

124. Quoted in Gologlu, vol. 2, 260.

125. Tunçay, *Türkiye Cumhuriyeti'nde*, 20–22, 349.

126. Hakan, *Türkiye Kurulurken Kürtler*, 283.

127. Though the same author praises these texts for creating "a definition of citizenship based on Islam, without any ethnic emphasis, in accordance with the historical and sociological reality of the Ottoman Empire," he ignores the fact that the "reality" he refers to is not historical but contemporary, created by the state and the Muslim majority after 1915 around a Muslimness Contract. In fact, when he criticizes the Turkification project of the "Kemalist mentality, which does not coincide with historical and scientific facts," he also lays bare just how subjective such "facts" can be. See Hakan, *Türkiye Kurulurken Kürtler*, 216, 328–330, 363.

that "our homeland would not be trampled under Armenian feet."[128] He strove to isolate the Kurdish delegation at the Paris Peace Conference—they had reached an agreement with the Armenian delegation for the establishment of an Independent Greater Armenia and Independent Kurdistan—as traitors who had sold the Kurds to Armenians.

Kurds were undoubtedly well aware of the Turkist and assimilationist vein in the Unionist tradition. But, in the world of the 1910s, fears of Armenians prevailed over those of Turks.[129] Further exacerbating Kurdish fears were two facts: the Treaty of Sèvres, which granted autonomy to Kurdistan and envisioned an Armenia that would include the Kurdish-majority provinces, left the southern border of this Greater Armenia (i.e., the northern border of Kurdistan) vague (Articles Eighty-Eight and Eighty-Nine); it also regulated the return of both the expelled Armenians and their "abandoned property" (Article 144).[130] Mustafa Kemal and Kazım Karabekir, who knew well the Kurdistan/Armenia issue and its region of relevance, exploited this fear and repeatedly stated in various ways that Kurdistan would become Armenia and would be divided and destroyed were it not struggled for in unison.[131] The fact that the Koçgiri Rebellion,[132] the only Kurdish revolt during the War of Independence, was also an Alevi revolt reveals only more so the limits of the Muslimness Contract. Unlike Sunni Kurds, Alevi Kurds were not afraid of Armenians. Rather, their real fear was to be exterminated like the Armenians.

The horizontal, negotiated, contractual, democratic, and pluralist character (alongside its simultaneous status as open to and meant only for Muslims) of the War of Independence is further evident in the first Grand National Assembly, initiated in Ankara. As in the congresses, the First Assembly included no non-Muslim representatives. Ideological, ethnic, and, to an extent, class differences among Muslims are reflected in the diversity and discourse of members of parliament.[133] This diversity, embodied in the congresses and in the associations—particularly through the idea of autonomy, which would guarantee Kurdish participation in the convention—was codified in the constitution adopted on January 20, 1921. With Article One, which states, "Sovereignty belongs to the nation unconditionally," sovereignty was taken away from the sultanate and given to the Muslim nation.[134] Also, some ten articles

---

128. E.g., see Atatürk, *Nutuk*, 927–931, 937–945.
129. Bozarslan, "Tehcir'den Lozan'a Türkler, Kürtler ve Ermeniler," 485–486.
130. Meray and Olcay, *Osmanlı İmparatorluğu Çöküş Belgeleri*, 67–68, 74–75, 86–87.
131. Beşikçi, *Kürdistan Üzerine Emperyalist Bölüşüm Mücadelesi*, 192–193.
132. For a comprehensive study of the uprising, see Soileau, *Koçgiri İsyanı*.
133. See Demirel, *Birinci Meclis'te Muhalefet*.
134. Dinçer Demirkent (*Bir Devlet İki Cumhuriyet*) analyzes the period 1919–1924 as one of struggle between the decentralist, pluralist, and populist republican understanding embodied in

granted autonomy to provinces and even subdistricts. One must see the democratic and decentralized nature of the 1921 constitution as tied deeply to the horizontal nature of the Muslimness Contract.

Consequently, the Muslimness Contract was successful and the War of Independence against the Armenians in Eastern Anatolia and the Greeks in Western Anatolia was won thanks to the unity of Anatolian Muslims. This is not to say that all Muslims were united or trusted. The situation, beyond generalizations, was far more complex. Already, during World War I, hundreds of thousands of Muslims, especially Kurds—for whom, based on sociological and ethnic characteristics, the government had little trust—were deported to various parts of Anatolia.[135] During the War of Independence, rebellions against the war broke out in many parts of Anatolia, in which the governments of İstanbul played a role.[136] Revolts led by Ahmet Anzavur and Ethem the Circassian in Western Anatolia underscore how, even for Circassians, long considered a loyal element of the Ottoman and Turkish states since their migration from the Caucasus,[137] the object of loyalty was subject to change; Circassians could follow their own specific agendas.[138] Still, Anatolian Muslims were able to forge a sufficiently powerful force of unity and defense around common feelings and interests. Without this unity—without the real and burning need to unite the Muslims of Anatolia against common enemies—things may have turned out far differently.

---

the 1921 constitution and the centralist, monist, and nationalist republican understanding embodied in the 1924 constitution. On the minutes of the parliamentary discussions about the 1921 constitution, see Sevinç and Demirkent, *Kuruluşun İhmal Edilmiş İstisnası*.

135. See Dündar, *İttihat ve Terakki'nin*.

136. Akşin analyzes these uprisings, launched by the governments of İstanbul, through the concept of civil war, in *İstanbul Hükümetleri ve Milli Mücadele*.

137. For an ambitious and, in equal measure, controversial book about the role of the Circassians in the periods of Abdülhamid, the constitutional monarchy, and the War of Independence, as well as their importance in the Turkish state system, see Avagyan, *Osmanlı İmparatorluğu ve Kemalist Türkiye'nin*.

138. Gingeras, *Dertli Sahiller*.

2

The Transition to the Turkishness Contract

The Social Contract and the Turkishness Contract

From the perspective of the Ottomans, the period spanning 1912 to 1922—that is, from the Balkan Wars to the end of the War of Independence—was one of almost uninterrupted war. Everyone was, in a sense, at war with everyone, and anyone could lose everything: life, relatives, property, country. It is, perhaps, not an exaggeration, in this context, to recall Thomas Hobbes's description of the state of war as a condition of "continual fear, and danger of violent death; and the life of man, solitary, poor, nasty, brutish, and short."[1] It was from within such an atmosphere that the Muslim nation, Muslim state, and Muslim morality emerged simultaneously, in a horizontal historical process that I term the Muslimness Contract. The making of a Muslim nation was shaped by similar pains that Muslims suffered on account of being Muslim and by having similar feelings and expectations. In this sense, the formation of a Muslim nation largely fits Ernest Renan's description of the nation, at his famous 1882 conference: "A nation is a soul, a spiritual principle. Two things, which in truth are but one, constitute this soul or spiritual principle. One lies in the past, one in the present. One is the possession in common of a rich legacy of memories; the other is present-day consent, the desire to live together, the will to perpetuate the value of the heritage that one has received in an undivided form . . . the fact of sharing, in the past, a glorious heritage and regrets, and of having, in the future, [a shared] programme to put into effect, or the fact having suffered,

---

1. Hobbes, *Leviathan*, 84.

enjoyed, and hoped together. . . . I spoke just now of 'having suffered together' and, indeed, suffering in common unifies more than joy does."[2]

Shared pains, feelings, and expectations also enabled the emergence of a moral contract among Muslims, according to which one felt no moral obligation to those outside the contract, particularly when the contract was under threat. As the comparative study of national ethnic cleansing demonstrates, homogenization policies routinely distinguish, through unequivocal terms and boundaries, between inside and outside or us and them, in their efforts to bring about uniformity and unity between state and society and build a new state and nation. By this logic and feeling, one is free to wrong those beyond certain abstract and concrete boundaries, since to do so is seen not as a wrong but as one's right. Moral obligations (doing good, abstaining from evil, protecting one's rights, honoring memories) and moral sentiments (gratitude, responsibility, guilt, shame) address insiders.[3] Thus, if a Muslim ventures to step beyond the moral contract and begins to sympathize with non-Muslims excluded from the contract, she is branded as immoral and treated as a traitor by both the state and the nation. Behaviors characterized as moral by insiders are, of course, seen as immoral by the excluded. Within and beyond the contract exist two different moral worlds.

Seen in this light, then, the widespread disinterest in and ignorance of the Armenian Genocide among Muslims (and, more generally, of the elimination of non-Muslims from Anatolia) have also been shaped by moral and epistemic contracts underlying the Muslimness Contract. The colossal forgetting of the ethnic and religious violence directed at groups beyond the contract is a typical example of the relationship between nation and memory, which Renan calls attention to in another famous passage: "Forgetting, I would even go so far as to say that historical error is a crucial factor in the creation of a nation, which is why progress in historical studies often constitutes a danger for [the principle of] nationality. Indeed, historical enquiry brings to light acts of violence which took place at the origin of all political formations, even those whose consequences have been altogether beneficial."[4] Such forgetting cannot be explained solely by the vertical influence of official state ideology or top-down historiography. At times voiced openly, often held implicitly, the feeling-thought that violence against non-Muslims has been "beneficial" is something shared among Muslims. After all, the construction of a Muslim country and state—of an environment where Muslims feel safe and at home—is held to have become possible due to this constituent violence.

---

2. Renan, "What Is a Nation?" 52–53.
3. Rae, *State Identities and the Homogenisation of Peoples*, 3–4, 14, 130.
4. Renan, "What Is a Nation?" 45.

The horizontality of the Muslimness Contract, as noted in Chapter 1, led to the transformation of the multinational Ottoman Empire—beginning in 1878 but essentially after 1912—into a state solely protecting the interests and lives of Muslims. Of particular interest, in terms of social contract theory, is the state of statelessness between 1919 and 1922.[5] It was then that a new state belonging to and represented only by Muslims was formed, as the local congresses formed by Muslims united into national congresses and a national assembly. However, after the war was won and the new state gained international recognition with the Treaty of Lausanne, the leadership Turkified the Muslimness Contract through a top-down, vertical push, shifting to a narrowing of the contract's basic principle. Such a transformation meant that, to be able to live in safety and with privilege in Turkey, being Muslim was no longer enough; one also had to be Turkish. Which is to say, one had to be both Muslim and Turkish. There are three main reasons, perhaps, for this partial narrowing. First, the founders believed that this new state and society would not be able to stay together solely through a Muslim partnership; other ethnic groups, ethnic cultures, and forms of ethnic consciousness within the Muslim nation also had to be eliminated. Thereby, it was thought, the ethnic divisions and forms of nationalist separatism that marked the last century of the Ottoman Empire would be brought to an end. Second, the founding leaders, chiefly Mustafa Kemal, hailed from a Turkist generation that seized control of the Committee of Union and Progress after 1906. All were Turkish nationalists, and, after Anatolia was liberated and a new state established, they set in motion the project of Turkification. Third, Mustafa Kemal, in particular, was a radical and unequivocal supporter of Westernization and secularism, unlike the majority of the Unionist generation to which he then belonged. It was thus impossible for the Muslimness Contract to sustain its earlier Islamic discourse. The transition from the Muslimness to the Turkishness Contract was not only a step in the direction of Turkishness, then, but also a step toward secularism, symbolizing the transition from a religious to a secular nation.

That said, the Turkishness of the Turkishness Contract was not necessarily an innate ethnic feature. Rather, it was a world of language, sentiment, and knowledge to which every Muslim and every Muslim family, even if not Turkic by birth, could switch if they so decided; one had only to be born Muslim. Yet, this same openness to Muslims also meant that the gates of the Turkishness Contract remained closed to non-Muslims, no matter how hard they endeavored to convert to Turkishness. Indeed, the second article of the Muslimness

---

5. The fact that Mustafa Kemal was influenced by Jean-Jacques Rousseau's *Social Contract* further underscores the significance of this concept for Turkish history. See Turan, *Atatürk'ün Düşünce Yapısını*, 13–14; Hanioğlu, *Atatürk*, 109–110.

Contract—a prohibition on both speaking truths about what is done to and sympathizing with non-Muslims—was transposed directly onto the Turkishness Contract. According to the first and second articles of the Turkishness Contract (variously expressed in writing, but often held implicitly), both non-Muslims excluded from the Turkishness Contract as well as Muslims who refuse to convert to Turkishness—that is, Muslims who did not consent to be a part of the Turkishness Contract—were condemned in Turkey to lives marked by insecurity, inauspiciousness, and a lack of access to privileges. A sense of security and expectations of privilege were reserved strictly for Turks and those who consented to (or were able to consent to) Turkification.

There is no clear or singular date for the transition from the Muslimness Contract and its horizontality to the Turkishness Contract imposed from above. For example, Mustafa Kemal's press conference in January 1923 on the matter of Kurdistan's autonomy implies still-partial adherence to the Muslimness Contract: "Rather than considering Kurdishness in and of itself, there will already be some sort of local autonomy in line with our Constitution. As such, wherever there are Kurds, they will govern themselves autonomously. . . . Currently, the Grand National Assembly of Turkey is composed of the representatives of both Kurds and Turks, and the two elements have united all their interests and destinies. So they know that this is something in common. It would not be right to try to draw a separate border."[6]

MustafaKemal's March 1923 statements in Adana are an early example of the partial narrowing of the first article of the Muslimness Contract and the retention of the second: "Armenians have no rights in this prosperous country. Your homeland is yours, the Turks'. This homeland was Turkish in history, is thus Turkish, and will be forever Turkish. . . . Armenians and the like have no rights here. These plentiful and blessed places are the homeland of Turks, deeply and essentially."[7] The extent to which Adana's Muslim population in 1923 considered themselves to be Turkish is unclear. Nevertheless, through this speech, Mustafa Kemal, effectively marking the end of the Cilician-Armenian issue (unsettled since at least the 1909 Adana massacre), declared that the Turkishness Contract would continue to protect any Muslim who accepted Turkishness.

The 1924 constitution is, in many ways, the most important written document for understanding the transition from the Muslimness Contract to the Turkishness Contract. The new constitution marked the end of the horizontal and deliberative nature of the Muslimness Contract and suggested a shift

---

6. Mustafa Kemal [Atatürk], *Eskişehir-İzmit Konuşmaları*, 104–105.
7. Quoted in Bardakçı, *İttihadçı'nın Sandığı*, 7.

from horizontality to verticality, from a decentralized to a centralized administrative structure. Particularly interesting for my purposes are the discussions, during the preparation of the constitution, about who could and could not be a Turk. The Constitutional Council's proposal that "the people of Turkey are to be called Turks without regards to religion and race" elicited objections from deputies, as did statements to the effect that non-Muslims could not be considered as Turks. The relevant article (Article Eighty-Eight) was subsequently modified to read, "The people of Turkey are to be called Turks in terms of citizenship, without regards to religion and race," and was adopted as such.[8] Thus, as Mesut Yeğen notes, the "Law ranks Turkishness as 'Turkishness-as-citizen' and 'Turks as something more than citizenship.'"[9] One can also take Article eighty-eight of the constitution as the written embodiment of the otherwise tacit first and second articles of the Turkishness Contract. Moreover, this constitutional statement, in terms of the imperatives of the modern state, seems rather kind or civil, and, at first glance at least (that is, if one is unaware of the debates during the preparation of the constitution), would seem to be egalitarian. Yet, as I demonstrate later, the Turkishness Contract operates fundamentally through unwritten rules, institutional structures, de facto practices, everyday habits, and strategies of not knowing and not caring—a way of operating that is, at times, far from kind.

The transition from the Muslimness Contract to the Turkishness Contract did not render Muslimness insignificant. On the contrary, Muslimness continued to be the basic conditionality of Turkishness. The Contract and Protocol on Turkish-Greek Population Exchanges—signed between Greece and Turkey on January 30, 1923, as negotiations over the Treaty of Lausanne continued—set out who could and could not be considered a Turk, according to which: "as from the 1st May, 1923, there shall take place a compulsory exchange of Turkish nationals of the Greek Orthodox religion established in Turkish territory, and of Greek nationals of the Moslem religion established in Greek territory."[10] In other words, even if a Greek person spoke Greek and was ethnically Greek, he would be considered Turkish if he was Muslim, and, even if a Turkish person spoke Turkish and was ethnically Turkish, he would be considered Greek if he was an Orthodox Christian. Despite Bishop Papa Eftim's efforts throughout the national struggle to prove that the Turkish-speaking Anatolian Orthodox Christians, or "Karamanlides," were faithful

---

8. Özbudun, *1924 Anayasası*, 62–63; Alpkaya, *Türkiye Cumhuriyeti'nin Kuruluşu*, 416.

9. Yeğen, *Müstakbel Türk'ten Sözde Vatandaşa*, 72–73.

10. Quoted in Grigoriadis, *Instilling Religion*, 100. Grigoriadis describes how, despite the efforts of Turkish and Greek nationalists to establish secular states, both nevertheless took Muslimness and Orthodox Christianity as the fundamental criteria of Turkishness and Greekness, respectively.

Turks (including the establishment of the Turkish Orthodox patriarchate in
contrast to the ecumenical patriarchate he described as traitorous and Greek),
the Turkish state's attitude remained unchanged.[11] The deportation of some
1.5 million Orthodox Christians and 500,000 Muslims marked the final
major step in the Muslimization of Anatolia. In 1913, one in five people in the
geography that is today Turkey was Christian; by the end of 1923, the ratio was
one in forty.[12]

Many Christian and Muslim contemporaries noted that, whereas the majority of Christians exchanged were urban merchants and tradesmen, the majority of new arrivals were peasants and farmers. The exchanges thus amounted
to an economic loss for the Turkish side. But, even weighed against this loss,
what was to be gained was far more valuable: the Muslimization and Turkification of the population and economy.[13] For example, the new Ankara-based
state adopted, with only minor changes, the *Emval-i Metruke* laws legalizing
the extortion of Armenian property by Unionists and donated the remaining
property of Armenians to the families of Unionist leaders killed by Armenian
assassins.[14] One member of parliament, known to be close to Mustafa Kemal,
underscored the logic of the law, enacted in 1926,[15] that regulated the alloca-
tion of Armenian property to the families of such Unionist leaders as Talat
Pasha, Cemal Pasha, and Bahaeddin Şakir: "Warning message to assassins:
you may execute a Turk through an assassination! But, we will raise his off-
spring with your money so that tomorrow he will gouge your eye and break
your head."[16]

---

11. See Benlisoy and Benlisoy, *Türk Milliyetçiliğinde Katedilmemiş Bir Yol.*
12. Keyder, *Memâlik-i Osmaniye'den Avrupa Birliği'ne*, 105. Keyder emphasizes that with
this demographic change, which includes the elimination of a non-Muslim bourgeoisie with
worldwide economic and cultural ties, there existed no independent or autonomous bourgeoisie
before the Muslim bureaucracy—a bourgeoisie that may have also represented a democratic political stance. See Keyder, *State and Class in Turkey.* Yet, when viewed not through a distinction between
state and civil society but through the concept of the Muslimness Contract, and keeping in mind
how Muslims in the center and the provinces, elite and ordinary Muslims, united to rid themselves
of non-Muslims and establish a state belonging only to them and protecting only them, the argument, then, can be made that what Keyder describes as a loss (of an autonomous civil society or
its potential) was not seen as terribly important by Muslims. Indeed, while some contemporary
observers noted the economic loss caused by the elimination of non-Muslims at the time, none, as
far as I know, noted a democratic loss.
13. Kemal Arı summarizes this logic, which he also follows: "After all, the significance of the
economy taking on a national character was, even with the lost material opportunities, greater
than could be measured in monetary terms." Arı, *Büyük Mübadele*, 177.
14. Akçam and Kurt, *Kanunların Ruhu.*
15. On the text of the law, and on properties allocated through the signatures of Mustafa Kemal
and İsmet Pasha, see Bardakçı, *İttihadçı'nın Sandığı*, 36–56.
16. Quoted in Çağaptay, *Islam, Secularism, and Nationalism*, 37.

Seen from the Turkish side, the basic logic behind the population exchange (the roots of which run far back and deep and were thought to be confirmed anew during the War of Independence) was this: non-Muslims could not, under any circumstances, be trusted; Muslims could be. In 1926, the British ambassador articulated this logic: "As the Republic [of Turkey] is full of deep distrust of all non-Turkish elements—the reason for this insecurity is the policy that [European] states have applied against Turkey for a hundred years!—he seems driven to build a great wall of China around himself [and in it] to leave no room for the influence of foreign influence in the state he will build—even if it comes from individuals or even merchants. This policy, supported by the entire population, continues to be implemented with relentless determination."[17]

Trust in Muslims meant trusting their loyalty in the face of external and internal enemies; it also implied faith in their ability to be assimilated easily to Turkishness. For Hamdullah Suphi, Turks were characterized as "Turkish-speaking, Muslim, and possessing a love of Turkishness." For Ziya Gökalp, articulating precisely this fundamental logic and trust, "Pomaks today are Bulgarian, Muslims in Crete speak Greek, but tomorrow they will learn Turkish with the help of Muslimness and abandon their present languages. Then, the individuals of a nation manifest themselves not only through their languages, but also through their religion."[18] Such an understanding of Muslimness as the yeast, so to speak, of Turkishness has also shaped immigration policy in the Republic of Turkey to this day. While Turkish Muslims are typically granted permission to migrate to Turkey and non-Turkish Muslims occasionally so, Turkic and Turkish-speaking Christians (such as the Gagauz) are typically refused.[19]

In practice, as one might expect, the majority of the Muslim population complied with this narrowed sense of the contract. Although facilitating cultural factors—the fact, for instance, that the majority of Anatolian Muslims already spoke Turkish—played some role in compliance, my sense is that the main factor lies in the logic of the contract itself.[20] It was Muslims who con-

---

17. Quoted in Aktar, *Varlık Vergisi ve "Türkleştirme" Politikaları*, 59.
18. Quoted in Benlisoy and Benlisoy, *Türk Milliyetçiliğinde Katedilmemiş Bir Yol*, 291, 303.
19. For an exploration of the migration of minority Muslim Turks from Bulgaria to Turkey through the lens of such emotions such as entitlement and hope, see A. Parla, *Precarious Hope*.
20. According to the 1927 census, the portion of the population whose native language was Turkish was around 86 percent (though one can assume that the actual number was lower). This high value, made possible by the ethnic cleansing of non-Muslim populations from Anatolia and the migration of Muslim populations across the past century, forms the demographic basis of both the Muslimness and the Turkishness Contracts. See Aslan et al., *Türkiye'nin Etnik Coğrafyası*, 226–229.

structed the Muslimness Contract, on the idea that their protection could only be ensured by a state of their own. Indeed, both the Ottoman Empire under Unionist leadership (by means of ethnic cleansing) and the Turkish state led by the Kemalists (by means of a War of Independence against Armenians and Greeks and population exchange of the latter) were able to accomplish this most vital mission: ushering Muslims from a world of insecurity, of everyone at war with everyone, and offering them a secure life. One must thus bear in mind the insecurity of the preceding state of war in order to understand the state that ensued as well as the subsequent forms of obedience to the state. That said, having executed this vital mission, new clauses were added that did not conform (as was the case with other states) to certain aspects of the original pact.[21] In other words, the new state forged the Turkishness Contract from within the Muslimness Contract, which Muslims constructed collectively and, thereby, set out the framing rules to which society and individuals must adhere.

Thinking through both the contract and the metaphor of the contract may offer further insights bearing on discussions of the formation of the Turkish nation and how these relate to theories of nationalism. In light of Ernest Gellner and Eric Hobsbawm's emphases,[22] the Turkish nation appears not as an ancient historical reality but as a modern political and emotional constellation invented by Turkish nationalism and the Turkish state. Or, by Benedict Anderson's formulation, one can see the Turkish nation as an imagined community that, with regard to its consequences, is quite real: members of the nation have a sense of solidarity with (though do not know) one another and will risk death for one another and for the nation.[23] Indeed, Turkish nationalism and the Turkish state founded by Turkish nationalists undertook a thorough and deliberate project to forge a collective Turkish identity and a Turkish self among individuals, mobilizing institutions and social fields (schools, mosques, the army, the press) to this end. But this act of creation was not carried out from scratch. By this, I mean not only in the sense of shared cultural ties or roots preceding nationalism and the nation but also such conditions as a shared homeland, myths, symbols, memories, and an economy, which Anthony

---

21. One can also see this narrowing as the second stage of the social contract—or, the political contract following the social contract. The will of Muslims to form a society and a state emerged through the Muslimness Contract, which itself took shape as they united under conditions of war. Meanwhile, the state (which began to find its footing with the end of war conditions) constructed both itself and Turkish society through a political contract—namely the Turkishness Contract.

22. Gellner, *Nations and Nationalism*, 48–49; Hobsbawm, *Nations and Nationalism*, 9–10.

23. Anderson, *Imagined Communities*.

Smith sees as key to a nation's formation.[24] Arguably, these conditions exist, but more important is the existence of the contract. The Turkish nation was created from within the Muslim nation, Turkishness from Muslimness, and the Turkishness Contract from the Muslimness Contract, through which the Muslim nation emerged. Muslims from all walks of life built this together, owing to common interests and common emotions and accompanied by decades of bloody struggles, massacres, and wars. And the Muslim nation, having taken shape within the contract and within struggle, likewise established a state belonging solely to Muslims within this contract. Therefore, it seems to me that the process of the formation of the Turkish nation can be seen as a synthesis of (1) the horizontal dynamics of a largely spontaneous Muslim nation, and (2) features imposed vertically and top-down by the new Turkish state formed within such horizontality. In other words, the Turkish nation may be an imagined community invented by the Turkish state, but such imagining and invention is founded upon genuine common interests, crimes, pains, and feelings, to which the state also stakes a claim.[25]

But was the contract's narrowed (Turkified) nature the sort of "vain and contradictory" contract that Jean-Jacques Rousseau said must be avoided, when he noted, "I make a covenant between us which is entirely at your expense and entirely for my good, which I will observe as long as I please, and which you will observe as long as I please"?[26] To be sure, the Turkishness Contract is not, as with any concrete national contract, the kind that Rousseau dreamed of, where all are united, yet one obeys only herself and maintains her original freedom. Not only has the state quashed those who left (or were left out of) the national contract; among those Turks who took part in the contract, the state also systematically favored the upper classes and did not refrain from suppressing the lower (read "dangerous") classes and their political representatives when deemed necessary. But beyond such forms of suppression and inequality, there are also common interests and expectations of privilege that unite Turks and the Turkified, in other words, all who adhere to the Turkishness Contract. As Rousseau notes, "The social bond is formed by what these interests have in common; if there were no point at which every interest met,

---

24. Smith, "Origins of Nations," 106–130; Smith, *Nationalism and Modernism.*

25. Both theorists of the social contract and of nationalism share an interest in emotions. Although contract theorists tend to speak of individual emotions and "human nature" while theorists of nationalism tend to take up collective emotions, this important overlap allows us to think about the concepts of contract and nationalism together and can be useful for contemplating the formation of modern nations through the idea of a national contract.

26. Rousseau, *Discourse on Political Economy and the Social Contract,* 50, 53.

no society could exist. And it is solely on the basis of this common interest that society must be governed."[27]

More concretely, the state imposed a range of new rules for those it rescued from the fear of loss of property and life. And as long as these new rules were adhered to, the state would continue to protect the lives and property of Turks. That is, in the future, as in the past, the state would ensure the security of life and property and would further equip those who adhered with both material and immaterial privileges and political and civil rights. Stemming from Turkishness is also a sense of psychological superiority (pride, righteousness, normality, and the like) as well as the possibility or hope of rising in the social/political hierarchy (class or status mobility). The value of these actual and potential interests and privileges was apparent, particularly to Anatolia's immigrant Muslims, who made up approximately 20 percent of the general population in 1923.[28] Thus, while those who took part in the contract perhaps lost some of their cultural and ethnic characteristics, what they gained was invaluable.[29] Recall Rousseau in this context: "Nothing is truly renounced by private individuals under the social contract; but instead their situations become preferable, in reality, as a result of the contract, to what it was before. Instead of abandoning anything they have simply made a beneficial transfer, exchanging an uncertain and precarious mode of existence for a better and more secure one, natural independence for liberty, the power of hurting others for their own safety, and reliance on their own strength, which others might overcome, for a position of right that social unity makes invincible."[30] In *Discourse on Political Economy*, Rousseau remarks: "Let their country there-

---

27. Rousseau, 63.

28. For a population estimate maintaining that immigrant Muslims accounted for one-fifth of Turkey in 1923, see McCarthy, *Ölüm ve Sürgün*, 356. Known for his proximity to the Turkish state, this U.S. historian viewed the bloody struggles in Ottoman geography through the eyes of Muslims and Turks and, in a sense, translated the emotions of Muslims and Turks into historical works. When read through such a lens, his work contains important information and interpretations regarding why and how the Muslimness and Turkishness Contracts were accepted.

29. Relaying a number of interviews he carried out, Suavi Aydın (*Amacımız Devletin Bekası*, 38) demonstrates the continued central place, into the 2000s, of interest and fear in Turkish Muslim immigrants' perceptions and embrace of the Turkish state. He concludes, in short: "A large part of the elements that make up Turkish society are groups who have taken shelter here, fleeing oppression and the fear of massacre in places mostly beyond [Turkey's] borders, and who have thereby come to consider here 'their state.' The National Struggle reinforced this feeling and united all these elements under the common denominator of Islam. Since 1924, the emphasis on Turkishness and the pressure of the state regarding Turkishness, at times through acts of violence, has also had an assimilating effect on such groups, which were already fragmented across the country. Rather than emphasizing their 'differences,' most of these groups find integration into 'broader society' beneficial (or feel compelled to feel so), and strive for this."

30. Rousseau, *Discourse on Political Economy and the Social Contract*, 70.

fore be a common mother to all the citizens; let the advantages which they enjoy there make them cherish it; let the government allow them a share in public administration sufficient to make them feel that they are in their home country, and let the laws, in their eyes, be nothing less than the guarantee of liberty for all."[31] Society and individuals trust the state established through contract, assuming their rights and privileges will be protected. This trust in the state, in both its explicit and tacit forms, shapes John Locke's idea of a social contract.[32] Moreover, a key founding principle of the new regime—that *sovereignty belongs unconditionally to the nation*—is not entirely a hollow idea or demagoguery. It was within the framework of this principle that multiparty politics emerged, and the general population was granted the right to elect and be elected. Possibilities for social mobility expanded in unprecedented ways; those who began life at the lowest economic strata could even become president.

But just as there are rewards that ensure compliance with the contract, there are also penalties; the Turkishness Contract is at once a mechanism of rewards and punishment. Noncompliance must be punished, for such acts demonstrate that noncompliance is a viable possibility, that such an option exists. Furthermore, noncompliance with the contract may lead to the voicing of views on issues at the heart of the contract's establishment, about which discussion is forbidden. This, in turn, lays bare certain implicit clauses of the contract, known to all but unvoiced; it exposes the contract. Punishment may take many forms, from death to exile, from unemployment to exclusion, but the fact that one will be punished is certain.

In an entirely different context, Rousseau describes this aspect of the social contract: "In order therefore that the social pact should not be an empty formula, it contains an implicit obligation which alone can give force to the others, that if anyone refuses to obey the general will he will be compelled to do so by the whole body."[33] According to Rousseau, one who does not abide by the contract or who insists on not abiding is a traitor and, as such, is either exiled or killed "as an enemy rather than as a citizen."[34] Gökalp, who laid out the basic terms of the Muslimness Contract in 1913, published the *Türkçülüğün Esasları* (*Principles of Turkishness*) in 1923, arguably the founding book of the Turkishness Contract. There, Gökalp summarizes the basic rule of the new contract: "Just as every individual who says 'I am a Turk' must be recognized

---

31. Rousseau, 21.
32. Locke, *Two Treatises of Government*, 381.
33. Rousseau, *Discourse on Political Economy and the Social Contract*, 58.
34. Rousseau, 71.

as such, there is no other remedy than punishment for those seen as betraying Turkishness."[35]

The Sheikh Said Rebellion in the early years of the contract made abundantly clear how and by what methods noncompliance with the Turkishness Contract would be punished. As noted earlier, throughout the Muslimness Contract, Unionist and Kemalist leaders were especially mindful of the Kurds, whose support was vital; they tried to persuade the Kurds, in particular, and were compelled to make promises of equality and autonomy, especially during the War of Independence. However, with victory in the War of Independence and the establishment of the Republic of Turkey, it was as if these earlier promises of autonomy and equality across the horizontal Muslimness Contract were never made. In other words, the narrowing of the contract's Muslimness and its Turkification had two crucial meanings for Kurds: the promise of autonomy gave way to centralization, and the promise of equality between Kurds and Turks gave way to Kurds being compelled to Turkify.

As reflected in British documents, the 1924 views and grievances of the *Azadi* (Liberty) organization (thought to have been founded by Kurdish intellectuals and officers in 1923) can be summarized as follows: plans were in place to remove a large number of Kurds from the region and replace them with resettled Turks; "among the few ties remaining between Turks and Kurds is the Caliphate, the elimination of which by the Turkish government severed this bond"; Kurdish was banned in courts and schools; madrasas, the only educational institution of Kurds, were closed; the word Kurdistan was done away with and Kurdish geographic names were replaced by Turkish names; Turks were very careful about who was hired into the bureaucracy, with no one suspected of being a Kurdish nationalist appointed even to lower positions; elected representatives from Kurdish regions were determined by the Turkish government; and infighting among Kurdish tribes was provoked.[36]

Although Kurdish nationalists differed in their reactions to the policies of the new state—broadly, some were more modern and secular and others more traditional and religious—nevertheless, these differences did not stand in the way of their uniting in resistance to the Turkishness Contract. Organized largely by secular and nationalist Kurdish intellectuals and officers, an uprising was launched in February 1925. Under the leadership of Sheikh Said, a Nakshibendi cleric, it aimed to establish an independent Kurdish state. Around fifteen thousand armed Kurdish militants took part in the uprising, which, after approximately three months, was eventually quashed by the state,

---

35. Gökalp, "Türkçülüğün Esasları," 185.
36. For all relevant British reports, see Yeğen, *İngiliz Belgelerinde Kürdistan*, 158–171.

though with difficulty.[37] Following the rebellion, a number of confidential reports on a resolution of the Kurdish issue were penned by various ministers, eventually synthesized and combined in the confidential Eastern Reform Plan. According to the plan, the geography of Kurdistan was to be governed under emergency rule. Government buildings, military outposts, highways, and rails would be built. The judiciary and bureaucracy were to be fully Turkified, and Turkish officers serving in the region were to be paid an increased salary. Kurdish children—girls, in particular—were to be assimilated through schools and other cultural institutions; dangerous and rebellious tribes were to be separated from their leaders and forcibly relocated, and Turks were to be resettled in the evacuated geographies. And the Kurdish language was to be banned, including even speaking Kurdish. A confidential report by then Minister of Interior Cemil Uybadin even openly stated that the necessary structure of state to be established in the area of the uprising was a "colonial type of administration" (*müstemleke tarz-ı idaresi*).[38] This is a striking example, in my view, of the synchronicity of the logics of contractual and colonial powers, which I briefly mentioned at the outset of this book and to which I return in more detail at the end: a contractual model and logic was introduced for Turks and those who Turkified, and a colonial model and logic was introduced for those who did not Turkify.

The written articles of the Eastern Reform Plan took aim at the geography of Kurdistan—that is, a geography standing defiantly outside the Turkishness Contract. As for those who stood with the Turkishness Contract or wished to do so, a third article was added after the Sheikh Said Rebellion. This article, unwritten but known to all, forbade engaging in politics and organizing for the benefit of Kurds, sympathizing with Kurds, telling the truth about what was done to the Kurds and systematically studying these facts, and even merely saying that Kurds and the Kurdish language exist. But, with the Sheikh Said Rebellion, the Turkish opposition within the Turkishness Contract was also suppressed. The *Takrir-i Sükûn* (Maintenance of Order) Law and "Independence Courts" paved the way for the arrest of many Turkish dissidents and the closure of both a number of newspapers and the opposition Progressive Republican Party.[39]

Such a pattern—taking advantage of an opportunity to suppress Turkish dissidents alongside a Kurdish resistance or opposition—would repeat throughout the history of the republic. The typical pattern is this: during a Kurdish

---

37. On the history and ideology of the rebellion, see Olson, *Emergence of Founding Nationalism*; van Bruinessen, *Agha, Shaikh and State*.

38. For these government documents, see Bayrak, *Şark Islahat Planı*, 109–132.

39. See Zürcher, *Political Opposition*.

uprising, Turks who sympathize with Kurds (that is, who do not adhere to the Turkishness Contract) are punished; at the same time, movements and individuals who abide by the contract but also oppose the ruling political movement are suppressed. This second suppressed group had supported the contract and thus had consented to the harsh suppression of Kurdish uprisings, but when subjected to the same harshness, it had little resort. Indeed, as discussed in Chapter 4, the conflict that began in 2015 (some ninety years after the Sheikh Said Rebellion) and the ensuing suppression are another iteration of this familiar boomerang pattern.

What was to be done to those opposing the Turkishness Contract? Prime Minister İsmet Pasha summarized this in a speech in April 1925: "Our task is to make all those residing in the Turkish homeland Turks, no matter what. We will extirpate those elements who oppose Turks and Turkishness. The qualities that we seek in those who serve the homeland are, foremost, that the person is a Turk and a Turkist."[40] However, despite İsmet Pasha's emphasis on Turkism, one way to understand how the Turkishness Contract worked across the long twentieth century is to appreciate that participation in the contract does not necessarily have to be active. In other words, in order to benefit from the material and immaterial privileges of the Turkishness Contract, one need not actively take part in the persecution of non-Muslims and non-Turks. Nor must one constantly praise Turkishness and denigrate non-Turks or even be a Turkist or Turkish nationalist. At stake is rather *structural Turkishness*.

Structural Turkishness refers to an institutional structure that systematically advantages Turks and disadvantages non-Turks. Just as structural racism in the United States privileges all white people, including nonracist white individuals, structural Turkishness in Turkey is a power relationship that privileges all Turks, including non-Turkist and non-Turkish-nationalist Turks. To benefit from structural Turkishness, rather than actively participating, often simply not violating the contract is enough. Which is to say, one may participate in the contract by staying silent and not violating the rules of the contract—by *not* doing something rather than doing something. Put abstractly, every interaction, action, thought, and emotion that does not violate the contract indirectly reproduces it. If, for example, an academic or a journalist does not systematically study, report on, or take a stand on issues prohibited by the Turkishness Contract, this means participating in and reproducing the contract. *Participating and reproducing through not doing*—we can make sense of this operation through Hobbes's remarks on "signs of contract by inference": "Signs by inference, are sometimes the consequence of words;

40. Quoted in Üstel, *İmparatorluktan Ulus-Devlete Türk Milliyetçiliği*, 173.

sometimes the consequence of silence; sometimes the consequence of actions; sometimes the consequence of forbearing an action: and generally a sign by inference, of any contract, is whatsoever sufficiently argues the will of the contractor."[41]

As important as *how* to participate in the contract is the question of *why*. One possible answer lies in the privileges allocated to those who participate, and another in the punishment of those who variously resist. Consider the famous words of the Minister of Justice Mahmut Esat (Bozkurt) Bey: "Those who are not truly Turks have only one right in the Turkish homeland, and that is to be a servant, to be a slave." Today, those critical of these words generally approach them as either a contemptible form of racism or an excessive statement by an otherwise great jurist and statesman. But recalling the context of this statement while situating it alongside the statements immediately preceding it allows one to interpret Bozkurt's words as, in fact, an expression of the rules, privileges, awards, and punishments of the Turkishness Contract. These words, voiced in September 1930, had a dual context. Bozkurt spoke in the wake of the Kurdish Rebellion of Ağrı (which was in many ways a continuation of the Sheikh Said Rebellion and which the state struggled to suppress) and amid growing interest in the newly formed Free Republic Party, particularly among non-Muslim voters.[42] As such, his words were a stern warning to Kurds, non-Muslims, and opposition parties resisting the Turkishness Contract. Further, Bozkurt's broader statement clearly underscores not only the penalties of the contract but also its rewards:

Until recently, on the steamboats, the railways, and in all the commercial and financial institutions of our homeland, who were the workers and who were the owners? It was non-Turks, was it not? And today, who are the owners? The Turks . . . all these are the gains of the Republican People's Party. The vineyards, gardens, even the mountains, the plains, the goods, the property, the country's economic life, were they not entirely in the hands of non-Turks? . . . Until just yesterday, was it not rare to find a Turk, working at the hand of foreigners, who owned a vineyard, a garden, or property? I am of the Republican People's Party, because this party has, through all it has done to date, restored the status of the Turkish Nation, the true masters. My idea, my conviction, is this: may the friends and the enemies know, the master of this

---

41. Hobbes, *Leviathan*, 89.
42. Emrence, *99 Günlük Muhalefet*, 167–168.

country is the Turk. Those who are not truly Turks have only one right in the Turkish homeland, and that is to be a servant, to be a slave.[43]

These last harsh and hard-line words of Bozkurt speak of the *punishments for noncompliance with the Turkishness Contract.*

The following words from Prime Minister İsmet Pasha, on a visit to the eastern provinces in 1932 following the suppression of the Ağrı Rebellion (only after great struggle, and through changes to the border with Iran), are polite and delicate, for they speak of the *rewards of complying with the Turkishness Contract*:

Who is a Turkish citizen? We are truly and seriously sincere in the description, provided by official state laws, of a Turkish nationalist and Turkish citizen. In order to become a Turkish nationalist and a Turkish citizen, we do not expect anything out of the ordinary of any individual living in this homeland. In order to possess all the rights granted by the Turkish nation, it is sufficient to choose to be Turkish, to accept to be Turkish. This is our legal duty. Such is our deep and sincere conviction and our duty. When we roamed this country, East and West, I did not allow any citizen of ours who knew and accepted that he was a Turk to worry about being deprived by anyone of any of the rights that every Turk enjoys. I satisfied everyone that a citizen, like me . . . who wholeheartedly accepts being a Turkish as a privilege to be proud of, and who strives accordingly, has every reason to possess every right. I have voiced my conviction everywhere, and I am very sincere in my words. Such an administration and mindset only reinforce the principles of the state as a national state and a Turkish state.[44]

Between Justice Minister Mahmut Esat Bey, who freely uses racist and exclusionary language due to his emphasis on punishment, and Prime Minister İsmet Pasha, whose language is more inclusive and inviting as it emphasizes rewards, is a vital difference: inclusion in or exclusion from the Turkishness Contract. So significant and far reaching is this difference that it splits the practical worlds and the ways of thinking, feeling, and acting between those who do and those who do not adhere to the contract. Those who abide by the contract become Turkish subjects as a part, an extension, an embodiment of the Turkish state and nation.

---

43. Quoted in Uyar, *"Sol Milliyetçi" Bir Türk Aydını*, 207–208.
44. Quoted in Yıldız, *Ne Mutlu Türküm Diyebilene*, 290.

Constructing the Turkish State, the Turkish Nation, and the Turkish Individual

Founded through a two-stage contract, with Muslimness and Turkishness as its main principles, the new state found the power to impose laws, rules, and norms through the centralization and monopolization of various forms of capital. In this process, the first matter of business for the new Turkish state was the monopolization of the means and use of violence. The suppression of the Sheikh Said and Ağrı Kurdish Rebellions—continuations of one another—was, in this context, more than just a simple military operation. In suppressing the rebellions, the state also eliminated those forces capable of launching a regional mass armed uprising. The horizontality of the Muslimness Contract, as noted earlier in different terms, was also related to the presence of forces, in various parts of Anatolia, capable of effectively employing violence. Unable to ignore these forces, Unionist and Kemalist leaders had little choice but to negotiate and make a number of compromises. Therefore, it is certainly no coincidence that the process of seizing a monopoly over the use of violence coincided with the transition from the horizontality of the Muslimness Contract to the verticality of the Turkishness Contract.

The notion of a monopoly over the use of violence, of course, recalls Max Weber's famous definition of the modern state as "a human community that (successfully) claims the monopoly of the legitimate use of physical force within a given territory. . . . Specifically, at the present time, the right to use physical force is ascribed to other institutions or to individuals only to the extent to which the state permits it. The state is considered the sole source of the 'right' to use violence."[45] Yet the Turkish state's power to impose the laws and rules of the Turkishness Contract was made possible not only through the state's successful seizure and monopolization of the legitimate use of physical violence but also through the centralization, around the principle of Turkishness, of other forms and means of capital. As Pierre Bourdieu has noted, "The state is the *culmination of a process of concentration of different species of capital*: capital of physical force or instruments of coercion (army, police), economic capital, cultural or (better) informational capital, and symbolic capital. It is this concentration as such which constitutes the state as the holder of a sort of meta-capital granting power over other species of capital and over their holders."[46]

In the economic sphere, the founding cadre of the new Turkey and its Muslim-Turkish (national) bourgeoisie agreed, at the February 1923 İzmir Economic Congress, on the basic economic principles to be implemented. The most

---

45. Gerth and Mills, *From Max Weber*, 78.
46. Bourdieu, "Rethinking the State," 4.

important partnership between the two groups was a desire to maintain relations with "foreign capital" (i.e., international capitalism) via a Muslim-Turkish bourgeoisie rather than a non-Muslim bourgeoisie, the elimination of which continued.[47] In this sense, this economic congress was the continuation of the political-military congresses that took place during the War of Independence. Indeed, Mustafa Kemal Pasha also underscored such similarities and continuities between the congresses in his opening speech: "For full independence, there is this principle: national sovereignty should be consolidated through economic sovereignty." A few days before the congress, a piece in the newspaper *Akşam* declared: "After Erzurum and Sivas Congresses is the İzmir Congress. . . . Its vital significance is through the political and historical meaning of what came before. I would not hesitate today to describe them as having the same gravity, the same value. . . . The Congress should and will be the economic manifestation, in İzmir, of Turkishness's will to exist, manifested with power and grandeur in Erzurum and Sivas." The newspaper *Hakimiyet-i Milliye* noted that representatives coming for the congress would be very pleased to see the transformation of "Infidel İzmir into Muslim İzmir" but will also "harbor a deep and everlasting sense of economic revenge against the ungrateful."[48] As the congress came to a close, the twelve-item Economic Pact, a continuation of the National Pact, was made public. Article Nine of this text—filled with such phrases as "Turks develop, are hardworking, non-monopolistic, clean and hygienic, and avoid waste"—is especially significant in the context of the Turkishness Contract: "The Turk is always friendly to nations that are not hostile to its religion, nationality, land, life and institutions; they are not opposed to foreign capital. However, they have no intercourse with institutions in their own lands that do not conform to his language and laws."[49]

This last sentence concerns the fact that companies not using the Turkish language in their transactions and without Turkish employees were to be eliminated or excluded. An article published in *Tevhid-i Efkar* in 1925 about the Ottoman Bank—a symbol of the economic sovereignty of non-Muslim Ottomans and of the Ottoman Empire's dependence on the Great Powers— articulated a key principle of the Turkishness Contract: "The Turkish nation, state and government have on every occasion suffered much damage from this

---

47. Boratav, *Türkiye'de Devletçilik*, 24–31.

48. At issue here is a kind of exuberance in the face of the population exchanges that would "cleanse" İzmir of its Christian "infidel" population.

49. For congressional citations and information, see Ökçün, *Türkiye İktisat Kongresi, 1923-İzmir*, 30, 36, 251, 256, 371, 387–389. On the population exchange's impact on İzmir, the approach of Muslim elites to the exchange, and the tense relations between settled and newly arrived Muslims, see Kolluoğlu, "Excesses of Nationalism," 532–550.

bank, whose entire staff is made up of foreigners and local Christians. . . . To be sure, there is a need to examine in earnest all the irregular acts, abuses and crimes of this institution to date. And if this bank is, subsequently, to be named the Bank of Turkey, then we must ensure that all its staff is made up of Turks."[50] While the Bank did Turkify its staff in time as promised, it never gained the trust of the state. Eventually, it ceded its prominent position to Turkish İş Bank, founded in 1924 through "wholly national capital, and entirely Turkish-staffed."[51]

Such shifting of roles (in this case, among banks) and the Turkification of workplaces came to affect all other institutions and fields. Private companies and public institutions alike were Turkified, and those resisting Turkification were eliminated. Indeed, the Civil Servant Law, enacted in 1926, established "being a Turk" as a primary condition for being an officer or employee.[52] The story of the making of the "national economy" should thus be told not simply in the narrow sense of the accumulation of capital in national hands or the creation of a national bourgeoisie through patronage, incentives, and wealth transfer[53] but, crucially, in the broader sense of the Turkification of the economy (in terms of ownership, production, consumption, trade, and employment).[54] In this context, consider the following words of Gökalp, the founding ideologue of Turkish nationalism: "In Turkey, the Turkish people had no status. Today, every right belongs to the Turk. Sovereignty in this land means the sovereignty of the Turk; in politics, culture, and economics, the Turk is always dominant. . . . Turkishness means exalting the Turkish people."[55] The rewards for being a Muslim-Turk and for fealty to the Muslimness and Turkishness Contracts were allotted by the state in the form of real and potential benefits. That is, the Turkishness Contract provides vital advantages not only to the upper classes but also to middle-class and lower-class Turks. Indeed, it seems to me that one way of understanding why and how different social classes (owner of capital, the unpropertied) converge around basic principles when their economic interests consistently, in Marxist terms, contradict one another involves understanding this nature of the Turkishness Contract.

---

50. Eldem, *Osmanlı Bankası Tarihi*, 411.

51. Kocabaşoğlu, Güven Sak, Sinan Sönmez, Funda Erkal, Özgür Gökmen, Nesim Şeker, and Murat Uluğtekin, *Türkiye İş Bankası Tarihi*, 43.

52. Article Ten of the law provides that the nationality and denomination of each officer shall also be indicated in the register. The full text of the law, accessed April 2, 2017, is available at http://www.memurlar.net/haber/550893/.

53. For national economics and statist policies in the first fifteen years of the Republic, see Kuruç, *Mustafa Kemal Döneminde Ekonomi*.

54. On the Turkification of employment, see Onaran, *Osmanlı'da Ermeni*, vol. 2, 353–361.

55. Gökalp, "Türkçülüğün Esasları," 180.

102 / Chapter 2

In Chapter 3, I describe, when adhering to the logic of the contract and the basic principles of the contract are known to all, how one living in the contract is like a fish in water, and the performances and strategies of Turkishness have become second nature. But this ability to spontaneously reproduce the contract does not mean, of course, that the state does not pursue conscious policies in this domain. In other words, an emphasis on the logic of the contract does not substitute for the fact that education and ideology are still deployed to ensure interclass alliance. On the contrary, the Turkish state labored intensively and deliberately in the early years of state-making to create the Turkish individual and, thereby, the nation.[56] Efforts were made to integrate the lower classes into capitalism through an ideology of solidarism (which preached that there existed not classes in conflict but occupations in complementary harmony) and into the nation-state through nationalism (which preached that the members of these different occupations belong not to different cultures but to a singular, superior Turkish culture). The attempt was to mold the lower classes into pieces of—foot soldiers for—both the National Pact (as Turks who thought and felt like a Turk and took pride therein) and the Economic Pact (as hardworking, clean, frugal, and docile bodies and minds).[57]

Education was, naturally, one field in which the policy of Turkifying the minds of individuals could be carried out most efficiently. Monopolization and centralization in the cultural sphere, in general, and in the field of education, in particular, began with the March 3, 1924, Law on the Unity of Education (*Tevhid-i Tedrisat Kanunu*), whose justification and purpose were to ensure "unity of the nation in terms of emotions and thoughts."[58] The law resulted in the closure of madrasas, potent symbols of actual autonomy and multiplicity in the field of education. It also brought an end to dual education (secular and religious), which had marked the last century of the Ottoman Empire. Established in the same year as the abolition of the caliphate, the Head of Religious Affairs has, since its creation, both favored only Islam among religions and only Sunni Islam among Muslim sects and ensured the sole public visibility of Sunni Islam. The institution further aided in the Turkification of Muslims through the education it offered in mosques. Thus, as with schools,

---

56. For a discussion of how the Turkish nation-state creates nation-individuals or nation-subjects who think and feel like a state and nation, see Açıkel, "Devletin Manevi Şahsiyeti ve Ulusun Pedagojisi," 117–139.

57. Gökalp holds that different professions and generations are "necessary and essential to each other" and considers professional moralities as the limbs of a general morality of the homeland. See Gökalp's "Türkçülüğün Esasları," 224, 267–271. On Gökalp, see T. Parla, *Social and Political Thought of Ziya Gökalp*.

58. Kaplan, *Türkiye'de Milli Eğitim İdeolojisi*, 159.

mosques were centralized around the principle of Muslim Turkishness, providing both an intellectual and an emotional education.[59]

For Durkheim, modern education possesses a dual character, aiming to create at once both homogeneity and diversity. On the one hand, schools provide specific training according to social class and professional specialization. On the other hand, general education cuts across an entire society and aims to render it a nation. Durkheim has this to say about general education and its vision of "fixing certain thoughts and emotions in consciousness" and "deeply affecting minds": "Society can survive only if there exists among its members a sufficient degree of homogeneity; education perpetuates and reinforces this homogeneity by fixing in the child, from the beginning, the essential similarities that collective life demands."[60] Precisely through such a process of fixing, education has created a Turkish presence or existence within individuals: Turkish individuals with common ways of thinking, feeling, perceiving, and seeing. Consider, further, the emphasis in Article Five of the 1927 Statute of the Republican People's Party: "[Party] is predicated upon the proper dissemination and development of Turkish language and culture, convinced that linguistic unity, a unity of feeling, and a unity of ideas are the strongest bond between citizens."[61]

The Minister of National Education Esat (Sagay) Bey, meanwhile, described the purpose of education in 1931 as follows: "The Turkish school is obliged to make every Turkish child it receives into a Turkish citizen who fully comprehends the psychology and ideology of the Republican regime and is maximally useful for the Turkish nation and the Republic of Turkey."[62] The desired outcome was, in essence, to create individuals who speak, think, feel, and behave like Turks, to render them members of the broader Turkish family and nation—in other words, members of the national contract. This was precisely what a book on morality, published in 1926 for elementary school fourth graders, exhorted:

A nation means a family. They live in the same climate and bear the same feeling. They receive the same upbringing. They make the same

59. Article Two of the Village Law, adopted in the same year, acknowledges the mosque and the school as the two main pillars of the village. Accessed April 28, 2017, available at www.mev zuat.gov.tr/MevzuatMetin/1.3.442.pdf.

60. Durkheim, *Education and Sociology*, 70–71.

61. Quoted in Beşikçi, *Cumhuriyet Halk Fırkası'nın Tüzüğü*, 81. On the relationship between solidarism and nationalism, see Besikçi, *Cumhuriyet Halk Fırkası'nın Programı*.

62. Quoted in Akyüz, *Türk Eğitim Tarihi*, 365. People's Houses, established starting in 1932, brought national education beyond the school walls. See Lamprou, *Nation-Building in Modern Turkey*.

sacrifice for the preservation and defense of their shared homeland. So then, just as the house in which we were born and raised is our family hearth, so too is the country in which we live the hearth of our nation. The elders of the nation are our spiritual fathers, mothers, older brothers and sisters, and those younger than us are our brothers and sisters. Then we must make our best sacrifice to preserve the law, possessions, and honor of our fellow countrymen. Because the honor and dignity of a citizen before foreigners amounts to our shared honor and dignity. If any corner of the homeland is harmed, then all countrymen suffer.[63]

Parallel to the state's monopolization and centralization of means and power across the fields of violence, economy, and culture/education was the monopolization and centralization of symbolic power. Symbolic capital is the power to attribute positivity or negativity to all kinds of capital (means of violence, economic means, cultural means, etc.) and characteristics. In other words, the state, as the holder of symbolic power, has the capacity to say what is right and wrong, legitimate and illegitimate, valuable and worthless, beautiful and ugly, or moral and immoral, as well as the power to impose and to affect the adoption of what it says. It was this monopoly of the state that Bourdieu pointed out when describing the state as the "central bank of symbolic capital." In this sense, one of the most vital stages in the construction of the Turkish nation, individual, and nation-state was the declaration of a single culture from within the cultures of Anatolia and, in parallel, a single language among its languages, as legitimate and valuable.[64] Thus was the culture/language market unified and made singular, with those possessing the dominant culture and legitimate language (as well as those who assimilated) receiving a range of material advantages/expectations. Prominent among these were finding a job, advancing in one's career, and enjoying class mobility. The most important psychological advantages are feelings of pride, superiority, and normalcy stemming from being a part of the legitimate culture, all of which nourish one's self-worth and self-esteem. Of course, just as there are rewards, privileges, and expectations, there are also penalties, disadvantages, and despondency. Or, more concretely, the state accepts only one culture and language as legitimate, declaring others illegitimate, worthless, and primitive; those who persist, or choose to persist, in these other cultures and languages are also seen as illegitimate, worthless, and primitive. Though the *use value* of one's culture and

---

63. Quoted in Üstel, *'Makbul Vatandaş'ın Peşinde*, 164.

64. On the importance of language policies in the construction of the Turkish nation, see Bayar, "Trajectory of Nation-Building through Language Policies," 108–128.

language may persist in part within a certain social environment, the *exchange value* of languages rendered other is nil, for instance, as one cannot study or find employment in such languages. In other words, because the illegitimate person of an illegitimate culture remains outside the legitimate linguistic and cultural market, and because cultural capital can only be accumulated within the legitimate culture, she also remains outside the labor market.[65] Knowing only one's own language also brings with it a form of psychological punishment, as that language is associated with primitivity, a lack of culture, and a lack of history. Legitimate culture and language mean civilization; illegitimate culture and language mean barbarism.

The psychological wage of the Turk or the Turkified—no matter how poor or uneducated—is the feeling of pride in one's Turkishness. This pride is undergirded by systematic historical studies carried out by the state and academy, passed on socially through schools, the army, the media, and the mosque. Thereby have Turks and the Turkified come to take pride in civilizations and states founded by Turks, the martial spirit of the Turks, the formation of Turkish as a language of civilization and science, and other similar myths. Considered in this context, the Turkish History thesis and Sun-Language theory (which emerged in the 1930s and pointed to Turks and the Turkish language as the origin of almost all civilizations and languages) were not exceptional. They merely amounted to taking the existing historiography to an extreme. Otherwise, the main claim behind these intellectual trends—that the Turks are a heroic, civilized ("a thousand years of state tradition"), and unique nation—is still maintained today, with institutions devoted to history and language and universities as the institutional guarantors of this continuity.

Now, it is partially true that such praise for Turkishness arises from the need to create a Turkish nation from within a population that had not previously described itself as Turkish, to instill self-confidence in its individuals, and to prove to the Western (external) world that one is at least as civilized as Westerners. But this same praise is also a form of belittlement when directed internally. However much the Turk is praised, so much is the non-Turk indirectly belittled. When Mahmut Esat (Bozkurt) Bey said that the "worst Turk is better than the best non-Turk,"[66] he also summed up this inversely proportional structure of praise (glorifying one as humiliating the other). Moreover, just as such humiliation can be indirect (extolling the Turks), it can also take quite direct forms (openly humiliating Kurds). The most well-known and most impactful example is a discourse reproduced by even the most educated Turks: Kurds

---

65. On the relationship between state and nation building and official/legitimate language, see Bourdieu, *Language and Symbolic Power*, 45–49.

66. Quoted in Uyar, *"Sol Milliyetçi" Bir Türk Aydını*, 115.

lack the ability to form a state; there is no such thing as the Kurdish language; or, even if there is, it is certainly not a language of civilization and science. This discourse "aims to make Kurds ashamed of their own history, reject Kurdishness, and become Turkish. This was the assumption, that Kurds, ashamed of and fed up with their own history, would reject Kurdishness and become Turkish."[67] In this sense, Turkishness has been built on exalting Turks and shaming non-Turks.[68] A 1930 confidential document sent by the Ministry of Internal Affairs to governorships clearly demonstrates the deliberateness with which the state belittled non-Turkish cultures, the endowment of Turkishness with material and immaterial privileges, and the punishment of non-Turks through material and immaterial disadvantages. Here are a few articles from the circular:

> 9. . . . to de facto demonstrate that true Turkishness and, in particular, speaking Turkish are not only honorable, but also materially profitable . . . 12. One should not forget that clothes, songs, games, weddings and social traditions and custom are ties that perpetually awaken feelings of nationality and race, and bind societies to their pasts; hence, seeing such contrary traditions, including dialects, as negative and harmful, and in particular to showing them as negative, they should be disparaged and condemned as in no way desirable, and on every occasion should be presented as base and primitive characteristics to be discouraged.[69]

Just as physical violence directed at those outside the Turkishness Contract often goes unpunished, so does symbolic violence. For example, one almost never pays a price for humiliating Armenians and Armenianness or Kurds and Kurdishness. This applies both to the highest and lowest levels of social and political life. Yet, while Armenianness and Kurdishness are constantly belittled with impunity, belittling Turkishness has always been among the gravest of crimes, and never goes unpunished.[70] Turkishness has been maintained and defended physically through means of violence, but a range of state institutions (judiciary, directorate of religious affairs, schools, institutions devoted to history and language) have also defended and maintained Turkish-

---

67. Besikçi, *Türk Tarih Tezi*, 78–79.

68. On the ways in which the construction of Turkishness as associated with civilization, Westernism, and modernity ran parallel to and relied crucially on an image of Kurdishness as Eastern, savage, and backward, see Demir, "Humbling Turkishness," 381–401.

69. Quoted in Bayrak, *Şark Islahat Planı*, 150–151.

70. On the history of the crime of "defaming and inveighing against Turkishness" since 1926, see Sancar, *Alenen Tahkir ve Tezyif Suçları*.

ness symbolically. National law, displacing the multiplicity of imperial law and forged through the centralization and monopolization of law, favored those within the Turkishness Contract and punished those without.[71]

Perhaps the most dramatic and tragic example of how the state monopolized and employed physical and symbolic violence, of how the two monopolies functioned as an inextricable whole, occurred in Dersim. The cultural and ideological expansion of Kurdistan has been a chief concern of the state since the republic's establishment. To prevent such expansion, the state sought to attract a powerful rampart of Turkishness to the north and west of *core Kurdistan*, and, through a range of means, to assimilate core Kurdistan.[72] In the eyes of the state, the most favorable region for the expansion of Kurdistan was Dersim, which, due to a combination of geographic and cultural characteristics and singularities, had long resisted control and assimilation. Since the second half of the nineteenth century, Dersim's denizens, in open resistance to the state's centralization policy, also took in a large number of Armenians, saving them from genocide. Furthermore, just as the Turkishness of the people of Dersim was suspect in the eyes of the state, so (as Alevis) was their Muslimness. Thus, if Dersim partially "Armenianized" in the 1910s, its "Kurdistanization" was also a possibility in the 1920s and 1930s. Consequently, in the 1930s, at a peak in the state's confidence in its own strength, debates flourished within the bureaucracy about resolving the so-called Dersim issue, yielding a number of confidential reports. A 1930 report from the chief of staff (among the most important of such documents) expresses pithily, in my opinion, the distinction I have made between the logics of contractual and colonial power and sovereignty: "Dersim should be considered primarily as a colony, Kurdishness should be dissolved within the Turkish community, and should subsequently, gradually, be subjected to real Turkish law."[73]

Following the confidential reports on Dersim, a number of explicit laws were adopted in the 1930s. For example, the Settlement Law, enacted in 1934, classified Turkey's geography into those places affiliated and unaffiliated with

---

71. For a comprehensive study of how Turkishness, Turks, and Turkish culture were systematically protected through legal texts and court decisions across the history of the republic, and how non-Turkish peoples and cultures were systematically overlooked and punished, see Bayır, *Türk Hukukunda Azınlıklar ve Milliyetçilik.*

72. E.g., Prime Minister İsmet Pasha, in a 1935 report, had this to say about regional differences: "One must be gravely concerned about the formation of a truly dreadful Kurdistan in short time, with Erzincan as a Kurdish center. . . . The plains of Van, Mus and Erzincan are vulnerable to Kurdish expansion. Urgently, in Van and Erzincan, gradually in the plain of Muş, and in the plain of Elazığ, we must incorporate powerful Turkish masses." Quoted in Bayrak, *Kürdoloji Belgeleri,* 402, 408, 412.

73. Çalışlar, *Dersim Raporu,* 251.

Turkish culture and race and targeted Dersim in particular (as well as, in part, Thracian Jews). It aimed to uproot people not belonging to Turkish culture, to disperse and resettle them among Turks, and to settle Turks and the easily Turkified in the geographies thus evacuated. The report of the commission that drafted the law highlighted the connection between the law and Turkishness as a realm of emotions and privileges: "The Turkishness of anyone in the Republic of Turkey who calls himself a Turk should be clear and transparent to the state. Here, the state does not want to harbor the slightest suspicion of the Turkishness of any Turk."[74] During parliamentary talks on the law, the Interior Minister Şükrü Kaya described the principle of Turkishness: "This law will make a homeland that speaks one language, that thinks as one, that has the same feeling."[75] Through the Tunceli Law, enacted in 1935, Dersim's name was changed and the legal basis for future military operations and massacres was prepared by granting extraordinary powers to the commander governor. The Dersim Operations of 1937 to 1938 took the form of genocide, with more than ten thousand people killed and at least as many exiled.[76]

Thus was the Turkishness Contract's last space of noncompliance conquered, militarily and culturally. Regarding the events in Dersim, to see what happened to its people through their eyes, to speak their language, and to sympathize with them was strictly prohibited by the unwritten Article Three of the Turkishness Contract. It was symbolic violence that legitimized physical violence of this scale and brutality, defined its people as savage and barbarian, described them in zoological terms, and marked them as a subhuman species. The campaign was presented by the Turkish state as a civilizing mission.[77] Brutality at this scale was perceived as civilization and was explained away with reference to the brutality of the brutalized. That this explanation was able to appear reasonable is itself a product of symbolic power and symbolic violence.

Consequently, the construction of a new state, nation, and individual, set in motion after 1913 through the Muslimness Contract and carried out after 1923 through the Turkishness Contract, was largely finalized with the 1938

74. Quoted in A. Parla, *Precarious Hope*, 19.

75. Beşikçi, *Kürtlerin Mecburi İskânı*, 111–129, 135, 146.

76. See Beşikçi, *Tunceli Kanunu*.

77. For one of the classic texts on this topic, see Uluğ, *Tunceli Medeniyete Açılıyor*. The entirety of the text concerns the civilizing mission and construction of the Turkish state in Dersim, e.g., "When the bayonets of the Republican army shone and their cannons were fired, tens of thousands of oppressed people in Dersim gained freedom and human rights; the bandit mentality delivered its last breath. How blessed is he who says I am a Turk!" (p. 67). For a historical study examining the continuity between genocide and the civilizing mission in the context of Dersim and through the concept of "maternal colonialism," see Z. Türkyılmaz, "Maternal Colonialism," 162–186. On how the Turkish press presents violence against Dersim and the methods it legitimizes, see Baran, *Yılları Arasında Basında Dersim*.

Dersim Operations. It was during this period that the state monopolized—within a specific territorially bound piece of land, internationally recognized after Lausanne—the means of violence and taxation, cultural and informational capital, and symbolic power. The state centralized certain forms of knowledge and emotions while prohibiting others. It constructed shared cognitive and emotional structures and schemas by instilling certain ways of seeing, sensing, thinking, evaluating, and feeling in the minds of its people, enabling them to experience the world they inhabit as a Turk. In other words, the state produced the Turkish individual.

So ends the historical process I have analyzed in terms of the formation of the Muslimness and Turkishness Contracts. Yet, this is not a history of the past but very much a living history of the present. It is repeated every day, everywhere, in many forms. It colors everyday social relationships. It continues to shape and influence life, from the functioning of institutions to the everyday performances of individuals, from individual schemas of thinking and feeling to the ways people use their bodies. Thinking through this history, I now turn to an analysis of the relationship between the historical and social formation of the Turkish nation/state and the psychological formation of individuals, focusing on the minds and bodies of individuals.

3

The Privileges, Performances, and States of Turkishness

To better understand the formative power of the Turkishness Contract in institutional and daily life, I believe it is crucial to attend to the individual states and performances of Turkishness, individual ways of being and acting within spaces and institutions, interactions between individuals colored by Turkishness, and ways in which the difference between being Turkish and not being Turkish permeates minds and bodies. Accordingly, in this chapter, I analyze how the Turkishness Contract shapes the ways in which individuals see, hear, know, care, feel, and behave—in other words, how these ways are historically and socially constructed. Why and how does one become Turkified? How are Turkification and the privileges of Turkishness entwined? What performances and strategies of Turkishness does one develop to be included in the contract? How do these transform into states of Turkishness, into an individual's character even, acquiring a certain social naturalness? How does one come to see and not see, to be informed and ignorant, to be interested and indifferent, to be moved and apathetic? How does Turkishness work on the mind and body? What is the connection between the most private and seemingly individual forms of knowing and feeling and the most general and social?

I begin by developing some thoughts on why Turks and the Turkified participate in the Turkishness Contract, and examine the types of performances, strategies, and states that define this participation. I further explore how the mediation and manners of such participation works to continuously reproduce the contract. However, the formative effect of the Turkishness Contract is not limited to Turks and the Turkified. It also shapes the minds and bodies of the individuals excluded, historically and today, from the contract. Someone outside the contract, aware of her situation, may behave according to the contract; at certain times and places, she may act as though she were inside the contract. Moreover, the knowledge of being outside the contract begins to work on the noncontractual person's body from childhood. Thus, in this chapter, I also analyze how the Turkishness Contract has shaped individual lives, behavioral schemas, and the public presentation of self for non-Muslims and Kurds outside the contract.

I suggest that looking at the lived experiences of noncontractual non-Muslims and Kurds also enables us to better understand the privileges and states of Turkishness of the Turks inside the contract. Looking at what life is like and how it feels to live on the outside may offer clues about living and feeling on the inside. To return to a metaphor I employ throughout the book, shifting our gaze to what goes on out of water may help us understand and be more aware of how life in water works. In other words, it is difficult to understand the nature of privilege solely by examining the privileged, since the existence of privilege, insofar as it has been naturalized and normalized, is often invisible to the privileged. But the unprivileged are never unaware of the absence of privilege. Thus, seeing what sorts of privilege the unprivileged lack may lay bare what the privileged enjoy. The ways of seeing, thinking, feeling, and behaving of these two sociological categories—contractual and noncontractual groups—came into being within a certain historical and social relationality. Hence, looking at noncontractual groups may further elucidate this relationality.

The Strategies, Feelings, and Thoughts of Turkishness

Being Turkish means learning to speak, think, see, be informed, and be moved in certain ways. Certain *positive performances*, in the sense of *doing certain things*, are expected of those who are part of, and so wish to benefit from, the Turkishness Contract.[1] These performances differ according to the social classes, fields, and institutions in which individuals operate as well as according to

---

1. The theoretical framework in this chapter is largely inspired by Pierre Bourdieu's conceptual set. But there are also certain similarities between the performative nature of race/ethnicity and that of gender. Judith Butler links gender ("stylized repetition of acts") to a certain contractual logic: "We regularly punish those who fail to do their gender right. . . . The various acts of gender create the idea of gender, and without those acts, there would be no gender at all. Gender is, thus, a construction that regularly conceals its genesis; the tacit collective agreement to perform, produce, and sustain discrete and polar genders as cultural fictions is obscured by the credibility of those productions" (*Gender Trouble*, 178).

the political conjuncture. But there is also a fundamental performance, transcending class and ideology, that is expected of everyone: speaking Turkish.

If the basic innate condition of Turkishness is Muslimness, the basic learned condition is speaking Turkish. It is through speaking Turkish, primarily, that individuals become Turkish and are able to participate in the Turkishness Contract. Beginning in the 1920s, the Turkish state called on citizens to speak Turkish through the "Citizen Speak Turkish!" campaigns and stated bluntly that those who did not speak Turkish would not be accepted as Turks. The use of languages other than Turkish was forbidden, at times through overt regulations but more often through more covert mechanisms of social control. Of course, speaking or not speaking a language is not simply a theatrical act, or at least not most of the time. (As I discuss later, language can also be displayed in deliberate performances meant to give the impression of Turkishness, yet allowing the "real person" to hide behind the scenes.) Someone who stops speaking a language stops thinking and feeling in that language if she has truly stopped—that is, if she has stopped speaking not only in public life but also in private. She begins to think and feel in a new language. Transitioning to another language thus also amounts to inhabiting another world of thought and feeling. Indeed, the emphasis of many modern nation-states on a single official language aims not only to facilitate communication or measure the loyalty of individuals but also to create common schemas of seeing, thinking, and feeling.[2] To put it another way, the actual expected performance is not to speak in a certain way, but to see, think, and feel in a certain way. In a 1932 list of the conditions of Turkishness, Celal Nuri (İleri) nicely summed up this expectation: "The following conditions are obligatory to be a Turk: 1. Turkish should be an individual's own language; in his home and in his family, he should speak Turkish and think in Turkish . . . in his dreams he should talk in Turkish, and if he takes a note, he should take it in Turkish, 2. Whether he is indifferent to religion, a free thinker, irreligious, or an atheist, he must be of Muslim descent or have converted, and, above all, his official religion must not be anything other than Islam."[3] Seen from this angle, one of the main goals of a host of linguistic reforms in the early republic—the transition from the Arabic to the Latin alphabet in 1928; a ban on educating,

---

2. For a discussion of the connection between the construction and functioning of modern states and emotion education, emotion control, and emotion management, see Stoler, "Affective States," 4–20.

3. İleri, *Devlet ve Meclis Hakkında Musahabeler*, 78. For the third condition of Turkishness, İleri introduces a racial and physiognomic logic: "They must not have obvious signs of yellow or black human beings." For a study examining the racist components of imagining Turkishness (especially prevalent in the 1930s) through the development of the discipline of anthropology in Turkey, see Maksudyan, *Türklüğü Ölçmek*. Also see Ergin, "Is the Turk a White Man?" 827–850.

publishing, and speaking in languages other than Turkish; efforts to "purify" Turkish of the influence of other languages—was to create a filter for thoughts and feelings, a means to exclude certain thoughts and feelings and to let through only certain others. Lexical repertoires are also ideational and emotional repertoires.

Turkishness's ways of speaking, seeing, knowing, thinking, and feeling are resources that offer certain tangible and intangible advantages to individuals, enabling them to gain a foothold and advance in different social fields. These resources can be leveraged as capital by one wishing to advance in different fields and institutions—that is, in different areas of investment. But the critical point here is that one does not make these investments based on rational calculations. Rather, at stake are states and strategies of Turkishness so internalized as to have practically become one's character.[4] These states and strategies, as the *habitus of Turkishness*, are inculcated in homes through the words and body language of parents and relatives, in schools, mosques, and the army through education and training, in the neighborhood through routine socialization, in professional life through the roles and performance expectations of institutions and fields, and through the implicit knowledge and intuition about power relations and hierarchies that, in theory, everyone possesses.

As is well known, Pierre Bourdieu refers, through the notion of *strategy*, to a course of action that one follows in a certain field, which, owing to one's systematic predispositions and inclinations (habitus) formed by adaptation to a field, displays certain regularities, and, to the extent that it is internalized, is largely unconscious. Each field is dominated by a different type of capital: social capital in politics, economic capital in the economy, or cultural-scientific capital in academia. Each field and its attendant institutions have their own rules for gaining a foothold and advancing. Moreover, each field is also a field of struggle; different actors and social positions in the field struggle with each other for control, by the rules of that field. In this sense, every field is the site of its own idiosyncratic game. The actors, though in competition, agree on the rules of the game and possess knowledge and a sense of the game. Through knowledge and sense of the game, then, one invests in a field of vested interests and expectations and follows a certain line of action within that field.[5] That said, such concepts as strategy, habitus, and the game do not imply a continuous rational calculation of gains and losses. The point is rather feeling like

---

4. On the relationship between institutional expectations and individual character, see the sociological classic by Gerth and Mills, *Character and Social Structure*.

5. Bourdieu, *Sosyoloji Meseleleri*, 41–42; Bourdieu, *Seçilmiş Metinler*, 163–164.

a "fish in water" in the spaces in which one lives, works, and plays: "It does not feel the weight of the water, and it takes the world about itself for granted."[6]

If we approach the process through which one becomes a Turk—that is, how one learns to think, feel, and see like a Turk—through Bourdieu's terms, then, crucial to this process is how one adapts to the functioning and expected roles of professional fields and institutions. To be sure, in Turkey as elsewhere, each field and institution has its own rules, different from other fields. However, in addition to specific professional rules and professional knowledge, every field also has its own set of rules and knowledge of Turkishness. That is, Turkishness is central to the game of each field, and one lacking in Turkishness's predispositions simply cannot play the game. Turkishness is the basic condition for entry, survival, and ascendance across a range of professions. In other words, to gain entry to an institution, one must possess a certain minimum level of Turkishness capital. Once in, it is necessary to know how to meet the expectations of Turkishness specific to that field and institution and to develop Turkishness capital. Such expectations of Turkishness, as well as the development of Turkishness capital according to these expectations, comprise doing certain things in certain ways and *not* doing certain things in certain ways, always doing certain things and *never* doing certain things. Turkishness, in short, as a metarole and metaperspective, is the unifying principle of different institutions and fields.

A person's habitus is shaped as much by *negative performances* (not doing certain things) as by *positive performances* (doing certain things one is expected to do). Just as positive performances turn into *positive states of Turkishness* as internalized *forms of doing*, negative performances likewise turn into *negative states of Turkishness* as *forms of not doing*. More concretely, Turkishness not only designates certain states of seeing, hearing, knowing, and caring but also certain states of not seeing, not hearing, not knowing, and not caring. One whose personality and ways of doing things are shaped by Turkishness sees certain things repeatedly but never sees others. She is informed about certain things repeatedly but never about others. She is moved by certain things repeatedly but never by others. It seems to me that these negative states of Turkishness, often experienced unconsciously, are shaped by the Indifference Contract and the Ignorance Contract, which can be seen as subcontracts of the Turkishness Contract.

Feelings and indifference are shaped by historical and social contexts. The form they take depends on social and ethnic relations of power and inequalities in particular places and times. They are either regulated or left unregu-

6. Bourdieu and Wacquant, *Invitation to Reflexive Sociology*, 127.

lated by the state. The emotional repertoire and lexicon of Turkey's Muslims was formed through a certain spontaneity and horizontality, expressed in the Muslimness Contract. The new state, established through the feelings of Muslimness, centralized both itself and the emotional repertoire of Muslims through the Turkishness Contract, imposed from above and to some extent narrowed. According to the Indifference Contract that grew out of this centralization and narrowing, there can be no sympathy with non-Muslims and non-Turkish Muslims outside the contract, no moral obligations and moral feelings toward them, and no concern for the injustices, lawlessness, oppression, and massacres committed against them. At issue here is the creation of a moral circle that draws emotional borders between those inside and those outside the contract. The feelings that should be felt by those inside the border turn first into moral obligation and, over time, into moral habit, while feelings that should not be felt for those outside the border turn into habits of indifference.

This state of indifference and callousness—the absence of moral feelings toward those outside the contract—is so widespread, so socially diffuse, that the state or institutions often need not even take any action. When someone inside the contract is moved by the situation of someone outside, mechanisms of control and warning kick in. In 1935, for example, the state demanded an investigation into the nationality of a police officer who had provided assistance and protection to an "Armenian woman, named Bedia, also known as Tırvanda."[7] The significance of this investigation is, to my mind, twofold. First, it functions as a warning: similar things should not be repeated by that policeman or any other policemen. It is an attempt to keep emotions in line and under control. Second, the suspicion is raised that a police officer capable of such an act might not be Turkish but another nationality. The reason for such suspicion has to do with the sheer exceptionality of this case—in other words, a Turkish police officer simply would not normally do such a thing. Recall, now in the context of this example, the first condition for becoming a civil servant in the 1926 Civil Servant Law: one had to be a Turk, and the nationality and sect of civil servants was to be indicated in their registry records. We thus see in clear and concrete terms how an institution's expectations of the performance of Turkishness connect with the emotional world of its employees.

Moreover, seen from a sociological perspective, this anecdote about a particular Turkish police officer has significance beyond its singularity. Because just as a Turkish policeman is expected not to protect an Armenian woman, a Turkish judge is expected not to protect an Armenian, and a Turkish histo-

---

7. Quoted in Çağaptay, *Islam, Secularism, and Nationalism*, 79.

rian is expected not to be interested in the Armenian issue, or, if she is, she is expected to sympathize with Muslims, not Armenians. If a Turkish judge or historian does not behave and feel as expected, then the mechanisms of warning, control, and punishment are set in motion. Such emotional dissonance is rare, however, because the overwhelming majority of Turks have internalized the feelings and indifference of Turkishness. In other words, socially constructed lines and strategies of feeling are a constituent component of Turkish individualization; the nation and the nation-state inhabit the individual. In Norbert Elias's terms, what I describe here is a parallelism between a sociogenetic process (the monopolization of various sources of power by the Turkish nation-state) and a psychogenetic process (the emotional constitution of Turkish individuals).[8]

The history and sociology of emotions cannot be separated from the history of thought and the sociology of knowledge. There is a direct relationship between forms of knowing and ignorance and forms of caring and indifference. In practice, feelings, knowledge, and thoughts constantly interact and bleed into one another. It is often difficult to separate thought from feeling, feeling from knowledge, or ignorance from feeling. Emotions are shaped by how and about what one is informed, but they also determine how information is perceived and processed. For example, one can be indifferent not only by ignoring information but also by taking in that information along with emotion—say, anger—and thus not taking it seriously. Just as knowledge and emotion are tightly linked, there is a close link in Turkey between the Indifference Contract and its regulation of emotions and the Ignorance Contract and its regulation of knowledge.

The Ignorance Contract[9] prohibits the production and dissemination of knowledge about persons and groups excluded, historically or today, from the contract. The fields of media and academia, which in theory possess both the ability and the professional ethics to bring such information to light, have played an especially vital role in perpetuating the Ignorance Contract. For decades, these fields simply did not touch individuals and groups outside the contract—or, if they did, they did so from the perspective of the Turkishness Contract. For example, the Turkish nation-state's policy of denial surrounding the events of 1915 also has echoes in academia, where it is often pre-

---

8. As is well known, Elias (see *Civilizing Process*), in examining the psychogenesis of individuals in the context of the sociogenesis of the state, describes how, with the monopolization and centralization of the instruments of violence and finance by the modern state, human behavior, impulses, and emotions are brought under control and how this control transforms over time into internalized modes of control and coercion in individuals.

9. For a study on South Africa through this concept, see Steyn, "Ignorance Contract," 8–25.

tended that the Armenian issue did not exist and never happened, or else is seen and analyzed through the eyes of the state and the Turkishness Contract. To do otherwise—to try to analyze the Armenian issue from the perspective of Armenians—is simply prohibited. Yet, this prohibition derives its power primarily through its transformation of individuals—here, academics—into something of an inner law, not from the threat of violence and punishment.

A similar dynamic applies to the Kurdish issue. The Turkish nation-state, to paraphrase M. Malmîsanij, prohibited the emergence of Kurdology as an autonomous field of study about Kurdish history and culture. Instead, it encouraged an "anti-Kurdology," arguing that Kurds were, in fact, Turks and that there was no such language as Kurdish. At the same time, however, the state also produced more factual but confidential documents on Kurds and Kurdistan (a kind of "secret Kurdology") to be able to resolve the Kurdish issue, which it very well knew existed.[10] Consequently, Turkish academics—with few exceptions—did not produce knowledge independent of the state on the Armenian and Kurdish issues until the late 1990s. Turkish history and society were analyzed as though the Armenian and Kurdish issues simply did not exist. Not surprisingly, the knowledge and perspectives this yielded on the state, society, and the individual were inevitably limited, incomplete, and rather weak.

It is clear by examining the trajectory in Turkey of the disciplines of history and sociology, two fundamental social sciences, that these disciplines were established and developed within the framework of the Ignorance and Indifference Contracts. Beginning in the 1910s, the disciplines furnished historical, sociological, and theoretical knowledge useful for the making of the Muslimness and Turkishness Contracts. The resulting knowledge ignored those people and groups outside the contracts. Overlooked were ways of knowing that might allow for the contract to be questioned. History and sociology were mobilized and instrumentalized to induce individuals inside the contract to see, know, and feel in certain ways. Consider the words of Yusuf Akçura, one of the founding figures of Turkish history: "History is important because it can give us knowledge, thoughts and feelings that will benefit . . . the human society to which we belong."[11] The discipline of history in Turkey has examined the history of the Turks and written the history of the Ottoman Empire and Turkey from the perspective, knowledge, and feelings of Turkishness. This is not to say that every historical work has praised and glorified Turkishness. There are countless historical studies that are, prima facie, quite

---

10. Malmîsanij, "Anti-Kürdolojiden Kürdolojiye Giden Yol ve İsmail Beşikçi," 65–85.
11. Quoted in Karal, "Önsöz"; Akçura, *Üç Tarz-ı Siyaset*, 3.

universal, scientific, impartial, and objective and that appear to not be written from a nationalist perspective. Crucially, however, insofar as such work omits topics prohibited by the Turkishness Contract, it aids in the contract's reproduction. Even a cursory look, from this perspective, at the leading historians of the long twentieth century of history writing in Turkey shows this to be the general rule.

Institutionalized by Ziya Gökalp, the science of sociology in Turkey was, from its nascence, a national science. From the 1910s onward, Turkish sociology sought to demonstrate who, in demographic terms, was to be eliminated and who assimilated, or how existing feelings among Muslims might serve as a social glue of sorts, or else how new feelings might be created. The resulting theoretical and informational capital constituted the scientific buttress of first the Muslimness Contract, and later, the Turkishness Contract.[12] Following Durkheim, Gökalp saw education as a form of "applied sociology" capable of mooring certain feelings and ideas to the mind. As Taha Parla summarizes, "Gökalp sees sociology, which he defines as a scientific discipline, not only as a science *of* society but also as a science *for* society: the findings of sociology can be put into practice to create a more salubrious society. The social function of education, for example, is to socialize individuals and to ensure the internalization of those moral and cultural norms that are part of the national collective conscience."[13]

That said, the concepts of "society" and "the social" as used earlier are in a sense misleading. Sociology in Turkey has not been a social science in the true sense of the word; its main object of analysis has not been society. It is not interested in the complex and intricate relations and contradictions within society as a whole but only in the complex and intricate relations within the nation as a whole. As with historiography, in the field of sociology, there is no such expectation that every sociologist write about how to constitute the Turkish nation. In fact, most sociologists are not interested in Turkishness per se; they are interested in a range of topics such as urbanization, squatting, migration, rural sociology, industrialization, or interclass relations and contradictions. What is expected of sociologists is not that they concern themselves in this or that way with *what is inside the nation*, but rather that they not concern themselves with *what is outside the nation*. Sociology is thus not in-

---

12. After claiming the science of sociology had proved that what makes a group of people a nation is a connection "common to upbringing and culture, that is, feelings," Gökalp proceeds to define the nation as "a group consisting of individuals who have the same language, religion, morals and arts in common, that is, who have received the same upbringing. As Turkish peasants describe it, 'same language, same religion'" ("Türkçülüğün Esasları," 184). For a history of Turkish sociology up to the 1940s, see Ünsaldı and Geçgin, *Sosyoloji Tarihi*.

13. T. Parla, *Ziya Gökalp, Kemalizm ve Türkiye'de Korporatizm*, 103.

terested in society beyond the Turkishness Contract; it is as if this part of society does not exist. It concerns itself with society beyond the Turkishness Contract only insofar as it disregards it, or insofar as it inquires into how that part of society might be assimilated and integrated into the nation. Sociology thus emerged and developed in Turkey as not a *social science* but a *national science*.[14]

Consequently, when a sociologist in Turkey examines an issue, he does so not as a sociologist but as a Turkish sociologist. The content and method of his sociology is determined as much by his Turkishness as by his sociology. The same can be said for other social-scientific disciplines: economics developed as Turkish economics, yielding Turkish economists, not economists; likewise with political science, anthropology, and psychology. But unlike those blatantly Turkish-nationalist thinkers who founded the disciplines,[15] most social scientists do not know that this is the case and do not see things this way. Most assume their areas of interests and disinterest are determined by individual character, preferences, and scientific outlook. To most, the idea that what one does and does not look at or what one includes and excludes from analysis may be related not to a discipline but to Turkishness simply does not occur.

However, ignorance of the Armenian and Kurdish issues is not passive; one remains ignorant not because of a lack of knowledge. Rather, by various psychological mechanisms, most Turks avoid the scattered information they hear or read regarding these issues. At worst, they are angered by such information; at best, they do not take it seriously.[16] The mechanisms and operations of active ignorance by which universalist intellectuals avoid knowledge are particularly interesting. An intellectual with such an ideological stance might be expected to be sensitive to crimes committed by states and nations or to the oppression of peoples and, perhaps, to produce and disseminate information on such matters. Yet surveying the history of Turkish thought reveals that intellectuals who adhere to such universalist ideologies as Marxism (internationalism), Islamism (ummahism), and Kemalism (Enlightenmentism) simply do not produce knowledge on the Armenian and Kurdish issues and often avoid what knowledge there is. This avoidance is necessary, even if it clashes in theory with their universalism, because to confront such informa-

---

14. Of course, this situation is not unique to Turkey. As numerous studies have shown, especially in recent years, modern social sciences have been shaped by national (contractual) and colonial contexts. This is particularly evident in their formative decades. E.g., see Steinmetz, *Sociology and Empire*.

15. Already by the time of the second constitutional monarchy, Turkists viewed economics and sociology as essentially nonnational sciences, on par with mathematics and chemistry, and criticized their universality. They argued that both sciences should be national, and they were institutionalized accordingly. See Toprak, *Türkiye'de "Milli İktisat,"* 29.

16. For a discussion of the strategies of ignorance and denial, see Zerubavel, *Elephant in the Room.*

tion and to take it seriously would oblige them, as universalist intellectuals, to disseminate it, and this would amount to exceeding the Turkishness Contract and its subcomponent, the Ignorance Contract.[17] Confronting knowledge also involves the risk of caring about that knowledge—that is, the risk of sympathizing, which could lead one to exceed not only the Ignorance Contract but the Indifference Contract.

The intellectual strategies and lines of thought developed by intellectuals to avoid knowledge frequently involve questioning the source and nature of knowledge. For example, one need not take alternative information seriously, because it is not the sort of true information that would warrant seriousness. It is biased, manipulative, even polluted (tainted) information. It has been manipulated by particularist intellectuals for their own self-interests rather than presented by one, like himself, who does not take self-interest into consideration, who, as a universalist, transcends interest. Thus, a Marxist can criticize and accuse Kurds of being nationalists or of playing into the hands of imperialists; thus, she maintains her self-image as an internationalist. An Islamist can criticize and accuse Kurds of tribalism and of dividing the ummah; he maintains his universalism (ummahism) in painting his opponent as divisive and tribalist. A Kemalist can criticize and accuse the Kurds of being reactionary and feudal; she maintains her universalism (Enlightenmentism), contra the reactionary other.[18] In the end, since one's opponents are nationalists, tribalists, and reactionaries and can only speak from vested interests, the information they present cannot be taken seriously. In this sense, blaming the other provides a useful intellectual path of escape from information coming from the other. Further, an intellectual making use of such a path assumes that the other speaks and thinks the way he does because he is Kurdish or Armenian. In other words, the universalist intellectual thinks the way he does because

---

17. In a manner similar to the conceptual framework I have employed in this book, Taner Akçam (*Ermenilerin Zorla Müslümanlaştırılması*, 15–47) explains the long-standing lack of interest among leftist and democratic groups on the Armenian issue through the idea of a "tacit agreement of silence." According to Akçam, the main reason for this silence is the belief that the Armenian issue has been "imposed on Turkish national identity from the outside"; silence represents a reaction to this imposition.

18. In an important book, Mesut Yeğen (*Devlet Söyleminde Kürt Sorunu*) analyzes the Turkish state's description of the Kurdish issue as based in reactionism, banditry, and separatism driven by imperialism and regional backwardness. Yeğen's Foucauldian approach offers an archaeology of state discourse that moves beyond a Marxist focus on ideological distortion. The state is not denying reality through an ideological narrative; it *actually sees* the issue through a modernizing, centralist, nationalist, and authoritarian discursive establishment, formed within a certain historical and institutional framework, and it speaks accordingly.

he is a Marxist or an Islamist; the other person thinks the way he does because he is a Kurd or an Armenian. Not recognizing one's own Turkishness goes hand in hand with possessing an advanced radar for the Kurdishness and Armenianness of the other. Thus, one can criticize the other for pursuing identity politics instead of class politics, or tribal politics instead of ummah politics.

All these lines of thought function as intellectual paths for escaping certain truths. Yet, because these paths are universalist, they are able to appear noble. Universalist intellectuals are able to conceal the powerful interests behind their escape and to present themselves as disinterested. Even if they fail to convince those outside the contract, they convince those within, and, most important, they convince themselves. In other words, these intellectual strategies are not consciously deployed. Escape, in any true, authentic sense, must leave no trace of shame and guilt. Escape is thus not conscious. It is secured by well-established intellectual strategies and lines of thought, which are constantly validated and never questioned by the social and institutional environment in which one is embedded. Moreover, these strategies and lines can only be sustained through profound self-ignorance. The universalist intellectual does not recognize her thoughts as motivated by interests; she does not know that her thoughts are shaped by Turkishness. She thinks that she is truly universalist and disinterested and that her thoughts are formed by her beliefs and ideology. This is why, for example, a Marxist intellectual may oppose the creation of a Kurdish state, on the basis of various Marxist or Leninist principles, yet never consider the possibility that Turkishness may have influenced her opposition. An Islamist intellectual may feel pride as a Muslim at seeing a Palestinian child throw a stone at an Israeli soldier yet horror as a Turk when a Kurdish child throws a stone at a Turkish soldier. It is often unthinkable to the universalist intellectuals that the difference between these feelings is determined by their Turkishness.

This state of righteousness and certitude, unquestioned by those within the contract, inevitably engenders a paternalistic aura in the universalist intellectual. He is certain that he represents true Marxism or Islamism, whereas his opponent is a Marxist tainted by Armenianness or an Islamist tainted by Kurdishness. He represents universal and rational thought; the other is particularist and emotional. His lack of self-awareness leads him to see himself as the embodiment of knowledge and reason and to adopt a patronizing and didactic air. This is how the universalist intellectual is able to maintain his intellectual and emotional comfort. Sacrificed, as the inevitable cost of this all, is the capacity to analyze the institutional, ideological, and class structure of Turkey; to examine the psychoformation of individuals, including himself;

or to convince any of the oppressed outside the contract of his universalist
ideology and politics.

Non-Muslims and Turkishness

Insofar as Turks have internalized the ways of speaking, thinking, feeling,
and behaving that are proper to Turkishness (through education, socialization, performances, and strategies), they experience them as states of Turkishness. Which is to say, they are not experienced consciously. One is simply
unaware of being in the water and swimming with the current. As long as
one can pass easily through open doors, the significance of doors—which
both allow entry *and* exclude—goes unnoticed. But one outside the water is
aware of the water, and when she enters the water, she does so with the rules
of the water in mind. One who swims against the current is aware of the current, because the current constantly makes its obstructive force known. One
to whom doors remain closed has little choice but to recognize the exclusionary function of doors.

As long as privilege goes unnoticed, so, too, does the close relationship
between privilege and ways of speaking, thinking, feeling, and behaving. Yet
the unprivileged are well aware of the ties between the privileges and states
of Turkishness. Take the Union of Secular Turkish Christians, founded by
"Turkish Christians" in 1935, who summarized their goal of assimilation and
integration as follows: "We will particularly focus our activities on the following principles: to owe obedience to Turkish culture, to feel and think like
a Turk, to speak, read and write Turkish."[19] This and many other instances
underscore my sense that to better understand the privileges and states of
Turkishness—life in water—we must turn our gaze to life outside.

In thinking about the relationship between Turkishness and assimilation,
it may be useful to make an analytical distinction between *being assimilated
to Turkishness* and *assimilating to Turkishness*. Examining the phenomenon of
assimilation solely in terms of individuals *being assimilated* may limit one's
understanding of the matter to a state-centered story, in which the state is
active, and the individual is passive. Yet examining the phenomenon through
the experience of assimilating to Turkishness attributes a certain consciousness
and agency to the individual and calls attention to a more dynamic interaction
between states and individuals. In more concrete terms, I understand assimilation as the transition, or attempted transition, to a dominant culture and le-

---

19. Quoted in Benlisoy and Benlisoy, *Türk Milliyetçiliğinde Katedilmemiş Bir Yol*, 336.

gitimate language by as-yet-un-Turkified individuals or "heads of family" who see material and immaterial advantages to assimilation.

However, when approached from the perspective of non-Muslims, the phenomenon of assimilation grows a bit more complicated. On the one hand, non-Muslims are categorically excluded from Turkishness. No matter how much they may want to assimilate and no matter how hard they try, as non-Muslims, they cannot.[20] On the other hand, the state has repeatedly invited non-Muslims to assimilate. In other words, the very same state that rejects their Turkification also demands it. From the state's perspective, this is a paradox in name only. The state expects from non-Muslims, in essence, loyalty to the Turkishness Contract from which they were excluded. They are expected to comply with the second and third articles of the contract: not to produce information about what has been done to non-Muslims and Kurds, not to engage in politics, and to carry out certain performances of Turkishness in public life, such as speaking Turkish or openly indicating their loyalty to the state. As long as these conditions are met, the state can allow non-Muslims to reside in Turkey and work, for example, in the private sector. Even if not every door is open, some are. Even if non-Muslims cannot be *real Turks*, they can still benefit in part from some advantages of being *de jure Turks*. Those who can perform their Turkishness well enough, who do not oppose Turkish supremacy in general, and who do not flaunt their own identity will be accepted as passable and reasonable non-Muslims. Those who oppose the Turkishness Contract, meanwhile, will be punished.

The fact that the state never recognized non-Muslims as real Turks, whatever their performance of Turkishness, generated near-insurmountable contradictions and tensions for non-Muslims in Turkey. No matter how hard a person tries to be Turkish, she cannot be fully so. Plus, she is blamed for this and lives under constant threat. This tension accompanies non-Muslims in Turkey from birth to death. Examining the Jewish experience in Turkey sheds particularly clarifying light on this tension. Unlike Armenians and Greeks, Jews

---

20. The recollections of a Christian Gagauz Turk on how he became Turkish are not simply an isolated example; they contain important clues about the Turkishness Contract: "When I became a Turkish citizen, my old name did not fit Turkish names. I applied to the court to change that too. . . . Finally, it was time for the last procedure, the final procedure regarding my religion. Without any difficulty, I went to my teacher and after repeating the prayer he recited, I accepted Islam. After changing my mother's name to Nadiye and my father's to Giray, I became a Turk by lineage, and changed my name to Özdemir, a wholly Turkish name, and I was no longer objectionable in the eyes of society. So, I have been a Muslim Turkish citizen for sixty years." Quoted in Benlisoy and Benlisoy, 339.

were seen as loyal by the state and were thought to be capable of Turkifying. At the same time, in practice, they were never accepted as real Turks.[21]

In 1928, Tekinalp (Moiz Kohen), perhaps the most Turkified Jew, published *Turkification*,[22] a book addressing both the state and Jews in the hope of addressing this problem of acceptance. Tekinalp wanted all who consider themselves Turks, who "participate in the aspirations and wishes of Turkish society, in all its emotions, in its material and immaterial future," should be treated as Turks: "When presented with an Albanian, a Persian, an Arab or a Jew who says he is a Turk, one must consider his background, the environment he lives in, the education he has received, and the constant factors that determine his material and immaterial interests. If all these factors are of such a quality as to demonstrate that his belief in being a Turk has substance, then his claim to be Turkish must be considered valid." Tekinalp believed (as he himself had been trying to do since the 1910s) that non-Muslims could become Turks in terms of the ways they thought and felt. But he was also aware that they could not be accepted into the Turkishness Contract, since they did not fulfill the condition of being Muslim. Yet, in the above quote, he lists Jews alongside Arabs, avoiding any mention of religion, as though there was no such obstacle before anyone becoming a Turk.

However, Tekinalp also thought that Jews themselves were a significant part of the problem; they were not doing enough. Accordingly, he offered ten recommendations or commandments, inspired by the Torah: "1. Turkify your names. 2. Speak Turkish. 3. In synagogues, read at least some prayers in Turkish. 4. Turkify your schools. 5. Send your children to public schools. 6. Get involved in the affairs of the country. 7. Make friends with the Turks. 8. Eradicate entirely your spirit of community. 9. Do your part in the national economy. 10. Know your rights." Among these strategies of Turkishness, the last commandment is particularly apposite to our topic, for it states that if the first nine articles are fulfilled, that is, if certain performances are demonstrated and Turkishness is internalized, then one can enjoy the rights and privileges

21. For a book suggesting that loyal Jews should be seen differently from the rebellious Armenians and Greeks in the context of Turkification, but that this difference is often ignored, see Avner Levi's *Türkiye Cumhuriyeti'nde Yahudiler*. Levi also states that in concrete cases the state could distinguish between Jews, on the one hand, and Armenians and Greeks, on the other (53–54). For the international support given by the Jews of Turkey to the Turkish state regarding "Armenian Genocide Allegations," see Bali, *Devlet'in Örnek Yurttaşları*, 299–344.

22. Translator's note: the word here is *Türkleştirme*, which adds the causative suffix *-tir* to *Türkleşme*. Thus, Turkification, in the context of Tekinalp's book, should be read transitively, as in "causing someone to Turkify" or "making someone Turkify," rather than the intransitive sense of *Türkleşme*, "oneself Turkifying." This grammatical distinction echoes the author's analytical distinction between assimilating and being assimilated.

of Turkishness. Indeed, in a passage expanding on the details of the article, he continues: "Know your rights: The Constitution has designated you 'Turk.' This is such a right, such a privilege, that it cannot be properly appreciated without being Turkish in worldview, spirit and consciousness. If you believe that through your worldview, you are, or soon will be, a Turk, then know your right, do not tolerate anyone assailing this right, and defend, with jealous determination and resiliently through legal means, the rights and privileges provided by the title of Turk."[23]

The Turkish press made frequent and explicit mention of the performance of Turkishness expected of Jews. Necmettin Sadak, a statesman and one of the founding figures of Turkish sociology, wrote in 1925, "Those who wish to live and earn a living in Turkey, regardless of their religion or race, must think like Turks, speak like Turks and live like Turks." Yunus Nadi, one of the founding figures of the Turkish press, wrote in 1927 that, while the principle of equality before the law was a blessing, "our compatriots must be worthy of this grace and make every effort to obtain the advantages promised to them by this high social formula." In another article he published in the same year, Nadi expected Jews—along with, of course, all citizens—to be "free citizens, constantly competing with one another to demonstrate their loyalty to the motherland, in this free Turkey." Orhan Seyfi Orhon, a Turkist poet and politician, simultaneously counseled Jews to become Turks and made them feel that, as non-Muslims, they could never be true Turks: "I don't know how it is in Judaism. True faith in Islam is based on two things: one, affirmation with one's heart! We trust that all our Jewish citizens affirm Turkishness with their hearts. But there is another condition, without which faith is incomplete: and that is to profess with one's tongue! Our Jewish citizens fulfill this condition only when they speak Turkish like other Turks, that is, when they profess with their tongues what they affirm with their hearts. Otherwise this faith is incomplete. And Muslims call those with incomplete faith not believers, but hypocrites!"[24]

Non-Muslims in Turkey know very well the vital difference between being and not being Turkish. Avram Galanti, a prominent figure in the Jewish community, articulated this awareness in 1925, writing on the issue of the Turkification of Jews in Turkey: "All minorities are well aware that assimila-

---

23. Tekinalp, *Türkleştirme*, 25, 28, 75, 78.
24. For these excerpts, see Bali, *Bir Türkleştirme Serüveni*, 66, 117, 133, 257. In 1934, the Turkist Nihal Atsız wrote in the periodical *Orhun*: "Just as mud cannot become iron no matter how much it is baked, the Jew cannot become a Turk no matter how hard he tries. Turkishness is a privilege, not granted to every mortal, especially not to mortals like Jews. The warning to them is this: they should know their limits." Quoted in Levi, *Türkiye Cumhuriyeti'nde Yahudiler*, 110.

tion with the Turks is in their own interests, and understand the meaning of the adage 'he who strays from the herd is lost.'" However, for reasons tied to both the Turkishness Contract and their own communal life, Jews were some-how unable to Turkify and were subjected to constant threats and insults from the state, the media, and Muslims. This is why, as Marsel Franko im-plied, some Jews had been reluctant to perform, knowing their performance of Turkishness would be found insufficient and would go unrewarded: "The state should treat as genuine Turks those who have adapted themselves. So that those who are hesitant may understand that the path of deliverance, the right path, is the path to Turkishness." To overcome this vital problem of non-Turkification and to create a good impression in the eyes of the Turkish community, in 1932 the Jewish community of İzmir made its members sign a Turkishness Contract of sorts: "Letter of Commitment: I declare that I will endeavor to adopt Turkish culture and to ensure national cohesion among our citizens, and that, to achieve this aim, I will always speak the Turkish language . . . and that I will strive to spread this idea everywhere." A promi-nent figure in the Jewish community warned Jews in 1936: "You shout out in Spanish or French in public places. This has a bad effect. There's a rising trend against us. So speak Turkish, and speak softly. Live a meek life!"[25]

Living meekly succinctly characterizes the modes of public existence and survival of Jews for whom inclusion in the Turkishness Contract was unattain-able. Of course, meekness, as a recommended way of life, is not specific to the 1930s; it is a strategy that Jewish parents and community leaders still teach children and young people today in order to live safely in everyday life. Jews possess knowledge of Turkishness and the Turkishness Contract because such knowledge is vital; potentially a matter of life and death, its acquisition is a necessity.[26] Jewish knowledge of Turkishness entails executing certain perfor-mances of Turkishness in public life: speaking and behaving like a Turk,

---

25. For excerpts, see Bali, *Bir Türkleştirme Serüveni*, 68, 159, 274, 282–283. Levi reports that as early as 1923, Marsel Fresko warned Jews not to stand out, not to dress ostentatiously, and not to arouse jealousy. Levi, *Türkiye Cumhuriyeti'nde Yahudiler*, 35.

26. Ivo Molinas, editor in chief of *Shalom* newspaper, describes how Jews in Turkey have adapt-ed to the Turkishness Contract: "Now we have a Ladino saying with Turkish words mixed in: '*No moz karışayamoz a la eços del hükümet.*' It means 'We do not interfere in the affairs of the government.' We want to live a normal life. . . . To live well here, we should not get into trouble with the government. We will always be good citizens. 'Citizen, speak Turkish,' and we immedi-ately start speaking Turkish. At what cost, at the cost of our language. Jews pay their taxes on time and do not comment on political issues. They feel sad about Israel, but they say nothing. In the same way that we don't interfere in the affairs of the government. . . . The aim is always to get along. So you can't get any opinions from our society; at most you can hear good wishes for the government" ("No moz karışayamoz a la eços del hükümet," available at http://www.agos.com.tr /tr/yazi/10577/no-moz-karisayamoz-a-la-ecos-del-hukumet).

adopting Turkish names, and praising the tolerance of the Turkish state when and where appropriate. These performances are accompanied by strategies of concealing and erasing their Jewishness—that is, their difference from Turkishness—in public life. In Turkey, Jews learn from childhood to live their Jewishness in terms of "being inconspicuous," "not attracting attention," "being invisible," or "being quiet." Judaism is a way of being that is reserved for the private sphere, or for public spaces where only Jews are present. The result is a dual existence, as Turks and as Jews. Separating these two lives is a stage curtain, with Turkishness on stage and Judaism behind the scenes.[27]

The double lives lived on and behind the stage are, of course, not unique to Jews. After all, it is the relations of power, produced by the Turkishness Contract, between groups inside and outside the contract, rather than something particular to Jewishness, that engender double lives.[28] In encounters between a Muslim and a non-Muslim Turkish individual (between one inside and outside contract), the crucial difference that marks the encounter is that one has a state while the other does not. This difference inevitably affects the nature of the encounter. More precisely, the Turkish individual knows that the state constituting one side of the contract is his state and will protect him should the need arise. Knowing that one is backed up by a state gives a form of confidence mirrored in behaviors and in the body as self-confidence. The non-Turkish individual, existing outside the contract, knows that the state is not his and will not protect him when needed. Knowing this is reflected in the non-Turkish person's behavior and body as timidity and meekness.[29] To summarize, when two people meet, one inside the contract and one not, they are

---

27. For a recent fieldwork-based study of the tensions Turkish Jews experience between being Jewish and being Turkish, of such survival strategies as silence, inconspicuousness, and invisibility, and of their performances of Turkishness, see Brink-Danan, *Yirmi Birinci Yüzyılda Türkiye'de Yahudiler*. As an anthropologist, Brink-Danan is particularly careful not to jeopardize the people she is researching; therefore, she does not share much of the data that could add value to her book. At the same time, she is already aware of the fact that the people she is investigating are protecting themselves. As one Turkish Jew told her, "I wouldn't tell you anything that would endanger us anyway!" (201).

28. On the relationship between multiple lives and spaces, a Turkish Greek says the following: "You are in your own country but your country does not accept you. You live with that feeling. You go from one place to another. So you go from school to home, to the sports club, to your friends' houses, to church. . . . These are places that belong to you, but beyond these, [places] don't belong to you. You live in a kind of fragmented mosaic. Some areas belong to you more, some areas don't belong to you at all." Quoted in Koçoğlu, *Azınlık Gençleri Anlatıyor*, 278.

29. For an article by literary figure Murat Uyurkulak on the behavior of his non-Muslim neighbors, in his apartment building in the Kurtuluş neighborhood of İstanbul, and on the timidity and fear that permeated their bodies, see "Şişli'de bir apartman," available at http://t24.com.tr/yazarlar/komsu/sislide-bir-apartiman,17877.

two people, one with and one without a state, with the state embedded in the minds and bodies of each in different ways.

For example, a non-Turkish person may carry her body as though it were a burden that could expose her in a crowd. She may thus try to render her body invisible or indistinct by minimizing its presence through the way she walks or sits. She may shy away from glances directed at her for fear of being seen and noticed, or, unable to respond with the same ease and self-confidence, she may fix her gaze elsewhere. In moments of interaction with Turks or in areas dominated by Turkishness, she may have difficulty speaking, or stutter, and her cheeks and ears may blush. I mean to point out here that differences between Turkishness and non-Turkishness are lived through and as bodies, just as are such sociological categories as masculinity and femininity or whiteness and blackness.[30]

When two people meet, one in the contract and one not, just as one has a state and one does not, so too, one has a nation and one does not.[31] "Nation" refers here not to a collective with a common history, language, and sense of solidarity but, rather, to a state-recognized network of power that offers material and immaterial advantages of the kind I describe in this book to those it recognizes as part of the nation. In this sense, there is only the Turkish nation in Turkey. However, since those inside the nation are not aware of the water they are in and do not recognize the role of Turkishness and structural Turkism in shaping their thoughts, they may criticize those who are not in the water (the nation) as nationalists in certain encounters. In other words, those with a nation and state can accuse those without the same of nationalism. Two Armenians describe such encounters and the helplessness they experience as follows: "I am in a leftist environment. They are more democratic. But even among them I have difficulties from time to time. Of course, I can't talk to them like I talk to an Armenian. And I feel it's not the same. You talk about something, the other person sees you as a nationalist"; "I am not a nationalist, but when I say 'I am Armenian,' many of my friends from leftist circles call me 'nationalist.' When I say I am Armenian, it is not because I am a nationalist."[32]

In 1915 and afterward, Armenians and Assyrians, who went through similar processes of annihilation and extermination, were excluded from the Muslimness and Turkishness Contracts on the grounds of their Christianity.

---

30. For an analysis of the ways in which whiteness and Blackness operate on the body, see Ahmed, "Phenomenology of Whiteness," 149–168.

31. A Christian Arab from Hatay notes, "For example, I don't say 'I am a Christian.' I say 'I am from Samandağ.' . . . We are here but our arms and wings are broken. The state is not ours; the nation is not ours." Quoted in Kentel, Ahıska, and Genç, *"Milletin Bölünmez Bütünlüğü."*

32. Quoted in Koçoğlu, *Azınlık Gençleri Anlatıyor*, 133, 191.

The fear and terror they experienced, especially in 1915, has haunted them ever since, even if the intensity has diminished over time. For instance, in the eastern provinces where they were subjected to the most intense forms of massacre, Armenian survivors, or the *remnants of the sword* by their historical name, either concealed their Armenian identity entirely and pretended to be Muslim or, indeed, converted to Islam and became Turks or Kurds. Two researchers describe the fundamental features of such lives as follows: "Those Armenians who converted to Islam or concealed themselves mostly married among themselves. They abandoned everything, hid in remote areas cut off from the rest of the world, and for decades scrupulously followed the most basic rule of survival: silence."[33] An Armenian "remnant of the sword" summarizes the experience of fear as follows: "We have always, always been afraid; this is the reason why Armenians continue to cover their heads and remain Muslim even today. That's why you get lost in the crowd, why you lay low. This is also the reason why we always want to be us, to marry our own, from our region, from our village, or, even worse, from our own family."[34] An Armenian from Diyarbakır emphasizes the historicity of this timidity rooted in fear: "My father is very timid. Our whole family line is timid. . . . This persecution, this tragedy that the Armenian people went through made them like this. Unfortunately, there is a historical timidity."[35] This fear is such that Armenians can hide their Armenianness for their entire life,[36] concealing it for protection, even from those closest to them. Today, there are perhaps hundreds of thousands of such hidden Armenian lives, known and unknown.[37]

---

33. Ritter and Sivaslian, *Kılıç Artıkları*, 9.

34. Quoted in Ritter and Sivaslian, *Kılıç Artıkları*, 177.

35. Quoted in Balancar, *Diyarbakırlı Ermeniler Konuşuyor*, 9–10.

36. There are many examples of this in the world of cinema. E.g., Samuel Uluçyan, known as Sami Hazinses, would for years refuse to admit to a journalist who approached him that he was Armenian. When he finally did, he said, "The old sympathy is gone. That's why I don't want it. Don't write this down. Let me die, then do it. Write after I die, never mind now." See "Ermeni Hemşehrilerimi Ararken," accessed April 4, 2025, available at https://bianet.org/haber/ermeni-hemsehrilerimi-ararken-200195.

37. E.g., only many years later, in her grandmother's old age, could Fethiye Çetin learn that her grandmother was Armenian, that most of her family had been massacred in 1915, and that some of the survivors had emigrated to the United States. See Çetin, *Anneannem*. Or, a bureaucrat who later learns that his grandmother was Armenian becomes aware that the state also knows this when he is dismissed from his post during the September 12, 1980, coup period, after serving as a district governor and property inspector for years. At a striking point in his narrative, he notes, "I think many people in similar situations in Turkey have experienced these feelings. If they have worked in state institutions like me, I believe they have also experienced great traumas. I've been through it. I have lived in such a way that . . . you break into a cold sweat thinking about what would happen if this 'other identity' of yours became known. I broke out in a cold sweat." Quoted in Altınay and Çetin, *Torunlar*, 75. Erhan Başyurt's book (*Ermeni Evlatlıklar*), meanwhile, tries to create the impression that it was written with a "sense of empathy," even as it raises suspicions

Intense fear and timidity also color the lives of Armenians, Assyrians, and Jews living in the west of Turkey, even if they did not experience the most brutal massacres in Turkey's east. So, too, with Turkey's Greeks,[38] who, though not subjected to extermination, were targeted by purges, perhaps unlike any other groups, and today number only in the thousands.[39] A Greek who migrated to Greece after spending his childhood and youth in Turkey describes the impact of fear: "We have concretized fears inside us. Living as a minority is something quite different, it gives you certain abilities. You can get into trouble at any time. There might be an obstacle, you have to think about how to overcome it when you are a minority."[40] This is the main factor that requires double lives (another factor being the effort to maintain the unique features of one's community). Ordinary non-Muslims perform Turkishness (speaking Turkish, using Turkish names[41]) in a public life dominated by Turkishness. Community leaders, from time to time, when necessary, emphasize their loyalty to the Turkish state, underscoring crucially that this is a loyalty born of love and gratitude, not fear. Such strategies of Turkishness allow non-Muslims to survive in daily life and in the private sector. Parallel to these performances, they hide their religious symbols and rituals and languages (Syriac, Greek, Armenian, Ladino) as well as any thought or feeling outside of or unacceptable to Turkishness, either by holding it in (both figuratively and literally—e.g., by tucking their crosses into their clothes) or by confining such practices to homes or churches.[42]

---

that covert Armenians seeking revenge played an important role in the Kurdish uprisings and the PKK (Partiya Karkerên Kurdistanê or the Kurdistan Workers' Party).

38. See Akgönül, *Türkiye Rumları*.

39. If the ratio of Greeks to the total population were the same today as it was in the early 1910s, there would now be around eight million to ten million Greeks in Turkey. The same is true for Armenians. In other words, about 25 percent of today's Turkey would be Greek and Armenian, whereas, in fact, they now make up around 0.1 percent of the population.

40. Quoted in Türker, *Vatanım Yok Memleketim Var*, 190.

41. In a speech in Ankara on May 4, 2017, the *Agos* editor in chief Yetvart Danzikyan told of how the "name issue" (the practice of hiding Armenian names in public life and replacing them with Turkish names, such as Vartan with Altan) is still very common among Armenians. On non-Muslim names, see Ender, *İsmiyle Yaşamak*.

42. For a field study on the dual lives of Assyrians and their "adaptation strategies" to Turkishness, see Su Erol's *Mazlum ve Makul*. Erol draws distinctions, for example, between the Assyrians of Mardin and İstanbul. Since the former live in a geography where the dominance of Turkishness is more limited and which has long been their own, they are able to live with less fear; they do not have to live double lives separated by clear boundaries, like those in İstanbul. An Assyrian living in İstanbul describes this fear as follows: "Assyrians are a people who want to feel safe, they are very afraid. . . . For example, I chose an apartment where my next door neighbor is Assyrian, even though it was very expensive. It is impossible to get rid of this fear" (182). Similar to the Assyrians of Mardin, the Christians of Antakya are able to live relatively fearless lives compared to, say, the Christians of Ankara: "I can express my identity very easily in Antakya.

One outside the contract hesitates to speak her mother tongue, to emphasize her ethnic or religious qualities (e.g., through dress), and to speak and write about the contract. Compelled to live meekly, she hides herself as much as possible in the fields and institutions of her professional life. Similarly, she must be excessively wary and prudent in her communication and interaction with individuals inside the Turkishness Contract. Pretending to be Turkish is one manifestation of this wariness and prudence. If she speaks Turkish and avoids mention of matters forbidden by the Turkishness Contract, she may be taken as Turkish, and the relationship can proceed smoothly. An exceptional story from an Assyrian living in İstanbul proves the rule: "Because you live in İstanbul, no one knows about anyone else. If you don't divulge, no one will know. My name doesn't reveal what I am anyhow. You can be more Muslim than a Muslim. I celebrated Eid al-Adha (*Kurban Bayramı*) with a friend who I didn't know was Assyrian, and he didn't know I was Assyrian. The man thought I was a Muslim and said, 'Happy Bayram.' I didn't want to spoil things for him, so I thanked him and said, 'Happy Bayram to you too.' Later, we saw each other in church."[43] An Armenian in Ankara employed the metaphor of a drop in the sea to describe the necessity of changing one's name due to powerlessness and scarcity: "You have to change. They blacklist you. Because you are a drop in the sea."[44] In this context, forms of Turkishness capital such as speaking Turkish well and having a Turkish name offer significant advantages relative to those lacking such capital.[45]

Borrowing Erving Goffman's concept and expanding its scope to some extent, we can conceive of the Turkishness Contract as constituting an *interaction order* that regulates the nature and form of everyday encounters between individuals/bodies.[46] Since the "whole social structure is present in

---

When I went to Ankara, I saw the difference between the Christian community there and here. They cannot address each other by their own names there, they change their names outside. You can wear a Virgin Mary, a cross, here, but not there. Of course, you cannot do this in every part of Antakya, you cannot walk around every neighborhood of Antakya with a cross. It varies from neighborhood to neighborhood, I don't want to name names, but it varies. Some neighborhoods are very conservative, we have no relations with such neighborhoods, we are very good in our neighborhood." Quoted in Doğruel, *"İnsaniyetleri Benzer,"* 249. The relative comfort of non-Muslims in Antakya is partly related to the region's significant Alevi population.

43. Quoted in Koçoğlu, *Azınlık Gençleri Anlatıyor*, 318–319.

44. Quoted in Balancar, *Ankaralı Ermeniler Konuşuyor*, 127.

45. A young Jewish man described, in the 2000s, the difference between himself and his girlfriend: "When my girlfriend and I go out with our friends, she has no trouble fitting in: She doesn't have a foreign name or a Jewish accent and she looks like a Turkish girl. But I have an accent because I speak Spanish [Judeo-Spanish] at home with my parents." Quoted in Brink-Danan, *Yirmi Birinci Yüzyılda Türkiye'de Yahudiler*, 115.

46. Goffman, "Interaction Order," 1–17.

each interaction,"[47] the Turkishness Contract seeps into the interactions of everyday life, giving them shape and color. For example, when someone outside the contract, but with knowledge and a sense of the basic rules of the contract, encounters someone inside the contract, she speaks and acts as if she, too, were inside, thereby minimizing potential personal risks.[48] My point here is that many thoughts, character traits, presentations of self, and body language that might seem personal are, in fact, determined by the Turkishness Contract. Thus, in a conversation between someone inside the contract and someone outside, the speakers are not simply human beings; they are bodies socialized and individuated at the two extremes of a power relation.

Even if one is known to be non-Turkish or non-Muslim, still, if he is meek and leads an unobtrusive life (i.e., if he erases his differences), then Turks can tolerate this. Indeed, this is the function of meekness: to survive and remain standing without attracting attention or garnering reactions. And this state of meekness is often internalized in non-Turks, just as self-confidence and self-righteousness are in Turks. Families and communities teach and inculcate such survival strategies from childhood. Thus, even the most seemingly personal character traits can be historically and socially constructed. As a Greek from Turkey put it, "We often carry out such auto-control upon ourselves. We try not to cause problems. Let's say we went to a restaurant, for example, and the soup is cold. I'd never say 'hey, the soup's cold.' This is a matter of habit for me. And I don't behave differently when I go to Europe. Because this is imprinted on us. We try not to call attention to ourselves, to disturb our surroundings, or create tension. This is my character."[49] An İstanbul Greek who later emigrated to Athens had this to say about the formation of character and the embodiment of Greekness: "When I was six or seven, I was naturally speaking Greek. 'Hush' became second nature to us, and I'm not sure when I became aware of this. It took me about 5–6 years after coming to Greece for me to speak audibly in public spaces. If you notice, Greeks from İstanbul are always rather genial. They speak gently, don't yell too much, refrain from being seen too often in public, and aren't noisy. Why? Because this is unthinking, second nature to them. This feeling runs that deep."[50]

47. Bourdieu, *Language and Symbolic Power*, 67.
48. To be sure, this is not unique to Turkey. For a sociological analysis of the interactions between Norwegians and Lapps in a fjord community in northern Norway, see Eidheim, "When Ethnic Identity Is a Social Stigma," 39–57.
49. Quoted in Koçoğlu, *Azınlık Gençleri Anlatıyor*, 291. Another Greek individual describes a similar state of mind: "As much as possible, we don't get into trouble" (286).
50. Quoted in Türker, *Vatanım Yok Memleketim Var*, 130. One of Nurdan Türker's Greek interviewees said that he was startled when he saw Greek tourists talking loudly in Beyoğlu, which he found outrageous. It was only much later that he realized this was not something crass but

In other words, non-Muslims in Turkey have to learn to be docile, soft, gentle people and to walk softly to minimize the possible risks they may face in interactions with Turks (at work, on the street, in restaurants, in their apartments, at the police station, in military service).[51] If one has not fully learned and internalized this way of being, he will continue to be constantly admonished by his family and community.[52] The various problems he has during encounters with Turks in public life are themselves instructive and allow him to gain experience.

The most extreme form of the internalization of performances of Turkishness among non-Muslims can be observed in cases where one fully embraces Turkishness and truly sees himself as a Turk. In these cases, the non-Muslim still lives a double life; he hides his religious and linguistic qualities in public, confining them to the private sphere. But he perceives this as normal; he thinks this is the way it should be. Consider the response (the logic, the feeling) of an Armenian to a question about the "Citizen Speak Turkish!" campaigns: "The Greeks were taken to task a bit. Not me. Because I wouldn't give them a reason. I wouldn't speak Armenian to an Armenian when a Turk is standing there. It's inappropriate."[53] The best performances of Turkishness depend on the ability to erase differences and to do so with conviction. Later, a Jewish man describes his ability to convincingly accomplish this, and how

---

rather that he had perceived it as such because of the timidity that permeated his own Greekness (131–132).

51. E.g., Rober Koptaş describes the historical relationship between being Armenian and being a good neighbor as follows: "If you live in Turkey, if you are Armenian, if you live in an apartment, what choice do you have but to be a neighbor who is understanding toward your neighbors, who puts up with any problems they may create, who does not make noise, who is clean, tidy, who pays his dues without delay, who comes to the aid of his neighbors? If you have lived for decades with all kinds of harassment of your life and property, if you have been made to feel, and still are made to feel in various ways, that you are a second-class citizen, that you are not trusted, that you are not wanted here, but that you are 'tolerated' and that this is a blessing for you, is there any other way for you to feel at least a little bit comfortable in your living space, in your home, which is your shelter, and in its primary environment, other than being a good neighbor?" ("Yandı bitti kül oldu," available at http://t24.com.tr/yazarlar/komsu/yandi-bitti-kul-oldu,16930).

52. Similar anecdotes are common from other non-Muslims whose mother tongue is not Turkish: "I have a very striking memory. One day on the street I asked my mother something in Greek. 'When are we going home?' 'When are we going to do this?' She shook my hand and got angry with me. 'Shut up, don't speak Greek on the street,' she said. . . . Later, as you grow up, you gradually understand why you can't speak while walking on the street. One always fears." Quoted in Koçoğlu, *Azınlık Gençleri Anlatıyor*, 264. Another anecdote: "There is a state of timidity, uneasiness. Extreme shyness is reflected in behaviors. I especially remember my mother's suggestions: 'When these kinds of issues come up, don't get involved, stay in the background,' and so on. I don't think it has had any obvious impact on my life. But this is perhaps difficult for me to understand. Perhaps it could be a deeper state of unease" (237).

53. Quoted in Koçoğlu, *Hatırlıyorum*, 31.

he was able to be loved almost as if he were a Muslim—how, that is, he could become a real Turk: "I never thought I was different. Everyone at my workplace says to me, 'You are a Muslim Jew.' Because we live together in a society. I think my only difference is my religion. We live in the Republic of Turkey. We live according to the laws and rules of this place. The majority of people is Muslims. You are always around them. I think this integration does away with this difference after a while. If you don't insist on being different, I think it's already gone."[54] Again, an İstanbul Jew underscores an ancient presence in this land. But, presumably knowing this to be insufficient, here homeland is equated to the Turkish language (in which the interviewee thinks and feels): "I told you that my roots in İstanbul go back about 500 years. I have another homeland; it is Turkish. Yes, as a writer, as a thinker, as a translator, I think, speak and feel in Turkish. . . . I walk in the soil of that language in my brain. In other words, both Turkey is my homeland and Turkish is my homeland. I mean, I am utterly Turkish."[55] The way of thinking of another Jewish person, meanwhile, sheds light on the connection between the official state slogan *Ne mutlu Türküm diyene* ("How blessed is one who says I am a Turk") and the performances and efforts of Turkishness: "*Ne mutlu Türküm diyene* is something very meaningful for me. This phrase is something exciting for me. It reminds me that a lot of work needs to be done on this. Atatürk is everywhere and I do this with love and feeling. It's a positive exclamation that I like to say."[56]

It is not my intent here to question the sincerity of these words and thoughts. Rather, I wish to underscore the historicity and sociality of this "sincerity": how the feelings and ideas of Turkishness are shaped through the performances expected of an individual, and how these performances can, in time, become who one is. However, the more Turkified one becomes, that is, the more one internalizes the ideas and feelings of Turkishness, the more likely she is to be disappointed, because even she is reminded from time to time that she is not fully accepted as a Turk. The realization that her love and labor have gone unrequited or have not been adequately reciprocated can lead to feelings of anger and betrayal. Moreover, not only the state but also the society she lives in remind her that her differences are not forgotten, despite all her efforts. An Armenian pointed to this when describing an uncle's life: "He had become ten times more a practicing Muslim than the Kurds there. Why did they do that? I think it was to make him forget himself, to alleviate that pressure, to be able to say, 'Look, we are Muslims now, too.' . . . He prayed so much, he went on pilgrimage, yet still, it wasn't forgotten that he was Armenian."[57] But even if society forgets or ignores, the state does not: "I am a Turk. I'm a Turk from my grandfather's side. I am Christian and Orthodox. What bothers me is that I am not accepted as a Turk in Turkey. If I want to be a garbage man, I can't. I want to be a fireman, but I can't. The state looks at me in a different way because it does not grant me the right to be a civil servant."[58] Another Armenian citizen, despite both ancient ancestry in these lands and a deep corporeal internalization of Turkishness ("having goosebumps"), experienced the sadness of not being seen as Turkish enough. "I am a citizen of the Republic of Turkey of Armenian descent; there are approximately 60,000 people like me in İstanbul. We all do our military service proudly when the time comes. When the National Anthem is played, it gives me goosebumps and fills me with pride, but I wish I had rights on another level. Today, if a Turkish citizen who immigrated to Germany thirty years ago can work in a municipality or a government office, then sometimes I ask myself why I can't, seeing as how I have been in these lands for two thousand years? Why can't I be a captain in the military?"[59] This situation enraged a Jewish citizen: "Shame on those who did not make me chief of general staff. I am no less Turkish than the chief of staff. Would I have been an ambassador? Would I be a representative at NATO or UNESCO? I am a Turkish citizen, my friend. Is my only crime to not be a Muslim Turkish citizen?"[60]

Kurds and Turkishness

As I have stressed a number of times, Islam has been the main port of entry to the Turkishness Contract; if one is a Muslim, one can proceed to Turkishness. This introduces certain differences, in terms of their relationship to Turkishness, between non-Turkish Muslims and non-Muslims.[61] In light of the fact that Turkishness is endowed with material and immaterial privileges and its absence with material and immaterial penalties, millions of Muslims who were not originally Turks converted to Turkishness and became assimilated by adopting the state's assimilation policy. In other words, millions of Muslims stopped being Kurds, Arabs, Circassians, Pomaks, Georgians, Laz, Albanians, or Bosnians. In addition to the many Muslims who have been fully Turkified,

57. Quoted in Balancar, *Diyarbakırlı Ermeniler Konuşuyor*, 9–10.
58. Quoted in Koçoğlu, *Hatırlıyorum*, 125.
59. Quoted in Caymaz, *Türkiye'de Vatandaşlık*, 72.
60. Quoted in Caymaz, *Türkiye'de Vatandaşlık*, 135.
61. However, certain purported physical or linguistic features (being "dark-skinned" or speaking with an accent) can also be used by the dominant group (Turks) as a means of racializing Kurds. See Ergin, "Racialization of Kurdish Identity in Turkey," 322–341.

millions more have been Turkified but nevertheless retain some of their ethnic characteristics, or, those who, even if they want to Turkify, cannot entirely meet the conditions of Turkishness due to a lack of cultural and economic capital (e.g., speaking Turkish with an accent). These individuals are aware that they are outside of Turkishness in certain respects, albeit to different degrees and in different forms. To avoid contempt and exclusion, a combination of negative and positive strategies are employed: concealing, erasing, or making oneself invisible in public life; speaking Turkish; living dual lives. Ayşe Serdar, in her studies on Lazness, describes the strategies of Laz people to assimilate to (and thus reap the benefits of) Turkishness: for example, distinguishing themselves from Kurds, in particular, and, thereby, enjoying the support of the state, or expressing Lazness as a depoliticized cultural identity, within the limits permitted by the state.[62] In a similar vein, Ayhan Kaya analyzes the Circassians' strategies of participation in and assimilation to Turkishness, attending both to a "double discourse" by which they can only emphasize their Circassianness alongside their Turkishness and to double lives wherein Circassianness is confined to private spaces.[63]

In the following section, I attempt to relay something of the experiences of Kurdishness and Turkishness of people who consciously resist or at least try to resist Turkification—that is, who have a certain awareness of Kurdishness in both political and cultural terms, even if some are partially Turkified in cultural terms. This section is largely based on in-depth interviews with Kurds born and raised in different places and working in different fields.[64] What emerges is a picture of differentiated Kurdishnesses according to geography, parentage (namely, whether one's mother is Turkish or not), political views, professions, and social classes. Parallel to this differentiation are shifting relations in interactions with Turkishness and Turks as well as shifting performances and emotions engendered by these interactions. That said, certain commonalities surface as well, across classes, professions, and ideologies.

62. Serdar describes the Turkishness of the Laz and their knowledge of Turkishness: "In sum, 'being Turkish' can be read as an attitude directly linked to enjoying equal citizenship and being sovereign. This is of course reproduced anew every day, in everyday life. The knowledge of where to behave like a Laz and where to behave like a Turk is embedded in habitus, and is embedded in unconscious attitudes, such as the automatization of where to slip into an accent and where to correct it" ("Etnik İlişkiler Bağlamında Lazlığın İnşası," 100–101; also see Serdar's "Making and Unmaking Ethnic Boundaries," 335–369).
63. Kara, *Türkiye'de Çerkezler*, 4–5, 32–35.
64. I interviewed sixteen people in total, fifteen face-to-face and one over email. Only three of my interviewees were women. Because of this imbalance, which I realized too late, I was not able to explore gender dynamics sufficiently.

Earlier, when discussing the double lives of non-Muslims, I noted that the main reason for this is related to their exclusion from the Turkishness Contract as well as to oppression and massacres and to the ensuing forms of fear. The same can be said for many Kurds, for a lot of the same reasons. A religious figure from Iğdır, in his mid-sixties,[65] put it this way: "The personality of every Kurd, *every* Kurd, is behind the scenes, no Kurd's personality is open." According to him, Kurds are "evasive when they speak," "speak differently at the mosque, at school and at home, speak according to the environment," and even tolerate insults against Kurds. The main apparent reason for this is "diffidence," and behind diffidence is the fear of being punished—or rather the awareness that one will be punished for expressing one's true views. For example, according to him, among Kurds, himself included, there is no one like İsmail Beşikçi:[66] "Whatever was in his head, he put it in writing. He never hid his personality behind the curtain."

A fifty-year-old researcher and translator[67] described the double life of Kurds through the concept of "hidden lives":

I can give many examples about hairdressers. These are spaces full of talk, everyone talks a lot, everyone's out-of-the-blue free and easy. But for me this is frustrating. I immediately put up walls. But everything is open to conversation there. They talk about Kurds, about Turkey's politics related to Kurds. You hear so many negative, foulmouthed, offensive, and degrading statements, yet you sit there and keep silent. You already put up your walls. I'd say you automatically put up those walls with your Kurdish identity. What I mean by walls is, let no one ask me a thing, let the conversation not continue. Because either you will expose your true self and get into an argument, or you will stay silent. And because it would be even worse to act like you think like them, the best is to make no contact, to try to cut off the interaction, see?

Shame—specifically, the shame of speaking Kurdish and of not speaking Turkish well—is another emotion that compels Kurds to live double lives, one as strong as the fear of being Kurdish and not being Turkish. Shame and fear are both powerful sources of self-concealment. One is ashamed to speak Kurdish because Kurdish is identified with coarseness; one is ashamed not to

---

65. Male. Interview in Ankara on September 13, 2014.

66. Translator's note: İsmail Beşikçi is a Turkish sociologist who spent more than seventeen years in prison due to his work on the Kurdish issue. See Chapter 4 for more on Beşikçi.

67. Woman. Interview in Ankara on May 24, 2017.

speak Turkish because Turkish is identified with civility.[68] Almost all of my interviewees whose mother tongue is Kurdish described how not knowing Turkish when they first started school led to feelings of inferiority and shame within them, whether their teachers were "good" (democratic/leftist) or "bad" (oppressive/rightist).[69] For example, a lawyer in his fifties, born in one the Kurdish villages outside the central Anatolian city of Konya,[70] stated that although his teacher was very good, learning Turkish later in childhood made him timid and asocial. When his family moved to the city of Konya, he struggled when interacting with Turks and avoided literature and theater groups in secondary school because he was not fluent. A thirty-year-old graduate student born in Malazgirt[71] evaluated his first encounter with the Turkish language and Turkish power, as embodied in the teacher, not in terms of physical violence, which he had seen in his family and was accustomed to, but in terms of psychological violence: "You feel bad, someone is talking there and you don't understand. You see yourself as inferior, you say there is something wrong with me, what am I? You're saying there's something wrong with me, since there can't be anything wrong with him. There's a well-dressed man before you. I would feel very bad, frankly, I would feel inferior. At the beginning I questioned myself because I didn't understand." Timidity and inhibition stemming from a sense of inferiority and inadequacy followed him into his later years: "As you become more aware, as you comprehend the situation, I mean, when you understand why the state is there, why that school is there, you get over it, but there are still psychological effects. I am not comfortable talking to a professor, or anyone else. I'm still like that kid. I cannot fully express myself

---

68. Consider these two accounts of the relationship between language and shame: "Not knowing Turkish is something that can get you belittled and ridiculed, I remember this the most, that even speaking two words of Turkish is a source of happiness. . . . Teaching anything by force, against your will, and making you forget what you knew before, constantly telling you that it is bad, constantly imposing on you that you are inferior, in other words, constantly imposing on you that it is an inferior situation, ultimately makes you become like that thing"; "We are always such an assimilated society, you know, as if Turkish is the important language; Kurdish is a wild, barbaric language." Quoted in Neyzi and Darıcı, *Diyarbakırlı ve Muğlalı Gençler Anlatıyor*, 104, 109.

69. The injury of sorts caused by not knowing Turkish or not knowing it well enough is a state of Kurdishness one often finds in the autobiographical narratives of Kurds. In a field study describing these and similar psychological conditions as "language wounds," a Kurd is quoted as saying: "You can't express yourself, you feel downtrodden, you don't trust yourself. . . . When we were educated in another language, we started to distance ourselves from our own language. . . . We are neither good at Turkish nor Kurdish. We spoke one language on the way home and another on the way to school. There is a disconnect there. Even today I experience the difficulty of this." Quoted in Coşkun, Derince, and Uçarlar, *Dil Yarası*, 46.

70. Male. Interview in Ankara on September 11, 2014.

71. Male. Interview in Ankara on June 3, 2017.

in an environment where Turks are the majority. It's something from elementary school."[72] A professor who has taught at one of Turkey's most liberal universities for nearly thirty years and is fluent in several foreign languages[73] maintains that Kurds are reticent to speak Turkish in front of crowds and that this is related to a sense of childhood shame ("the fear of 'will they laugh?'"): "My heart still beats like so when I speak in public. We don't have the habit of speaking in public, in Turkish."

It seems to me that such timidity can be interpreted as a general state of Kurdishness created by the interlacing of fear and shame—at times fear, at times shame. For example, Kurds avoid speaking Kurdish in public spaces dominated by Turkishness and Turks for fear of getting into trouble. However, they may also avoid speaking Turkish in the same settings because they feel ashamed of not speaking Turkish well enough. The researcher-translator drew attention to this state of "muteness" stemming not from fear, but shame. She told of how an acquaintance from Diyarbakır was embarrassed to say where she wanted to alight from a minibus in Ankara, and instead she got off where another passenger requested. Another acquaintance avoided asking for three (*üç*) or four (*dört*) kilograms of any product at the market, since one raised in Kurdish (which does not employ the vowel sounds "ü" and "ö") may struggle to pronounce these words in an unmarked way.[74]

This sort of shame stems from measuring oneself against the values of the dominant group—that is, against the dominant values of Turkishness. It results from seeing oneself through the eyes of others and judging one's self-worth accordingly. To borrow from Du Bois, Kurds live with a *double consciousness* that evaluates them through the eyes of Turks and is constantly vigilant about how they speak and how they are seen from the outside. In the same context, Bourdieu's description of the physical and linguistic challenges of the petty bourgeoisie, who measure themselves against the values and inclinations of the bourgeoisie, may also shed light on the position of Kurdishness vis-à-vis Turkishness: "Although it is not a petit-bourgeois monopoly, the petit-bour-

---

72. Consider a remarkably similar narrative: "Since I didn't ask questions in primary school, even now at university I prefer to remain silent when a topic is being discussed as long as it doesn't push my buttons. . . . I guess it comes from primary school times." Quoted in Coşkun, Derince, and Uçarlar, *Dil Yarası*, 46.

73. Male. Interview in Ankara on June 30, 2017.

74. Here is one Kurdish woman's experience of shopping in Turkish after coming to a big city as a result of forced migration: "I didn't know anyone, I didn't even know the name of bread in Turkish. . . . I remember one day I learned the name of bread in Turkish, but I didn't know how to ask for it. . . . You have a hard time going outside the house. You don't speak Turkish. You don't know the environment. You're in a strange place. All that you have experienced, all that you know has disappeared. . . . I was sick for a long time. I lost my language." Quoted in Çağlayan, Özar, and Doğan, *Ne Değişti?* 63.

geois experience of the world starts out from timidity, the embarrassment of someone who is uneasy in his body and his language and who, instead of being 'as one body with them,' observes them from outside, through other people's eyes, watching, checking, correcting himself, and who, by his desperate attempts to reappropriate an alienated being-for-others, exposes himself to appropriation, giving himself away as much by hyper correction as by clumsiness."[75]

Further, on the matter of language, the fact that the majority of Kurds are bilingual may, at first glance or theoretically, seem like an advantage. However, this is not the case in practice, since a significant proportion of Kurds begin to forget and can no longer use Kurdish sufficiently well once they learn Turkish. Moreover, the *low market value* of Kurdish also reduces the worth and importance of knowing Kurdish.[76] Nor does the problem end there, as a significant number of Kurds (for various reasons) are unable to learn Turkish well enough or in an accent that is unmarked. Thus, instead of bilingual people, we have people who cannot speak and write adequately and who "do not feel at home" in either language.[77] They are rendered speechless, both literally (as they speak neither language very well) and figuratively (as they avoid speaking out of fear or shame). The aforementioned graduate student described this state of speechlessness as leading not only to basic linguistic confusion but also, and, perhaps, far more significantly, to confused thought: "Confusion of language leads to confusion of thought. I think this is one of the main problems Kurds face. We are not talking about thousands, we are talking about millions."

Language problems also create substantial miscommunication problems between the generations within families. For example, a grandson who has lost his Kurdish cannot communicate with his grandfather and can only partially understand his mother. At the same time, as he was not able to fully learn Turkish, miscommunication marks his public life, and he is unable to advance professionally. The material inequalities generated by all these linguistic situations between Kurds and Turks, often expressed by Kurds through such metaphors as "losing before the game begins," are typically never overcome; they

---

75. Bourdieu, *Distinction*, 207.

76. A Kurdish teacher interviewed by Handan Çağlayan explains the Kurdish language's lack of market value through her students: "But this is the language (Turkish) that works for them. This is our biggest handicap. We can try as hard as we want. . . . As soon as that child starts school, his/her relationship with Kurdish will end, there will be no job opportunities. They don't know where to use Kurdish. . . . Turkish works better for them." Quoted in Çağlayan, *Aynı Evde Ayrı Diller*, 118.

77. As Brubaker et al. note, "Language is a deeply embodied competence, and the experience of speaking 'one's own' language is often associated with a feeling of phenomenological comfort, a sense of being at home in the social world" (*Nationalist Politics and Everyday Ethnicity*, 264).

pursue one throughout life, and in all areas of life (education, work, family). Moreover, for Kurdish students, the first year of their education is often spent learning a foreign language instead of subject matter.[78] For example, a high school teacher from Dersim[79] noted that compared to Turkish students, Kurdish students start school at a disadvantage, and, no matter how hard they work, it is very difficult to close that initial gap. Even if this academic gap, over time, is made up for by working harder than Turks, other gaps may remain open—in job interviews, for instance, for political reasons.

The *eziklik*[80] of Kurds vis-à-vis Turks and how this is mirrored in the behavior and bodies of Kurds came up often in interviews. The teacher just mentioned, from Dersim, went on to describe, in the district of Ankara where he teaches physics, how forcibly migrated Kurdish students from Mardin behave in their interactions with Turkish students: "We educated both of them. And I mean that class dominance is in children of Turkish origin. The other can only assert himself through the use of violence. Or he can do so by entering into shady relationships. . . . He tries to make himself known by bearing the values of Turkish society." He diagnosed and classified Kurds more generally, in a similar manner, arguing that powerlessness, albeit in contrasting forms, has always permeated the Kurdish body: "You feel it in his behavior, in the way he walks in the streets. There are two styles. A significant number of Kurds walk very rigidly. As if to say 'I have the power.' It is actually a disguise of powerlessness. There must be a psychological equivalent. Or he walks very cynically, it reflects in his body, you can see it when you look at him." A sixty-year-old retired primary school teacher from Kars[81] exemplified her ex-husband's *eziklik* as follows: "For example, you go to a restaurant, he waits a long time to ask the waiter for something. He would speak in due time. We are more confident, my relatives would scold the waiter.[82] [My husband] would

---

78. One Kurd described his sense of alienation due to education in a foreign language as follows: "I was scared. I remember being scared. My father took me. You go to school with a language you don't know. I remember entering a different world. Someone was talking but I didn't know what they were talking about. It is a very different language. You don't know anything. So you're sitting there and someone is talking to you. So you can't express that sentence of emotion. Teachers would beat you for speaking Kurdish. You know, you go to any country, you don't know anything and you don't have anyone you know. You don't know the language, you don't know the system, there is no one to hold your hand." Quoted in Neyzi and Darıcı, *Diyarbakırlı ve Muğlalı Gençler Anlatıyor*, 104.

79. Male. Interview in Ankara on June 3, 2017.

80. Translator's note: *eziklik* suggests an internalized sense of inferiority that mainly manifests itself as meekness, timidity, or cowardice. *Ezik*, the word's adjectival root is sometimes used to mean something close to "lame" or "loser." It is arguably best left in the original.

81. Woman. Interview in Ankara on October 21, 2017.

82. Here, she refers to the Turkish side of her family. I address this issue later.

drive a person nuts by the time he asked the waiter for something. . . . He always had an *ezik* side, I attribute this to his Kurdishness." The professor, on the other hand, explained in Kurdish how this timidity stemming from Kurdishness permeated his body: "It's automatic, when you speak Kurdish you immediately lower your voice. When I switch over to Kurdish, as if by bodily habit I lower my voice. The body is used to this, I mean." While explaining this, he leaned over to his friend sitting next to him and spoke very quietly, demonstrating how the body conceals Kurdishness from the outside world.

However, the majority of the men I interviewed attributed Kurdish *eziklik* and timidity, and the resulting forms of self-concealment and double lives, to Kurds *other than themselves*. For example, one interviewee in his sixties, who was born in Bitlis, worked as a laborer in a state office, and was active in the Republican People's Party (as a member of the municipal council and a delegate),[83] expressed the difference between himself and others as follows: "It's *eziklik*, because he can't express himself. It's because he faces constant humiliation that he does such *eziklik*. But as for me, I am proud to say, never!" The graduate student I mentioned earlier emphasized that masculinity can affect the way Kurdish men see and evaluate themselves: "I think most Kurdish men don't talk about these psychological processes and difficulties in order not to appear weak, in order not to weaken their masculinity. It's all about masculinity. He wants to protect his manhood. 4–5 years ago I wouldn't have said these things. I can talk about it more easily now, I think it's about masculinity."[84] This young Kurdish man attributes the change in the way he sees himself to his studies and readings on gender. He started to change, to be more honest with himself and his environment, as he realized that his perception and presentation of self have also been shaped by his masculinity—in other words, as he realized that he measures his self-worth not only in terms of being Kurdish or not being Turkish but also through his masculinity.

---

83. Male. Interview in Ankara on June 6, 2017.

84. The relationship between masculinity and Kurdishness and the wounds Kurdish masculinity has suffered due to Turkish power would make for an intriguing research topic. E.g., a Kurd describes the crisis of masculinity they experienced due to the collapse of gender roles in their family as follows: "I really think that in this process, masculinity, that patriarchal vein of Kurds, has really taken a beating, in other words, it has been really offended. The same with women. Imagine, for example, he pushes my mother, he searches her, I mean, imagine how much the man is hurt in such a thing. That man who was raised with patriarchal codes, who has a traditional attitude, is actually experiencing incredible shame. It's that *ezik* state of not being able to do anything. . . . For example, when people leave after such a [police] search, they [family members] can't talk to each other for hours, because both are ashamed, it's difficult for both of them, they are aware that they have taken on a role other than their normal daily roles. My father seemed quite *ezik* to me too, for example, I felt that." Quoted in Neyzi and Darıcı, *Diyarbakırlı ve Muğlalı Gençler Anlatıyor*, 63.

Interviewees agreed, significantly, that Turkishness provides privileges and advantages in professional life.[85] For example, the lawyer said that it was impossible to progress to a judgeship or to the prosecutor's office as a Kurd if one remained a Kurd, even if this were not strictly true for practicing law. The teacher from Dersim described how, despite a very successful educational background, he "could only become a teacher" and could not progress further to become an academic. A minor contractor born in Bitlis, working in construction,[86] said that Kurds were not able to win large state tenders and often did not even bother. According to the religious figure from Iğdır, "If you insist on Kurdishness, you can't move forward." In the opposite situation, that is, when a Kurd advances in a certain field, a number of interviewees interpreted this as Turkification, using such phrases as "losing one's soul," "betraying Kurdishness," "pledging allegiance to the state," or "converting to their religion." The religious figure summed up the difference in privilege between Turks and Kurds as follows: "A Turk is always at an advantage. He has no disadvantages, only disadvantages stemming from one's personality, backwardness, or poverty. But a Kurd is always at a disadvantage. Even if he is the President, he has to present himself as a Turk." "In a sense, the state is buying them," noted the lawyer, describing Kurds advancing in various fields (adding that he may have put this somewhat harshly). The Kurd from Bitlis mentioned earlier saw this self-abnegation as quite common among wealthy Kurds living in nice neighborhoods in Ankara—he called them "Milan Kurds, Paris Kurds"—who "camouflage" themselves and pretend to be Turkish.

A major contractor I interviewed, a man in his seventies[87] who grew very wealthy, rising to the top of the economic ladder, is an interesting case in point. His family was forced to move from their village to the city center because of relatives who had participated in one of the Kurdish uprisings before the 1940s. "We were like Syrian refugees today," he says, to describe the hardships and poverty they faced. When he was eighteen, his father sold a cow and sent him to Ankara to study. As a student, he says, he could think of little else but "what can I do to avoid going hungry?" At first, like other Kurds, he was timid and hung-up ("Kurds are *ezik* and hung-up because of state oppression, they see themselves as second class. . . . Turks also have a superiority complex. Just as Sunnis have a superiority complex over Alevis, Turks

---

85. An interviewee from Kars, who speaks Turkish without a marked accent and, in his own words, "looks Turkish" from the outside, explained to me that one of the most important advantages of being Turkish is that "there are no extra problems": "I didn't have a problem, I didn't have an extra problem. Work is easier."

86. Male. Interview in Ankara on June 6, 2017.

87. Male. Interview in Ankara on February 4, 2015.

have one over Kurds"), but, over time, overcoming difficulties and growing stronger, he "got over [his] hang-ups." Although he believes (and, indeed, knows it to be the case) that Turkishness is a great advantage in the business world, he emphasized that, as he became stronger, he "embraced his Kurdishness" and "made people accept his Kurdish identity." That said, he was quick to add that he is an exception; other Kurdish businessmen hide their Kurdishness and say, "At most, 'I am from the East.'" Despite all the psychological and material disadvantages of Kurdishness, he attributes his great success in the business world to his "personal skills" and "very healthy relationships." He also thinks that his significant ambition came into play and wonders if this ambition may be related to his hang-ups stemming from his Kurdishness: "Maybe if we weren't so *ezik*, I wouldn't be so ambitious."

But while ambition may play a part in an individual's exceptional success, it lacks explanatory power in sociological terms. Otherwise, it would be necessary to attribute the prominence of Turks (who are, on the whole, much more successful in all areas of social life) to ambition and hard work, and the failure of Kurds (who struggle to advance) to lack of ambition and laziness. Indeed, such explanations are not uncommon in popular discourse on Turkishness and Kurdishness. In fact, there is an element of truth in this statement, though here, as is often the case in how dominant groups perceive the world, cause and effect are confused when assessing a lack of ambition. Not only does this way of thinking allow one to look down on Kurds; it also makes the dominant group feel superior, thinking that they have earned their position (through hard work or talent). But the absence of ambition, especially its widespread absence, has to be read as a historical and social product. Individuals belonging to certain social groups learn to curtail their desires from a young age, internalizing the idea that certain professions and fields are not suitable for or compatible with them or are out of their depth. For example, a Kurdish restaurant owner in Konya[88] said that, whereas he continued in his studies because he had a Turkish mother and thus spoke fluently, the majority of his primary school friends whose mother tongue was Kurdish cut short their education on the idea that "it would not pave the way for us anyway, what would happen anyhow if we studied." The lawyer, a Kurd from Konya, said that his daughter, born and raised in Ankara, wants to study international relations and become a diplomat, but he thinks that she will be punished for his political background and her (Kurdish) name. Fearing that she "will get nowhere in that field," he is trying to steer her toward another area of interest, psychology. Thus, behind the student's choice of psychology over diplomacy is not a

---

88. Male. Interview in Ankara on September 6, 2014.

lack of ambition but rather a social and historical logic, whereby Kurdishness colors and delimits aspirations. A Turk can aspire to be a president, a diplomat, a judge, a professor; a Kurd cannot aspire to these because he knows that the condition for attaining these positions is leaving his Kurdishness behind. Indeed, there are countless examples in Turkish history of Kurds who abandoned their Kurdishness and rose to the top of social and political life. An academic in his forties whom I interviewed in Diyarbakır[89] described Turkishness, in this sense, as a "centralized examination system." According to him, to succeed in this exam, the rules are clear: "One must set out on this path without any internal struggle, to live accordingly, to build a life accordingly, and to work hard. This chosen life determines one's life, relationships, way of thinking, and emotional life."

The price for not giving up one's Kurdishness is mandatory adaptation and the curtailing of one's ambitions and desires. Moreover, even if one wishes to Turkify, she may be confronted with the Kurdish past of her mother or father; the decision of whether to Turkify transcends the individual. In this context, the restaurant owner from Konya described raising one's children as Turks and never mentioning Kurdishness to them as the best way to ensure their success. In fact, he says, many Turks who have reached certain positions today learned much later of their Kurdish origins (these are in addition, he adds, to the many who know but conceal their Kurdishness). That said, a significant number of my interviewees held that no matter how much you Turkify, the state does not forget Kurdishness and may one day confront you with it.

Another point that my interviewees agreed on was the role of differences in material and psychological power in coloring interactions between Kurds and Turks across a range of fields—differences that Turks reportedly do not appreciate or simply ignore. It is reasonable to assume that such differences in power come down to the fact that Turks have a state, and Kurds do not. Indeed, none of the Kurds I interviewed see the Turkish state as their state. Consider the teacher from Dersim: "There is still a lack of self-confidence when we confront the state. You can't see it like you do, for example, when you enter an institution, you can't enter thinking 'it's mine.' Even when they see your place of birth [e.g., on one's ID card] it's enough to create a perception about you." There is a deep awareness among Kurds that the environs and institutions of daily life are dominated by Turks. And this awareness largely structures their behavior in these environs and institutions. A Kurd's behavior is structured, then, not only by some abstract sense of statelessness or fear of a lack of state protection but also by the power relations of the spe-

---

89. Male. Interview in Diyarbakır on April 9, 2016.

cific institutions in which one is embedded. Which is to say that Kurdish behavior is also shaped by a lack of institutions. The graduate student mentioned earlier describes a sense of "institutionlessness," even in one of the most liberal environments in Turkey, and characterizes institutions as a "theater of Turkishness." "To tell you the truth, everywhere that Turks control is like a theater of Turkishness to me. It's as if you have to take on the role of a Turk, to speak you have to be a Turk. Maybe this is something I made up. If you're a Turk, you can speak, you can express yourself. As a Kurd, you can't speak. I feel that my words are worthless." A teacher from Midyat, nearly sixty years old,[90] attributed his daughter's lack of Kurdish culture—she married a man from the eastern Black Sea district of Hemşin—not to her marriage but to the Turkishness of institutions: "The other side is very organized, the state. It has schools, education, newspapers, movies, it is active in every way. You have nothing. We carry Kurdishness as our heritage, but I could not pass it on to most of my children."

As most of my interviewees were leftists who move in leftist circles, their observations on interactions with leftist Turks made up an important part of the interviews. All noted both that Turkish leftists did not discriminate against them on the basis of their Kurdishness and that Turkish-leftist attitudes on the Kurdish issue were far more progressive than those of other groups in Turkish society and across the political spectrum. Still, interviewees also noted, at times angrily, that many of the acts and thoughts of leftists were colored by Turkishness. There is a fundamental reason for this anger, as far as I have observed: not feeling understood and being "looked down upon" by the very person you thought would understand. The graduate student remarked: "It's worse with them [leftists] because you expect something from them, you expect them to understand." About certain Marxists and Marxist groups, he continued, "They use Marxism as a weapon against us, they cast a veil over Kurdistan through Marxism." The current example he had in mind was Rojava: "Regarding Rojava, the Marxists say, 'You are working with America, you receive support from there,' and they try to attack us from there. It's such a shaky understanding. When we ask, 'Then why don't you support us?' . . . If the Turks help, why wouldn't the Kurds accept it? They'd love to." The lawyer described how he had criticized, for example, the fact that the penal code and the civil code are designated as the Turkish Penal Code and the Turkish Civil Code, or that judges sometimes state "on behalf of the Turkish nation" when reading their rulings. Yet, this criticism was not taken seriously by Turkish-leftist lawyers and was dismissed as trivial. He said that,

---

90. Male. Interview in Ankara on May 30, 2017.

when he raised the matter of including statements on the Kurdish issue in the written proceedings of the bar association elections, some leftists objected, citing the bar's status as a professional organization. The religious figure from Iğdır said that Turkish and Kurdish Islamists, clerics, and religious orders have always sided with the Turkish state and the state religion ("everyone who calls himself a Muslim is responsible for the Kurdish issue and is an accomplice of the state. These Muslims, who are so denialist, so guarded about the Kurdish issue"). "Conscientious" Turkish socialists, he continued, should be given their due and have helped the Kurds a great deal. He described the debt that this fact imposes on him, saying, "He who denies the truth is the speechless devil." Nevertheless, he added, he had heard objections, from time to time, from some of his socialist acquaintances—"What do you want, what do you lack?"—whom he characterized as "socialists who do not know real socialism."

What explains this insufficient understanding and support from leftists? The professor introduced earlier, who identified as a social democrat, employed the metaphor of a vein to explain why his close friends at university, Marxist professors, rejected the Kurdish movement and showed little interest in the Kurdish question: "The regime pierces the vein. . . . Every Turk has a national vein." The graduate student underscored, among other causes, inequality between Kurds and Turks: "We know that we are not equal wherever we are, not even in leftist environments. No leftist in this country has experienced what I have experienced. Who is ashamed of their language and culture?"[91] The lawyer attributed this to the tendency of Turkish leftists to preserve their comfort ("a conformist ease") and privileges. The teacher from Dersim observed much the same, if in different terms:

The people we struggle alongside [leftists] do not discriminate against you because of your ethnic identity. But there is a logic to it: he defines your fight, your struggle, through nationalism. There is the question of how open the left is to radical change. This is the reason behind not putting the Kurdish issue on the agenda. They don't embrace Kobani the way they embraced Gezi. . . . They don't dare to confront the tyrannical state. He sets the limits of his own struggle with you. He sets the limits of how far he is able to struggle against the state. In

---

91. Similar stories are often told by Kurdish children. E.g., "There is a huge difference between a child here and a child in the west. He's lived here, he has experienced things. He has seen more than his age. Let's say a 20-year-old boy in the West and a 7-year-old boy here, he hasn't seen anything like him. The children here are surrounded by fire, by the war. But there is no such thing there, no such problem." Quoted in Tuzcuoğlu, *Ben Bir Taşım*, 67.

theory, he knows that you are right. But he sets limits to his own struggle. He doesn't put it like this, of course. Because then he would stray from socialism.

A Kurd from Nusaybin employed in a municipality in Ankara[92] detected a "big brother complex" in many Turkish leftists and leftist organizations, which precludes them from recognizing the development of the Kurdish movement. Whatever the Kurdish movement does, they label it as nationalism. When I asked him to explain what he meant by big brother, he replied: "I mean a part of the leftist movement in Turkey. There is an understanding that 'we will spearhead socialism, women's equality, the rights of laborers, whatever values there are on the left.'" The teacher from Kars described big brother leftists in similar terms: "There is a perception that Kurds cannot do it alone, and that's there for Turkish leftists, too. There is arrogance among the leftists too. I don't mean to say that Kurds did everything right. I am very critical of the Kurdish movement." A trade unionist and researcher in her fifties whom I interviewed[93] noted, with a caution stemming from her sociological training, that the Turkish/Kurdish distinction can be misleading, as class differences generate multiple Turkishnesses and Kurdishnesses. Nevertheless, reflecting on her years in academia, she attributed the attitude of a leftist professor (who had always thought of herself as a "principal") to "Turkishness as a position, not as an ethnic identity." The big brother issue also came up spontaneously in correspondences with a devout Kurd:[94] "The discourse of 'Ummah/Ummahism' by Turkish Islamists has been used even to prevent Kurds from defending their most basic rights. . . . Sometimes there are even attempts to denigrate someone for speaking Kurdish through this discourse. Many Islamic groups have banned speaking Kurdish in their dormitories. The concept of 'brotherhood' most commonly resorted to has never included 'equality,' it always conveyed a sense of hegemony. The expression 'we are brothers' actually means that we will be your 'big brother,' and in their perception, a 'big brother' is always dominant." Analogies such as big brother and teacher are tied to the paternalism often observed in individuals belonging to dominant groups.

The researcher-translator thinks that even in friendships between leftists, Kurdishness and Turkishness can be divisive. A wish to not upset things defines the boundaries of a relationship:

---

92. Male. Interview in Ankara on June 3, 2017.
93. Woman. Interview in Ankara on October 26, 2014.
94. Male. Interview dated February 11, 2014 (email).

For example, your friend is very close to you, she thinks like you, I mean, you can easily share even your most radical thoughts with her, she agrees or understands, even if she doesn't agree, she understands, she puts what you say into perspective, but in that person's circle beyond you, there are settings you never take part in, that you are not included in. Almost all Turkish friends have this. Because . . . she has a wider circle around her that is not like her or she has a family environment, a business environment, and your entering that environment will disrupt her balance with them. . . . I mean, for example, if she takes me to such a setting, let's say a business environment, she should include me in it, she should reflect what kind of a person I am, and if she doesn't, it would be unfair to me. I mean, say, '[my friend] is a translator, she translated such and such books.' But when she says this, she disrupts things in that setting, and her relationship with me is disrupted. She will reflect me as I am, she will back me up. But she can't back me up everywhere, she has to keep this job. She has to behave in a way that is not herself, and this is something that unsettles everything, that upsets the balance, that upsets her relationship with me, that upsets her relationship with them.

The same person also talked about Kurdish-Turkish interactions and, related to that, intermarriage. She said that she did not intend to marry, but that, if she did, she would never marry a Turk, because in Kurdish-Turkish marriages, it is always Kurds who lose culturally and who are disregarded: "A Kurd has almost no identity. Kurdish culture, language, ways of living, [for example] if the parents come from the Kurdish side, they have no opportunity to make their presence known. They are as invisible as possible. One lives by the culture of the Turk. There isn't a single thing about Kurdish culture. For example, if a Turk marries a European or an African . . . the culture, characteristics, parents, favorite music of the person he or she marries, a Turk who marries such a person talks about such a marriage as an honor, and is praised for this. But when she marries a Kurd, she never, ever, ever talks about the Kurd. Nothing about a Kurd becomes a part of that marriage."

After hearing these reflections on Kurdish-Turkish marriages,[95] which I had not really considered before, I spoke both with a female interviewee

---

95. It is often stated by politicians and nationalist social scientists that inter-Muslim marriages are one of the most important elements holding the nation together. E.g., Kemal Karpat (*Osmanlı Nüfusu*, 17) believes that one of the factors uniting Anatolian Muslims from different ethnic backgrounds is their common family structure. According to Karpat, while Muslim families marry among themselves, they do not want to unite with, say, a French family. Evren Dayar

whose mother's side is Turkish and who married a Kurd and with three male interviewees who married Turks about their experiences. The father's side of the teacher from Kars is one of the leading Kurdish tribes in the region. Her mother's side is part Turkish, part Azerbaijani. She explains that there have always been problems between her father's and mother's sides of the family because Kars Azerbaijanis consider themselves to be "true Turkish" (*öz-Türk*). When she was young, although Azerbaijanis were a minority in terms of population, they were economically stronger and considered themselves culturally superior to Kurds. She also said, "There is this idea that Azerbaijanis are right-wing and Kurds are left-wing." In such a mixed family structure, she was only able to learn her mother tongue, Turkish. Nor did her father make any effort to teach her Kurdish. She describes herself: "I am a person without an identity. If my mother tongue were Kurdish, if I had lived as a Kurd, I might have thought differently. For me, Turkishness and Kurdishness were never important, but I felt more Kurdish. When there is a debate about Kurds, I defend my Kurdish side." Her children from her marriage to her Kurdish cousin were not given Kurdish names and were not taught to speak Kurdish. Her husband, she said, did not want—was, in fact, frightened of having—Kurdish names for the children, though she herself very much wanted this.

The teacher from Dersim had significant marital problems, at least at first, having married a woman from a conservative Sunni family from Kayseri: "We didn't have a normal marriage. They wouldn't even allow us to come and ask for [their daughter's hand]. Because of both Kurdishness and Alevism. They would say, 'I will never give my child to an easterner.'" Although their relationship later settled down somewhat, there seems to have been a power struggle over naming their children. The father gave his first daughter a Kurdish name, but the grandmother and grandfather never use her Kurdish name, preferring Yağmur instead. Their second daughter was given a Kurdish and a Turkish name, suggesting an atmosphere of negotiation between the families. But, here too, while the family always calls their daughter by her Kurdish name, the grandmother and grandfather avoid the Kurdish name in favor of her Turkish name, Damla. On the issue of culture, the teacher from Dersim

---

("Antalya'da Girit Göçmenleri," 64–73) criticizes Karpat's thesis by showing that Cretan Muslims who migrated to Antalya married only among themselves for a long time. Something similar to what Karpat said was also said in the 1910s by Gökalp ("Türkleşmek, İslamlaşmak, Muasırlaşmak," 48): "A Turk can give his daughter to an Arab, an Albanian, a Kurd, a Circassian, but never to a Finn or a Christian Hungarian; he cannot take the daughter of a Buddhist Mongol or a shamanic Tunguz without Islamizing them." In 1923, Gökalp ("Türkçülüğün Esasları," 269) also emphasized a vital function of the family: "Families are the cells of this social entity [nation, homeland] and professional groups are its limbs." For a discussion of how the nation-state enters into the "privacy" of the family, see Balibar, "Nation Form," 86–106.

described his children as politically close to the Kurdish movement but as culturally Turkified and unable to speak Kurdish.

For a Kurd from Nusaybin who married a Turk from Trabzon, a disagreement surfaced between the two families over the names of children: the Turkish side of the family never uses the children's Kurdish names. But, though they have Kurdish names, the children do not speak a word of Kurdish. The father from Nusaybin described two situations, both of which he saw as leading to Turkification. In one, the mother is Kurdish, and the father is Turkish; state ideology and nationalism predominate, and the children are thus Turkified. In the other, the mother is Turkish, and the father is Kurdish, as in his case; the mother/child relationship naturally leads to Turkification. This, to him, confirms the fact that Kurdish/Turkish marriages necessarily produce cultural Turkification. He also drew on his own experience to illustrate how such marriages entail not only cultural and political struggles but economic ones as well: "After she married me, my father-in-law started selling his land. When I joined this family, his friends started talking, saying these lands would all go to a Kurd."

The Kurd from Bitlis confirms that in his marriage with a Turkish "officer's daughter," the children were culturally Turkified, owing to the influence of the mother. Nevertheless, he says he has never regretted this marriage and would marry the same person again. To state, "I would not marry a Turk," would, he feels, "reek of nationalism." He also underscores that he has never been met with any negative words or behavior from his wife's military father, who, to his estimation, is a very democratic person. That said, he had significant problems with his wife's uncles, especially at the beginning; they kept asking his wife's father, "Where did you find this Kurd?" My interviewee attributed the uncles' attitude to their Circassianness. Indeed, throughout the interview he repeatedly stated that Turkism in Turkey and the oppression of minorities stemmed not from "real and native Turks" but from Caucasian and Balkan immigrants. "In this country, non-Turks engage more in Turkism. For example, those who come from the Balkans and Caucasus are more Turkist. The true owners of this country are the Turks, and they never, ever have such a hang-up. But those who come from elsewhere, in order to prove themselves. . . . The real owners of this country are the concierge, the tea seller, the custodian. The real Turks of this country do not benefit." My interviewee's relative, the minor contractor, repeatedly made it clear through his facial expressions that he agreed with this strong and negative stereotype of immigrant Muslims. When it was his turn to speak, for example, after recounting an argument he had with a Bulgarian immigrant, he said, "You don't have two drops of blood in this country [but] you came and got the best lands, the best jobs, the best salaries." When his daughter wanted to marry a Turk, this contractor looked into the man's family. Satisfied that they were "Turcoman" and not immigrants, he decided to "give his daughter away."

These two relatives from Bitlis repeatedly emphasized, without my prompting, that the real owners of this country are those Kurds and Turks who shed blood and were martyred together for this country. The real problems stem, they posit, from those immigrants who later became Turks, and who, through Turkification, took over the state and enjoyed all manner of privileges. They emphasized often that Kurds and Turks are brothers and sisters, and that, were it not for the interference of the state, immigrants, and imperialism, there would never have been, nor would there ever be, any problems between them. Keeping in mind that one of these two Kurds is a card-carrying member of a major national political party, and the other is a businessman, we can assume that such a discourse of brotherhood grew out of a strategy of integration that shifts blame to the outside *and* exonerates the inside. Indeed, the metaphors of brotherhood and family surfaced repeatedly in other interviews, though, tellingly, such metaphors took on more negative tones the less someone had contact with mainstream Turkish society and politics. For example, regarding the rhetoric of "we are brothers of a thousand years," the restaurant owner said that Turks never ask, "What do I have and what does my brother lack?" For the religious figure, according to Islam, "those who believe are brothers," whereas in Turkey, they say, "We are brothers if you believe in us."[96] For the lawyer, the father discriminates between his children, which "has a very bad effect on a child."

Across classes, professions, ideologies, and genders, my interviewees further agreed that the Kurdish movement had, since the 1980s, empowered Kurds psychologically and politically. This empowerment, they maintained, is evidenced in the behavior and attitudes of Kurds, from those living in Turkish provinces to the remotest villages of Kurdistan. The major contractor pointed to Abdullah Öcalan, rather than the movement as a whole, as the agent of

---

96. According to Mücahit Bilici, Turkish superiority complexes and teacher complexes are mirrored in Kurdish childhood complexes and student complexes. Kurds are afraid of being labeled as racists, Kurdists, or nationalists because they need the approval, acceptance, and affection of their "Turkish teachers." The most respectable way to get rid of these stigmas is to become a leftist or an Islamist: "The Kurd had to become leftist and Islamist because he could not be Kurdish. These ideologies, both of which are universalist in relation to being Kurdish, would provide Kurds with the opportunity to at least . . . not be Turkish . . . in an environment where it was no longer possible to be Kurdish." Bilici makes a similar observation about Armenians: "In the end, the Armenian cannot be an equal human being. Because he cannot be a Turk. That is why he is doomed to be a very good person, to spread goodness. . . . He is obliged to be a good person, because he can only achieve Turkishness through humanity" (*Hamal Kürt*, 14, 55, 107–108).

this empowerment, whom he said, "made the biggest reform." He summed up Öcalan's contribution: "Öcalan's statement, 'I gave the Kurds a personality' is true." The graduate student thinks similarly about the relationship between the Kurdish liberation movement and self-confidence and adds, "removing shame, making you feel that you are human," to Öcalan's contributions: "Kurds want to rise in every field. This wasn't so before. This is about self-confidence, as I said, we used to be ashamed, but the new generation is not ashamed of being Kurdish. For example, one's name is Turkish on the ID card, but on Facebook she writes her name in Kurdish, so she is not ashamed." Drawing on his own experience, the teacher from Dersim describes the relationship between the Kurdish movement and the demand for self-assertion and recognition as follows: "It gave us a chance to express ourselves more clearly. In the past we weren't able to take a stand against the state. But with the Kurdish movement, we became insistent. So there was a need to not back down, to state with persistence 'this is who I am.' It gives us strength. I feel stronger with it. You believe that they can organize you, take a stand against something imposed on you. And you see they do. . . . This is not a power to dominate. I'm talking about a demand to be accepted for who you are." The Kurd from Nusaybin said that through the "Kurdish struggle," there was less oppression, and that even in villages the state does not oppress people as it used to ("it is not like that anymore, people oppose, they don't bow down"). The Kurd from Bitlis believed it was to the PKK's (Partiya Karkerên Kurdistanê or the Kurdistan Workers' Party) credit that Kurds have begun to feel that "there is a power behind [us]"; the PKK "gives strength and confidence," a "wonderful effect." His relative, the minor contractor, noted that the PKK has transformed even Islamic conservative Kurds, such that this group now makes up the majority of the Kurdish movement's support base. The lawyer emphasized that the Kurdish movement has prevented assimilation and awakened the Kurdish people to this threat. Otherwise, he thinks, assimilation could have been entirely successful in the era of globalization, and Kurdish culture could have disappeared. My interviewee from Kars, a feminist, drew attention to the emancipation and empowerment of women: "It had a great impact on women. They developed self-confidence. They became stronger. They became valuable as women, they rose to many positions. Kurdish women becoming mayors, MPs."

Insofar as the rise of the Kurdish movement has empowered Kurds, Kurdishness ceases to be a source of shame and oppression, transforming into a source of pride and solidarity. Consequently, Kurds no longer assess themselves through the eyes of Turks or measure their self-worth in terms of Turkishness; they begin to shed the influences of double consciousness. Such a transformation in mind is naturally reflected in the body; bodies are freed from timidity. Moreover, the Kurdish movement has also entailed the economic and political empowerment of Kurds—a psychological empowerment of sorts accompanying material empowerment. Consequently, the market value of Kurdishness and the Kurdish language has, to some extent, grown. The benefits of Kurdishness, one can say, are not only immaterial but material, and interest in Kurdishness seems to be on the rise.[97]

The results of all these changes—Kurds taking pride in themselves and their culture, gradually shedding their timidness and oppression, emerging from hidden lives, not only growing more visible but desiring more visibility and recognition, demanding increased rights, ascending in various fields of social and political life—are not limited to the empowerment of the Kurds. This relative political, economic, and psychological empowerment of Kurds has also led to a relative weakening of Turks. Turks and those who abide by the Turkishness Contract have, to some extent, lost their power in various areas of life, including naturalized immaterial monopolies and privileges such as normality or righteousness; monopolies over how history is written; monopolies over defining, naming, and giving value; and the power to not see, not hear, and not care. All these losses, which amount to a weakening in power, have set in motion a large-scale crisis of Turkishness, which, though taking many forms, has undoubtedly registered with intensity and spread gradually. In the Conclusion of this book, I take up this dual process: the empowerment of the Kurds and the ensuing crisis of Turkishness.

---

97. One of Çağlayan's interviewees describes this transformation: "Some people who didn't know Kurdish until now, some people who didn't care, some people who don't care much about identity, are going to Kurdish courses. Because they think that Kurdish now brings money. . . . They are learning Kurdish. Because it will be useful for them tomorrow. . . . Learning it well won't bring any loss. It might even bring gains. In the past, it used to be profitable to know an additional foreign language, right? Now Kurdish is the second foreign language." Quoted in Çağlayan, *Aynı Evde Ayrı Diller*, 124.

4

The Crisis of Turkishness

So far, I have distinguished between two states of Turkishness: positive states, or certain ways of seeing, hearing, knowing, feeling, and caring; and negative states, certain ways of not seeing, not hearing, not knowing, not feeling, and not caring. In practice, of course, these states are inextricably bound. One comes to not see, hear, know, feel, and care in certain ways by seeing, hearing, knowing, feeling, and caring in certain ways. Similarly, because one does not see, hear, know, feel, or care about certain things, he sees, hears, knows, feels, and cares about certain other things in certain ways. Both the positive and negative states of Turkishness play a vital role in the reproduction of the Turkishness Contract within which they are formed—namely, the contract's relations of power and mechanisms of privilege. But, in terms of the continuity of the contract, the negative states are, in my view, more vital. They ensure that the Turkishness Contract be respected and not violated. They are also privileges; only the dominant group in a country has the right and the power to not see, not hear, not know, not feel, and not care. The dominant group does not concern itself with the powerless or with those outside the contract; it has the power to do so, and loses nothing thereby. Melissa Steyn's reflections on apartheid apply just as well to the Turkish context of ignorance deriving from the power to ignore: "Part of the privilege of being white was that one could choose not to hear, not to know."[1]

---

1. Steyn, "Whiteness Just Isn't What It Used to Be," 9.

Yet, since the second half of the 1960s, Turkishness has been in a state of crisis, intensifying and expanding into the present. This crisis is tied to the unsustainability of the negative states of Turkishness. And behind this unsustainability are the struggles and the forms of resistance of those outside the contract and the emergence of modes of power of their own making, capable of chipping away at the history of silence and invisibility. This power, forged out of struggle and resistance, has rendered not seeing, not hearing, not knowing, not feeling, and not caring difficult, if not, increasingly, impossible.

Seeing things and people not previously seen, heard, known, felt, or cared about has the potential to generate new forms of seeing, hearing, knowing, feeling, and caring. One may begin to feel shame, guilt, or responsibility for those beyond the contract, for instance, or shame, guilt, or responsibility for one's own self and identity, having realized, for the first time and in earnest, how one's self and identity has been constituted. In other words, the development of certain moral sentiments enables the radius of morality to expand to include those outside the contract. And because the transformation of someone inside the contract may result in her opposition to both the Turkishness Contract and the Contract of Indifference (which is its moral form), punishment and exclusion from the contract is a very likely result.

Yet, the resistance and visibility of those outside the contract may also induce greater intellectual and emotional rigidity among those inside the contract. A powerful challenge unsettles the world of knowledge and emotion to which they are accustomed—in which they feel like a fish in the water—and is registered as a loss of power by the dominant group. Before all else, this counterforce, in declaring that the world is not what the dominant group knows and thinks, chips away at the monopoly over symbolic power, over the act of defining, that was once the province of Turks—that is, the power to determine what is to be described and known and in what way, what is good or bad, what is valuable or worthless, what is right or wrong. Losing a monopoly over definition and valuation, Turks become themselves the object of definition and valuation. In other words, those at the top, no longer able to control and manage the gaze and speech of those at the bottom, experience the *shock of being seen*. All of this can elicit deep reactance and generate new mechanisms of escape and defense whereby those at the top try to avoid having to confront alternative information and feelings. For example, one may attempt to regain a sense of self-confidence and righteousness by amplifying anger toward those outside the contract. Deep suspicion of any new information coming from outside the contract and the production of new knowledge to counter this threatening alternative information are part of the same process.

In either case, whether creative transformation or reactionary backlash, at stake is the same crisis of Turkishness. As those outside the contract lay bare the nature of the Muslimness and Turkishness Contracts, those within are impelled to respond to this challenge; ignorance is no longer possible. The challenge is the cause of the crisis, and the stronger the challenge, the deeper the crisis. When and how, then, did the crisis of Turkishness begin? Which groups first registered its effect? How did these effects grow over time into a mass phenomenon? What sorts of change and transformation has the crisis given rise to in Turks? What forms of political discourse, what individual strategies, and what defense mechanisms have been developed and deployed to deal with the crisis? Is it not only Turkishness but also the Turkishness Contract that is now in crisis? I analyze these questions later, exploring and exposing how Turkishness, as a historical formation, continues to shift in time.

In the first section, I trace the historical contours of the crisis in terms of political and ideological affiliations. I then turn to the effects of this social crisis at the level of the individual, focusing on academics and intellectuals to better understand the transformative power of this crisis. Why academics and intellectuals? The erosion of the privilege of Turks to not know and not care is, to my mind, one of the most important causes of the crisis. Looking at academics and intellectuals, who simply work with knowledge more often and (possibly) with more intensity than much of the rest of society, may help bring into sharper relief the effects of this crisis.

Kurdish Empowerment, Turkish Crisis

From the late 1930s to the 1960s, the Kurdish geographies within Turkey's borders were largely quiet. Alevi Kurdistan was, in a sense, conquered anew through the suppression of the Kocgiri Rebellion in 1921 and the Dersim Operation of 1937–1938; so was Sunni Kurdistan, through suppression of the 1925 Sheikh Said Rebellion and the 1930 Ağrı Rebellion. Military responses led to thousands being killed and internally displaced, burnt villages, and the international exile of many Kurds. After the 1930s, the atmosphere was one of fear and silence, which went on for roughly two decades until a number of historical shifts in the mid- to late 1950s prompted change: the partial democratic opportunities brought about by the transition to multiparty life, the revival of the Barzani movement in Southern Kurdistan, and the emergence of a less traumatized generation of Kurdish intellectuals with no direct experience of the physical violence of the 1920s and 1930s. Kurdish intellectuals organized their own meetings, followed world politics closely, contacted Kurds in exile, and wrote articles and poems for a range of publications. The Democratic Party government, worried by the gains of the Barzani movement in Iraq and fearing its repercussions in Turkey, sought to thwart any new Kurdish awakening by arresting 50 Kurdish intellectuals[2] known as "the 49."[3] Nevertheless, an awakening gained momentum in the years following the military coup of May 27, 1960. The pluralistic and emancipatory political environment of the 1960s, unprecedented in the history of Turkey, set the stage for a range of new modes of Kurdish political engagement and organization. It was in the 1960s that a large part of the Kurdish intelligentsia joined such socialist movements as the Workers' Party of Turkey (TİP) and the Revolutionary Youth Federation of Turkey (Dev-Genç).

The growing presence of Kurds in leftist movements helps explain why it was among Turkish socialists that the crisis of Turkishness first began to appear. Bringing the Kurdish issue to the attention of the left amounted to a challenge, a defiance, that forced Turkish leftists to deal with a matter they had long overlooked. For example, an influential Kurdish group within TİP, the so-called Easterners (*Doğulular*), spoke about discrimination against Kurds within the party platform and set about organizing in Kurdish provinces. In the Eastern Meetings (*Doğu Mitingleri*) of TİP in 1967, the party chairman, Mehmet Ali Aybar, characterized the Kurdish issue, known then—in a telling omission—as the "Eastern Issue,"[4] as a problem not just of economic underdevelopment but also of cultural humiliation and contempt.

A critical early moment in the onset of the Turkishness Crisis among the Turkish left came as Kurds began to leave the existing leftist organizations of the late 1960s to establish their own. In particular, in 1968, divisions were prompted within the Turkish left along operational (parliamentarism or rev-

---

2. For a sociological profile of the "49," see Hamit Bozarslan's essay: "'49'ların Anıları Üzerine 127–143.

3. Musa Anter, one of the "49," details how the DP government hoped to solve the problem by exterminating about a thousand Kurdish intellectuals, a move opposed by Minister Tevfik İleri on these grounds: "Friends, you know me. I am no friend of the Kurds, but if we make such a move, dread to think that we bring Algeria to Kurdistan" (*Hatıralarım*, 149–150).

4. I have talked about how the Turkishness Contract has included bans on non-Turkish languages. There is also much work to be done on how the contract touches down/registers within the Turkish language, both as a set of negative restrictions ("do not use this word") and positive euphemisms/allusions/elisions ("use this word instead"). Thus, one should not use such words as "Kurd," "Kurdish," or (certainly not) "Kurdistan"; one should rather use vague references to "Easterners" or "the East." Of course, no one was/is really under any illusion about what they refer to when they say "Easterner." They function pragmatically as indexical signs; their deployment in the right context of speech marks the speaker as someone who signs on to the contract, who is "our guy," who agrees to play by the epistemic rules of the game. Here, in other words, is another example of the many micropractices of social signing through which one performs Turkishness, through which one actually becomes Turkish.

olutionism?), ideological (Kemalism or Marxism?), and theoretical (feudalism or the Asiatic mode of production?) lines. It was around this time, too, that Kurdish socialists first attempted to organize independently, informed and impelled by their critical understanding of the limited importance paid by Turkish socialists to the Kurdish issue (variously approached as a matter to be postponed until after the revolution or ignored entirely) as well as their critical diagnoses of the difficulties Kurds faced in trying to make their voices heard sufficiently within organizations dominated by Turks. Such was the context for the emergence of Revolutionary Eastern Cultural Centers (DDKO), founded by Kurdish socialists in the spring of 1969 to study, publish, and hold conferences on the history, language, and culture of Kurds.

The criticism of Turkish socialists by Kurdish socialists and the emergence of increasingly independent forms of Kurdish organizing helped push left movements to adopt more radical and emancipatory stances on the Kurdish issue. One of the first developments along these lines can be seen in the decisions adopted by TİP at its 1970 Grand Congress, when Behice Boran was elected chairwoman. These decisions would later lead to the banning of the party: "The Party accepts and declares that Kurdish people live in the East of Turkey, that from the very beginning the fascist powers of the ruling classes have put in place a policy of repression, terror and assimilation over the Kurdish people, at times manifest as bloody acts of oppression . . . that it is the normal and necessary revolutionary duty of our Party to support the struggle of the Kurdish people to exercise their constitutional citizenship rights and to realize all their other democratic aspirations and desires . . . [and] that Kurdish and Turkish socialists must work side by side within the Party."[5]

A similar process of change occurred in young revolutionaries. The fact that Mustafa Kemal liberated the country from foreign occupation and attempted to establish an independent, secular, and modern new country set in motion a deep tendency, in the history of the Turkish left, to view Kemalism as an anti-imperialist and progressive ideology. A certain historical affinity between socialism and Kemalism also led to a largely uncritical embrace of nationalism (another ideological element of Kemalism) by various left groups and intellectuals. Only in the late 1960s was this presumed affinity between Kemalism, nationalism, and socialism thrown more and more into question. The rapid adoption by the '68 generation—it only took a year or two—of such terms as "the left of Turkey" instead of "the Turkish left," or "the people(s) of Turkey" instead of "Turkish people" underscores the pace of change for this generation. The stance of certain legendary youth leaders of the left tells

---

5. Quoted in Aren, *TİP Olayı*, 291.

a similar story.[6] Deniz Gezmiş, for instance, famously shouted, moments before his imminent execution, "Long live the independence struggle of the Turkish and Kurdish peoples!" Mahir Çayan and his circle criticized the Old Left's denial of Kurdish self-determination.[7] And İbrahim Kaypakkaya, in a rare move of touching on a matter of almost secular sacred status, questioned leftist ties with Mustafa Kemal and Kemalism: "M. Kemal's whole life is full of examples of persecution and oppression of the Kurdish nation and other minority nationalities." Kaypakkaya went on to characterize those socialists who deny Kurds any right to self-determination and who conceal their biases with reference to Marxist-Leninist principles as hypocritical Turkish nationalists: "Without combating their insidious nationalism and erasing the traces of this nationalism among Turkish workers and laborers, mutual trust, unity and solidarity cannot be achieved between workers and laborers of various nationalities."[8]

The military intervention of March 12, 1971, targeted leftist movements and their rapid rise and radicalization, but these forces proved unstoppable. For instance, in the Diyarbakır prison, a group of Kurdish socialist inmates came forth with a rare political defense. Rather than reject the accusations of *Kürtçülük* and *bölücülük*,[9] the inmates made use of hearings as a forum to detail the oppression of Kurds and state efforts to erase the Kurdish language.[10] Such political radicalization, evidenced in these political defenses, was part of a broader intellectual radicalization encapsulated in the thesis that saw Kurdistan as an international colony divided into four parts (Turkey, Iran, Iraq, and Syria).

---

6. PKK leader Abdullah Öcalan had this to say about Deniz Gezmiş, Mahir Çayan, and İbrahim Kaypakkaya: "They did not deny (the Kurdish issue), and I am their classmate, so how can I deny it?" Quoted in Yücel, *Abdullah Öcalan*, 126.

7. Çayan, *Toplu Yazılar*, 159–160, 191–211.

8. Kaypakkaya, *Bütün Eserleri*, 228, 264.

9. Translator's note: each term is, for different reasons, only partially translatable. *Kürtçülük* begins with the root "Kurdish" (*Kürt*) and adds a case ending indicating affiliation or advocacy or association with something (-çü). At a very basic level, then, a *Kürtçü* simply means someone with some sort of connection to Kurdishness. The final ending simply transforms this adjective into an abstract noun. A possible translation is, perhaps, "pro-Kurdishness," but the reader should keep in mind that the ambiguity here ("pro" what? of what aspects of being Kurdish?) is built into the very legal pragmatics of the term when leveled as an accusation. That is, the political and legal usefulness of such a term is precisely its ambiguity—nearly anything in the life of a Kurdish person can be construed as *Kürtçü* if one wishes. The second term, *bölücülük* derives from a verb (*bölmek*) meaning to divide, to split up, to separate, to divvy up, and so on. Yet, this term should be translated differently, depending on the political conjuncture of state fears: at times separatism, when the fear was Kurds setting up an independent state; at other times divisiveness, when the fear was sowing internal social and communal divisions and upsetting the nationalist fiction of unity. Here, then, separatism is probably the correct translation (the dominant sense), though there are arguably pragmatic and connotative echoes of divisiveness as well.

10. See *Devrimci Doğu Kültür Ocakları Dava Dosyası*.

While the thesis of Kurdistan as a colony was first voiced early in 1971, the idea truly took shape after 1973.[11] All the different Kurdish organizations to have emerged after the 1974 amnesty shared in such an analysis, which both gave legitimacy to the idea of organizing independently of the Turkish left, and, more importantly, made the idea of struggle for national independence through violence and revolution inevitable, at least as a subject of discussion and debate. Indeed, all the Kurdish movements to emerge from this period favored independence, if by different means and with different emphases.[12]

The colonial thesis was also an intellectual undertaking,[13] calling for a rewriting of Turkey's history through completely different eyes—a historiographical dimension that constituted a particular challenge to Turkish socialists. In this new historiography, pioneered, in particular, by the Freedom Path (Özgürlük Yolu) movement and the Komal Publishing House (Rizgarî) circle,[14] many of the figures and acts once considered progressive by Turkish socialists were recast as colonialist. I have mentioned how socialist movements began to diverge from Kemalism in the late 1960s and, increasingly, the 1970s. Also, in the 1970s, most leftist organizations took as axiomatic that (1) the relationship between the Turkish and Kurdish nations was one of oppressor nation and oppressed, (2) the Turkish state was assimilationist and chauvinist, and (3) as a general principle, the Kurdish nation had the right to self-determination. But the idea of a "colonial Kurdistan" (which, by default, also declared Turkey to be colonialist) undermined the thesis, long put forward by Turkish socialists as the basis of their revolutionary strategy, that Turkey was itself a "semi-colony" or a "neo-colony." Thus the Communist Party of Turkey (TKP)[15] and Revolutionary Path (Dev-Yol), perhaps the two most powerful organiza-

---

11. Akkaya, "Kürt Hareketinin Örgütlenme Süreci olarak 1970'ler," 100–101.

12. For important texts containing the basic theses of Kurdish organizations in the 1970s, see Türkmen and Özmen, *Kürdistan Sosyalist Solu Kitabı*. See also Güneş, *Kurdish National Movement in Turkey*.

13. Bozarslan, "Türkiye'de Kürt Sol Hareketi," 1181.

14. On the Komal circle, see Maraşlı, "Rizgarî'nin Sosyalist Hareket," 68–93.

15. It is worth pointing out an important comparative difference between Turkey and South Africa. The Communist Party of the Soviet Union (CPSU) is known to have wanted the TKP to support the Turkish state against Kurdish rebellions, especially in the 1920s and 1930s. And the CPSU largely got what it wanted. This conjuncture arguably contributed to the emergence of the various problems between the Turkish left and the Kurdistan left that live on today. In South Africa, the same CPSU wanted the South African Communist Party (SACP) to be organized among Black people, not white people, and from the 1920s on, the SACP fought for the rights and national sovereignty of the Black majority. While this difference cast a shadow on the international prestige of the TKP, it made the SACP one of the most respected communist parties in the world for many years. The African National Congress (ANC) and the SACP fought together against apartheid and, since its collapse, have been coalition partners. See Ellis and Sechaba, *Comrades against Apartheid*.

tions of the Turkish socialist left at the time, argued that there was no such thing, according to Marxist thought, as a colonialist semicolony.[16] Yet, according to the Liberation (Kurtuluş) movement—an important exception among the major organizations of the Turkish left regarding the colonial question—Kurdistan was a colony of Turkey, and its independence was to be supported.[17]

In short, the increased visibility of Kurds in Turkish left circles in the 1960s, their independent organizing at the time, and the emergence of the thesis of a colonial Kurdistan in the 1970s forced Turkish socialists to reckon with the Kurdish issue. The imperative to see and care led to significant changes in socialist groups and among Turkish socialists, some of which I have noted earlier. Were it not for Kurdish demands and criticisms and their independent organization, the Kemalism of the Turkish left would have gone unquestioned. Nor would the right of nations to self-determination have been up for debate. That said, such changes did not, in themselves, spell a coming to terms with or, certainly, any abandonment of Turkishness and its power to structure ways of thinking, feeling, and acting. The changes to result from Kurdish demands and criticisms were largely political and ideological. Socialist political formations were compelled to revisit and revise their historical theses and conceptions of the nation to convince Kurds to struggle together. But the Kurdish issue cannot really be said to have dominated the left's agenda at the time; it was simply one issue among many.[18] This had to do with the fact that Turkish socialist movements were simply larger than Kurdish socialist movements in the 1960s and 1970s and enjoyed more mass support. Thus, in response to new Kurdish theses and new modes of Kurdish organization, Turkish socialist movements made do by pursuing certain modifications to their own thinking and courses of action in the name of greater inclusivity. Most of the changes were at the level of the group, not the individual. Histories of socialism in Turkey in the 1960s and 1970s thus often evaluate (or are compelled to evaluate) the changes brought about by the Kurdish issue in collective terms, as in "Dev-Yolcular thought this way while Kurtuluş thought that way." Things changed after 1980, however, as the Kurdish movement gained mass momentum, surpassing the Turkish left in scale and radicalism.

The Kurdistan Workers' Party, or Partiya Karkerên Kurdistanê (PKK), grew out of transformations in Kurdistan between roughly 1960 and 1980. In the mid-1970s, a group then known as the Revolutionaries of Kurdistan—

16. On the approach of the Turkish left to the Kurdish question, see Yeğen, "Türkiye Solu ve Kürt Sorunu," 1208–1236.
17. See "Türkiye'de Ulusal Sorun Üzerine," 24–61.
18. See Türkmen and Özger, *Türkiye Sosyalist Solu Kitabı 2*.

or Apocular, after an abbreviated form of the name of their leader, Abdullah Öcalan—published *The Path of the Kurdistan Revolution*, a pamphlet outlining their main theses and goals as of 1978, the year often cited as the founding of the PKK. According to party members, Turkey's form of colonialism made use of both physical violence and cultural or "cerebral colonialism," via the "institutions of depersonalization" (educational institutions). Socialists who denied Turkey's colonizer status were "social chauvinists" poisoned by Kemalism. The ultimate goal of the Kurdistan Revolution was to respond to colonialist-reactionary violence with revolutionary violence and to establish an "Independent, United and Democratic Kurdistan," which could only be possible through a protracted people's war.[19] While other Kurdish movements at the time mostly engaged in intellectual production and publishing, what distinguished the PKK was its direct organizing in Kurdish communities.

A number of commentators have described the PKK's emergence as a Fanonist movement (though it remains unclear whether its founders had read Frantz Fanon at the time). What this points to is a two-sided aim within the movement: putting an end to the domination of the colonizer through counterviolence and liberating the Kurdish personality[20] from the colonized and oppressed subject position, despised and colored by shame.[21] Accordingly, from the outset, the PKK's organizational efforts focused on rural and poor Kurds, and, accordingly, its guerrilla army consisted largely of the dispossessed. When imprisoned PKK members took action against the oppression and torture of Kurds, especially in the infamous Diyarbakır prison, during the September 12, 1980, coup d'état in Turkey, the movement's popularity in Kurdistan grew further. Meanwhile, the Turkish left had almost completely disintegrated and collapsed by the early 1980s (unlike the aftermath of the coup in 1971). Filling this gap, in part, the PKK launched a war of national liberation against the Turkish state in 1984.

If the state had long managed to suppress the Kurdish issue through physical violence and systematic and institutionalized mechanisms of denial, the PKK succeeded in returning the issue to the attention of Turkey and the world through the use of violence.[22] The Turkish state could do little to quell the

---

19. See Öcalan, "Kürdistan Devriminin Yolu," 445–528.

20. Öcalan has described his childhood and early youth as marked by shame (of his weakness and Kurdishness) and a desire to become Turkish. See, e.g., Öcalan, *Demokratik Uygarlık Manifestosu*, 19, 78–79, 146, 595.

21. For two studies attending to the ties between the PKK and Fanon, see Kaya, "Kürdistan'da Fanon Etkisi," 18–30; Jongerden and Akkaya, *PKK Üzerine Yazılar*, 22–23.

22. In a broadly similar way, the Armenian Secret Army for the Liberation of Armenia brought the Armenian issue to national and international attention—an issue that the state had also violently suppressed and systematically and institutionally denied—through the assassination of

PKK's military presence in the 1980s. Nor could it prevent the party's growing popular support, seen most clearly in such events as mass funerals, Newroz celebrations,[23] and the civil political process set in motion by the People's
Labour Party (HEP), founded in 1990. Under the leadership of Erdal İnönü,
who sought a solution to the Kurdish issue and recognized the support of
HEP candidates in Kurdish provinces, the Social Democrat Populist Party
built an alliance with HEP in the 1991 elections. President Turgut Özal attempted, to a degree, to encourage discussion on the resolution of the Kurdish issue, saying, "We should discuss everything, including federation." In a
speech in 1992, Prime Minister Süleyman Demirel recognized the "Kurdish
reality." And Necmettin Erbakan, the leader of the Islamist Welfare Party,
criticized the substitution of the pledge "I am a Turk, I am righteous, I am
hardworking" for the *basmala* (or opening prayer) in schools, saying that this
gives a "Muslim son" the right to say, "I am a Kurd, I am more righteous, I am
more hardworking," which may alienate the country's people from one another. Inasmuch as such statements point to a certain loosening of the state's
long-standing politics of denialism, they amount to the earliest Kurdish over-
tures in mainstream Turkish politics. Yet, for complex reasons that remain
somewhat unclear, any sense of opening quickly dissolved. The PKK ended a
ceasefire; HEP and subsequent Kurdish parties were shut down. Kurdish newspapers were banned, Kurdish parliamentarians were arrested, and military
evacuations emptied thousands of villages. Millions of Kurds were forced to
migrate from villages to cities. Counterinsurgency violence and the unsolved
murders (i.e., extrajudicial killings) of Kurdish civilians were widespread.[24]

Despite the growing repression and lawlessness, the will and courage of
Kurdish political agents continued, and they engaged in politics to create their
own forms of knowledge, their own new political parties, new newspapers,
and new politicians. Additional factors—economic and cultural globalization, the end of the Cold War, Turkey's EU candidacy process, and the opening of private TV channels—increased Kurdish visibility in the mainstream

Turkish diplomats abroad from the mid-1970s. On both the institutional and social denial of the
Armenian question and the historically shifting forms and strategies of denial, see Öztan and
Turan, "Türkiye'de Devlet Aklı ve 1915," 78–131; Göçek, *Denial of Violence*. For an article/inter-
view analyzing—through the concept of "habitus of denial"—the various forms that denial takes,
see Suciyan, "Dört Nesil," 132–149.

23. For an analysis of Newroz (organized by the Kurdish movement) and Nevruz (organized
by the state in opposition), see Demirer, *Tören, Simge, Siyaset*.

24. For a summary of the Kurdish issue during these years, see Kirişçi and Winrow, *Kurdish
Question and Turkey*.

media. The rise of the Justice and Development Party (AKP) in 2002 further strengthened this partial pluralization. The early years of AKP rule were marked by a degree of political insecurity, as the party had yet to establish control over such institutions and fields as the army, police, judiciary, and media. It was this insecurity that compelled AKP to embark on a series of legal and administrative reforms to gain international support, especially from the United States and the EU. A range of political projects meant to shore up its legitimacy both at home and abroad ensued, some short term, some longer: the Armenian Opening, the Cyprus Opening, the Alevi Opening, and the Kurdish Opening. Initiating such projects required acknowledgment, in some form, of the existence of a problem, amounting to a partial moderation of the Turkishness Contract. AKP's desire to erode and discredit Kemalism in the ideological field also played a major role in the making of this atmosphere of semidemocratic debate. The AKP government's confidence grew in direct proportion to its control over public and private institutions. AKP aimed at nothing less than the gradual and deliberate establishment of a new state, and it sought to destroy, one by one, the ideological foundations of the old state to ensure the success of their project of state building. This set in motion an uninterrupted and nearly inescapable flow of information—1915, the Sheikh Said Rebellion, Dersim, racist incidents and policies targeting non-Muslims, the systematic and brutal torture of Kurds in Diyarbakır prison, the unsolved murders of the 1990s, and more—enlisting TV debate programs, newspaper columns, books, doctoral and master's theses, magazines, the statements of politicians, and social media. The proliferation of knowledge rendered the crisis in Turkishness a mass phenomenon, exposing Turks to what was previously unseen, unheard, unknown, and ignored.

Nor were Kurds alone in making use of the unique possibilities of the partial pluralization of the 1990s and, particularly, the 2000s. As the Armenian Secret Army for the Liberation of Armenia waned, so did Turkish state pressure on Armenians, and one important product of this conjuncture is *Agos*, a newspaper founded by Hrant Dink and his associates in 1996. *Agos* set out to provoke public discussion of the Armenian question and the problems of Armenians, with Dink turning a critical eye primarily to the state: "It is a fact that, throughout the history of the Republic, Armenians have consistently been perceived, like other non-Muslim minorities, as a security problem. They've been consistently subjected to discrimination, treated something like, 'You're different, but you're inherently wrong. You can live in this country, but you can't progress past your present situation; you can't attempt to heal, to regain your health, to develop, to multiply. Live as long as you can in this situation, and, in time, decrease and go extinct on your own.'"[25] Dink targeted not only the Turkish state and its denialism but also the Armenian diaspora, particularly certain deep assumptions among the diaspora (e.g., Turks will never change, those Armenians who remained in Turkey are Turkified) obscuring any positive changes in Turks or Armenians in Turkey. Fostering civil debate about 1915 (in which Dink played a key symbolic role), he aimed to rescue both Armenians from their trauma and Turks from their paranoia (of demands for land, reparations, territorial division, etc.). Especially striking, for those who read his analyses and watched his interviews and TV appearances, was his language—at once courageous, calm, conciliatory, and peaceful—and his continued emphasis of his love for Turkey.

Dink, of course, was not alone but, rather, led a new and courageous generation within the Armenian community, critical not only of the Turkish state and media but also, in time, of the Armenian patriarchate. Patriarch Mesrob II criticized *Agos* as a "revolutionary left" newspaper controlled by "representatives of the 1968 generation and their children undergoing an identity crisis" and accused its editor in chief, in particular (Dink), of audacity.[26] Dink replied: "It is true that *Agos* is a left-wing and revolutionary newspaper. It is prepared with contributions from Turks, Armenians and Kurds, and read by them. *Agos* demands a civil society. When *Agos* finds fault in the disposition of His Majesty the Patriarch, it invites society not to take part in this, but to criticize it. It is also true that we have been audacious, that at times we have gone too far, pushed the boundaries, exceeded the limits. This is also our right. Revolutions happen when you go too far, when you step over the line."[27]

It seems to me that the audacity that the patriarch criticizes and that Dink embraces is no indiscriminate term. Audacity is indicative of a new character, a new mode of being, and is crucial to understanding the crisis of Turkishness. In Chapter 3, I described meekness as a strategy of survival and getting by for those (kept) outside of Turkishness and the Turkishness Contract. Social and historical meekness is doubtlessly still widespread and persistent. Millions hide their names, religions, languages, styles of dress, thoughts, and feelings. They speak softly so as not to attract attention and refrain from asking for even the smallest things to avoid trouble. That said, today there are also many living beyond Turkishness and the Turkishness Contract who refuse to lead meek lives. Having shed their fears and shame, they no longer hide their names, religions, languages, clothes, thoughts, or feelings; they lead

---

25. Dink, *İki Yakın Halk İki Uzak Komşu*, 25.
26. "Ermeni Cemaatinde 68'li Tartışması," Hürriyet, January 22, 2006, available at http://www.hurriyet.com.tr/ermeni-cemaatinde-68-li-tartismasi-3825821.
27. Quoted in Özdoğan et al., *Türkiye'de Ermeniler*, 224.

daring lives. Just as meekness is socially and historically constituted, so, too, is audacity. To live meekly can be a source of shame and to live with audacity, a source of pride. Meekness wanes as audacity waxes. But the same psychological transformation—the transition of those outside the contract from obscurity to audacity—may also register as a shock on those within the contract: the shock, that is, of shifting from seer to seen, definer to defined, and critic to criticized.

The dynamics of this crisis closely resemble the contemporary crises of whiteness and masculinity experienced today on a global, mass scale—crises that are rooted fundamentally in the empowerment and audacity of Black people and women. Robert Bernasconi, for example, links the crisis of whiteness to the "shock of being seen." His work draws on Jean-Paul Sartre, whom Bernasconi considers one of the few white philosophers to treat racism as a philosophical issue. White people are, from this lens, not used to being seen nor accustomed to knowing how they are seen from the outside: "What Sartre's analyses reveal is that the oppressor, as oppressor, remains unknown to himself. This is due to the presence of mechanisms that protect him from seeing himself as seen. . . . By controlling the Black gaze, whites were able to avoid experiencing themselves as Blacks saw them. Prejudice seeks to lose sight of those to whom it is directed." Black movements, in different forms, offered a position of strength and self-confidence, presenting the possibility to control the gaze of others, to hold one's head high, and to speak what one sees. It was no longer so easy for white people to escape the gaze of Black people, no longer so easy to not know how one is seen. And what they heard and learned about themselves was less than pleasant.[28]

Ongoing peace negotiations between the Kurdish movement and the AKP government were another important factor amplifying the crisis of Turkishness. The peace process threw into question many of the policies, practices, historical events, and historical figures that, for roughly the past century, had gone unmentioned, and whose legitimacy had remained unquestioned. Now up for debate were questions central to the making of political community: What is Turkishness? Is it race, ethnicity, culture, emotion, consciousness, speaking Turkish, being Muslim? Who is—who can and cannot be—a Turk? What redefinitions of Turkishness are required to resolve the Kurdish issue? Can the place-based concept "of Turkey" (*Türkiyeli*) replace the ethnicized concept of "Turk" or "Turkish" as a metaidentity? It is now not uncommon in the wake of such changes, as noted earlier, to find analysts

28. Bernasconi, *Irk Kavramını Kim İcat Etti?*, 123, 140, 150.

framing the real problem as not a Kurdish but a Turkish problem.[29] The very existence of such questions and discussions, transcending isolated groups and touching broad swaths of society, is a phenomenon unique to crisis periods, as both cause and consequence of crisis. By way of example, Bourdieu points to a similar process in France: "There is another situation in which questions are asked, that is in periods of decomposition. Movements of involution, as some biologists call them, periods of dissolution, 'pathological' situations, moments of state crisis, as for example the time of Algerian independence, are very interesting, since questions that, even if not repressed, were rejected because already resolved before even being raised, came forward again. Where do the borders lie? Do you need to speak French to be French? And if you don't speak French are you still French? Is it enough to speak French in order to be French?"[30]

It is no surprise that Kemalist Turks have been at the center of the crisis of Turkishness. After all, the Kurdish movement and Armenian intellectuals have sought to exclude the Muslim-Turkish majority from the debate and to criticize the consequences of Unionist/Kemalist ideologies and the state structure. The ruling AKP, too, has persistently called attention to the oppression and discrimination perpetrated by Kemalist elites against the pious. The history that Kemalist Turks knew and embraced was being turned upside down before their eyes; much of what they knew was said to be wrong. Not only did they lose their past; they began to think that they had also lost their future with the rise of political Islam. This double loss triggered and made widespread a sense of nostalgia for a lost past that was secular, modern, and in which Turkishness was not questioned.[31] Losses fed feelings of powerlessness and helplessness, which in turn stoked profound anger. Anger ensured that the flood of new information be met with hostility, not taken seriously. But this was not enough on its own; it did little to stop the loss of power, which was the main problem. This, in part, explains why millions have sought new means and put in place new strategies both to regain some sense of meaning and righteousness in life and thought and to feel strong again. The rising tide of nationalism in the 2000s, and its echoes in the main opposition party, the Republican People's Party (CHP), were directly related to this search for lost power. The nationalist newspapers and television channels that grew out of the same period, when many could not bear to read and watch anything that did not confirm their existing ideas, served to validate the thoughts and feel-

---

29. See, e.g., Kılıç, *Türk Sorunu.*
30. Bourdieu, *On the State,* 115.
31. For an analysis of forms of Kemalist nostalgia emerging in the second half of the 1990s, see Özyürek, *Nostalgia for the Modern.*

ings of a Kemalist audience and readership—in short, to make Kemalists feel good again. In a sense, these media outlets constituted new comfort zones and allowed one to close oneself off to the outside world. A related mushrooming of new history programs on television and popular history books—explaining to already sympathetic audiences the falsity and baselessness of the flood of new information (about state practices against Kurds, about 1915, about Dersim)—provided a certain intellectual ammunition to combat (which is to say, to not have to confront) this new information. Adding "TC" (short for Türkiye Cumhuriyeti, the Republic of Turkey) before one's name on social media accounts, pasting Atatürk stickers on car windows, hanging Atatürk posters on home windows, and tattooing Atatürk's signature on one's body emerged as common means to compensate, in some way, for this sense of weakness. Alongside these conjunctural micropractices of feeling strong was a proliferation of discourse, positing, for instance, that Kurds already have everything they need; that Turks, not Kurds, are the real victims; that it has become a disadvantage and a liability to be Turkish; and that Turks are increasingly asked to feel ashamed of their Turkishness, to fear saying "I am Turkish."

But the crisis was not limited to Kemalist Turks or the official ideology of Kemalism. The challenge of Kurds and Armenians also incited a crisis in Turkism and Islamism (the other two major Turkish-centered ideologies to emerge from the Muslimness and Turkishness Contracts) and their political pillars (the Nationalist Movement Party, or MHP, and AKP).[32] All three ideologies—having embraced Gökalp's foundational formula of "Turkification, Islamization, Modernization" from the 1910s, if with different understandings and different emphases (of one element above the other two)—had to confront the crisis of Turkishness. Turning to (certain constructions of) history to explain the legitimacy of Turkish rule and generating discourses about its persistence were the means deployed to alleviate and compensate for the crisis, among both intellectuals and voters.

It is from this context that one should make sense of a declaration penned at the time, the so-called Call to the Turkish Nation. The declaration brought together such Kemalist intellectuals as Mümtaz Soysal and Sina Akşin, Turkist

---

32. For an expansive field study conducted in the mid-2000s with Turks of different ideological affiliations providing a wealth of data on differing discourses of Turkishness, everyday nationalisms, and nationalist "tactics" developed in the face of change, see Kentel, Ahıska, and Genç, *"Milletin Bölünmez Bütünlüğü."* Anti-Armenian and, particularly, anti-Kurdish racism, on the rise since the 2000s, are plausibly related to the crisis of supraideological Turkishness. For two sociological discussions of the rise of racism, see Saraçoğlu, *Şehir, Orta Sınıf ve Kürtler*; Keneş, *Yeni Irkçılığın "Kirli" Ötekileri.*

intellectuals such as Ümit Özdağ[33] and İskender Öksüz,[34] centrist historians as Halil İnalcık and İlber Ortaylı (ideologically somewhere between the first two groups), and politicians from across the spectrum, all upset by Turkish-ness having been so openly thrown into question. Consider the declaration: "1. The Turkish nation, as founder and protector of the State of the Republic of Turkey, cannot be removed from the definition of citizenship and the Constitution. 2. Our precious citizens, equal and honorable members of our state, cannot be divided into races and sects. 3. The national state structure established by the great Atatürk and based on the uninterrupted sovereignty of the Turkish Nation, starting with the Seljuks and continuing with the Ottomans in the geography of Anatolia, cannot be eliminated."[35] Shortly after the publication of the declaration, then-President Abdullah Gül also referred, in a statement to journalists about the peace process, to the Seljuk and Ottoman states, stressing that Turkish rule would be maintained but that it should go forward based on the logic of empire rather than nation-state: "The Ottoman Empire and the Seljuk Empire are known in history as Turkish states. But these empires did not insist that 'all citizens are Turks.' Still, all have gone down in history as great states led by the Turks. We are not an empire today. We are a unitary state. But we can act with this imperial reflex and self-confidence, I believe."[36]

Gül's statement in part reflects how nationalist, conservative, and Islamist Turks (who make up AKP's real and potential electoral base) have sought to minimize the crisis of Turkishness. As the hegemonic party of the right, AKP had to compensate both for its own electorate's crisis of Turkishness and that of nationalist MHP voters in its effort to unite what Tanıl Bora conceptual-

---

33. To Özdağ, the fact that being Turkish is portrayed as a crime and has become a disadvantage in many areas constitutes "a 'Turkish Problem' that's very difficult to overcome." According to Özdağ, one consequence of the discourse of "Kurdish victimization" is the "Kurdish excuse"—that is, any action of Kurds can be excused. As a result, Turks have begun to feel victimized and to "undertake psychological preparations for the new War of Independence." For Özdağ, "The Turkish question is a double-edged sword." It may drive a political process capable of restoring the Republic of Turkey, or it may evolve into a dangerous anti-Kurdish psychology. See Özdağ, *Türk Sorunu*, 13–28. As of 2023, Özdağ is the founder and leader of the far-right Victory Party, the two main policies of which are anti-Kurdish and anti-Syrian.

34. Öksüz transformed the discourse positing Turks as the real victims and Turkishness as something one is made to feel ashamed of into an ironic and reproachful book title: *Sorry, I'm a Turk*. See Öksüz's *Türk'üm Özür Dilerim*.

35. "Solun tanınmış isimleri ülkücü camia ile aynı metne imza attı," OdaTV, March 28, 2013, available at http://odatv.com/-turk-solunun-babasi-ile-dogunun-basbugu-nasil-bir-araya-geldi-2803131200.html.

36. "Gül: İmparatorluk Refleksi ve Özgüveni ile Hareket Etmeliyiz," accessed August 7, 2017, available at http://www.rusencakir.com/Gul-Imparatorluk-refleksi-ve-ozguveni-ile-hareket-etme liyiz/1983.

izes as the three states of the Turkish right: nationalism (solid), conservatism (liquid), and Islamism (gas).[37] AKP thus spoke, implicitly and explicitly, of the making of a new imperial/Islamic nation-state in place of the old Western/ secular nation-state—a state under Turkish rule, with all the greatness and glory of the Ottomans. Throughout the peace process, AKP repeatedly referred both indirectly to the Muslimness Contract and directly to the battle of Çanakkale and the Independence War, activating a discourse positing Turks and Kurds as "religious brothers" who together shed blood for this country.[38] The aim, in short, was to replace—while including—the Turkish nation with an imperial form of Muslim nationalism in which Turks would dominate.[39]

A parallel strategy held "White Turks"—a relatively recent neologism, referring to the class privileged, who occupy a position of cultural alienation from their own country—responsible for all the oppression and ethnic crimes of the twentieth century. AKP leader Tayyip Erdoğan and pro-AKP intellectuals have consistently described White Turks as privileged, Western, arrogant, racist, with little or no religious convictions, fond of drinking, alien to this land and the values of the nation, and with roots abroad (the latter hinting at both European values and the Balkan roots of the founders of the Republic). White Turks, so the discourse goes, will fade away into history along with the old state and the old Turkey. The new state and the new Turkey will be the product of innocent, oppressed, aggrieved, pure, honest, religious, native, and national Turks (also called "Black Turks" or "*Zenci* Turks"[40]), who are said to have long been humiliated, despised, and ostracized by White

---

37. Bora, *Türk Sağının Üç Hâli.*

38. After 2009, expressions such as "Kurdish Opening (*Kürt Açılımı*)" and "Democratic Opening (*Demokratik Açılım*)" were replaced by "The Project of National Unity and Brotherhood (Milli Birlik ve Kardeşlik Projesi)." See Koyuncu, "*Benim Milletim,*" 213–229.

39. For the dynamics of the emergence of Muslim nationalism and its discursive strategies, see White, *Muslim Nationalism and the Turks.*

40. "Cumhurbaşkanı Erdoğan: 'Zenci bir Türk olmaktan şeref duyuyorum,'" *Sabah,* June 25, 2015, http://www.sabah.com.tr/webtv/turkiye/cumhurbaskani-erdogan-zenci-bir-turk-ol maktan-seref-duyuyorum.

Translator's note: terms for racial categories are, at best, only loosely translated. Translation risks only partially capturing the pragmatics of the original term, and, perhaps more direly, introducing irrelevant connotations and contexts via the new term. "Zenci" is used in Turkey to refer to people of African origin. It is fair to say that many Turkish speakers use the word without a second thought, but the term is hardly without injurious connotations. Thus, Turkish speakers sensitive to the micropractices of race and meaning tend to prefer *siyah*—Black. "Negro," then, is, perhaps, a reasonable translation, insofar as the term has (or, rather, had) a certain widespread use, but can also be deployed as an injurious term, depending on the context of speech. That said, readers familiar with the U.S. pragmatics and semiotic histories of "negro" are asked to put aside this context.

Turks.[41] An authentic and native Turkishness will, by this framing, replace forms of false and foreign Turkishness.[42]

The task of alleviating the crisis of Turkishness fell not only to the AKP government but also to the Kurdish movement—the other partner in the peace process. The Kurdish movement's abandonment of the goal of an independent state in favor of more ambiguous, flexible, and inclusive goals of democratic republicanism, democratic confederalism, and democratic autonomy further facilitated this process.[43] Of critical importance for our discussion is the fact that Abdullah Öcalan, the imprisoned leader of the PKK, began to employ discourses similar to those of the AKP government, invoking, for instance, religious brotherhood and the wars that Turks and Kurds fought together for this country and blaming "White Turkism" and "White Turkish fascism" for the Kurdish issue.[44] Öcalan's message, read aloud in Diyarbakır (in a sense, the de facto capital city of Kurdistan in Turkey) during the Newroz celebrations of 2013, constitutes one of the most important texts of the peace process. To Öcalan, the "Turkish people who live in what is called Turkey today—the ancient Anatolia—should recognize that their common life with the Kurds, under the flag of Islam, rests on the principles of amity and solidarity. . . . The last century's repressive, annihilationist, and assimilationist policies, based on capitalist modernity, represent the efforts of a ruling elite to deny a long history of amity. They do not represent the will of the people. . . . The time has come for dispute, conflict, and enmity to yield to alliance, unity, blessings, and a mutual embrace. The Turks and Kurds who fell as martyrs together at Çanakkale also went through the War of Independence together, and together they opened the 1920 assembly. Our common past is a reality that requires us to create a common future."[45]

Insofar as it helped alleviate the crisis of Turkishness, the discursive emphasis, by both AKP and the Kurdish movement, on the sentiments and alliances of the Muslimness Contract facilitated the peace process. That said,

---

41. For an analysis of AKP's discourse of establishing, through a war of independence against the internal-colonialist White Turks, a new state restored to its true owner (the nation, millet), see Aktoprak, "'Postkolonyal' bir Tahayyül," 293–321.

42. On both the typology of the White Turk and the White Turk resentment of Islamists, see the following works of Bora: "Beyaz Türkler Tartışması," 25–37; "Muhafazakâr ve İslamcı Söylemde Beyaz Türk Hıncı," 36–45.

43. For the ideological transformation of the Kurdish movement, see Jongerden, Akkaya, and Şimşek, İsyandan İnşaya; Küçük, "Yerelleşmenin ve Evrenselleşmenin Ötesinde Kürt Sorununu Yeniden Düşünmek," 62–84.

44. See, e.g., Öcalan, Demokratik Uygarlık Manifestosu, 125, 153. Öcalan is especially careful not to condemn Mustafa Kemal on the grounds of white Turkishness (125, 260).

45. "Öcalan's Historical Newroz 2013 Statement," accessed August 8, 2023, available at https://www.freeocalan.org/news/english/ocalans-historical-newroz-statement-2013.

the Kurdish movement also contains leftist, feminist, environmentalist, secular, and emancipatory discourses that do not sit well with the AKP government. Unlike the rhetoric of the Muslimness Contract, these discourses were not tactical but reflected the core ideology of the Kurdish movement. This ideology combined with (1) the claims of the main Kurdish party (the Peoples' Democratic Party [HDP]) to be the "party of Turkey,"[46] (2) HDP's strong women's movement, ensured by quotas, (3) the personal charisma of then party cochair Selahattin Demirtaş, and (4) the de-escalation process throughout the country, led to greater electoral successes for HDP, with more and more support from so-called White Turks. Not only socialist and radical Turks but also many who considered themselves Kemalists were drawn to HDP. This trend, evident in Demirtaş's candidacy in the 2014 presidential elections, rattled AKP. AKP intellectuals accused Demirtaş of having passed to the "White Turk class"[47] and of playing their games.[48] Thus, the stigma of outsider or nonlocal status that Islamists had always attached to White Turks was now applied to Demirtaş, a Kurdish citizen of Turkey.[49]

However, the trend of HDP's rise and growth proved unstoppable. In the June 7, 2015, general elections, the party comfortably passed the 10 percent threshold, gaining eighty deputies with over 13 percent of the vote. The Islamist AKP thereby lost its one-party rule, while the Turkist MHP lost its status as the third party in parliament. HDP not only made a significant difference in provinces where the Kurdish movement was already strong, chipping away at AKP's votes (the other powerful party in these provinces). Its vote share also expanded in Turkish-dominated provinces in the East. HDP received the most votes in all the provinces on Turkey's eastern border except Artvin, further underscoring the long-standing perception of the eastern border region—particularly the border with Armenia—as a security threat in the eyes of Turkish nationalism. Such changes in the eastern provinces thus constituted a significant problem not only for the AKP government but also for the century-old nation-state that has sought to build a barrier of Turkishness to prevent the expansion of Kurdistan. And, in another consequential development for this analysis of Turkishness, HDP increased its share of the vote

---

46. This slogan describes HDP's attempt to become a party not just of Kurdistan but of the entire country and thus gain support and votes from both Kurds and Turks.

47. Akdoğan, "Yazıklar Olsun," available at http://www.star.com.tr/yazar/yaziklar-olsun-yazi -915820/.

48. Miroğlu, "'Türkiyelileşmek' Anadolu'dan Geçer," available at http://www.star.com.tr /yazar/turkiyelilesmek-anadoludan-gecer-yazi-917219/.

49. E.g., in 2012, Islamist intellectual Mustafa Islamoglu noted, "We have to leave aside the foreigners. The locals, the Kurd of these lands and the Turk of these lands, will solve the state issue very easily" (Türköne, *Türküm Vicdanlıyım*, 46).

in an unprecedented way by attracting a large number of votes from Turks in western provinces. While AKP assumed that the crisis of Turkishness (in which it played a role) would wholly solidify the Kemalist position of White Turks, instead the conjuncture transformed urban and secular individuals, perhaps more than any other Turkish social category.[50]

Following the June 7, 2015, elections, AKP (Islamist) and MHP (Turkist) formed a far-right alliance, reinstating a war-based policy approach and putting an end to the peace process.[51] The PKK's efforts to seize control of Kurdish cities through armed force, in the name of self-government, also played a major role in the unraveling of de-escalation. But the extraordinarily harsh reaction of the state and of the Turkist-Islamist front, in particular, strongly suggests that PKK politics may have simply provided the pretext that government agents were already searching for. In the conflict that began in the summer of 2015, the state relied on heavy weaponry to completely demolish and destroy many Kurdish settlements and entire neighborhoods. Hundreds of thousands were left homeless. Thousands of militants and hundreds of civilians were killed. Numerous attacks were carried out on HDP buildings. A March 10, 2017, UN Human Rights Office report[52] detailed grave human rights violations by the state, though no state officials were investigated for crimes committed. The result was a reossification of the Turkishness Contract. In contrast to the previous period of democratic opening and détente, a complete ban was reinstated on the production of information about human rights violations in Kurdistan and on sympathizing with Kurds. In the November 1, 2015, early elections following a summer of conflict, AKP increased its votes by approximately 10 percent compared to elections five months ago

---

50. The Islamist newspaper *Yeni Akit* announced the election results for such İstanbul districts as Nişantaşı, Bebek, and Etiler with the headline "White Turks' Love for HDP Reaches Its Peak," accessed July 16, 2017, available at http://www.yeniakit.com.tr/haber/beyaz-turklerin-hdp-sevdasi-zirve-yapti-73868.html.

51. With the end of the peace process, Islamist intellectuals began to sound the same complaints that were once the province of Kemalist and Turkist intellectuals: "Turks are now victims," or "being a Turk has become something to be ashamed of." See, e.g., Kılıçarslan, "Türk olduğum için özür dilemeyeceğim," available at http://www.yenisafak.com/yazarlar/ismailkilicarslan/turk-oldugum-icin-ozur-dilemeyecegim-2040320. Hayrettin Karaman, meanwhile, concludes that since Iraq and Turkey are Islamic countries, the establishment of a separate state by the Kurds is "not legitimate and reasonable" according to Islam and ummahism: "Meşru ve makul olmayan bağımsızlık (2)," *Yenişafak*, October 12, 2017, available at http://www.yenisafak.com/yazarlar/hayrettinkaraman/mesru-ve-makul-olmayan-bagimsizlik-2-2040549. Both authors deliberately employ an anti-imperialist and anti-colonialist rhetoric in their opposition to the independence of Kurdistan.

52. The report, accessed July 31, 2017, is available at http://www.ohchr.org/EN/NewsEvents/Pages/DisplayNews.aspx?NewsID=21342&LangID=E.

and resumed single rule with 49.5 percent of the votes, while HDP's share of votes fell to 10.76 percent.

The emergence of the AKP-MHP de facto coalition should be read, I suggest, as an effort to stamp out not just the political change embodied in the rise of the HDP but also that of a larger sociopolitical transformation, of which HDP was but one part. The Gezi Uprising of 2013, in which millions participated, was a horizontal, democratic, emancipatory, (pro)feminist, leaderless, and environmentalist left opposition to neoliberalism and authoritarianism, similar to its counterparts in many parts of the world.[53] Gezi pointed to the emergence of new modes of left politics beyond such traditional left institutions as political parties or trade unions. More precisely, the Gezi Uprising laid bare and redoubled these existing trends. In the formation of this New Left vein, the transformative potential of the crisis of Turkishness also had an indirect but, in my opinion, quite powerful effect. The Kurdish civilian movement also owes its post-2013 rise in part to this New Leftist vein. The resumption of war in 2015 and the subsequent formation of a far-right alliance around the Turkishness Contract thus have much to do with the aim of suppressing these mutually reinforcing sociopolitical dynamics—that is, the aim of stemming the rise of the Turkish left and of HDP.

From İsmail Beşikçi to the Academics for Peace: A Brief History of Transformation

I have ascribed a significant role to intellectuals and academics in the construction of the Turkishness Contract as well as in the operation of its subcomponents, the Contracts of Ignorance and Indifference. Therefore, examining the effects of the crisis of Turkishness by studying academics and intellectuals will spell out its links to the previous chapters and make it easier to monitor change. Among the academics and intellectuals I selected for analysis, cases such as İsmail Beşikçi, whose work marks the beginning of a broader transformation, and the Academics for Peace, whose actions offer a snapshot of the transformation in its contemporary forms, have almost inevitably imposed themselves. I have also included, somewhat arbitrarily, a number of other examples in between; other examples, other names, could have just as easily been included. Behind my choices is not any desire to foreground the work of, or single out for particular criticism, any particular intellectual. What rather guided me was this: the words and actions of the intellectuals I have chosen are sim-

---

53. See Ağartan, *Gezi*.

ply apt reflections of the various aspects of Turkishness that I wish to highlight. Care was taken to select examples from different political traditions, with different relations to—and exhibiting different states and strategies of—Turkishness. I thus aim to demonstrate how Turkishness shapes the ways of perceiving, thinking, and feeling of intellectuals and academics at even opposite ends of the political spectrum.

One way to understand the nature of the Turkishness Contract and to analyze the effects of the crisis of Turkishness is to look at the millions of people who were born into and have remained within the contract. Still another is to examine a single person, to examine the biography of someone who was born into but came to exit the contract. To explore this way of thinking, I turn to the intellectual biography of Beşikçi, arguably the first Turk who understood the substance of the Turkishness Contract, and who exited the contract upon grasping its nature.[54] It is not my intention to propose Beşikçi's transformation as an ethical and intellectual model to follow. Nor am I interested in whether Beşikçi's opinion on this or that issue is right or wrong, fair or baseless. What interests me instead about Beşikçi are the ways in which his transformation helps shed light on a conceptual debate I have turned to throughout this book. The fact that Beşikçi was able to leave Turkishness behind entirely—by starting to think and feel in entirely new and different ways—demonstrates in reverse that Turkishness is, indeed, a world of thought and feeling. No Turk before Beşikçi recognized Turkishness as a world of thought and feeling, as a habitus that shapes ways of seeing and not seeing, hearing and not hearing, knowing and not knowing, taking interest in and ignoring, and caring about and being indifferent, the reason being simply that no Turk had yet to step out of the water. As a Turk born and raised in the water, having fully internalized life in the water, Beşikçi stepped out, and, only then, was he able to grasp the true nature of life in the water. As he began to see, hear, know, care, and feel in new ways, he also understood how he used to see, hear, know, care, and feel. The process was cognitively and emotionally challenging, however, and took a long time to complete. In a sense, tracing the process of Beşikçi's exit from the water might, in fact, amount to tracing a brief history of Turkishness.

Beşikçi was born into a poor Sunni Turkish family and won a scholarship from the Ministry of Internal Affairs, entering the Faculty of Political Science

---

54. In this telling of Beşikçi's biography, for brevity's sake, I do not refer to all I have mentioned elsewhere. For more information and an extended bibliography, see Ünlü, "İsmail Beşikçi Fenomeni," 11–44.

(SBF) at Ankara University in 1958. SBF was, at the time, an important center of opposition to Democratic Party rule. SBF academics and students, in
part, saw themselves as the flag bearers of Kemalist principles and, in part,
came more and more under the influence of left currents from different parts
of the world (Russia, China, Europe, the Middle East, North Africa). This
synthesis of Kemalism and socialism colored many of the left movements and
magazines to then emerge, especially in the pluralistic environment following
the 1961 constitution. Socialist-Kemalist intellectuals drew on socialism to
breathe new life into the progressive core of Kemalism, seeking new means
to create a true democracy free from the yoke of agas and sheikhs, and to create a genuine national independence, free from the comprador bourgeoisie and
imperialism. Beşikçi, graduating from SBF in 1962, was one of these intellectuals. Initially, at least.

An important feature distinguishing Beşikçi from his peers was his interest in the "Eastern Question." Of course, the Kurdish Question was garnering
more and more attention on the Turkish left in the 1960s, as I have noted.
So, in this sense, Beşikçi was not alone. What made Beşikçi exceptional was
that he did not settle for living in Ankara or İstanbul and reading a limited
number of books and writings about the East. He also lived and worked in
the eastern part of the country for many years and, in time, became an expert
on Eastern Anatolia. It was living and working in Kurdish provinces—namely, spending most of his time with Kurds who thought and felt in completely
different ways than Turks—that prompted in Beşikçi the realization that his
own thoughts and feelings had been shaped by Turkishness.

Beşikçi's first exposure to the eastern part of the country came in the
summer of 1961, between his third and fourth year in university, when he
went to the city of Elazığ for an internship with the district and provincial
governors. In 1963, Beşikçi was further brought to Bitlis for his compulsory military service. As Kurdish rebellions resurfaced at the time, led by
Barzani in northern Iraq, the Turkish state began to send military units to
Hakkari, in an effort to prevent the infiltration of rebels and the rebellion
into Turkey. Beşikçi was a part of one such unit and served for a number of
months as a platoon commander along the border. There, Beşikçi was able
to see firsthand the social and linguistic relations binding people in south-
eastern Turkey and northern Iraq. The border could be said, in this sense,
to divide not only two nation-states but also a single stateless country:
Kurdistan. But this thought had yet to occur to Beşikçi at the time. Such
an awareness required time, impeded as it was by those "police stations in
the mind" (a metaphor Beşikçi often employs). A certain spiritual transfor-

mation was also needed before Beşikçi could afford the cost of such an awareness. In the mountains of Hakkari, Beşikçi also saw many abandoned and burned churches, where some went looking for treasure.[55] But, as he later reflected, it had yet to occur to him to ask where the congregation was: "To ask, why are these churches in ruins, to ask, where are the congregations of these churches, this is a question related to historical consciousness, to social consciousness. Who hid their money, why did they hide it. And so on. I didn't have the consciousness to ask that question at the time. I had taken many courses, including The History of Political Ideas, Theory of the State, Political History, Comparative State Administration, Public Freedoms, Sociology, Economics, Finance, The Law of States, and the like. But I didn't have the consciousness, the historical and social consciousness, to ask such questions."[56] Beşikçi encountered something new in the East, but, because he still perceived what he saw from within Turkishness's diagrams of seeing, thinking, and feeling, the "something new" that he saw had yet to arouse in him new thoughts or feelings.

In late 1964, Beşikçi became an assistant in the Department of Sociology at Erzurum Atatürk University in Eastern Anatolia. The following year, after convincing his professors at SBF where his doctoral work was ongoing, he decided to write a thesis on the social structure and change of the nomadic Alikan tribe, which he first saw in Bitlis during his military service. In 1965–1966, he lived in tents with the Alikan tribe for a total of seven months, working alongside them as a nomad. His doctoral thesis, which he defended at SBF in 1967 and later published in book form, was highly appreciated within the Turkish academy and was seen as an important contribution to the social sciences. Behind this appreciation and recognition was the fact that Beşikçi noted, at the very beginning of his thesis, and voicing the same claim of supraideological rationality that many a Turkish sociologist self-attributes: "In this analysis, at no point was space devoted to a number of political and ideological debates on such ethnic roots as

---

55. Translator's note: the reference here to treasure may be unfamiliar to some readers. Across the east and southeast of Turkey, rumors of treasures left behind by departed (i.e., displaced, deported, and massacred) Christians (Armenians, in particular) are widespread. Early in my own doctoral fieldwork, for instance, I was approached by one man whom I somehow could not convince that I was not an archaeologist, and who wanted me to locate a ground penetrating radar machine to help him look for Armenian gold beneath his home in Diyarbakır. Another time, a young man brought me to a town outside of Diyarbakır ostensibly to interview his relatives; instead, he spent most of the time trying unsuccessfully to recruit me to go looking for treasure in some caves just outside of the town. These are but two small examples, the first to come to mind among many, from a landscape storied with histories of displacement and dispossession.

56. Personal correspondence with İsmail Beşikçi, September 1, 2011.

Turkish or Kurdish; such differences were not touched upon."[57] He remained loyal to this throughout his thesis. Yet, in his preface to the second
edition of the book, written some twenty-five years later, Beşikçi saw clearly—having already left Turkishness behind—that these words amounted
to little more than an escape strategy: "These are, in fact, circular words
with no content. As for circular words, they are a kind of lie told with the
aim of hiding, distorting and ignoring an unknown. . . . The use of circular
words points to a very important disease, one that prevents [us] from asking
the right questions."[58]

After around 1967, Beşikçi began to no longer ignore the ethnic dimension of the "Eastern Question"—in other words, he began to see the so-called
Eastern Question as a Kurdish problem. In this, he was affected by his time
spent as a sociologist amid the crowds in the Eastern Meetings, organized by
the TİP. His writings, based on field notes and observations inside the rallies,
were published in *Forum* in early 1968. Although he continued to attribute a
lack of capitalist development and modernization in the East to the domination of the sheikhs and agas, he also criticized the racist policies of the state
and its denial of the very existence of the Kurdish language:

Say as much as you want that there is no such thing as a Turkish-
Kurdish [distinction], that everyone who lives in this homeland is a
Turk, you still cannot hide a certain sociological fact. This fact is
language. . . . Claim as much as you want that there is no such language as Kurdish, that it is but a mixture of Arabic, Persian and Turkish,
or . . . that it is a distorted form of Persian and Turkish, you still cannot change the plain sociological fact. Because what is important from
a sociological point of view is not the relationship of a particular language with this or that language or its historical evolution, but rather
its role in ensuring communication, the consequent incommunicabil-
ity between Turkish-speaking and Kurdish-speaking groups, and the
emergence of different cultural groups.[59]

Beşikçi's transformation, coupled with his popularity among leftist and
Kurdish students at Atatürk University, set in motion a process that would
see him purged from the university. On January 26, 1968, Orhan Türkdoğan,
a Turkist intellectual and a colleague of Beşikci's in the same department,
denounced Beşikçi before the university administration, accusing him of be-

---

57. Beşikçi, *Doğu'da Değişim ve Yapısal Sorunlar (Göçebe Alikan Aşireti)*, 7.
58. Beşikçi, *Doğu'da Değişim ve Yapısal Sorunlar (Göçebe Alikan Aşireti)*, 21–22.
59. Beşikçi, *Doğu Mitingleri'nin Analizi*, 14–15.

ing a separatist and a Marxist and of poisoning "tender young minds." In the city of Erzurum—one of the strongholds of anti-communism and Turkism, cultivated with the specific mission of resisting communism and Kurdish nationalism—the presence of a thinker like Beşikçi was inadmissible, particularly in the wake of 1968 and the rise of the radical left. Immediately after the denunciation, he was removed from teaching, and, as a result of an investigation (in which his students were asked such questions as, "They call İsmail Beşikçi a communist, they call him a pro-Kurd, what do you say? . . . Do you approve of İsmail Beşikçi's article about the Kurds?"), he was dismissed on July 23, 1970.[60]

In 1968, Beşikçi went to a number of Kurdish provinces with two friends for the purpose of research. What resulted was *Doğu Anadolu'nun Düzeni* (*The Order of Eastern Anatolia*), a book based on the interviews conducted and data obtained in this trip, published in 1969. This was the first academic study of the social structure of Eastern Anatolia and, as such, can be seen as the starting point of Kurdology in Turkey, as a field of academic inquiry autonomous from the state. Indeed, in his book, Beşikçi is critical of the lack of interest in the East he saw among the left, a shortcoming (or what he describes as an "unforgivable flaw") he attributes to the ongoing influence of fascist education. Even the title of Beşikci's landmark book is a not-so-implicit criticism of, and attempt to find an alternative to, Doğan Avcıoğlu's *Türkiye'nin Düzeni* (*The Order of Turkey*), which had become something of a manual for Turkish leftists at the time. But *The Order of Eastern Anatolia* cannot be said to constitute a rupture in Beşikci's thought.[61] Although he discusses the ethnic dimension of the Eastern Question and criticizes the denialist, fascist, and chauvinist policies of the state, he also stresses the feudal relations and the sultanate of agas and sheikhs ruling over Kurds in collaboration with the state. And, on the question of the fundamental contradiction to shape the revolution (a matter of heated debate among left movements), he touches on this implicitly: "The contradiction is not between Turkish and Kurdish people, but between the Turkish and Kurdish working peoples and the Turkish and Kurdish ruling classes."[62] Beşikçi still held that the revolutions of Mustafa Kemal ought to be embraced and given new life in new circumstances.

---

60. Quoted in *İsmail Beşikçi Davası*, 71.

61. Avcıoğlu, criticized by Beşikçi for "drastically avoiding any mention of the economic, social, and cultural imbalances and ethnic differentiations between regions," tried to make up for this deficiency by referencing Beşikçi in the fourth edition of his book. See Avcıoğlu, *Türkiye'nin Düzeni (Dün-Bugün-Yarın)*, 715.

62. Beşikçi, *Doğu Anadolu'nun Düzeni*, 13, 262.

The ideas put forward in *The Order of Eastern Anatolia* began to test the limits of what the academic left could accept. An early indication of this came in February 1970 at the academic conference, "The Development of Social Research in Turkey." Beşikçi proposed a paper examining the fascist and assimilationist means by which Kurdish language, culture, and literature had been suppressed, the state's collaboration with feudalism, and the academic legitimization of this entire situation. Yet, on behalf of the organizing committee, which reviewed papers in advance, Prof. Mübeccel Kıray requested, on the morning of the conference, that Beşikçi not present his work. Kıray's warning was, as far as Beşikçi recalls it, something like this: "The statement was found to be very objectionable. I also find it personally objectionable. . . . The seminar can be raided and halted by the police. . . . You're too young. It would not be right for you to run into such mistakes so early in your career. . . . If people take a hit in their youth, they don't recover easily. Try not to get hit. Do not think of this conversation as an intervention, take it in stride. . . . Moving forward, you'll be more comfortable dealing with these kinds of issues."[63] Faced with such a warning from the most respected and authoritative name in Turkish sociology, Beşikçi agreed to present an abbreviated version of his text.

It seems to me that the pressure he encountered at this conference, although it stung at the moment, constituted an instructive moment of censorship for Beşikçi. That is, he began to grasp the nature of the Turkishness Contract not through the praises he received when inhabiting it but through the pressures and punishments he was subjected to when he began to act in ways contrary to the contract. Each warning and sanction allowed him to better comprehend life in the water and its normalized ways of thinking and acting, recalling the general rule of social life (or perhaps, more accurately, national life) that Durkheim spoke of: "Thus there are ways of acting, thinking and feeling which possess the remarkable property of existing outside the consciousness of the individual. Not only are these types of behaviour and thinking external to the individual, but they are endued with a compelling and coercive power by virtue of which, whether he wishes it or not, they impose themselves upon him. Undoubtedly when I conform to them of my own free will, this coercion is not felt or hardly felt at all, since it is unnecessary. None the less it is intrinsically a characteristic of these facts; the proof of this is that it asserts itself as soon as I try to resist."[64]

---

63. Beşikçi, *Kürt Toplumu Üzerine*, 13–15. The entirety of the censored declaration was published in this book.
64. Durkheim, *Rules of Sociological Method*, 51.

The fact that Beşikçi passed the qualifying exams at SBF in early 1971 and became a faculty member demonstrates that he had yet to be entirely excluded from the Turkish academy. But, with the intervening military memorandum of March 12, 1971, Beşikçi was arrested on June 19 of the same year. An important difference that distinguished Beşikçi from other SBF professors arrested at the time was that, in addition to being tried as a communist, he was also charged with pro-Kurdishness and thus sent to the Diyarbakır Martial Law Prison, where he would spend years with Kurdish prisoners. His years in the Diyarbakır prison functioned as something of a school for both Kurdish intellectuals and Beşikçi. In the prison commons, books were read and discussed, education was offered, and defenses were prepared together. The commons to which Beşikçi belonged, which would evolve into the Rizgarî/Komal movement after 1974, favored political advocacy. Beşikçi believed strongly in presenting political defenses and in doing so in Kurdish. His friend Mehdi Zana, later elected mayor of Diyarbakır, recalls: "He compelled us to speak Kurdish in the courts. He was brave, he gave new meaning to courage."[65] That said, although a significant number of Kurdish intellectuals presented political defenses, few did so in Kurdish. Many explained this through the idea that Kurdish defenses would amount to a form of nationalism incompatible with internationalism. Beşikçi, on the other hand, viewed these sorts of explanations as unconscious escape strategies developed to avoid certain costs: "Concepts such as internationalism, socialism, or revolutionism are employed not to truly make good on what these concepts call for, but as a cloak concealing self-escape—escape from fundamental problems."[66]

Presenting a political defense, especially in a manner that falls squarely within those spaces prohibited by the Turkishness Contract, came at a significant cost. A friend who visited Beşikçi in prison told him that, should he choose to not mount a political defense, his friends from the SBF would hire a famous and influential lawyer for him—underscoring that everyone was aware of the cost. After all, electing to present a political defense means not trying to prove one's innocence. It means accepting conviction from the outset and, instead, charging and judging the state—that is, mounting a rupture defense. Beşikçi's decision, in a sense and despite friendly warnings, thus amounted to a decision to break with the Turkishness Contract. And following his defense, he was sentenced to thirteen years in prison.

That Beşikçi violated the Turkishness Contract is evident not only in the punishment the state meted out but also in the attitude of his Turkish friends

---

65. Excerpted from the documentary *Sarı Hoca İsmail Beşikçi*, directed by Ahmet Soner.
66. İsmail Beşikçi, "Hapisteki DDKO," *Bir*, no. 5 (2006).

and professors. After serving three years in prison, Beşikçi was released through a general amnesty in 1974; he again applied to SBF to return to his job as a faculty member. However, unlike other SBF professors arrested on March 12, Beşikçi was told that he could not be reinstated since his sentence was final and that he would again have to take the qualifying exam. Beşikçi subsequently took the exam before the same sociology jury that had previously admitted him to SBF, but this time they deemed him unsuccessful. This should be interpreted, to my thinking, as an unofficial means of intellectual purge. And, indeed, Beşikçi was received very negatively by SBF professors and the Turkish social-scientific world more generally after 1974. In personal interactions with other left academics, Beşikçi was told that there is no such problem as the Kurdish problem, that this is simply a game of imperialism, or that, even if there is such a problem, it is too early to bring it up.[67] It also seems probable that in SBF, where left leanings predominated, Beşikçi's radicalism was perhaps seen as casting a disturbing shadow on the radicalism and socialism of other professors. In any case, the purge at SBF was carried out in a manner that appeared not as a purge but as scientific (a "jury decision"). The purge at Atatürk University, meanwhile, where Turkism predominated, was carried out openly, officially, and through the proud denunciations of Beşikçi's purgers.

The process of the independent organization and radicalization of Kurdish intellectuals, set in motion in 1969 and continuing in Diyarbakır prison, only intensified after the 1974 amnesty. The Rizgarî/Komal circle, to which, as I have noted, Beşikçi belonged, set about developing a new historiography through books contending the colonial and genocidal nature of the Turkish state (1915 and Dersim). For instance, Beşikçi came to understand the Kurdish families with relatives on both sides of the Turkish-Iraqi border, whom he encountered while serving in the military in 1963, as divided because of Kurdistan's status as an international colony, just as he came to understand the church ruins he came across in Hakkari's mountains as tied to the ethnic cleansing of non-Muslims. His ways of seeing had undergone a complete transformation. The four books published by Beşikçi in the second half of the 1970s, as part of his *Method of Science* series, are the product of these new ways of seeing. The first in the series considers the relationship between official ideology and the social sciences in Turkey. According to Beşikçi, official ideology works through various institutions to stifle the development of scientific thought (which should be based on facts); it limits academic thought as it shapes it. In a manner similar to the definition of Turkishness that I have

---

67. For more on this matter, see Baskın Oran's interview: "İsmail Beşikçi ve Mülkiye: Fevkalade Özel bir Mülkiyeliyle Söyleşi," 301–313.

tried to develop here, Beşikçi detects a contradiction between the researcher who is Turkish in terms of "content of consciousness" and the Kurd as object of research, and thus maintains that a Turkish researcher simply cannot examine Kurds in any factual and scientific manner.[68] In the remaining three books of the series, he examines the 1934 Settlement Law, the Turkish History Thesis and Sun Language Theory, and CHP's 1927 Charter primarily in their factual extent, through publicly available legal and charter texts, parliamentary deliberations, and contemporary texts all of which is to say that the documents he examines are not confidential. He goes on to criticize Turkish intellectuals and socialists for having overlooked racist and colonialist practices, so clearly visible if one simply takes the time to look for them, or for having interpreted such practices through the lens of official ideology when encountered.[69]

Beşikçi forwarded his critique of Turkish socialists in a series of letters in the 1970s. For instance, in a 1979 letter to Boran, the aforementioned near-legendary leader of the socialist movement, Beşikçi evaluates the Turkish left's opposition to the thesis of Kurdistan as a colony:

The Turkish left angrily opposes the colonial thesis developed by the Kurdish left. "A nation that is itself a colony or a semi-colony cannot have a colony," they say . . . all parties and all groups that claim to be on the left oppose the colonial thesis with the same terminology and the same concepts. On such an important issue, it cannot be seen as a coincidence that all parties and all groups come together and think in the same way. It is certainly no coincidence that the Communist Party of Turkey and Aydınlık[70] think the same thing, exactly the same thing. On the Kurdish national question, this is an attempt by the Turkish left to stay within the framework of official ideology as much as possible. Turkish left parties carry on with the business of communism even as they maintain their anti-Kurdish stance. As for this stance, it hardly upsets the Turkish bourgeoisie and the racist and colonialist state. Such, already, is the tacit agreement between the Turkish bourgeoisie and the Turkish left.[71]

---

68. Beşikçi, *Bilim Yöntemi*, 18–19.

69. See Beşikçi's *Kürtlerin Mecburi İskânı; Türk Tarih Tezi, Güneş-Dil Teorisi ve Kürt Sorunu;* and *Cumhuriyet Halk Fırkası'nın Tüzüğü (1927) ve Kürt Sorunu.* All were published by Komal Yayınları in the 1970s.

70. A controversial leftist movement and circle known for its Turkish nationalism.

71. Letter to Behice Boran dated August 31, 1979 (from the private archive of İsmail Beşikçi).

In the same year, in a letter to renowned SBF professor Mümtaz Soysal, Beşikçi commented on Turkish socialists' interest in national liberation movements in various parts of the world yet their lack of interest in the Kurdish question: "The basic condition for being a democrat in Turkey is one's stance on the Kurdish national problem. . . . Today, in Turkey, there is no price to pay, no cost, for pointed communist speech, for talking about Vietnam or Cambodia, for sending one's greetings to Angola, Namibia, or the Sandinistas. Yet to side with international-colonial Kurdistan, with the oppressed Kurdish nation, requires paying a price, a cost. A democrat has to pay that price."[72]

Beşikçi was made to pay a heavy price. Parallel to the gradual transformation he underwent, at every stage of transformation he was punished with increasing force: he was fired, not hired, ostracized by professors and friends, saw more than thirty of his books banned, and was imprisoned for a total of over seventeen years. The main reasons for this punishment were his noncompliance with the Turkishness Contract, the knowledge and thoughts he produced on subjects prohibited by certain subcomponents of the Contract of Ignorance, and his feelings forbidden by the Contract of Indifference. In addition, through the texts and defenses he penned, he revealed the content of the Turkishness Contract, even if he did not name it as such. In other words, he was not content simply with stepping out of life in the water; once out, he turned his attention to scrutinizing, demonstrating, and analyzing life in the water. By punishing Beşikçi, the state and Turkish-dominated institutions aimed to ensure that no one else dared do what he had done. But Beşikçi's exceptionality, in terms of his transcending the Turkishness Contract, cannot be made sense of solely with reference to the fear of punishment. For decades, countless Turkish socialists, fearless of punishment, have been killed, purged, exiled, and imprisoned. A more important factor than the fear of punishment is the inability to perceive Turkishness, the habitus of Turkishness—an inability, that is, to recognize the water in which one lives and the ways in which it determines one's thoughts and feelings. In this light, Beşikçi evaluates his own transformation:

You produce ideas. But the state confronts this with all its institutions and mechanisms of repression. That's what you become aware of. You become conscious of such obstruction. From the moment you become conscious of this obstruction, you try to overcome it. If you can overcome this, you have liberated yourself. From that moment on, your

---

72. For the letter, dated August 29, 1979, see Beşikçi, *Kürdistan Üzerinde Örgütlü Devlet Terörü ve İsmail Beşikçi*, 106.

mind is liberated. The pressure exerted by the state is no longer so important. You keep on persisting in the production of thought. Because you have overcome that mechanism of repression. But in order to overcome this, it is necessary to become conscious of it; that is what I am trying to emphasize.[73]

Beşikçi's individual transformation in the 1960s and 1970s was, in its radical and singular nature, a true exception. But, of course, this transformation did not occur in a vacuum. Beşikçi's change and transformation paralleled that of Kurds and Kurdistan. In a 1979 appeal to the court, he described this general transformation: "Nothing has changed, either in the attitude of the university and the professors, or in the attitude of the so-called 'independent judiciary.' It is Kurdistan that has changed. Kurdistan is not the old Kurdistan. It is changing rapidly. And Kurdish revolutionaries, democrats and patriotic elements are striving to comprehend, understand and explain the various aspects of this change. Despite all the oppression, persecution and imprisonment, the rapid increase in publications about Kurdistan, Kurds and the Kurdish language across the last five to six years is the most important evidence of this change."[74]

The Kurdish movement, born of the changes described by Beşikçi, emerged in the 1980s with a complex power of its own and rendered the ideas of Kurds visible and audible. The acceptance and acknowledgment, even within the state and mainstream politics, of the Kurdish problem in the early 1990s was a direct result of this movement of Kurdish empowerment. The first Turks to feel the effects of this process at an individual level hailed, naturally, from the intellectual left, and they began to feel the need to speak out and attend to a topic about which they had, to date, largely been silent and unconcerned. Among the first instances in which left intellectuals collectively took—or felt compelled to take—a position on the Kurdish question came in the form of a declaration published in 1991 by ninety-five intellectuals, under the banner, "There Is No Good Nationalism." The declaration chiefly criticized the Turkish state's suppression of Kurds and its denial of the Kurdish question. At the same time, though, as the title of the declaration suggests, it was also critical of nationalism, including Kurdish nationalism. It held that the distinction between the nationalism of the oppressor nation and that of the oppressed nation could not be likened to the distinction between bad and good nationalisms. Rather, all nationalisms were seen as mis-

---

73. Beşikçi, *Kirletilen Kavramlar*, 160.
74. Beşikçi, *Kürdistan Üzerinde Örgütlü Devlet Terörü ve İsmail Beşikçi*, 60–61.

guided. From such a perspective, the idea of an independent Kurdistan and the principle of "to every nation a state" was criticized as distant from a progressive stance. What was needed, the declaration said, were peaceful, solidaristic, and democratic ways of living together.[75]

Of particular interest for our concerns here is not whether the ideas in the declaration are right or wrong,[76] but their presentation—their framing—as if they were independent of Turkishness. It is very common among Turkish intellectuals to overlook or rule out the possibility that one's thoughts, feelings, and attitudes might have been shaped by Turkishness. This is perhaps tied to a certain mode of narcissism that Bourdieu sees as unique to the intellectual field: that the intellectual's thoughts belong to and spring from only the intellectual herself. Such is the illusion of the "knowing subject": that her thoughts take shape independently of the social and the everyday and are inherently disinterested.[77] Just as this delusion—especially particular to intellectuals from dominant ethnic and racial groups and with universalist orientations—may lead one to see himself as internationalist, scientific, humanist, rational, and even tempered, it may also lead one to view others as nationalist or emotional. A person who does not recognize herself as a Turk (and who, therefore, cannot imagine that her thoughts and feelings may have been shaped by Turkishness and the policed borders of the Turkishness Contract) immediately sees the Kurdishness of another, whose thoughts and feelings she takes to be inescapably formed by his Kurdishness—something the universalist intellectual advises the Kurd to rid himself of.

Increasingly, however, such ideas and assumptions have been questioned; it is this questioning that has, in part, generated the crisis of Turkishness. Metin Sever's *Kürt Sorunu: Aydınlarımız Ne Düşünüyor* (*The Kurdish Question: What Our Intellectuals Think*), published in 1992, constitutes, in this respect, an interesting example. The book presents thirty leftist, nationalist, and Islamist intellectuals with a range of general questions: What are the origins of the Kurdish problem? What might its solution look like? Is Kurdistan a colony or not? Why has the Turkish intellectual remained silent for so long about the Kurdish question? The answers vary, of course, according to the contributors' political backgrounds and ideological affiliations, from those who argue that Kurdistan is, in fact, a colony to others who label the PKK a terrorist organization with whom no state could possibly negotiate. Yet, regardless of the left

---

75. "Milliyetçiliğin 'Doğrusu' Yoktur."

76. For an article written around the time of the declaration's emergence that is critical of the signatories as liberals, see Savran, "Liberalizmin Doğrusu Yoktur."

77. See Bourdieu, *Pascalian Meditations*; Bourdieu and Wacquant, *Invitation to Reflexive Sociology*.

or right sympathies of the contributors, a significant proportion of the answers clearly demonstrates that the Kurdish question and Turkishness had yet to receive serious consideration. Even the best-educated left-wing intellectuals of Turkey were able, in this volume, to opine that Kurds can even become generals[78] or prime ministers, that it is not exclusively or specifically the Kurdish problem but rather all problems that Turkish intellectuals remain silent about, or that it is misguided to think that Kurdish culture is under pressure since Kurds lack a noteworthy culture in the first place.[79] Failing to realize how one's ways of seeing, thinking, and feeling have been shaped by Turkishness can lead to precisely such consequences, where little difference exists between the stances of the educated and uneducated or between the left and right intellectual.

One idea that at times unites right and left intellectuals in Turkey is the claim that, before the 1980s, one's ethnic identity was unimportant, that no one knew or asked about the ethnic identity of another. Of course, the 1960s and, in particular, the 1970s saw the emergence both of discussions around the Kurdish question and of independent Kurdish organizations writing their own histories. This claim would seem to stem, then, from Turkishness's ways of seeing and not seeing, of knowing and not knowing. For instance, the socialist Ömer Laçiner said, in a 2006 interview, "In the 1960s and '70s, we didn't ask about people's ethnicity or anything. We would learn three or four years later that our close friends were Kurds. Because ethnicity didn't matter to us. There was no talk of nationalities, but of common, universal, human values and ideas. The current climate is different."[80] Or, in an interview carried out by Mümtaz'er Türköne (a Turkish nationalist) with the Islamist Cemal Uşşak, the former labels as anachronistic Uşşak's observation that Islamists and religious people had long overlooked the Kurdish problem and the oppression of Kurds: "For 28 years now, there is the phenomenon of terrorism. 40–50 thousand people have died. And amid these acts of terror and the sounds of gunshots, society understood and learned that Kurds had a differ-

---

78. Attilâ İlhan (sympathetic to the nationalist left) notes, e.g., "The non-Muslim element was indeed treated harshly in the Republic. But there has been no such discrimination against the Kurds. Generals have emerged from among the Kurds." Quoted in Sever, *Kürt Sorunu*, 143.

79. E.g., according to Mete Tunçay (sympathetic to the liberal left), "There are many Kurds who serve as prime ministers and ministers in Turkey. It's not very justified for these people to complain about discrimination against Kurds. Of course there is a mass of Kurds who are discriminated against, but they aren't the ones who complain. That is, it doesn't seem that justified to me to see Kurds as having been oppressed like non-Muslim minorities, because in our traditions, no family has ever objected to one asking for their daughter's hand on the basis of his Kurdish blood. . . . I don't think Kurdish cultural production is being quashed. I also don't think it's such a cultural treasure as to be plundered." Quoted in Sever, *Kürt Sorunu*, 277, 280.

80. Laçiner, "Kimlikçilik Gericiliktir," 221.

ent language, a different identity. [Society] saw that they had demands. When you go back 28 years, when you go back to the 70s, 60s, don't you do injustice to the religious?" To Uşşak's answer, "Even when there was no PKK, there were Kurds," Türköne replied, "But we didn't know."[81]

It is not my intent here to obscure the significant differences, in terms of their approach to the Kurdish question, between Laçiner on the left and Türköne on the right, or to single out these two intellectuals by cherry-picking certain sentences. What I try to call attention to is, rather, how two intellectuals from very different political traditions simply do not recognize that their own conditions of not seeing and not knowing before the 1980s might be tied to Turkishness's conditions of not seeing and not knowing. Likewise, they seem to ignore the fact that the Kurds in their lives may have hidden or chosen not to highlight their Kurdishness as a necessary part of living within the Turkishness Contract. Insofar as they fail to appreciate the socially and historically constituted forms of seeing and not seeing, knowing and not knowing, and concealing and not concealing that are proper to both Turkishness and Kurdishness, their belief in the veracity and the scientific nature of their analyses remains unshaken. Thus, in a manner similar to discourses of color blindness in the United States, they develop forms of discourse that we might call ethnic blindness, which function to blind them not so much to the Kurdishness before them but to their own Turkishness.[82]

Turkish intellectuals like Laçiner and Türköne supported the peace process, even if, as I claim, they saw and thought within the schemas of Turkishness. Both worked to ensure that their different audiences supported the peace process. In this sense, they opened Turkishness up to discussion, albeit indirectly. That said, many Turkish intellectuals opposed the peace process and sought to reestablish (at least at an intellectual level) the notion of Turkishness and its dominance in the face of its interrogation; that is, they sought, thereby, to alleviate the crisis of Turkishness for their audiences. Within this second group, those who opposed the peace process, the historians who emphasized the accuracy of old information about modern Turkish history, against the explosion of the new, played an important role.

81. Türköne, *Türküm Vicdanlıyım*, 14–15. The interview was conducted in 2012. Also, "28 years" refers to 1984, when the PKK carried out its first armed attack.

82. For an article criticizing the blindness of Turkish socialists to the left ideology of the Kurdish movement and the left tendencies of its base (as well as their discomfort when they do recognize this), see Aktan, "Makul ve Makbul Kürtler," 45–53. For a critique of Marxist and liberal Turkish intellectuals' internalized self-confidence in their own knowledge and righteousness, see Yonucu, "Sömürgeci Devletin Aydını ve Muhalif Olmak," accessed August 24, 2017, available at http://www.birikimdergisi.com/guncel-yazilar/1255/somurgeci-devletin-aydini-ve-muhalifi-ol mak#.WZ7UIOlLfIU.

Let us consider, then, in this context of efforts to preserve and maintain Turkishness's ways of seeing, hearing, knowing, and feeling, İlber Ortaylı and Murat Bardakçı, perhaps Turkey's two most popular historians. Ortaylı and Bardakçı's books are bestsellers, and their television programs are viewed widely. It seems to me that both have responded to an important need, and it is mainly this to which they owe their popularity. Both figures, speaking from their authority as historians (and making a particular point to underscore this authority), have made use of their many media platforms to decry new ideas as "absurd," "stupid," or "ignorant" and to urge their audiences not to take such ideas and information seriously. Their audiences are told that what they already know is not wrong; on the contrary, it is true. They are relieved to hear that those who said they were wrong are, in fact, unfair and uninformed. For example, Ortaylı, who stresses both his academic authority and his authority as a historian, has spoken insistently on the impossibility of shifting from ethnic to place-based notions of identity and names (i.e., from *Türk* to *Türkiyeli*), describing such a shift as both historically inaccurate and politically harmful (in much more cynical and condescending terms, of course). In so doing, Ortaylı has, by his very presence, helped soothe and compensate for the crisis of Turkishness.[83]

In some ways following Ortaylı and in others exceeding him, the amateur historian Bardakçı contributed to the flood of new information by publishing a large number of new documents claiming that, since there is nothing like genocide in the history of Turkey to be ashamed of, there is thus nothing to be afraid of. And lest the reader suspect, from the documents he published, that something bad may have been done to non-Muslims, Bardakçı steps in here and tries to ensure that no new feelings be produced from this new information. A striking example, in this context, is a 1917 letter by novelist Halide Edip (Adıvar) to the Ottoman Minister of Finance Cavid Bey. At one point

---

83. See, e.g., Ortaylı, "Türkiyelilik." Ortaylı claims that the term "Turkey," "in the sense of the country of the Turks," was a place-name given by "Italy, which knew the world very well," in the Middle Ages. The main function of this sentence, which repeats a well-known knowledge, is conveyed by its emphasis on "Italy, which knew the world very well." Weak ideas are reinforced by such phrases as being very familiar with, knowing very well, and being a very good historian, which function to conceal and suppress their actual weakness. Consider, in this context, Ortaylı's interview with *Sözcü*: "Türkiyeli diye bir şey yoktur, Türk Türk'tür," available at http://www.sozcu.com.tr/2015/gundem/turkiyeli-diye-bir-sey-olmaz-turk-turktur-808575/. Kuban, one of Turkey's leading architectural historians, employed similar strategies in his writings on Turkishness, criticizing people who discuss Turkishness as ignorant of history. See, e.g., Kuban's "Ben Neden Türk'üm"; "Bir Toplumsal Varlık ve Kimlik Sorunu." What I criticize here is not their abilities as historians, but, rather, their conviction that their own subjective ideas on Turkishness are related to objective knowledge of history and historiography, as well as the ways in which they reflect this conviction.

in her letter from Beirut, Edip reflects on the Armenians deported to Syria and Lebanon: "They ended up here after eating grass in the deserts to fill their bellies, some losing their mothers, some their fathers, and many their children. . . . A wretched man who suddenly lost the ability to speak when his son was killed beside him does not know where they disposed of his other son and his family. . . . Can the new cabinet not at least mitigate the consequences of this unprecedented cruelty and murder?"

Here, the reader is confronted with the words of one of the most important names in Turkish literature, conveying to an Ottoman minister the pains and cruelties she personally observed. The reader thus risks, in the face of this new information, doubting what she once knew and experiencing new feelings that could lead to sympathizing with Armenians. To prevent this, the historian steps in, abusing his authority. In a personal comment at the outset of the letter he published, Bardakçı implies that Edip's words should not be taken seriously. He goes on to attempt to manage the reader's emotions, exhibiting the performance of Turkishness expected of him: "The exaggerated expressions in Halide Edip's letter should be attributed to her artistic personality as a novelist."[84] Unlike Edip, Bardakçı is not interested with making up for what happened to the Armenians. His concern is to show that he did not violate the Turkishness Contract in publishing such a document as well as to compensate for the crisis of Turkishness.

In his widely read newspaper articles, Bardakçı reminds us of the terms of the Muslimness and Turkishness Contracts and issues a warning of sorts to those who owe their security and privileges to these contracts. For example, he accuses the Circassians of Turkey of ingratitude (and, in a sense, threatens them) in light of their recent efforts to demand education and cultural rights in their mother tongue, even as he notes that at least half his ancestors were migrants from the Caucasia. I quote at length from this article, as I think it summarizes well the logic of the contract:

The Circassians living in Turkey today came to Turkey not with the enthusiasm of "seeing different places" or "going and trying their luck in the New World," but because of the extremely bloody Russian operations in the Caucasus, intensifying particularly in the middle of the 19th century. The reason for their migration was simply to escape the Russian sword, to save their lives. The troubled Turkey under Sultan Abdulaziz welcomed hundreds of thousands of Circassian immigrants, provided them with places, jobs and food, and even gave them im-

---

84. Bardakçı, *Talat Paşa'nın Evrak-ı Metrûkesi*, 149–151.

portant duties within the state. Today, in almost every publication by Caucasian associations, there is a section entitled "Circassians Who Made a Mark"; . . . When you look at the lists, you see many names from politicians to artists, from businessmen to scholars. In fact, there are Circassians who are presidents and prime ministers, and it is blatant ingratitude towards Turkey to say, in spite of all the titles and the positions they have gained, such things as "our identity is being oppressed" or "our rights are taken away from us"! . . . It is to their own shame that young people of Caucasian descent do not know [Caucasian] languages. . . . The fault for forgetting lies not with the state, but with families. . . . There is a place where those who still do not feel "from here," after so many generations, should demand their cultural, political, etc. rights: the Caucasus! . . . If you can afford it, go and ask for your rights there.[85]

Yet such solutions as offered by Ortaylı and Bardakçı are, relative to the scale of the crisis facing Turkishness and the Turkishness Contract, merely palliative; like a painkiller, they only serve to gloss over or postpone the crisis. Statist and nationalist historians are unable to develop a new and intellectually sophisticated historiography that can cope with the gravity of the problems facing Turkishness. Even if some readers are relieved by the language of "ignorant," "stupid," or "ungrateful," this does little to prevent the escalation of the crisis. To discount a real weakening and crisis through the misuse of the historian's authority only serves to amplify this weakening and crisis.

Alongside such reactions, the crisis of Turkishness, prompted by the growing strength of Kurds and Armenians, has also led to the emergence of a strong critical historiographical vein within Turkish thought. In the early 1990s, such publishing houses as Yurt and Belge began to issue Beşikçi's works, old and new.[86] While Fikret Başkaya's 1991 book *Paradigmanın İflası: Resmi İdeolojinin Eleştirisine Giriş* (*The Bankruptcy of a Paradigm: An Introduction to the Critique of Official Ideology*) resulted in Başkaya's imprisonment and expulsion from the university,[87] it left a great impression on a new generation of Marxist academics and intellectuals. Taner Akçam's pioneering works on the Ar-

85. Bardakçı, "Bir 'Çerkes Açılımı' Eksikti!" available at http://www.haberturk.com/yazar lar/murat-bardakci/609308-bir-cerkes-acilimi-eksikti. See also Bardakçı, "Vatana ve Millete Hayırlı Olmasın," available at http://www.haberturk.com/yazarlar/murat-bardakci/1032983 -vatana-ve-millete-hayirli-olmasin.

86. Belge Yayınları, headed by Ayşe Zarakolu (1946–2002) and Ragıp Zarakolu, has published a number of books that have contributed significantly to the understanding of the Armenian issue.

87. Başkaya, *Paradigmanın İflası.*

menian question, in the 1990s, began to attract the attention of liberal academics, especially in the 2000s. Also in the 2000s, Dink was perhaps the most influential figure in Turkey's intellectual world. That said, Dink's real and enormous influence is a result of his death as much as his life.

The process that would end with Dink's murder began with a story he wrote in the newspaper *Agos*, in early 2004, claiming that Sabiha Gökçen, well known as the first Turkish female pilot, may have been an Armenian taken from an orphanage (i.e., a "remnant of the sword"). As Dink said in his news commentary, "[Gökçen's] name became symbolic not only of Turkey, but also of Turkishness. Before all else, she was Atatürk's adopted daughter and represented a model for Turkish women through the power she received from him. What mainly brought her fame, though, was the fact that she was the first Turkish woman in the Air Force, and moreover, was among the heroes (!) who put down the Dersim rebellion." In other words, if Dink's claim is true, Gökçen, who participated in the Dersim Operation as a fighter pilot, was an Armenian orphan whose Armenianness was concealed both by the state and by Gökçen herself. This claim was enough by itself to set in motion a debate on the making of the Turkishness Contract and the ways in which it has shaped the lives of institutions and individuals—that is, it was enough to threaten the Turkishness Contract. Indeed, in response, the general staff issued a harsh statement demanding observance of the Turkishness Contract: "In this period, when our national unity and cohesion should be the strongest, the purpose of such publications taking aim at our national unity and cohesion and national values is now understood by a large part of Turkish society and is being monitored with concern. . . . In this context, it is expected, as a nation, that the Turkish media will be more sensitive to Atatürk's spiritual existence, his system of thought, the basic principles and values of the Republic of Turkey, and the unity and cohesion of the Turkish nation, and that they will review their publishing principles in light of such thoughts."[88]

In the wake of the news on Sabiha Gökçen and the statement of the general staff, nationalist and Turkist groups ramped up their actions against Dink. A phrase Dink used in an article he published in 2004 was deliberately distorted and presented as denigrating Turkishness, and a lawsuit was filed against Dink to that effect (the official charges were for insulting and denigrating Turkishness). Although the expert report ruled in Dink's favor, the court sentenced him to six months in prison on October 7, 2005, for insulting Turkishness. The statements in the court's decision—which normally should have no

---

88. Dink, "Sabiha-Hatun'ın Sırrı." The report and the statement by the general staff, accessed July 28, 2017, are available at http://www.agos.com.tr/tr/yazi/17528/sabiha-hatunun-sirri.

place in the legal text of a modern state—underscored the nature of this case, concerning someone who was outside the Turkishness Contract and who threatened the contract. Or, in other words, since the accused was tried as an enemy, the case was outside of normal conditions and was now a matter of enemy law:

> Freedom of thought, freedom of expression, is not unlimited. Everything has a limit. This limitation is sometimes by law and sometimes by moral rules. There can be no freedom of expression of a humiliating or hurtful nature. . . . Every country has its own values. There are such countries where you can make shorts out of your flag and it will be tolerated. There are such countries where if you touch their cow, it creates indignation. . . . There are such peoples for whom when you say blood, the blood of the ancestors found on every inch of this land is called to mind. Every square inch of this land is soaked in blood. Since Atatürk knew very well that it was this blood that saved this country, he told the youth that this blood held the power they needed in every difficult situation. However, the defendant has stated that this blood is poisonous. This is disrespectful to Turkish ancestors, martyrs, the values that make up the nation, and, of course, it is humiliating and hurtful.[89]

The campaign against Dink resulted in his murder by the far-right Ogün Samast on January 19, 2007. To date, it remains unclear who or what institutions or structures were behind the murder;[90] the AKP government first blamed nationalists and then the Fettullah Gülen movement, after relations between the two entities spoiled. More crucial for our subject, though, is the guilt that Dink's murder has engendered among, particularly, a new generation of left intellectuals. Dink was killed in plain sight, following a process that unfurled for all to see. Consequently, oppositional intellectuals felt a certain responsibility for the murder—an intense guilt, marked by feelings

---

89. Quoted in Çetin, *Utanç Duyuyorum*, 341.

90. Two days after the assassination, Serdar Turgut ("Türklüğün İsyanı"), a popular columnist at the time, wrote: "It does not matter who the killer was or what he served. What is important is the creation and explosion of an atmosphere of animosity. For quite some time, I've feared an explosion of the nationalism of Turks." He linked the sociological dynamic behind the assassination to the "rebellion of Turkishness": "For many years, being a Turk in this country was forced into the position of near criminality. Turks and Turkey were constantly humiliated. Citing European values, Turks were targeted, citing democracy, Turks were humiliated, Turks were always bad. They constantly toyed with the pride of our ordinary people. The Kurds have emerged from victimhood and have begun to be a dominant force. The chief murderer [Öcalan, B.Ü.] became the crown jewel of the defenders of democracy. The same people, meanwhile, humiliated Turkey at every opportunity."

and thoughts of having ignored the situation or having been unable to protect Dink. Such feelings were not only about Dink's murder; countless people saw Dink's murder as but a continuation of 1915 in 2007. Such a connection, drawn between the killing of hundreds of thousands of people in 1915 and the murder of a single person in 2007, points to the development of a certain historical consciousness of the Turkishness Contract. And such consciousness contributed to the development of such feelings as responsibility and guilt, stepping outside of the Contract of Indifference. In other words, there was as much guilt for Dink's murder as there was for 1915 as well as a sense of moral responsibility for the crimes committed. Embodying this new climate of consciousness and feeling was the slogan, "We are all Hrant, we are all Armenian," chanted by tens of thousands of people attending Dink's funeral.[91] The slogan reflected not just the ephemeral emotional state of that day but a broader intellectual and emotional transformation.[92] It was also an expression of determination born of guilt: to never again be complicit in crimes committed within the framework of the Turkishness Contract.

The magnitude of the transformation that Dink's death brought about for intellectuals once again became clear with the "I Apologize" campaign in 2008. The text of the apology, signed by more than thirty thousand people and written in the first person, states: "My conscience does not accept the insensitivity to the Great Catastrophe suffered by the Ottoman Armenians in 1915 and the denial of it. I reject this injustice, share the feelings and pain of my Armenian brothers and sisters, and apologize to them."[93] This two-sentence declaration pointed to an abandonment—a rejection—by tens of thousands of Turks of the world of knowledge and feelings proper to the Turkishness Contract. Yet this declaration was issued and signed at a time when both the Turkishness Contract had been partially softened and AKP was still careful to maintain the image of democratic rule. Indeed, while some in the AKP leadership were critical, their tone was, on the whole, mild.[94]

---

91. For an analysis of the emotional transformation embodied in the assassination of Dink through the concept of "moral shock," see Demirhisar, "Emotion and Protest in Turkey," available at https://www.opendemocracy.net/deniz-g-nce-demirhisar/emotion-and-protest-in-turkey -what-happened-on-19-january-2007.

92. For various forms and agents of collective guilt and its absence, see Branscombe and Doosje, *Collective Guilt.*

93. The signature text and the list of signatories, accessed August 12, 2017, is available at http:// web.archive.org/web/20160304054234/http://ozurdiliyoruz.com/.

94. In the wake of President Abdullah Gül's statement that the declaration reflected Turkey's democratic atmosphere of debate, CHP member of parliament Canan Arıtman claimed that Gül's mother was of Armenian descent. In response, Gül issued a new statement avowing that family was "Muslim and Turkish" and that this could be proven by family trees and official population registers. See "Gül'den 'Etnik Köken' Açıklaması," CNN Türk, December 21, 2008, accessed

Less than a decade later, the declaration released by the group Academics for Peace (BAK) on January 11, 2016, with the signatures of 1,128 academics/ researchers under the banner, "We will not be a party to this crime," came at a time of both renewed ossification of the Turkishness Contract and the wholesale abandonment, by the AKP government, of any claims to democracy. In a climate marked by the expectation that everyone perform Turkishness—through both the positive (active) and negative (passive) performances specific to various professions, classes, and ideologies[95]—and by profound indifference and silence about the experiences of Kurds, BAK signatories announced their noncompliance with the Turkishness Contract and with crimes committed:

> The Turkish state has effectively condemned its citizens in Sur, Silvan, Nusaybin, Cizre, Silopi, and many other towns and neighborhoods in the Kurdish provinces to hunger through its use of curfews that have been ongoing for weeks. It has attacked these settlements with heavy weapons and equipment that would only be mobilized in wartime. As a result, the right to life, liberty, and security, and in particular the prohibition of torture and ill-treatment protected by the constitution and international conventions have been violated.
>
> This deliberate and planned massacre is in serious violation of Turkey's own laws and international treaties to which Turkey is a party. These actions are in serious violation of international law.
>
> We demand the state to abandon its deliberate massacre and deportation of Kurdish and other peoples in the region. We also demand the state to lift the curfew, punish those who are responsible for human rights violations, and compensate those citizens who have experienced material and psychological damage. For this purpose we demand that independent national and international observers to be given access to the region and that they be allowed to monitor and report on the incidents.

August 12, 2017, available at https://www.cnnturk.com/2008/turkiye/12/21/gulden.etnik.ko ken.aciklamasi/505716.0/index.html.

95. There are countless instances of such performances: prosecutors launched or refrained from launching investigations, judges ruled or refrained from ruling, journalists reported or refrained from reporting, academics wrote or refrained from writing. For an example (among many) that almost approaches cliché, see that of journalist İsmet Berkan, who reported from inside armored police vehicles during the clashes in Sur (Diyarbakır): "İsmet Berkan Sur'da," *Sol*, December 29, 2015, available at http://haber.sol.org.tr/medya/ismet-berkan-surda-zirhli-aracta-poz -verdi-140973.

We demand the government to prepare the conditions for negotiations and create a road map that would lead to a lasting peace which
includes the demands of the Kurdish political movement. We demand
inclusion of independent observers from broad sections of society
in these negotiations. We also declare our willingness to volunteer as
observers. We oppose suppression of any kind of the opposition.

We, as academics and researchers working on and/or in Turkey,
declare that we will not be a party to this massacre by remaining silent
and demand an immediate end to the violence perpetrated by the state.
We will continue advocacy with political parties, the parliament, and
international public opinion until our demands are met.[96]

A day after the declaration was announced, President Recep Tayyip Erdoğan
disparaged the signatory academics, calling them "so-called intellectuals" and
"intellectual hacks" and accusing them of betrayal: "The mob that calls itself
academic accuses the state. Not content with this, they invite foreigners to
Turkey. This is called [an invitation to mandate rule]. There was the same
mentality 100 years ago."[97] Prime Minister Ahmet Davutoğlu said that he
believed the signatories had unknowingly and unwittingly signed the declaration, which, according to him, amounted to support for terrorism, and that
they should withdraw their signatures: "I invite every single signatory to read
and evaluate this text once again."[98] Erdoğan's harsh insults and Davutoğlu's
relatively mild warnings left no doubt that the signatories would be punished.
The threats of the mafia boss Sedat Peker can be interpreted historically—
leaving aside the fantasies of violence—in the context of the relationship
between the Turkishness Contract and punishment: those who step outside
the contract will be punished, often by unlawful means and with impunity.
Peker declared, "[THE SONS OF THE MOTHERLAND] will take the
declaration you have signed before them, they will come to your luxurious
workplaces, declaring you to be the truly dangerous ones. (Rest assured, they
won't kill you alongside your children and spouses.) They will take their revenge in a manner befitting a Muslim Turk, but they will not forget to bathe

---

96. "We Will Not Be a Party to This Crime! (in English, French, German, Spanish, Arabic,
Russian, Greek)," January 10, 2016, accessed September 4, 2023, available at https://barisicinak
ademisyenler.net/node/63.

97. "Erdoğan: Sözde Akademisyenlerin Haddini," BBC Turkish, January 12, 2016, accessed
July 20, 2017, available at http://www.bbc.com/turkce/haberler/2016/01/160111_erdogan_aka
demisyen_aciklama.

98. "Davutoğlu: Eminim Birçok Akademisyen," T24, January 15, 2016, accessed July 30,
2017, available at http://t24.com.tr/haber/davutoglu-yoku-yeniden-insa-etmeliyiz,324334.

in your blood. . . . I repeat: WE'RE GOING TO SPILL YOUR BLOOD IN STREAMS, AND WE'RE GOING TO BATHE IN YOUR BLOOD!!!"[99]
But the vast majority of signatories did not withdraw their signatures, despite all the insults, warnings, and threats. Furthermore, within ten days, more than one thousand additional academics signed the declaration. On January 20, 2016, the BAK group, in a new statement, announced the total number of signatories to have reached 2,212 and called an end to the signature campaign.[100] The second round of signatures are of particular importance, added as they were after the insults, warnings, and threats. A significant number of academics—a mass, one could say, considering the size of the field—supported the declaration, despite the very real likelihood of paying a price. And, in fact, as expected, hundreds of signatories were dismissed from their jobs in state and private universities by state of emergency decrees. Four signatories were arrested,[101] dozens received death threats, and hundreds were banned from traveling abroad.

Whereas in the 1960s and 1970s only one academic, Beşikçi, took a radical stance on the Kurdish issue and paid a price for it, in the 2010s this number reached the thousands. I do not mean to imply that all BAK signatories have gone through the sort of radical individual transformation that Beşikçi experienced, have entirely severed their ties with Turkishness, have stepped out of the water, or are prepared to pay a price as significant as what Beşikçi paid. BAK signatories are a heterogeneous group of academics from across the left spectrum, with different political affiliations, from different class backgrounds, and enjoying different degrees of privilege depending on the universities and cities where they work. While there were some signatories close to the Republican People's Party, many were close to the pro-Kurdish HDP and to other leftist movements. Just as there are those who hold the state entirely responsible for the clashes in 2015—the subject of the declaration—others find the PKK at least as responsible and guilty as the state. As such, many signatories felt the declaration to be one sided, as it solely criticizes the state, but they signed nevertheless. Across all these differences, though, thousands of academics risked exiting the contract based on a common will.[102] How,

99. Sedat Peker, "Sözde Aydınlar Çanlar," accessed July 30, 2017, available at http://sedatpeker.com/-552.htm. Emphasis is in the original text.
100. "Basına ve Kamuoyuna," January 20, 2016, accessed July 31, 2017, available at https://barisicinakademisyenler.net/node/69.
101. Esra Mungan, Muzaffer Kaya, Kıvanç Ersoy, and Meral Camcı.
102. There are many academics who, in theory, could have signed such a document, but who, in practice, opted out for various reasons (seeing little use in signing a declaration, or being uncomfortable of some of the statements and calls in the declaration). In other words, the impact of the transformation that I speak of goes far beyond BAK and the signatories.

then, to explain this partnership? Why were thousands of academics willing to pay the price for signing such a statement?

Many different answers have been put forth in response to these and similar questions.[103] To my mind, behind this partnership and the determination of many to pay the price are the echoes, in the academy, of a widespread crisis of Turkishness. Owing to the strength of the Kurdish movement and the increasing audacity of Kurds and Armenians, dissident academics began to see what they had not seen before, to hear what they had not heard, to know what they had not known, and to care about matters they were once indifferent to. In other words, as the negative states of Turkishness became unsustainable, they began to see, hear, know, and attend to those outside the Turkishness Contract, which, in turn, encouraged the development of a new awareness among academics regarding their own thoughts: about what they thought and how, about how their thoughts were formed, as well as about what they had once found unthinkable and why. I have in mind here the development of a capacity for thought that Bourdieu calls reflexivity, that "systematic exploration of the 'unthought categories of thought, which delimit the thinkable and predetermine the thought.'"[104]

These new ways of knowing and thinking have also generated new ways of feeling. Among these new feelings are sympathy with others as well as moral feelings directed at oneself, such as guilt and shame. One can thus speak both of a new morality constituted beyond the moral world of the Turkishness Contract and of new subjects following lines of action according to this new morality. Such new subjects no longer see, hear, know about, or care in the way expected of a Turk. As one's ways of seeing, hearing, and knowing are transformed, it becomes no longer possible to not see, not hear, ignore, or remain impassive. Such a transformation also renders universalist escape mechanisms useless. If, in the past, one could avoid such matters as the Armenian and Kurdish questions by maintaining one's self-esteem (insofar as universalism allowed one to link these problems to imperialism, feudalism, reactionism, tribalism, etc.), in time, as the crimes committed (and passed over in silence) within the framework of the Muslimness and Turkishness Contracts were revealed, such escape mechanisms lost their prestige and, therefore, their utility. This new repertoire of awareness and feeling about past crimes and their ongoing effects

---

103. A number of studies explore the case of Academics for Peace from different angles. See, e.g., Vatansever, "Partners in Crime," 3–25; Özatalay, "Purge, Exile, and Resistance," 1–46; Özdemir, Mutluer, and Özyürek, "Exile and Plurality in Neoliberal Times," 235–259; Biner, "Precarious Solidarities," 15–32; Tutkal, "Power, Knowledge, and Universities," 639–654.

104. Quoted in "Toward a Social Praxeology: The Structure and Logic of Bourdieu's Sociology," by Loïc Wacquant, published in Bourdieu and Wacquant, *Invitation to Reflexive Sociology*, 40.

has eliminated the possibility of remaining silent on present and future crimes. In this sense, it is particularly poignant that the conflict in 2015 at the heart of the declaration coincides with the centenary of 1915. In this way, the determination to not be complicit, rooted in a sense of historical and moral responsibility, overcame the fear of paying the price.

Conclusion

If one reason for the social process I have characterized as "a crisis of Turkishness" is the dynamics from the ground up of the Kurdish empowerment, the other reason is the top-down dynamics tied to the multilayered crisis of the Turkish state. The Turkishness Contract was founded on the promise that Turks and Turkified people would have various rights, protections, and opportunities granted by the Turkish state. And the Republic of Turkey could, in fact, offer Turks—consistent with the liberal contractual model—a more or less functioning democracy, meritocracy, rule of law, and social rights (including the autonomous and secular institutions guaranteeing all these). From time to time, and for various reasons, this contractual model was thrown into crisis and, therefore, needed modifications and restorations. This need for restoration was one of the causes of the relatively brief periods of military coups and interventions (in 1960, 1971, 1980, and 1997), which increasingly shifted to the right. However, over the past two decades, the AKP government has chipped away at, if not eliminated entirely, this liberal contractual model and its vital pillars of democracy, meritocracy, the rule of law, and secularism. The state has become synonymous with single-party rule, dominated by kleptocratic networks; legal institutions now simply function as an extension of the ruling party and one-man rule; the far-right ruling bloc has invaded such autonomous institutions as universities. While this state collapse has many consequences for the contractual logic, one crucial outcome at the level of individual lives can be summarized as follows: a Turkish individual can no longer ascend within any state institution by maintaining respect for herself, her profession, and her worldview; to put it the other way around, the individuals who rise can only do so by making major concessions and compromises in their character, profession, and worldview. The costs of Turkishness and Turkification rise as their benefits fall.

Here, by way of conclusion, I take up certain theoretical discussions and political reconfigurations, suggested by the idea of a national contract, building on the insight that the crisis of contract we see in Turkey today, certainly, assumes a particular social form specific to the conditions of its historical constitution, yet it is hardly a unique phenomenon in world history and politics. In particular, I call attention to the fact that "contract" is not an isolated logic of sovereignty but always operates in conjunction with another relational and parallel logic of sovereignty, "colonialism." Focusing on the relationship between these logics of power—one of constant mutual production and reproduction—may also shed light on the very operations of modernity and its current crisis.

Looking back on world politics from the present, the collapse of socialism in the early 1990s appears (contrary to the hopes of some mainstream thinkers) to have ushered in not so much the final triumph of liberalism as the process of its disintegration.[1] Already neoliberalism, globalization, and financialization, ascendant in the 1980s, had given rise to significant political corruption through the lifting of various institutional, ideological, and ethical barriers before the market economy. Opening Soviet and Chinese geographies to capitalism in the 1990s set in motion a channeling of plundered wealth to the rest of the world (through banks, real estate markets, lobbying and consulting firms, football clubs, and more), redoubling processes of corruption already in motion. The disappearance of the threat of socialism further took away one of liberalism's most important reasons for being and led to a growing perception of the liberal center (including its center right and center left) as an overly corrupt structure based on the rule of experts and elites. Consequently, a gradual decline in reverence for the various institutions and principles of the liberal contract model runs parallel to a gradual erosion of the liberal center—which is another way of saying, an erosion of the pillar of modern nation-states and, thus, of national contracts. And the ensuing vacuum is being filled by far-right movements and their chauvinist, racist, sexist, demagogic, and mafia-esque leaders.

I am far from alone in considering the global dissolution of the liberal center and the growing strength of the far right as a crisis of the social contract

---

1. For an insightful and foresighted study of the crisis of liberalism, see Wallerstein, *After Liberalism*.

model. Andreas Wimmer, for instance, well known for his work on nationalism, sees modern nation-states as formed on a contract in which the rulers promise to govern the country in the interests of the people, and, in return, they expect political loyalty, soldiers, and taxes from the people. This logic of the national contract, which nationalism both reflects and justifies, has benefited not only the new elites but also ordinary people "because the nation-state offered a better exchange relationship with the government than any previous model of statehood had. Instead of graduated rights based on social status, nationalism promised the equality of all citizens before the law. Instead of restricting political leadership to the nobility, it opened up political careers to talented commoners. Instead of leaving the provision of public goods to guilds, villages, and religious institutions, nationalism brought the power of the modern state to bear in promoting the common good. And instead of perpetuating elite contempt for the uncultured plebs, nationalism elevated the status of the common people by making them the new source of sovereignty and by moving popular culture to the center of the symbolic universe."[2]

In countries where these mutual promises, duties, and responsibilities are more or less fulfilled (where democracy, meritocracy, and the welfare state more or less function), the people begin to see themselves as a nation, as an extended family. That said, according to Wimmer, this model is undergoing a crisis even in those Western countries where it works best. Center-left governments in particular, he argues, have both neglected the interests of the nation through proimmigration and pro–free trade positions and marginalized the white working class as the putative reactionary enemies of progress. Right-wing populists fill this vacuum. They promise to put the interests of the nation first; they advocate, in other words, a return to the most basic principle of nationalism. According to Wimmer, instead of combating nationalism, the solution lies in building better, more inclusive, more democratic, and fairer nationalisms: "The challenge for both old and new nation-states is to renew the national contract between the rulers and the ruled by building—or rebuilding—inclusive coalitions that tie the two together."[3]

One can criticize Wimmer's prescription as conservative or unimaginative. But, in explaining the power of nation-states and nationalism in terms of the national contract, he points to something important. The main problem that I see with Wimmer's modern historical narrative is that he emphasizes only one of the models that have defined modernity. As such, he limits his attempt to analyze today's complex moment of crisis to developed Western

2. Wimmer, "Why Nationalism Works and Why It Isn't Going Away," 30.
3. Wimmer, 34.

countries, whereas, as I noted earlier, attending simultaneously to the two basic and parallel logics of power (contractual and colonial) that have shaped the modern world might offer a broader, more explanatory model. The contractual logic of power provides various rights, guarantees, and opportunities to a nation possessing certain characteristics (racial, ethnic, and/or religious) framed as somehow unique. It resides, in a sense, within the individuals who make up the nation and exercises sovereignty over them in an almost invisible and imperceptible way. Thus is the consent of the nation obtained. The colonial logic of power is constituted by, and continues to operate through, physical and cultural violence against peoples who do not belong to this or that unique nation and whose rights and demands are not seen as legitimate. This logic of power exerts an external, not internal, form of sovereignty over individuals; it is open, bare, and does not have the consent of these peoples. This dual and parallel structuring of power inherent to nation-states has become, with the spread of modernity and capitalism, a global phenomenon.

The logic of dual power unique to modernity has attracted the attention of many thinkers and social scientists, even if they do not name it as such. Mahmood Mamdani, for example, has suggested a revised timeline for the emergence of the nation-state. He points to 1492, when the Castilian Monarchy homogenized Iberia by purging it of Muslims and Jews and began building colonies in the Americas: "Modern colonialism and the modern state were born together with the creation of the nation-state. Nationalism did not precede colonialism. . . . The two were co-constituted."[4] Individuals of the nation were civilized over time and, thereby, endowed with liberal tolerance and rights, while, in uncivilized and uncivilizable colonies, violence reigned. Mamdani thus makes a conceptual and historical distinction between liberal modernity, which is oriented toward the nation, and colonial modernity, which is oriented toward the nonnation.[5]

Indeed, violence predominates in the making of national contracts. Those deemed incapable of belonging in any way to the nation are subjected to ethnic cleansing; those who are thought to belong, now or in the future, are, in a sense, reconquered and civilized. This is taken up by Eugen Weber in his renowned work on the making of modern France, where he concludes that the transformation of savage peasants into civilized Frenchmen entailed the application within France of something resembling colonialism in Algeria.[6]

---

4. Mamdani, *Neither Settler nor Native*, 1–2.

5. For another study that emphasizes the simultaneity of liberalism and colonialism, see Lowe, *Intimacies of Four Continents*. Decolonial thinkers, of course, also see coloniality as the dark side of modernity. See, e.g., Mignolo, *Darker Side of Western Modernity*.

6. Weber, *Peasants into Frenchmen*.

Michel Foucault, too, has described those disciplinary mechanisms that work to both domesticate and normalize individuals and render them productive as a mode of internal colonization.[7] From the middle of the nineteenth century, in fact, we see colonies established within the national borders of colonizing countries, where alcoholics, lunatics, beggars, criminals, and some indigenous peoples were confined.[8] That said, and as Weber points out, the physical and cultural violence that accompanies the processes of civilizing the nation is usually relatively mild and temporary. In a way, the internal colonization of the French—their civilization and incorporation into the nation—was desired and welcomed, for it meant development and prosperity.[9]

Whereas on the other side of the Mediterranean, in French-colonial Algeria, violence was uninterrupted,[10] because democratic governance can only be applied to the nation of a nation-state, not to other nations. The "specific imaginary of state" that Achille Mbembe describes as the colonial *commandement* is the opposite of the liberal model of discussion and debate. The logic of colonialism—not recourse to violence, but violence itself—rests on three types of violence: conquest, or constitutive violence; supreme right that perpetually denies the rights of the conquered; and perpetual violence, which ensures the continuation of colonial power and authority.[11] As Mbembe notes in a more recent book, "The sovereign right to kill is not subject to any rule in the colonies. In the colonies, the sovereign might kill at any time or in any manner. Colonial warfare is not subject to legal and institutional rules. It is not a legally codified activity."[12] This state of lawlessness in the colonies indicates the permanence of the state of exception and/or state of emergency and the suspension of the law; what is the exception of contractual societies is the rule in colonial societies.[13] It is thus not inconsistent that such liberals as Alexis de Tocqueville defend the rule of law for the French alongside a form of government with extraordinary and exceptional powers for Algerian Arabs.[14] Such is the vital (in all etymological senses) difference between the contractual and the colonial logics of power inherent to modernity.

These dual, simultaneous, and parallel logics of power are seen not only in cases where clear territorial boundaries or seas separate the colonial homeland from its colonies; contractual and colonial logics can also coexist and con-

7. Foucault, *Psychiatric Power*, 66–71, 108–109.
8. See Arneil, *Domestic Colonies*.
9. Weber, *Peasants into Frenchmen*, 490–496.
10. E.g., see Hannoum, *Violent Modernity*.
11. Mbembe, *On the Postcolony*, 25.
12. Mbembe, *Necro-Politics*, 78.
13. See Kohn and McBride, *Political Theories of Decolonization*, 77–97.
14. See Kohn, "Empire's Law," 255–278.

join within national borders. For example, the forms of sovereignty exercised over Black people, indigenous peoples, and Mexicans in the United States, over Kurds in Turkey, over Palestinians in Israel, or over nonwhite people in apartheid-era South Africa all point to the existence of a colonial logic operating on those excluded from the singular nation (on racial, ethnic, and religious grounds) *and* all exist alongside a contractual logic of power applied to the legitimate nation. Debates on internal colonialism, especially in the 1960s and 1970s, were attempts to conceptualize this very phenomenon.[15]

The transfer of colonialism debates to within the borders of the nation-state also calls into question certain regnant understandings in the social sciences, which make a categorical and qualitative distinction between empire and nation-state. For example, positing such clear distinctions between the Ottoman Empire, as a world-empire, and the Republic of Turkey, as a nation-state, has obscured certain continuities in the logic of sovereignty in the peripheries, where the line between the nineteenth-century Ottoman and the twentieth-century republican practices often blurs. Happily, many recent theoretical and historical-sociological studies have thrown into question the validity of such a distinction, with more and more studies underscoring the similarities and continuities between imperial states and nation-states, imperialisms and nationalisms, and nationalizing empires and imperializing nations.[16] Moreover, the logic of colonial power is not limited to Western colonial powers or former imperial powers such as China, Russia, and Turkey. In the case of postcolonial Africa, for instance, many observers have argued that the processes of ethnic cleansing in many postindependence African countries are inseparable from a colonial logic integral to the nation-state.[17] This is not to say that African states are colonialist. Rather, such historical dynamics points to the universality of the logic of colonial power and sovereignty in the modern world.

This universality of the logic of colonial power parallels, in its development, that of the logic of contractual power described earlier in this study. Just as looking at the simultaneity and relationality between the two logics enables us to analyze racism within a more global framework, it can also enable us to analyze colonialism within a more global framework. In other words, just as a discussion of racism confined to a Black/white dichotomy

---

15. See, e.g., Blauner, "Internal Colonialism and Ghetto Revolt," 393–408; More, "Colonialism," 463–472; Hechter, *Internal Colonialism*; Chávez, "Aliens in Their Native Lands," 785–809.

16. A special issue of *Thesis Eleven* is devoted entirely to this topic. For an introductory essay, see Malesevic, "Empires and Nation-States," 3–10. See also Kumar, "Empires and Nations," 279–299; Kumar, "Nation-States as Empires, Empires as Nation-States," 119–143.

17. See, e.g., Sharma, *Home Rule*.

speaks only partly to experiences in other geographies, so a discussion of colonialism focused solely on the dynamics of Western countries may not fully account for other modes of colonial experiences. A perspective on the relationality and universality of contractual and colonial logics of power may, at least in part, help transcend such epistemological limits.

This relationality—for example, that the logic of the contract almost inevitably gives rise to a colonial logic as well as to various strategies of ignorance, apathy, and escape within contractual society—is well known to those on the bottom of racial and ethnic hierarchies, or to those excluded from the contract. That Black people develop knowledge and a sense of what it means to be white, or that Kurds and Armenians do the same for Turkishness, also stems from an awareness of this relationality. But the same relationality typically passes unnoticed by those living within a contractual society. "Colonial unknowing" is how some have characterized such reactions to relational analysis, describing an "epistemological orientation that works to preempt relational modes of analysis."[18] The fact that even a thinker like Hannah Arendt, one of the most creative and earnest intellects of the past century, hardly mentions Black people and Indigenous people when analyzing the American Revolution through a contractual model (making no secret of her admiration for this model) is a striking example of the invisibility of contractual/colonial relationality—unseen not only by the founders of countries but also by social scientists analyzing the founders.[19]

But this relationality has grown more visible over the past seventy years, through the struggles of noncontractual and colonized peoples and their echoes in social analysis. Decolonization activism and thought, especially in recent years, have brought such relationality to the forefront of political and intellectual life. This political and intellectual challenge, led from the lower rungs of racial and ethnic hierarchies and from the outside of national contracts, has also generated rifts and polarization within contractual societies. As the ignorance of relationality gradually gives way to awareness, many within dominant societies are beginning to see and know, in other ways, and to question old ways of seeing and knowing. The crises in contract noted by Wimmer thus have less to do with the mistakes of liberal elites or their alienation of the white working class and more to do with emergent forms of dialectical relationality between contractual and colonial logics.

Whether our symbolic starting point is, with Mamdani, 1492, or some later date, arguably our world has been postcontractual and postcolonial for

---

18. Vimalassery, Hu Pegues, and Goldstein, "Introduction," available at muse.jhu.edu/article/633283.

19. Arendt, *On Revolution.*

centuries. These dual logics of power and sovereignty, directly tied to the principles and practices of capitalism and the modern nation-states that have permeated everywhere, everything, and everyone, are today undergoing a multidimensional crisis due to the relational dynamics originating from within (cultural polarization in contractual societies), outside (decolonizations), below (minority struggles and demands), and above (crises of legitimacy of states and the liberal center). The construction and functioning of these two logics of power, which have so marked modern world history, as well as their crises, are painful at both the national and the global scale. This is only natural; the struggle concerns matters of hierarchy and equality, of exclusion and inclusion, which are necessarily fraught with tensions. The proponents of hierarchy are strong, in force if not in intellect. The proponents of equality, whatever their stature in the world of thought, lack force and organization. Meanwhile, the left, which might offer an alternative to the existing state of the world, has increasingly become, over the past century, a national movement, losing its international character. This has made imagining another world almost unthinkable. Yet, even amid this disorganization and powerlessness, a culture of equality is expanding and deepening since 1968. In an age of pessimism, this culture of equality and social struggles around it should be a source of optimism.

Bibliography

Abadan, Yavuz. "Tanzimat Fermanı'nın Tahlili." In *Tanzimat: Değişim Sürecinde Osmanlı İmparatorluğu*, edited by Halil İnalcık and Mehmet Seyitdanlıoğlu, 37–64. Ankara: Phoneix Yayınları, 2006.

Abak, Tibet. "Kürt Politikasında Hamidiye Siyasetine Dönüş ve Kör Hüseyin Paşa Olayı, 1910–1911." In Adanır and Özel, *1915*, 277–292.

Açıkel, Fethi. "Devletin Manevi Şahsiyeti ve Ulusun Pedagojisi." In *Türkiye'de Siyasi Düşünce*. Vol. 4, *Milliyetçilik*, edited by Tanıl Bora, 117–139. İstanbul: İletişim Yayınları, 2002.

Adanır, Fikret. "'Ermeni Meselesi'nin Doğuşu." In Adanır and Özel, *1915*, 3–43.

Adanır, Fikret, and Oktay Özel, eds. *1915: Siyaset, Tehcir, Soykırım*. İstanbul: Tarih Vakfı Yurt Yayınları, 2015.

Ağartan, Kaan. "Beyazlık Çalışmaları Aynasında Türklüğe Bakmak: Tartışmaya bir Katkı." *Birikim*, no. 277 (May 2012): 67–75.

———. *Gezi: The Making of a New Political Community in Turkey*. Edinburgh: Edinburgh University Press, 2024.

Ahmad, Feroz. *İttihatçılıktan Kemalizme*. İstanbul: Kaynak Yayınları, 1996.

Ahmed, Sara. "A Phenomenology of Whiteness." *Feminist Theory* 8, no. 2 (2007): 149–168.

———. *Queer Phenomenology: Orientations, Objects, Others*. Durham, NC: Duke University Press, 2006.

Akçam, Taner. *Ermenilerin Zorla Müslümanlaştırılması: Sessizlik, İnkâr ve Asimilasyon*. İstanbul: İletişim Yayınları, 2017.

———. *'Ermeni Meselesi Hallolunmuştur': Osmanlı Belgelerine Göre Savaş Yıllarında Ermenilere Yönelik Politikalar*. İstanbul: İletişim Yayınları, 2010.

———. *İnsan Hakları ve Ermeni Sorunu: İttihat ve Terakki'den Kurtuluş Savaşı'na*. Ankara: İmge Kitabevi, 2002.

———. *Naim Efendi'nin Hatıratı ve Talat Paşa Telgrafları (Krikor Gergeryan Arşivi)*. İstanbul: İletişim Yayınları, 2016.

Akçam, Taner, and Ümit Kurt. *Kanunların Ruhu: Emval-i Metruke Kanunlarında Soykırımın İzini Sürmek*. İstanbul: İletişim Yayınları, 2012.

Akçura, Yusuf. "İttifak'a Dair." In *Türk Milliyetçiliğinin Kökenleri: Yusuf Akçura (1876–1935)*, edited by François Georgeon, translated by Alev Er, 175–176. İstanbul: Tarih Vakfı Yurt Yayınları, 1999.

———. "İttihad-ı Anasır Meselesi." In *Türk Milliyetçiliğinin Kökenleri: Yusuf Akçura (1876–1935)*, edited by François Georgeon, translated by Alev Er, 156–167. İstanbul: Tarih Vakfı Yurt Yayınları, 1999.

———. *Türkçülüğün Tarihi*. İstanbul: Kaynak Yayınları, 1998.

———. *Üç Tarz-ı Siyaset*. Ankara: Türk Tarih Kurumu Basımevi, 1998.

Akdoğan, Yalçın. "Yazıklar Olsun." *Star*, July 22, 2014.

Akgönül, Samim. *Türkiye Rumları: Ulus-Devlet Çağından Küreselleşme Çağına Bir Azınlığın Yok Oluş Süreci*. Translated by Ceylan Gürman. İstanbul: İletişim Yayınları, 2012.

Akın, Kadir. *Ermeni Devrimci Paramaz: Abdülhamid'den İttihat ve Terakki'ye Ermeni Sosyalistleri ve Soykırım*. Ankara: Dipnot Yayınları, 2015.

Akkaya, Ahmet Hamdi. "Kürt Hareketinin Örgütlenme Süreci olarak 1970'ler." *Toplum ve Bilim*, no. 127 (2013): 88–120.

Akşin, Sina. *İstanbul Hükümetleri ve Milli Mücadele*. Vol. 3, *İç Savaş ve Sevr'de Ölüm*. İstanbul: Türkiye İş Bankası Kültür Yayınları, 2010.

———. *Jön Türkler ve İttihat ve Terakki*. Ankara: İmge Kitabevi, 1998.

Aktan, İrfan, "Makul ve Makbul Kürtler," *Birikim*, no. 260 (December 2010): 45–53.

Aktar, Ayhan. *Varlık Vergisi ve "Türkleştirme" Politikaları*. İstanbul: İletişim Yayınları, 2001.

Aktoprak, Elçin. "'Postkolonyal' bir Tahayyül: 'Yeni Türkiye'nin Yeni Ulusu." In *21. Yüzyılda Milliyetçilik: Teori ve Siyaset*, edited by Elçin Aktoprak and A. Celil Kaya, 293–321. İstanbul: İletişim Yayınları, 2016.

Akyüz, Yahya. *Türk Eğitim Tarihi (Başlangıçtan 1988'e)*. Ankara: AÜ Eğitim Bilimleri Fakültesi Yayınları, 1989.

Allen, Ricky Lee. "Whiteness and Critical Pedagogy." *Educational Philosophy and Theory* 36, no. 2 (2004): 121–136.

Alpkaya, Faruk. *Türkiye Cumhuriyeti'nin Kuruluşu*. İstanbul: İletişim Yayınları, 1998.

Altınay, Ayşe Gül, and Fethiye Çetin. *Torunlar*. İstanbul: Metis Yayınları, 2013.

Anderson, Benedict. *Imagined Communities: Reflections on the Origins and Spread of Nationalism*. London: Verso, 1991.

Ansell, Amy. "Casting a Blind Eye: The Ironic Consequences of Color-Blindness in South Africa and the United States." *Critical Sociology* 32, nos. 2–3 (2006): 333–356.

Anter, Musa. *Hatıralarım*. İstanbul: Avesta Yayınları, 2007.

Arai, Masami. *Jön Türk Dönemi Türk Milliyetçiliği*. Translated by Tansel Demirel. İstanbul: İletişim Yayınları, 2011.

Aren, Sadun. *TİP Olayı (1961–1971)*. İstanbul: Cem Yayınevi, 1993.

Arendt, Hannah. *On Revolution*. London: Faber and Faber, 2016.

———. "Reflections on Little Rock." In *The Portable Hannah Arendt*, edited by Peter Baehr, 231–246. New York: Penguin Books, 2000.

Arı, Kemal. *Büyük Mübadele: Türkiye'ye Zorunlu Göç (1923–1925)*. İstanbul: Tarih Vakfı Yurt Yayınları, 1995.

Arneil, Barbara. *Domestic Colonies: The Turn Inward to Colony*. New York: Oxford University Press, 2017.

Arnesen, Eric. "Whiteness and the Historians' Imagination." *International Labor and Working-Class History* 60 (October 2001): 3–32.

Arrighi, Giovanni, Terence Hopkins, and Immanuel Wallerstein. *Anti-Systemic Movements*. London: Verso, 1995.

Aslan, Şükrü, Sibel Yardımcı, Murat Arpacı, and Öykü Gürpınar. *Türkiye'nin Etnik Coğrafyası: 1927–1965 Ana Dil Haritaları*. İstanbul: Mimar Sinan Güzel Sanatlar Üniversitesi Yayınları, 2015.

Atatürk, Kemal. *Nutuk*. Vol. 3, *Vesikalar*. İstanbul: Milli Eğitim Basımevi, 1962.

[Atatürk], Mustafa Kemal. *Eskişehir-İzmit Konuşmaları (1923)*. İstanbul: Kaynak Yayınları, 1993.

Ateş, Sabri. *Tunalı Hilmi Bey: Osmanlı'dan Cumhuriyet'e bir Aydın*. İstanbul: Tarih Vakfı Yurt Yayınları, 2009.

Avagyan, Arsen. *Osmanlı İmparatorluğu ve Kemalist Türkiye'nin Devlet-İktidar Sisteminde Çerkesler*. Translated by Ludmilla Denisenko. İstanbul: Belge Yayınları, 2004.

Avcıoğlu, Doğan. *Türkiye'nin Düzeni (Dün-Bugün-Yarın)*. Vol. 2. Ankara: Bilgi Yayınevi, 1969.

Aydın, Suavi. *"Amacımız Devletin Bekası": Demokratikleşme Sürecinde Devlet ve Yurttaşlar*. İstanbul: TESEV Yayınları, 2009.

———. "İki İttihat-Terakki: İki Ayrı Zihniyet, İki Ayrı Siyaset." In *Modern Türkiye'de Siyasi Düşünce*. Vol. 1, *Tanzimat ve Meşrutiyet Birikimi*, edited by Mehmet Ö. Alkan, 117–128. İstanbul: İletişim Yayınları, 2002.

Aydınkaya, Fırat. "1880'den 1915'e Kürt-Ermeni Hinterlandındaki Kısmi Soykırım ve Soykırımdaki Kürt İştiraki Üzerine." In *Utanç ve Onur: Ermeni Soykırımı'nın 100. Yılı (1915–2015)*, edited by Aydın Çubukçu et al., 91–108. İstanbul: Evrensel Basın Yayın, 2015.

Bajalan, Djene Rhys. *Jön Kürtler: Birinci Dünya Savaşı'ndan Önce Kürt Hareketi (1898–1914)*. Translated by Burcu Yalçınkaya. İstanbul: Avesta Yayınları, 2010.

Balancar, Ferda, ed. *Ankaralı Ermeniler Konuşuyor*. İstanbul: Hrant Dink Vakfı Yayınları, 2013.

———, ed. *Diyarbakırlı Ermeniler Konuşuyor*. İstanbul: Hrant Dink Vakfı Yayınları, 2014.

Baldwin, James. *Collected Essays*. Edited by Toni Morrison. New York: Library of America, 1998.

———. *The Fire Next Time*. Austin: Holt, Rinehart and Winston, 1990.

Bali, Rıfat N. *Cumhuriyet Yıllarında Türkiye Yahudileri: Bir Türkleştirme Serüveni (1923–1945)*. İstanbul: İletişim Yayınları, 2010.

———. *Cumhuriyet Yıllarında Türkiye Yahudileri: Devlet'in Örnek Yurttaşları (1950–2003)*. İstanbul: Kitabevi Yayınları, 2009.

Balibar, Etienne. "The Nation Form: History and Ideology." In *Race, Nation, Class: Ambiguous Identities*, edited by E. Balibar and I. Wallerstein, translated by Chris Turner, 86–106. London: Verso, 1991.

Baran, Taha. *1937–1938 Yılları Arasında Basında Dersim*. İstanbul: İletişim Yayınları, 2014.

Bardakçı, Murat. "Bir 'Çerkes Açılımı' Eksikti!" *Haber Türk*, March 11, 2011.

———. *İttihadçı'nın Sandığı*. İstanbul: Türkiye İş Bankası Kültür Yayınları, 2014.

———. *Talat Paşa'nın Evrak-ı Metrukesi*. İstanbul: Everest Yayınları, 2009.

———. "Vatana ve Millete Hayırlı Olmasın." *Haber Türk*, January 21, 2015.

Başkaya, Fikret. *Paradigmanın İflası: Resmi İdeolojinin Eleştirisine Giriş*. İstanbul: Doz Yayınları, 1991.

Başyurt, Erhan. *Ermeni Evlatlıklar: Saklı Kalmış Hayatlar*. İstanbul: KaraKutu Yayınları, 2007.

Bayar, Yeşim. "The Trajectory of Nation-Building through Language Policies: The Case of Turkey during the Early Republic." *Nations and Nationalism* 17, no. 1 (2011): 108–128.

Bayır, Derya. *Türk Hukukunda Azınlıklar ve Milliyetçilik*. Translated by Ülkü Sağır. İstanbul: İstanbul Bilgi Üniversitesi Yayınları, 2017.

Bayrak, Mehmet. *Kürdoloji Belgeleri*. Vol. 2. Ankara: Öz-Ge Yayınları, 2004.

———. *Şark Islahat Planı: Kürtlere Vurulan Kelepçe*. Ankara: Öz-Ge Yayınları, 2009.

Beauvoir, Simone de. *The Second Sex*. Translated by H. M. Parshley. London: Jonathan Cape, 1956.

Benlisoy, Foti, and Stefo Benlisoy. *Türk Milliyetçiliğinde Katedilmemiş Bir Yol: "Hıristiyan Türkler" ve Papa Eftim*. İstanbul: İstos Yayın, 2016.

Bernasconi, Robert. *Irk Kavramını Kim İcat Etti? Felsefi Düşüncede Irk ve Irkçılık*. Edited by Zeynep Direk. Translated by Zeynep Direk. İstanbul: Metis Yayınları, 2011.

Beşikçi, İsmail. "Behice Boran'a yazılmış 31.08.1979 tarihli mektup." İsmail Beşikçi Private Archive.

———. *Bilim Yöntemi*. Ankara: Yurt Kitap-Yayın, 1991. Originally published in 1976, Ankara: Komal.

———. *Cumhuriyet Halk Fırkası'nın Programı (1931) ve Kürt Sorunu*. İstanbul: Belge Yayınları, 1991.

———. *Cumhuriyet Halk Fırkası'nın Tüzüğü (1927) ve Kürt Sorunu*. Ankara: Yurt Kitap-Yayın, 1991. Originally published in 1978, İstanbul: Komal.

———. *Doğu Anadolu'nun Düzeni: Sosyo/Ekonomik ve Etnik Temeller*. Ankara: E Yayınları, 1969.

———. *Doğu'da Değişim ve Yapısal Sorunlar (Göçebe Alikan Aşireti)*. Ankara: Doğan Yayınevi, 1969.

———. *Doğu'da Değişim ve Yapısal Sorunlar (Göçebe Alikan Aşireti)*. Ankara: Yurt Kitap-Yayın, 1992.

———. *Doğu Mitingleri'nin Analizi (1967)*. Ankara: Yurt Kitap-Yayın, 1992.

———. *İsmail Beşikçi Davası*. Vol. 1, *Danıştay Davaları-İddianame-Esas Hakkında Mütalaa*. Ankara: Yurt Kitap-Yayın, 1993.

———. *Kirletilen Kavramlar: Bilim, Eşitlik, Adalet*. Ankara: Yurt-Kitap Yayın, 1994.

———. *Kürdistan Üzerinde Emperyalist Bölüşüm Mücadelesi (1915–1925)*. Ankara: Yurt Kitap-Yayın, 1992.

———. *Kürdistan Üzerinde Örgütlü Devlet Terörü ve İsmail Beşikçi (Biyografi-Savunmalar-Mektuplar)*. İzmir: Komal Yayınevi, 1980.

———. *Kürtlerin Mecburi İskânı*. Ankara: Yurt Kitap-Yayın, 1991. Originally published in 1977, İstanbul: Komal.

———. *Kürt Toplumu Üzerine*. Ankara: Yurt-Kitap Yayın, 1993.

———. "Mümtaz Soysal'a yazılmış 29.08.1979 tarihli mektup." In *Kürdistan Üzerinde Örgütlü Devlet Terörü ve İsmail Beşikçi (Biyografi-Savunmalar-Mektuplar)*, edited by İsmail Beşikçi, 99–109. İzmir: Komal Yayınevi, 1980.

———. *Tunceli Kanunu (1935) ve Dersim Jenosidi*. Ankara: Yurt Kitap-Yayın, 1992.

———. *Türk Tarih Tezi, Güneş-Dil Teorisi ve Kürt Sorunu*. Ankara: Yurt Kitap-Yayın, 1991. Originally published in 1977 by Ankara: Kamal.

Bilici, Mücahit. *Hamal Kürt: Türk İslamı ve Kürt Sorunu*. İstanbul: Avesta Yayınları, 2017.

Biner, Zerrin Özlem. "Precarious Solidarities: 'Poisonous Knowledge' and the Academics for Peace in Times of Authoritarianism." *Social Anthropology* 27, no. 2 (2019): 15–32.

Black Past. "Combahee River Collective Statement." Accessed July 16, 2024. Available at https://www.blackpast.org/african-american-history/combahee-river-collective-statement-1977/.

Blauner, Robert. "Internal Colonialism and Ghetto Revolt." *Social Problems* 16, no. 4 (Spring 1969): 393–408.

Bloxham, Donald. *The Great Game of Genocide: Imperialism, Nationalism, and the Destruction of the Ottoman Armenians*. Oxford: Oxford University Press, 2005.

Bogues, Anthony. *Black Heretics, Black Prophets: Radical Political Intellectuals*. New York: Routledge, 2003.

Bonilla-Silva, Eduardo. *Racism without Racists: Color-Blind Racism and the Persistence of Racial Inequality in the United States*. Lanham, MD: Rowman and Littlefield, 2006.

Bonilla-Silva, Eduardo, Carla Goar, and David G. Embrick. "When Whites Flock Together: The Social Psychology of White Habitus." *Critical Sociology* 32, nos. 2–3 (2006): 229–253.

Bora, Tanıl. "Beyaz Türkler Tartışması: Kirli Beyaz." *Birikim*, no. 260 (December 2010): 25–37.

———. "Muhafazakâr ve İslamcı Söylemde Beyaz Türk Hıncı: Beyaz Türk'e Kahretmek." *Birikim*, no. 305 (September 2014): 36–45.

———. *Türk Sağının Üç Hâli: Milliyetçilik, Muhafazakârlık, İslamcılık*. İstanbul: Birikim Yayınları, 2008.

Boratav, Korkut. *Türkiye'de Devletçilik*. İstanbul: Gerçek Yayınevi, 1974.

Boucher, David, and Paul Kelly, eds. *The Social Contract from Hobbes to Rawls*. London: Routledge, 1994.

Bourdieu, Pierre. *Distinction: A Social Critique of the Judgment of Taste*. Translated by Richard Nice. Cambridge: Harvard University Press, 2007.

———. *Language and Symbolic Power*. Translated by Gino Raymond and Matthew Adamson. Oxford: Polity, 1991.

———. *On the State: Lectures at the Collège de France, 1989–1992*. Edited by Patrick Champagne et al. Translated by David Fernbach. Cambridge: Polity, 2014.

———. *Outline of a Theory of Practice*. Translated by Richard Nice. Cambridge: Cambridge University Press, 2010.

———. *Pascalian Meditations*. Translated by Richard Nice. Stanford, CA: Stanford University Press, 2000.

———. "Rethinking the State: Genesis and the Structure of the Bureaucratic Field." *Sociological Theory* 12, no. 1 (March 1994): 1–18.

———. *Seçilmiş Metinler*. Translated by Levent Ünsaldı. Ankara: Heretik Yayınları, 2014.

———. *Sosyoloji Meseleleri*. Translated by Filiz Öztürk et al. Ankara: Heretik Yayınları, 2016.

Bourdieu, Pierre, and Loïc Wacquant. *An Invitation to Reflexive Sociology*. Chicago: University of Chicago Press, 1992.

Bozarslan, Hamit. "'49'ların Anıları Üzerine: Tarihsel-Sosyolojik Okuma Notları ve Bazı Hipotezler." *Tarih ve Toplum*, no. 16 (Summer 2013): 127–143.

————. "Tehcir'den Lozan'a Türkler, Kürtler ve Ermeniler." In Adanır and Özel, *1915*, 471–487.

————. "Türkiye'de Kürt Sol Hareketi." In *Modern Türkiye'de Siyasi Düşünce*. Vol. 8, *Sol*, edited by Murat Gültekingil, 1169–1206. İstanbul: İletişim Yayınları, 2007.

Branscombe, Nyla R., and Bertjan Doosje, eds. *Collective Guilt: International Perspectives*. Cambridge: Cambridge University Press, 2004.

Brink-Danan, Marcy. *Yirmi Birinci Yüzyılda Türkiye'de Yahudiler: Hoşgörünün Öteki Yüzü*. Translated by Barış Cezar. İstanbul: Koç Üniversitesi Yayınları, 2014.

Brubaker, Rogers. "Ethnicity, Race, and Nationalism." *Annual Review of Sociology* 35 (2009): 21–42.

Brubaker, Rogers, Mara Loveman, and Peter Stamatov. "Ethnicity as Cognition." *Theory and Society* 33 (2004): 31–64.

Brubaker, Rogers et al. *Nationalist Politics and Everyday Ethnicity in a Transylvanian Town*. Princeton, NJ: Princeton University Press, 2008.

Buck-Morss, Susan. "Hegel and Haiti." *Critical Inquiry* 26, no. 4 (Summer 2000): 821–865.

Butler, Judith. *Gender Trouble: Feminism and the Subversion of Identity*. New York: Routledge, 1999.

Çağaptay, Soner. *Islam, Secularism, and Nationalism in Modern Turkey: Who Is a Turk?* London: Routledge, 2006.

Çağlayan, Handan. *Aynı Evde Ayrı Diller: Kuşaklararası Dil Değişimi*. Diyarbakır, DİSA Yayınları, 2014.

Çağlayan, Handan, Şemsa Özar, and Ayşe Tepe Doğan. *Ne Değişti? Kürt Kadınların Zorunlu Göç Deneyimi*. Ankara: Ayizi Yayınları, 2011.

Cahen, Claude L. "Zimme." In *İslam Ansiklopedisi* [*Encyclopedia of Islam*]. Vol. 13, 566–571. Eskişehir: MEB Yayınları, 2001.

Çalışlar, İzzeddin, ed. *Dersim Raporu*. İstanbul: İletişim Yayınları, 2019.

Carmichael, Stokely, and Charles V. Hamilton. *Black Power: The Politics of Liberation in America*. New York: Vintage Books, 1967.

Çayan, Mahir. *Toplu Yazılar*. Ankara: BirGün Kitap Yayınları, 2013.

Caymaz, Birol. *Türkiye'de Vatandaşlık: Resmi İdeoloji ve Yansımaları*. İstanbul: İstanbul Bilgi Üniversitesi Yayınları, 2008.

Çelik, Adnan, and Namık Kemal Dinç. *Yüz Yıllık AH! 1915 Diyarbekir*. İstanbul: İsmail Beşikçi Vakfı Yayınları, 2015.

Çetin, Fethiye. *Anneannem*. İstanbul: Metis Yayınları, 2016.

————. *Utanç Duyuyorum: Hrant Dink Cinayetinin Yargısı*. İstanbul: Metis Yayınları, 2013.

Çetinkaya, Y. Doğan. *Osmanlı'yı Müslümanlaştırmak: Kitle Siyaseti, Toplumsal Sınıflar, Boykotlar ve Milli İktisat (1909–1914)*. İstanbul: İletişim Yayınları, 2015.

————. *Young Turks and the Boycott Movement: Nationalism, Protest and the Working Classes in the Formation of Modern Turkey*. New York: I. B. Tauris, 2021.

Chávez, John R. "Aliens in Their Native Lands: The Persistence of Internal Colonial Theory." *Journal of World History* 22, no. 4 (December 2011): 785–809.

Chen, Jun Mian. "The Contentious Field of Whiteness Studies." *Journal for Social Thought* 2, no. 1 (December 2017): 15–27.

Collins, Patricia Hill. *Intersectionality as Critical Social Theory*. Durham, NC: Duke University Press, 2019.

Coşkun, Vahap, Şerif Derince, and Nesrin Uçarlar. *Dil Yarası: Türkiye'de Eğitimde Anadilin Kullanılmaması Sorunu ve Kürt Öğrencilerin Deneyimi*. Diyarbakır: DİSA Yayınları, 2010.

Crenshaw, Kimberlé. "Demarginalizing the Intersection of Race and Sex: A Black Feminist Critique of Antidiscrimination Doctrine, Feminist Theory and Antiracist Politics." *University of Chicago Legal Forum*, no. 1 (1989): 139–167.

———. "Mapping the Margins: Intersectionality, Identity Politics, and Violence against Women of Color." *Stanford Law Review* 43, no. 6 (July 1991): 1241–1299.

———. "Twenty Years of Critical Race Theory: Looking Back to Move Forward." *Connecticut Law Review* 43, no. 5 (July 2011): 1253–1352.

Crenshaw, Kimberlé, Neil Gotanda, Gary Peller, and Kendall Thomas, eds. *Critical Race Theory: The Key Writings That Formed the Movement*. New York: New Press, 1995.

Dadrian, Vahakn N. *Ermeni Soykırımı Tarihi: Balkanlardan Anadolu ve Kafkasya'ya Etnik Çatışma*. Translated by Ali Çakıroğlu. İstanbul: Belge Yayınları, 2008.

Dağlıoğlu, Emre Can. "Diyarbakır'da Soykırım Nasıl Örgütlendi?" *Toplum ve Bilim*, no. 132 (2015): 232–236.

Davison, Roderic H. "Turkish Attitudes concerning Christian-Muslim Equality in the Nineteenth Century." *American Historical Review* 59, no. 4 (July 1954): 844–864.

Dayar, Evren. "Antalya'da Girit Göçmenleri: Göç, İskân ve Siyaset." *Toplumsal Tarih*, no. 279 (March 2017): 64–73.

Delgado, Richard. "Rodrigo's Eleventh Chronicle: Empathy and False Empathy." In *Critical White Studies: Looking behind the Mirror*, edited by Richard Delgado and Jean Stefancic, 614–618. Philadelphia: Temple University Press, 1997.

Demir, İpek. "Humbling Turkishness: Undoing the Strategies of Inclusion and Exclusion of Turkish Modernity," *Journal of Historical Sociology* 27, no. 3 (September 2014): 381–401.

Demirel, Ahmet. *Birinci Meclis'te Muhalefet: İkinci Grup*. İstanbul: İletişim Yayınları, 2011.

Demirer, Yücel. *Tören, Simge, Siyaset: Türkiye'de Newroz ve Nevruz Şenlikleri*. Ankara: Dipnot Yayınları, 2012.

Demirhisar, Deniz Günce. "Emotion and Protest in Turkey: What Happened on 19 January, 2007?" *Open Democracy*, January 22, 2016.

Demirkent, Dinçer. *Bir Devlet İki Cumhuriyet*. İstanbul: Ayrıntı Yayınları, 2017.

Deringil, Selim. *İktidarın Sembolleri ve İdeoloji: II. Abdülhamid Dönemi (1876–1909)*. İstanbul: Yapı Kredi Yayınları, 2002.

Der Matossian, Bedross. *Parçalanmış Devrim Düşleri: Osmanlı İmparatorluğu'nun Son Döneminde Hürriyetten Şiddete*. Translated by Renan Akman. İstanbul: İletişim Yayınları, 2016.

Devrimci Doğu Kültür Ocakları Dava Dosyası, Vol. 1. Ankara: Komal Yayınevi, 1975.

Dinçer, Sinan. "Adana Katliamı ve Göçmen İşçiler Meselesi." In Adanır and Özel, *1915*, 256–263.

Dink, Hrant. *İki Yakın Halk İki Uzak Komşu*. İstanbul: Hrant Dink Vakfı Yayınları, 2012.

———. "Sabiha-Hatun'ın Sırrı." *Agos*, February 6, 2004.

Doğruel, Fulya. *"İnsaniyetleri Benzer": Hatay'da Çoketnili Ortak Yaşam Kültürü*. İstanbul: İletişim Yayınları, 2013.

Du Bois, W.E.B. *Black Reconstruction in America, 1860–1880*. New York: Free Press, 1995.

————. *The Souls of Black Folk*. New York: Signet Classic, 1995.

Dündar, Fuat. *İttihat ve Terakki'nin Müslümanları İskân Politikası (1913–1918)*. İstanbul: İletişim Yayınları, 2011.

————. *Kahir Ekseriyet: Ermeni Nüfus Meselesi (1878–1923)*. İstanbul: Tarih Vakfı Yurt Yayınları, 2013.

————. *Modern Türkiye'nin Şifresi: İttihat ve Terakki'nin Etnisite Mühendisliği (1913–1918)*. İstanbul: İletişim Yayınları, 2008.

Durkheim, Émile. *Education and Sociology*. Translated by Sherwood D. Fox. New York: Free Press, 1956.

————. *The Rules of Sociological Method*. Translated by W. D. Halls. New York: Free Press, 1982.

Eidheim, Herald. "When Ethnic Identity Is a Social Stigma." In *Ethnic Groups and Boundaries: The Social Organization of Culture Difference*, edited by Fredrik Barth, 39–57. Boston: Little, Brown, 1969.

Eldem, Edhem. "'Banka Vakası' ve 1896 İstanbul Katliamı." In Adanır and Özel, *1915*, 176–198.

————. *Osmanlı Bankası Tarihi*. İstanbul: Tarih Vakfı Yurt Yayınları, 2000.

Elias, Norbert. *The Civilizing Process: Sociogenetic and Psychogenetic Investigations*. Translated by Edmund Jephcott. Oxford: Blackwell, 2000.

Ellis, Stephen, and Tsepo Sechaba. *Comrades against Apartheid: The ANC and the South African Communist Party in Exile*. Bloomington: Indiana University Press, 1992.

Emrence, Cem. *99 Günlük Muhalefet: Serbest Cumhuriyet Fırkası*. İstanbul: İletişim Yayınları, 2006.

Ender, Rita. *İsmiyle Yaşamak*. İstanbul: İletişim Yayınları, 2016.

Ergin, Murat. "'Is the Turk a White Man?' Towards a Theoretical Framework for Race in the Making of Turkishness." *Middle Eastern Studies* 44, no. 6 (November 2008): 827–850.

————. "The Racialization of Kurdish Identity in Turkey." *Ethnic and Racial Studies* 37, no. 2 (2014): 322–341.

Erol, Su. *Mazlum ve Makul: İstanbul Süryanilerinde Etno-Dinsel Kimlik İnşası ve Kimlik Stratejileri*. İstanbul: İletişim Yayınları, 2016.

Esin, Taylan, and Zeliha Etöz. *1916 Ankara Yangını: Felaketin Mantığı*. İstanbul: İletişim Yayınları, 2015.

Evans, Richard J. "The Road to Slaughter." *New Republic*, December 5, 2011. Available at https://newrepublic.com/article/98085/the-road-slaughter.

Fanon, Frantz. *Black Skin, White Masks*. Translated by Richard Philcox. New York: Grove, 2008.

————. *The Wretched of the Earth*. New York: Grove Press, 1963.

Foucault, Michel. *Psychiatric Power: Lectures at the Collège de France*. Translated by Graham Burchell. New York: Picador, 2006.

Frankenberg, Ruth. "The Mirage of an Unmarked Whiteness." In *The Making and Unmaking of Whiteness*, edited by Birgit Brander Rasmussen, Eric Klinenberg, Irene Nexica, and Mat Wray, 72–96. Durham, NC: Duke University Press, 2001.

————. *White Women, Race Matters: The Social Construction of Whiteness*. Minneapolis: University of Minnesota Press, 2005.

Fredrickson, George M. *Black Liberation: A Comparative History of Black Ideologies in the United States and South Africa*. New York: Oxford University Press, 1995.

————. *The Comparative Imagination: On the History of Racism, Nationlism, and Social Movements*. Berkeley: University of California Press, 2000.

Gellner, Ernest. *Nations and Nationalism*. Oxford: Basil Blackwell, 1983.

Georgeon, François. *Türk Milliyetçiliğinin Kökenleri: Yusuf Akçura (1876–1935)*. Translated by Alev Er. İstanbul: Tarih Vakfı Yurt Yayınları, 1999.

Gerçek, Burçin. *Akıntıya Karşı: Ermeni Soykırımında Emirlere Karşı Gelenler, Kurtaranlar, Direnenler*. İstanbul: İletişim Yayınları, 2016.

Gerhart, Gail. "Interview with Steve Biko." In *Biko Lives! Contesting the Legacies of Steve Biko*, edited by Andile Mngxitama, Amanda Alexander, and Nigel Gibson, 21–42. New York: Palgrave Macmillan, 2008.

Gerlach, Christian. "İştirak ve Vurgun: Ermenilerin İmhası, 1915–1923." In *Kıyam ve Kıtal: Osmanlı'dan Cumhuriyet'e Devletin İnşası ve Kolektif Şiddet*, edited by Ümit Kurt ve Güney Çeğin, 151–194. İstanbul: Tarih Vakfı Yurt Yayınları, 2015.

Gerth, Hans, and C. Wright Mills, eds. and trans. *Character and Social Structure: The Psychology of Social Institutions*. New York: Harcourt, Brace, 1953.

————. *From Max Weber: Essays in Sociology*. New York: Oxford University Press, 1946.

Gingeras, Ryan. *Dertli Sahiller: Şiddet, Etnisite ve Osmanlı İmparatorluğu'nun Sonu, 1912–1923*. Translated by Melike Neva Şellaki. İstanbul: Tarih Vakfı Yurt Yayınları, 2014.

Göçek, Fatma Müge. *Denial of Violence: Ottoman Past, Turkish Present, and Collective Violence against the Armenians (1789–2009)*. Oxford: Oxford University Press, 2015.

Goffman, Erving. "The Interaction Order." *American Sociological Review* 48, no. 1 (February 1983): 1–17.

Gökalp, Ziya. "Türkçülüğün Esasları." In *Kitaplar*. Vol. 1, edited by Şevket Beysanoğlu et al., 173–298. İstanbul: Yapı Kredi Yayınları, 2007.

————. "Türkleşmek, İslamlaşmak, Muasırlaşmak." In *Kitaplar*. Vol. 1, edited by Şevket Beysanoğlu et al., 45–88. İstanbul: Yapı Kredi Yayınları, 2007.

Gölbaşı, Edip. "1895–1896 Katliamları: Doğu Vilayetlerinde Cemaatler Arası 'Şiddet İklimi' ve Ermeni Karşıtı Ayaklanmalar." In Adanır and Özel, *1915*, 140–163.

————. "Hamidiye Alayları: Bir Değerlendirme." In Adanır and Özel, *1915*, 164–175.

Goloğlu, Mahmut. *Milli Mücadele Tarihi*, Vol. 1, *Erzurum Kongresi*. İstanbul: İş Bankası Kültür Yayınları, 2011.

————. *Milli Mücadele Tarihi*. Vol. 2, *Sivas Kongresi*. İstanbul: İş Bankası Kültür Yayınları, 2017.

Grigoriadis, İoannis N. *Instilling Religion in Greek and Turkish Nationalism: A "Sacred Synthesis."* New York: Palgrave Macmillan, 2013.

Güneş, Cengiz. *Kurdish National Movement in Turkey: From Protest to Resistance*. London: Routledge, 2012.

Hakan, Sinan. *Türkiye Kurulurken Kürtler (1916–1920)*. İstanbul: İletişim Yayınları, 2013.

Halaçoğlu, Ahmet. *Balkan Harbi Sırasında Rumeli'den Türk Göçleri (1912–1913)*. Ankara: Türk Tarih Kurumu, 1995.

Hall, Stuart. "Teaching Race." In *Selected Writings on Race and Difference*, edited by Paul Gilroy and Ruth W. Gilmore, 123–135. Durham, NC: Duke University Press, 2021.

Hanioğlu, Şükrü. *Atatürk: An Intellectual Biography*. Princeton, NJ: Princeton University Press, 2011.

————. *Bir Siyasal Düşünür Olarak Doktor Abdullah Cevdet ve Dönemi*. İstanbul: Üçdal Neşriyat, 1981.

————. *A Brief History of the Late Ottoman Empire*. Princeton, NJ: Princeton University Press, 2008.

————. *Preparation for a Revolution: The Young Turks, 1902–1909*. Oxford: Oxford University Press, 2001.

————. *The Young Turks in Opposition*. Oxford: Oxford University Press, 1995.

Hannoum, Abdelmajid. *Violent Modernity: France in Algeria*. Cambridge: Harvard University Press, 2010.

Harris, Cheryl I. "Whiteness as Property." *Harvard Law Review* 106, no. 8 (June 1993): 1707–1791.

Hartigan Jr., John. "Establishing the Fact of Whiteness." *American Anthropologist* 99, no. 3 (September 1997): 495–505.

Hartman, Andrew. "The Rise and Fall of Whiteness Studies." *Race and Class* 46, no. 2 (October 2004): 22–38.

Hechter, Michael. *Internal Colonialism: The Celtic Fringe in British National Development, 1536–1966*. Berkeley: University of California Press, 1975.

Hobbes, Thomas. *Leviathan*. New York: Oxford University Press, 1998.

Hobbs, Allyson. *A Chosen Exile: A History of Racial Passing in American Life*. Cambridge: Harvard University Press, 2014.

Hobsbawm, Eric. *Nations and Nationalism since 1780: Programme, Myth, Reality*. Cambridge: Cambridge University Press, 1992.

Ignatiev, Noel. "Treason to Whiteness Is Loyalty to Humanity." In *Critical White Studies: Looking behind the Mirror*, edited by Richard Delgado and Jean Stefancic, 607–612. Philadelphia: Temple University Press, 1997.

İleri, Celal Nuri. *Devlet ve Meclis Hakkında Musahabeler*. İstanbul: Emre Yayınları, 2007.

İpek, Nedim. *Rumeli'den Anadolu'ya Türk Göçleri (1877–1890)*. Ankara: Türk Tarih Kurumu, 1999.

İzrail, Nesim Ovadya. *24 Nisan 1915: İstanbul, Çankırı, Ayaş, Ankara*. İstanbul: İletişim Yayınları, 2013.

Jongerden, Joost. "Diyarbekir'de Seçkinlerin Şiddete Dayalı Karşılaşmaları: Milli İbrahim Paşa, Ziya Gökalp ve 20. Yüzyıl Başında Siyasal Mücadele." In *Diyarbekir'de Toplumsal İlişkiler (1870–1915)*, edited by J. Jongerden and J. Verheij, 57–85. İstanbul: İstanbul Bilgi Üniversitesi Yayınları, 2015.

Jongerden, Joost, and Ahmet Hamdi Akkaya. *PKK Üzerine Yazılar*. Translated by Metin Çulhaoğlu. İstanbul: Vate Yayınevi, 2012.

Jongerden, Joost, Ahmet Hamdi Akkaya, and Bahar Şimşek, eds. *İsyandan İnşaya: Kürdistan Özgürlük Hareketi*. Ankara: Dipnot Yayınları, 2015.

Joseph, Gloria. "The Incompatible Ménage à Trois: Marxism, Feminism, and Racism." In *Women and Revolution: A Discussion of the Unhappy Marriage of Marxism and Feminism*, edited by Lydia Sargent, 91–107. Montreal: Black Rose Books, 1981.

Jupp, James C., and Pauli Badenhorst. "Second-Wave Critical White Studies." In *Encyclopedia of Critical Whiteness Studies in Education*, edited by Zachary A. Casey, 596–608. Leiden: Brill, 2021.

Jwaideh, Wadie. *Kürt Milliyetçiliğinin Tarihi: Kökenleri ve Gelişimi*. Translated by İsmail Çekem and Alper Duman. İstanbul: İletişim Yayınları, 2009.

Kaiser, Hilmar. *The Extermination of Armenians in the Diarbekir Region*. İstanbul: İstanbul Bilgi University Press, 2014.

Kaplan, İsmail. *Türkiye'de Milli Eğitim İdeolojisi ve Siyasal Toplumsallaşma Üzerindeki Etkisi*. İstanbul: İletişim Yayınları, 2011.

Kara, Ayhan. *Türkiye'de Çerkezler: Diasporada Geleneğin Yeniden İcadı*. İstanbul: İstanbul Bilgi Üniversitesi Yayınları, 2011.

Karal, Enver Ziya. "Gülhane Hatt-ı Hümayunu'nda Batı'nın Etkisi." In *Tanzimat: Değişim Sürecinde Osmanlı İmparatorluğu*, edited by Halil İnalcık and Mehmet Seyitdanlıoğlu, 65–82. Ankara: Phoenix Yayınları, 2006.

———. "Önsöz." In Akçura, *Üç Tarz-ı Siyaset*, 1–18.

———. *Osmanlı Tarihi*. Vol. 8. Ankara: Türk Tarih Kurumu Basımevi, 1995.

Karaman, Hayrettin. "Meşru ve makul olmayan bağımsızlık (2)." *Yenişafak*, October 12, 2017.

Karpat, Kemal. *Osmanlı Nüfusu (1830–1914): Demografik ve Sosyal Özellikleri*. İstanbul: Tarih Vakfı Yurt Yayınları, 2003.

———. *The Politicization of Islam: Reconstructing Identity, State, Faith, and Community in the Late Ottoman State*. Oxford: Oxford University Press, 2001.

Kaya, Ramazan. "Kürdistan'da Fanon Etkisi." *Kürd Araştırmaları Dergisi*, no. 2 (February 2020): 18–30.

Kaynar, Reşat. *Mustafa Reşit Paşa ve Tanzimat*. Ankara: Türk Tarih Kurumu Basımevi, 1985.

Kaypakkaya, İbrahim. *Bütün Eserleri*. İstanbul: Umut Yayıncılık, 2013.

Keneş, Hatice Çoban. *Yeni Irkçılığın "Kirli" Ötekileri: Kürtler, Aleviler, Ermeniler*. Ankara: Dipnot Yayınları, 2015.

Kentel, Ferhat, Meltem Ahıska, and Fırat Genç. *"Milletin Bölünmez Bütünlüğü": Demo-kratikleşme Sürecinde Parçalayan Milliyetçilik(ler)*. İstanbul: TESEV Yayınları, 2009.

Kévorkian, Raymond. *The Armenian Genocide: A Complete History*. New York: I. B. Tauris, 2011.

———. *Ermeni Soykırımı*. Translated by Ayşen Taşkent Ekmekci. İstanbul: İletişim Yayınları, 2015.

Kévorkian, Raymond, and Paul B. Paboudjian. *1915 Öncesinde Osmanlı İmparatorluğu'nda Ermeniler*. İstanbul: Aras Yayıncılık, 2013.

Keyder, Çağlar. *Memâlik-i Osmaniye'den Avrupa Birliği'ne*. İstanbul: İletişim Yayınları, 2007.

———. *State and Class in Turkey: A Study in Capitalist Development*. London: Verso, 1987.

Kieser, Hans-Lukas. *Iskalanmış Barış: Doğu Vilayetleri'nde Misyonerlik, Etnik Kimlik ve Devlet (1839–1938)*. Translated by Attila Dirim. İstanbul: İletişim Yayınları, 2013.

Kili, Suna, and Şeref Gözübüyük. *Türk Anayasa Metinleri (Sened-i İttifaktan Günümüze)*. İstanbul: Türkiye İş Bankası Kültür Yayınları, 2000.

Kılıç, Mustafa, ed. *Türk Sorunu*. İstanbul: Profil Yayıncılık, 2013.

Kılıçarslan, İsmail. "Türk Olduğum İçin Özür Dilemeyeceğim." *Yenişafak*, September 26, 2017.

Kılıçdağı, Ohannes. "Ermeni Toplumu ve Meşrutiyet: Umut ve Umutsuzluk Arasında Yükselen Beklentiler." In Adanır and Özel, *1915*, 264–276.

Kimmel, Michael S., and Abby L. Ferber, eds. *Privilege: A Reader*. Boulder: Westview, 2014.

King, Deborah. "Multiple Jeopardy, Multiple Consciousness: The Context of a Black Feminist Ideology." *Signs* 14, no. 1 (Autumn 1988): 42–72.

Kirişçi, Kemal, and Gareth M. Winrow. *The Kurdish Question and Turkey: An Example of a Trans-State Conflict.* London: Routledge, 2004.

Kırmızı, Abdülhamit. "Feelings of Gratitude: Muslim Rescuers of Armenians in Adana 1909." In *History from Below: A Tribute in Memory of Donald Quataert,* edited by Selim Karahasanoğlu and Deniz Cenk Demir, 643–660. İstanbul: İstanbul Bilgi University Press, 2016.

Klein, Janet. *The Margins of Empire: Kurdish Militias in the Ottoman Tribal Zone.* Stanford, CA: Stanford University Press, 2011.

Kocabaşoğlu, Uygur, Güven Sak, Sinan Sönmez, Funda Erkal, Özgür Gökmen, Nesim Şeker, and Murat Uluğtekin. *Türkiye İş Bankası Tarihi.* İstanbul: Türkiye İş Bankası Kültür Yayınları, 2001.

Koçoğlu, Yahya. *Azınlık Gençleri Anlatıyor.* İstanbul: Metis Yayınları, 2004.

———. *Hatırlıyorum: Türkiye'de Gayrimüslim Hayatlar.* İstanbul: Metis Yayınları, 2008.

Kohn, Margaret. "Empire's Law: Alexis de Tocqueville on Colonialism and the State of Exception." *Canadian Journal of Political Science* 41, no. 2 (June 2008): 255–278.

Kohn, Margaret, and Keally McBride. *Political Theories of Decolonization: Postcolonialism and the Problem of Foundations.* New York: Oxford University Press, 2011.

Kolluoğlu, Biray. "Excesses of Nationalism: Greco-Turkish Population Exchange." *Nations and Nationalism* 19, no. 3 (2013): 532–550.

Koptaş, Rober. "Yandı Bitti Kül Oldu." *T24,* April 3, 2017.

Koyuncu, Büke. *"Benim Milletim . . .": AK Parti İktidarı, Din ve Ulusal Kimlik.* İstanbul: İletişim Yayınları, 2014.

Kuban, Doğan. "Ben Neden Türk'üm." *Cumhuriyet Bilim Teknik,* no. 1389 (November 1, 2013).

———. "Bir Toplumsal Varlık ve Kimlik Sorunu: Türk Olmak." *Cumhuriyet Bilim Teknik,* no. 1446 (December 5, 2014).

Küçük, Bülent. "Yerelleşmenin ve Evrenselleşmenih Ötesinde Kürt Sorununu Yeniden Düşünmek." *Mülkiye Dergisi* 39, no. 2 (2015): 62–84.

Kumar, Krishan. "Empires and Nations: Convergence or Divergence?" In *Sociology and Empire: The Imperial Entanglements of a Discipline,* edited by George Steinmetz, 279–299. Durham, NC: Duke University Press, 2013.

———. "Nation-States as Empires, Empires as Nation-States: Two Principles, One Practice?" *Theory and Society* 39, no. 2 (March 2010): 119–143.

Kuran, Ahmet Bedevi. *İnkılap Tarihimiz ve Jön Türkler.* İstanbul: Kaynak Yayınları, 2000.

Kurt, Ümit. *"Türk'ün Büyük, Biçare Irkı": Türk Yurdu'nda Milliyetçiliğin Esasları (1911–1916).* İstanbul, İletişim Yayınları, 2012.

Kuruç, Bilsay. *Mustafa Kemal Döneminde Ekonomi.* İstanbul: Bilgi Yayınevi, 1987.

Laçiner, Ömer. "Kimlikçilik Gericiliktir." In *Zehir ve Panzehir, Kürt Sorunu: Faşizmin Şartı Kaç?* edited by İrfan Aktan, 211–225. Ankara: Dipnot Yayınları, 2006.

———. "Sola Düşen Süreci Desteklemek." *Yenişafak,* April 22, 2013.

Lamprou, Alexandros. *Nation-Building in Modern Turkey: The "People's Houses," the State and the Citizen.* London: I. B. Tauris, 2015.

Landau, Jacob M. *Tekinalp: Bir Türk Yurtseveri (1883–1961).* İstanbul: İletişim Yayınları, 1996.

Levi, Avner. *Türkiye Cumhuriyeti'nde Yahudiler: Hukuki ve Siyasi Durumları.* Edited by Rıfat Bali. İstanbul: İletişim Yayınları, 2010.

Lipsitz, George. *The Possessive Investment in Whiteness: How White People Profit from Identity Politics.* Philadelphia: Temple University Press, 2006.

Locke, John. *Two Treatises of Government.* Cambridge: Cambridge University Press, 1988.

Loveman, Mara. "Is 'Race' Essential?" *American Sociological Review* 64, no. 6 (December 1999): 891–898.

Lowe, Lisa. *The Intimacies of Four Continents.* Durham, NC: Duke University Press, 2015.

Maksudyan, Nazan. *Türklüğü Ölçmek: Bilimkurgusal Antropoloji ve Türk Milliyetçiliğinin Irkçı Çehresi (1925–1929).* İstanbul: Metis Yayınları, 2007.

Malesevic, Sinisa. "Empires and Nation-States: Beyond the Dichotomy." *Thesis Eleven* 139, no. 1 (2017): 3–10.

Malmîsanij, M. "Anti-Kürdolojiden Kürdolojiye Giden Yol ve İsmail Beşikçi." In *İsmail Beşikçi,* edited by Barış Ünlü and Ozan Değer, 65–85. İstanbul: İletişim Yayınları, 2011.

Mamdani, Mahmood. *Neither Settler nor Native: The Making and Unmaking of Permanent Minorities.* Cambridge: Harvard University Press, 2020.

Maraşlı, Recep. "Rizgarî'nin Sosyalist Hareket ve Kürdistan Ulusal Kurtuluş Mücadelesindeki Yeri Üzerine Bir Deneme." *Mesafe,* no. 4 (2010): 68–93.

Mardin, Şerif. *Jön Türklerin Siyasi Fikirleri (1895–1908).* İstanbul: İletişim Yayınları, 2000.

———. "Osmanlı Bakış Açısından Hürriyet." In *Türk Modernleşmesi, Makaleler 4,* edited by Mümtaz'er Türköne and Tuncay Önder, 103–122. İstanbul: İletişim Yayınları, 1992.

———. *Yeni Osmanlı Düşüncesinin Doğuşu.* Translated by Mümtaz'er Türköne, Fahri Unan, and İrfan Erdoğan. İstanbul: İletişim Yayınları, 1998.

Matsuda, Mari J. "Beside My Sister, Facing the Enemy: Legal Theory out of Coalition." *Stanford Law Review* 43, no. 6 (July 1991): 1183–1192.

Maurice, Frederick. *The Armistices of 1918.* New York: Oxford University Press, 1943.

Mbembe, Achille. *Necro-Politics.* Translated by Steven Corcoran. Durham, NC: Duke University Press, 2019.

———. *On the Postcolony.* Berkeley: University of California Press, 2001.

McCarthy, Justin. *Ölüm ve Sürgün: Osmanlı Müslümanlarının Etnik Kıyımı (1821–1922).* Translated by Fatma Sarıkaya. Ankara: Türk Tarih Kurumu Yayınları, 2012.

McIntosh, Peggy. "White Privilege and Male Privilege: A Personal Account of Coming to See Correspondences through Work in Women's Studies." Working Paper no. 189, Wellesley College, Center for Research on Women, 1988.

McMeekin, Sean. *The Russian Origins of the First World War.* Cambridge: Harvard University Press, 2013.

Meray, Seha L., and Osman Olcay. *Osmanlı İmparatorluğu Çöküş Belgeleri (Mondros Bırakışması, Sevr Andlaşması, İlgili Belgeler).* Ankara: AÜSBF Yayınları, 1977.

Mignolo, Walter D. *The Darker Side of Western Modernity: Global Futures, Decolonial Options.* Durham, NC: Duke University Press, 2011.

"Milliyetçiliğin 'Doğrusu' Yoktur." *Cumhuriyet,* August 8, 1991.

Mills, Charles W. *Blackness Visible: Essays on Philosophy and Race.* Ithaca: Cornell University Press, 1998.

———. *The Racial Contract.* Ithaca: Cornell University Press, 1997.

———. "White Ignorance." In *Race and Epistemologies of Ignorance,* edited by S. Sullivan and N. Tauna, 13–38. Albany: State University of New York Press, 2007.

Mills, C. Wright. *The Sociological Imagination.* Oxford: Oxford University Press, 2000.

Miroğlu, Orhan. "'Türkiyelileşmek' Anadolu'dan Geçer." *Star*, July 24, 2014.

Molinas, Ivo, "No Moz Karışayamoz a la Eços del Hükümet." *Agos*, February 13, 2015.

More, Joan W. "Colonialism: The Case of the Mexican Americans." *Social Problems* 17, no. 4 (Spring 1970): 463–472.

Morrison, Toni. *Playing in the Dark: Whiteness and the Literary Imagination*. New York: Vintage Books, 1993.

Naimark, Norman M. "Preface." In *A Question of Genocide: Armenians and Turks at the End of the Ottoman Empire*, edited by der. R. G. Suny, F. M. Göçek, and N. M. Naimark, xii–xix. Oxford: Oxford University Press, 2011.

Nash, Jennifer C. *Black Feminism Reimagined: After Intersectionality*. Durham, NC: Duke University Press, 2019.

Neyzi, Leyla, and Haydar Darıcı. *Diyarbakırlı ve Muğlalı Gençler Anlatıyor: "Özgürüm ama Mecburiyet Var."* İstanbul: İletişim Yayınları, 2013.

Öcalan, Abdullah. *Demokratik Uygarlık Manifestosu*. Vol. 5, *Kürt Sorunu ve Demokratik Ulus Çözümü (Kültürel Soykırım Kıskacında Kürtleri Savunmak)*. İstanbul: Ararat Yayınları, 2012.

———. "Kürdistan Devriminin Yolu." In *Kürdistan Sosyalist Solu Kitabı: 60'lardan 2000'lere Seçme Metinler*, edited by Emir Ali Türkmen and Abdurrahim Özmen, 445–528. Ankara: Dipnot Yayınları, 2014.

Ökçün, Gündüz. *Türkiye İktisat Kongresi, 1923-İzmir: Haberler-Belgeler-Yorumlar*. Ankara: AÜSBF Yayınları, 1981.

Öksüz, İskender. *Türk'üm Özür Dilerim*. Ankara: Panama Yayın, 2016.

Olson, Robert. *The Emergence of Founding Nationalism and the Sheikh Said Rebellion, 1880–1925*. Austin: University of Texas Press, 1989.

Onaran, Nevzat. *Osmanlı'da Ermeni ve Rum Mallarının Türkleştirilmesi (1914–1919): Emvâl-i Metrûkenin Tasfiyesi*. Vol. 1. İstanbul: Evrensel Basım Yayın, 2013.

———. *Osmanlı'da Ermeni ve Rum Mallarının Türkleştirilmesi (1920–1930): Emvâl-i Metrûkenin Tasfiyesi*. Vol. 2. İstanbul: Evrensel Basım Yayın, 2013.

Oran, Baskın. "İsmail Beşikçi ve Mülkiye: Fevkalade Özel bir Mülkiyeliyle Söyleşi." In *İsmail Beşikçi*, edited by Barış Ünlü and Ozan Değer, 301–313. İstanbul: İletişim Yayınları, 2011.

Ortaylı, İlber. "İlk Osmanlı Parlamentosu ve Osmanlı Milletlerinin Temsili." In *Armağan: Kanun-u Esasi'nin 100. Yılı*, edited by Bahri Savcı, 169–183. Ankara: AÜSBF Yayınları, 1978.

———. *İmparatorluğun En Uzun Yüzyılı*. İstanbul: İletişim Yayınları, 2000.

———. "Türkiyeli diye bir şey yoktur, Türk Türk'tür." *Sözcü*, April 20, 2015.

———. "Türkiyelilik." *Milliyet Pazar*, April 5, 2015.

Özatalay, Cem. "Purge, Exile, and Resistance: Rethinking the Conflict of the Faculties through the Case of Academics for Peace in Turkey." *European Journal of Turkish Studies*, no. 30 (2020): 1–46.

Özbudun, Ergun. *1924 Anayasası*. İstanbul: İstanbul Bilgi Üniversitesi Yayınları, 2012.

Özdağ, Ümit. *Türk Sorunu*. Ankara: Kripto Yayıncılık, 2017.

Özdemir, Seçkin Sertdemir, Nil Mutluer, and Esra Özyürek. "Exile and Plurality in Neoliberal Times: Turkey's Academics for Peace," *Public Culture* 31, no. 2 (2019): 235–259.

Özdoğan, Günay Göksu, Füsun Üstel, Karin Karakaşlı, and Ferhat Kentel. *Türkiye'de Ermeniler: Cemaat-Birey-Yurttaş*. İstanbul: İstanbul Bilgi Üniversitesi Yayınları, 2009.

Özel, Oktay. "Tehcir ve Teşkilat-ı Mahsusa." In Adanır and Özel, *1915*, 377–407.

Özoğlu, Hakan. *Osmanlı Devleti ve Kürt Milliyetçiliği*. Translated by Azat Zana Gündoğan. İstanbul: Kitap Yayınevi, 2005.

Öztan, Güven Gürkan, and Ömer Turan. "Türkiye'de Devlet Aklı ve 1915." *Toplum ve Bilim*, no. 132 (2015): 78–131.

Özyürek, Esra. *Nostalgia for the Modern: State Secularism and Everyday Politics in Turkey*. Durham, NC: Duke University Press, 2006.

Parla, Ayşe. *Precarious Hope: Migration and the Limits of Belonging in Turkey*. Stanford, CA: Stanford University Press, 2019.

Parla, Taha. *The Social and Political Thought of Ziya Gökalp, 1876–1914*. Leiden: E. J. Brill, 1985.

———. *Ziya Gökalp, Kemalizm ve Türkiye'de Korporatizm*. İstanbul: İletişim Yayınları, 2001.

Pateman, Carole. *The Sexual Contract*. Stanford, CA: Stanford University Press, 1988.

Pateman, Carole, and Charles W. Mills. *Contract and Domination*. Cambridge: Polity, 2007.

Petersen, Roger D. *Understanding Ethnic Violence: Fear, Hatred, and Resentment in Twentieth-Century Eastern Europe*. Cambridge: Cambridge University Press, 2002.

Quataert, Donald. "Clothing Laws, State, and Society in the Ottoman Empire (1720–1829)." *International Journal of Middle East Studies* 29, no. 3 (August 1997): 403–425.

Rae, Heather. *State Identities and the Homogenisation of Peoples*. Cambridge: Cambridge University Press, 2002.

Ramsaur, E. E. *Jön Türkler ve 1908 İhtilali*. Translated by Nuran Yavuz. İstanbul: Sander Yayınları, 1982.

Renan, Ernest. "What Is a Nation?" In *Becoming National: A Reader*, edited by Geoff Eley and Ronald Grigor Suny, 42–56. New York: Oxford University Press, 1996.

Reynolds, Michael A. *Shattering Empires: The Clash and Collapse of the Ottoman and Russian Empires, 1908–1918*. Cambridge: Cambridge University Press, 2011.

Ritter, Laurence, and Max Sivaslian. *Kılıç Artıkları: Türkiye'nin Gizli ve Müslümanlaşmış Ermenileri*. Translated by Alev Er. İstanbul: Hrant Dink Vakfı Yayınları, 2013.

Roediger, David R., ed. *Black on White: Black Writers on What It Means to Be White*. New York: Schocken, 1998.

———. *The Wages of Whiteness: Race and the Making of the American Working Class*. London: Verso, 2007.

———. *Working toward Whiteness: How America's Immigrants Became White*. New York: Basic, 2006.

Rousseau, Jean-Jacques. *Discourse on Political Economy and the Social Contract*. Translated by Christopher Betts. New York: Oxford University Press, 1999.

Sabahaddin, Prens. *Bütün Eserleri: Gönüllü Sürgünden Zorunlu Sürgüne*. Edited by Mehmet Ö. Alkan. İstanbul: Yapı Kredi Yayınları, 2007.

Sancar, Türkan Yalçın. *'Türklüğü, Cumhuriyeti, Meclisi, Hükümeti, Adliyeyi, Bakanlıkları, Devletin Askeri ve Emniyet Muhafaza Kuvvetlerini' Alenen Tahkir ve Tezyif Suçları (TCK.m.159/1- YTCK 301/1–2)*. Ankara: Seçkin Yayınları, 2006.

Saraçoğlu, Cenk. *Şehir, Orta Sınıf ve Kürtler: İnkâr'dan "Tanıyarak Dışlama"ya*. İstanbul: İletişim Yayınları, 2011.

Sargent, Lydia, ed. *Women and Revolution: A Discussion of the Unhappy Marriage of Marxism and Feminism*. Montreal: Black Rose Books, 1981.

Savran, Sungur. "Liberalizmin Doğrusu Yoktur." *Cumhuriyet*, August 23, 1991.

———. "Sınıf Mücadelesi Olarak Ermeni Soykırımı." *Devrimci Marksizm*, no. 23 (Spring 2015): 40–101.

Scott, James C. *Domination and the Arts of Resistance: Hidden Transcripts*. New Haven, CT: Yale University Press, 1990.

Şekeryan, Ari, ed. *1909 Adana Katliamı: Üç Rapor*. İstanbul: Aras Yayıncılık, 2015.

Serdar, Ayşe. "Etnik İlişkiler Bağlamında Lazlığın İnşası." *Toplum ve Kuram*, no. 11 (2016): 75–104.

———. "Strategies of Making and Unmaking Ethnic Boundaries: Evidence on the Laz of Turkey." *Ethnicities* 19, no. 2 (2019): 335–369.

Sever, Metin. *Kürt Sorunu: Aydınlarımız Ne Düşünüyor*. İstanbul: Cem Yayınevi, 1992.

Sevinç, Murat, and Dinçer Demirkent. *Kuruluşun İhmal Edilmiş İstisnası: 1921 Anayasası ve Tutanakları*. İstanbul: İletişim Yayınları, 2017.

Sharma, Nandita. *Home Rule: National Sovereignty and the Separation of Natives and Migrants*. Durham, NC: Duke University Press, 2020.

Smith, Anthony D. *Nationalism and Modernism*. London: Routledge, 2003.

———. "The Origins of Nations." In *Becoming National: A Reader*, edited by Geoff Eley and Ronald Grigor Suny, 106–130. New York: Oxford University Press, 1996.

Soileau, Dilek Kızıldağ. *Koçgiri İsyanı: Sosyo-Tarihsel Bir Analiz*. İstanbul: İletişim Yayınları, 2017.

Somel, Selçuk Akşin. "Osmanlı Reform Çağında Osmanlıcılık Düşüncesi (1839–1913)." In *Modern Türkiye'de Siyasi Düşünce*. Vol. 1, *Tanzimat ve Meşrutiyet Birikimi*, edited by Mehmet Ö. Alkan, 89–116. İstanbul: İletişim Yayınları, 2002.

Sönmez, Erdem. *Ahmed Rıza: Bir Jön Türk Liderinin Siyasi-Entelektüel Portresi*. İstanbul: Tarih Vakfı Yurt Yayınları, 2012.

Steinmetz, George, ed. *Sociology and Empire: The Imperial Entanglements of a Discipline*. Durham, NC: Duke University Press, 2013.

Steyn, Melissa. "Feeling White." In *Unveiling Whiteness in the Twenty-First Century: Global Manifestations, Transdisciplinary Interventions*, edited by Veronica Watson, Deirde Howard-Wagner, and Lisa Spanierman, 3–8. Lanham, MD: Lexington Books, 2015.

———. "The Ignorance Contract: Recollections of Apartheid Childhoods and the Construction of Epistemologies of Ignorance." *Identities: Global Studies in Culture and Power* 19, no. 1 (January 2012): 8–25.

———. "Whiteness Just Isn't What It Used to Be": White Identity in a Changing South Africa. Albany: State University of New York Press, 2001.

Stoler, Ann Laura. "Affective States." In *A Companion to the Anthropology of Politics*, edited by David Nugent and Joan Vincent, 4–20. Oxford: Blackwell, 2007.

Suciyan, Talin. "Dört Nesil: Kurtarılamayan Son." *Toplum ve Bilim*, no. 132 (2015): 132–149.

Sullivan, Shannon. *Revealing Whiteness: The Unconscious Habits of Racial Privilege*. Bloomington: Indiana University Press, 2006.

Suny, Ronald Grigor. "Writing Genocide: The Fate of the Ottoman Armenians." In *A Question of Genocide: Armenians and Turks at the End of the Ottoman Empire*, edited by R. G. Suny, F. M. Göçek, and N. M. Naimark, 15–41. Oxford: Oxford University Press, 2011.

Tanör, Bülent. *Osmanlı-Türk Anayasa Gelişmeleri (1789–1980)*. İstanbul: Yapı Kredi Yayınları, 1998.

————. *Türkiye'de Kongre İktidarları (1918–1920)*. İstanbul: Yapı Kredi Yayınları, 1998.

Tekinalp, Munis. *Türkleştirme*. Edited by Özer Ozankaya. Ankara: Kültür Bakanlığı Yayınları, 2001.

Toksöz, Meltem. "Çukurova'da Sosyoekonomik Dönüşüm ve 1909 Adana Katliamı." In Adanır and Özel, *1915*, 244–255.

Toprak, Zafer. *Türkiye'de "Milli İktisat" (1908–1918)*. Ankara: Yurt Yayınları, 1982.

Trouillot, Michel-Rolph. *Silencing the Past: Power and the Production of History*. Boston: Beacon, 1997.

Tunaya, Tarık Zafer. *Türkiye'de Siyasal Gelişmeler (1876–1938): Kanun-ı Esasi ve Meşrutiyet Dönemi*. İstanbul: İstanbul Bilgi Üniversitesi Yayınları, 2001.

————. *Türkiye'de Siyasal Partiler*. Vol. 1, *İkinci Meşrutiyet Dönemi*. İstanbul: İletişim Yayınları, 1998.

————. *Türkiye'de Siyasal Partiler*. Vol. 3, *İttihat ve Terakki: Bir Çağın, Bir Kuşağın, Bir Partinin Tarihi*. İstanbul: İletişim Yayınları, 2000.

Tunçay, Mete. *Türkiye Cumhuriyeti'nde Tek-Parti Yönetimi'nin Kurulması (1923–1931)*. İstanbul: Tarih Vakfı Yurt Yayınları, 1999.

Turan, Şerafettin. *Atatürk'ün Düşünce Yapısını Etkileyen Olaylar, Düşünürler, Kitaplar*. Ankara: Türk Tarih Kurumu, 2006.

Turgut, Serdar. "Beyaz Türklerin Demirtaş Sevgisi." *Haber Türk*, August 8, 2014.

————. "Türklüğün isyanı." *Akşam*, January 21, 2007.

Türker, Nurdan. *Vatanım Yok Memleketim Var. İstanbul Rumları: Mekân-Bellek-Ritüel*. İstanbul: İletişim Yayınları, 2015.

"Türkiye'de Ulusal Sorun Üzerine." *Kurtuluş Sosyalist Dergi*, no. 2 (July 1976): 24–61.

Türkmen, Emir Ali, and Ümit Özger, eds. *Türkiye Sosyalist Solu Kitabı 2: 70'lerden 80'lere Seçme Metinler*. Ankara: Dipnot Yayınları, 2014.

Türkmen, Emir Ali, and Abdurrahim Özmen, eds. *Kürdistan Sosyalist Solu Kitabı: 60'lardan 2000'lere Seçme Metinler*. Ankara: Dipnot Yayınları, 2014.

Türköne, Mümtaz'er. *Siyasi İdeoloji Olarak İslamcılığın Doğuşu*. İstanbul: İletişim Yayınları, 1991.

————, ed. *Türküm Vicdanlıyım: Kürt Sorunu ve Türk Aydını*. İstanbul: Ufuk Yayınları, 2012.

Türkyılmaz, Yektan. "Devrim İçinde Devrim: Ermeni Örgütleri ve İttihat-Terakki İlişkileri, 1908–1915." In Adanır and Özel, *1915*, 324–353.

Türkyılmaz, Zeynep. "Maternal Colonialism and Turkish Woman's Burden in Course: Educating the 'Mountain Flowers' of Dersim." *Journal of Women's History* 28, no. 3 (2016): 162–186.

Tutkal, Serhat. "Power, Knowledge, and Universities: Turkey's Dismissed 'Academics for Peace.'" *Critical Studies in Education* 63, no. 5 (2022): 639–654.

Tuzcuoğlu, Müge. *Ben Bir Taşım*. İstanbul: Evrensel Basım Yayın, 2012.

Twine, France Winddance, and Charles Gallagher. "The Future of Whiteness: A Map of the 'Third Wave.'" *Ethnic and Racial Studies* 31, no. 1 (January 2008): 4–24.

Twine, France Winddance, and Bradley Gardener, eds. *Geographies of Privilege*. New York: Routledge, 2013.

Uluğ, Naşit Hakkı. *Tunceli Medeniyete Açılıyor*. İstanbul: Kaynak Yayınları, 2007. Originally published in 1939 by Cumhuriyet Matbaası in İstanbul.

Üngör, Uğur Ümit. *The Making of Modern Turkey: Nation and State in Eastern Anatolia, 1913–1950*. Oxford: Oxford University Press, 2012.

Üngör, Uğur Ümit, and Mehmet Polatel. *Confiscation and Destruction: The Young Turk Seizure of Armenian Property.* New York: Continuum Books, 2011.

Ünlü, Barış. "İsmail Beşikçi Fenomeni: Bir *Parrhesiastes*'in Oluşumu." In *İsmail Beşikçi*, edited by Barış Ünlü and Ozan Değer, 11–44. İstanbul: İletişim Yayınları, 2011.

———. "The Kurdish Struggle and the Crisis of the Turkishness Contract." *Philosophy and Social Criticism* 42, nos. 4–5 (May–June 2016): 397–405.

———. "Türklüğün Kısa Tarihi." *Birikim*, no. 274 (February 2012): 23–34.

———. "Türklük Sözleşmesi'nin İmzalanışı (1915–1925)." *Mülkiye Dergisi* 38, no. 3 (2014): 47–81.

———. "Türklük Sözleşmesi ve Türk Solu." *Perspectives*, no. 3 (2013): 23–27.

———. "Türklük ve Beyazlık Krizleri: Türkiye ve Güney Afrika Üzerine Karşılaştırmalı Notlar." *Birikim*, nos. 289–290 (May–June 2013): 103–111.

Ünsaldı, Levent, and Ercan Geçgin. *Sosyoloji Tarihi: Dünya'da ve Türkiye'de.* Ankara: Heretik Yayınları, 2015.

Uras, Esat. *Tarihte Ermeniler ve Ermeni Meselesi.* İstanbul: Belge Yayınları, 1987.

Üstel, Füsun. *İmparatorluktan Ulus-Devlete Türk Milliyetçiliği: Türk Ocakları (1912–1931).* İstanbul: İletişim Yayınları, 1997.

———. *'Makbul Vatandaş'ın Peşinde: II. Meşrutiyet'ten Bugüne Vatandaşlık Eğitimi.* İstanbul: İletişim Yayınları, 2011.

Uyar, Hakkı. *"Sol Milliyetçi" Bir Türk Aydını: Mahmut Esat Bozkurt (1892–1943).* İstanbul: Büke Yayınları, 2000.

Uyurkulak, Murat. "Şişli'de Bir Apartman." *T24*, August 14, 2017.

Van Bruinessen, Martin. *Agha, Shaikh and State: The Social and Political Structures of Kurdistan.* London: Zed Books, 1992.

Vatansever, Aslı. "Partners in Crime: The Anti-Intellectual Complicity between the State and the Universities in Turkey." *Journal of Interrupted Studies*, no. 1 (2018): 3–25.

Vimalassery, Manu, Juliana Hu Pegues, and Alyosha Goldstein. "Introduction: On Colonial Unknowing," *Theory and Event* 19, no. 4 (2016). Available at https://muse.jhu.edu/article/633283.

Wallerstein, Immanuel. *After Liberalism.* New York: New Press, 1995.

———. *The End of the World as We Know It: Social Science for the Twenty-First Century.* Minneapolis: University of Minnesota Press, 1999.

———. *World-Systems Analysis: An Introduction.* Durham, NC: Duke University Press, 2004.

Weber, Eugen. *Peasants into Frenchmen: The Modernization of Rural France, 1870–1914.* Stanford, CA: Stanford University Press, 1976.

Wekker, Gloria. *White Innocence: Paradoxes of Colonialism and Race.* Durham, NC: Duke University Press, 2016.

West, Michael O. "Global Africa: The Emergence and Evolution of an Idea." *Review* 28, no. 1 (2005): 85–108.

White, Jenny. *Muslim Nationalism and the Turks.* Princeton, NJ: Princeton University Press, 2013.

Wiegman, Robyn. "Whiteness Studies and the Paradox of Particularity." *boundary 2* 26, no. 3 (Autumn 1999): 115–150.

Wimmer, Andreas. "Elementary Strategies of Ethnic Boundary Making." *Ethnic and Racial Studies* 31, no. 6 (September 2008): 1025–1055.

————. "The Making and Unmaking of Ethnic Boundaries: A Multilevel Process Theory." *American Journal of Sociology* 113, no. 4 (January 2008): 970–1022.

————. "Why Nationalism Works and Why It Isn't Going Away." *Foreign Affairs* 98, no. 2 (March–April 2019): 27–35.

Wittig, Monique. "On the Social Contract." In *The Straight Mind and Other Essays*, 33–45. Boston: Beacon, 1992.

Yalçın, Hüseyin Cahit. *Tanıdıklarım*. İstanbul: Yapı Kredi Yayınları, 2001.

Yeğen, Mesut. *Devlet Söyleminde Kürt Sorunu*. İstanbul: İletişim Yayınları, 2006.

————, ed. *İngiliz Belgelerinde Kürdistan (1918–1958)*. Ankara: Dipnot Yayınları, 2012.

————. *Müstakbel Türk'ten Sözde Vatandaşa: Cumhuriyet ve Kürtler*. İstanbul: İletişim Yayınları, 2014.

————. "Türkiye Solu ve Kürt Sorunu." *Modern Türkiye'de Siyasi Düşünce*. Vol. 8, *Sol*, edited by Murat Gültekingil, 1208–1236. İstanbul: İletişim Yayınları, 2007.

Yıldız, Ahmet. *Ne Mutlu Türküm Diyebilene: Türk Ulusal Kimliğinin Etno-Seküler Sınırları (1919–1938)*. İstanbul: İletişim Yayınları, 2013.

Yonucu, Deniz. "Sömürgeci Devletin Aydını ve Muhalif Olmak." *Birikim Güncel*, September 17, 2015.

Yücel, Müslüm. *Abdullah Öcalan: Amara'dan İmralı'ya*. İstanbul: Alfa Yayınları, 2014.

Zerubavel, Eviatar. *The Elephant in the Room: Silence and Denial in Everyday Life*. Oxford: Oxford University Press, 2007.

Zürcher, Erik Jan. *Milli Mücadele İttihatçılık*. Translated by Nüzhet Salihoğlu. İstanbul: Bağlam Yayıncılık, 1995.

————. *Political Opposition in the Early Turkish Republic: The Progressive Republican Party, 1924–1925*. Leiden: Brill, 1991.

Index

Abadan, Yavuz, 35
Abdülhamid II, 33, 40–57, 65–66, 69, 76
Abdullah Cevdet, 46, 50, 53, 78n121
Academics for Peace, 31, 175, 196–200
Adana Massacre, 54–55, 58, 66, 86
Adıvar, Halide Edip, 190–191
Ağrı Rebellion, 97–99, 157
Ahmed, Sara, 22
Ahmet Rıza, 46–47, 48n41, 49
Akçam, Taner, 120n17, 192
Akçura, Yusuf, 48, 59n70, 60, 70, 117
AKP (Justice and Development Party), 165, 167–175, 194–196, 201
Akşin, Sina, 169
Alevi, 3, 25n66, 44, 63, 68, 76, 81, 107, 143, 157
Ali Suavi, 39
ANC (African National Congress), 161n15
Anderson, Benedict, 90
Arendt, Hannah, 23n60, 207
Armenian Genocide, 32, 55, 65–76, 84, 195
Armistice of Mudros, 77–78
Atatürk, Mustafa Kemal, 79–81, 85n5, 86, 88, 100, 134, 159–160, 169–170, 172n44, 180, 194
Atsız, Nihal, 125n24
Avcıoğlu, Doğan, 180
Aybar, Mehmet Ali, 158

Bahaeddin Şakir, Dr., 49–50, 73, 77n118, 88
Baldwin, James, 6–8
Balkan Wars, 59–60, 66, 83
Bardakçı, Murat, 190–192
Başkaya, Fikret, 192
Beal, Frances M., 10
Beauvoir, Simone De, 2
Bernasconi, Robert, 167
Beşikçi, İsmail, 30, 137, 175–186, 198
Biko, Steve, 7–8
Bilici, Mücahit, 152n96
Black Consciousness, 7–8
Black Power, 6–8
Body, 2, 7, 22–24, 30, 102, 109–111, 113, 127–128, 131–132, 140–142, 154
Bora, Tanıl, 170
Boran, Behice, 159, 184
Bourdieu, Pierre, 27, 99, 104, 111n1, 113–114, 139, 168, 187, 199
Bozkurt, Mahmut Esat, 97–98, 105
Butler, Judith, 111n1

Cahen, Claude, 34n2
Carmichael, Stokely, 7
Çayan, Mahir, 160
Çetin, Fethiye, 129n37
CHP (Republican People's Party), 97, 103, 142, 168, 184, 198

Civil Rights Movement, 6
Colonial logic of power, 21–22, 204–207
Combahee River Collective, 9
Committee of Union and Progress, 46–76.
  See also Young Turks; Unionists
Contractual logic of power, 21–22, 201,
  204–207. See also colonial logic of power
CPSU (Communist Party of the Soviet
  Union), 161n15
Crenshaw, Kimberlé, 10–12
Critical race theory (CRT), 2, 4, 10–12, 17
Cultural revolution of 1968, 8–9, 12, 29,
  208

Danzikyan, Yetvart, 130n41
Dashnak Party, 43, 51–52, 57–58, 64, 68n87
Davutoğlu, Ahmet, 197
DDKO (Revolutionary Eastern Cultural
  Centers), 159
Demirel, Süleyman, 164
Demirkent, Dinçer, 81n134
Demirtaş, Selahattin, 173
Democratic Party, 158, 177
Dersim Operations and Massacre, 108–109,
  157, 193
Dev-Genç (Revolutionary Youth Federation
  of Turkey), 158
Dev-Yol (Revolutionary Path), 161–162
Dink, Hrant, 165–166, 193–195
Diran Kelekian, 49
Du Bois, W.E.B., 5, 139

Eastern Reform Plan, 95
Elias, Norbert, 116
Emval-i metruke, 70–71, 88
Enver Pasha, 50, 67, 73
Erbakan, Necmettin, 164
Erdoğan, Tayyip, 171, 197

Fanon, Frantz, 7, 22–23, 163
Feminism, 9–10, 13
Foucault, Michel, 205
Frankenberg, Ruth, 12–13
Franko, Marsel, 126

Galanti, Avram, 125
Gaze, 16, 23, 128, 156, 167
Gellner, Ernest, 90
Gerlach, Christian, 74
Gezmiş, Deniz, 160
Goffman, Erving, 131

Gökalp, Ziya, 59–61, 75, 89, 93, 101, 118,
  169
Gökçen, Sabiha, 193
Gül, Abdullah, 170, 195n94

Habitus, 15, 17, 26, 113–114, 176, 185
Haitian Revolution, 5
Hakan, Sinan, 80
Hall, Stuart, 23–24
Hamidiye regiments, 43–44, 56–58, 66,
  74–75
Hanioğlu, Şükrü, 37n13, 78n121
Harris, Cheryl, 14
Hazinses, Sami (Samuel Uluçyan), 129n36
HDP (Peoples' Democratic Party), 173–175,
  198
Hobbes, Thomas, 83, 96
Hobsbawm, Eric, 90
Hunchak Party, 43, 51–52, 58, 69n89
Hüseyin Pasha, 57

İbrahim Pasha, 75
İbrahim Temo, 46, 50, 53
Ignorance Contract, 114, 116, 120
İleri, Celal Nuri, 112
İnalcık, Halil, 170
Indifference Contract, 114–116, 120
İnönü, Erdal, 164
Interaction order, 131
Intersectionality, 3, 9–13, 16, 29
İshak Sukuti, 46
Islahat Edict, 36, 37, 39
Islamism, 28, 40, 54, 61–62, 119, 121, 169,
  171
İsmet Pasha (İnönü), 96, 98, 107n72
İzmir Economic Congress, 99–100

Joseph, Gloria, 9

Kaiser, Hilmar, 75
Kanun-u Esasi, 36
Karabekir, Kazım, 81
Karpat, Kemal, 41, 149n95
Kaya, Ayhan, 136
Kaya, Şükrü, 108
Kaypakkaya, İbrahim, 160
Kemalism, 28, 119, 159–163, 165, 177
Kemalists, 29, 62, 90, 169, 173
Keyder, Çağlar, 88n12
King, Deborah, 10
Kıray, Mübeccel, 181

Klein, Janet, 43
Koçgiri Rebellion, 81, 157
Koptaş, Rober, 133n51
Kuran, Ahmed Bedevi, 55
Kurtulmuş, Numan, 38
Kurtuluş (Liberation) movement, 162

Laçiner, Ömer, 188–189
Liberalism, 8, 17, 37, 49, 62–63, 72, 202
Lipsitz, George, 14
Locke, John, 93

Mahmud II, 34–35
Mahmut Şevket Pasha, 61–65
Malmîsanij, M., 117
Mamdani, Mahmood, 204, 207
Mardin, Şerif, 40n19
Marxism, 9, 28, 50, 72, 119, 121, 146, 159
Matsuda, Mari, 11
Mbembe, Achille, 205
McIntosh, Peggy, 12
Mehmed Reşid, 46, 75
Mehmet (Muhammed) Ali Pasha, 34
MHP (Nationalist Movement Party),
    169–170, 173–175
Midhat Pasha, 36, 40
Mills, Charles W., 15, 17–20, 23–24
Mills, C. Wright, 25
Mizancı Murat, 46, 50
Molinas, Ivo, 126n26
Morrison, Toni, 14

Nadi, Yunus, 125
Naimark, Norman M., 73
National contract, 21–25, 91, 103, 202–204,
    207
Nazım, Dr., 49–50, 56, 73

Öcalan, Abdullah, 152–153, 160n6, 163, 172
Öksüz, İskender, 170
Orhon, Orhan Seyfi, 125
Ortaylı, İlber, 170, 190, 192
Ottoman-Russian War of 1877–1878, 41, 59
Özal, Turgut, 164
Özdağ, Ümit, 170
Özgürlük Yolu (Freedom Path), 161

Parla, Taha, 118
Pateman, Carol, 24
Patriarch Mesrob II, 166
Peker, Sedat, 197

Petersen, Roger, 72
Phenomenology, 7, 17, 22
PKK (Partiya Karkerên Kurdistanê;
    Kurdistan Workers' Party), 153, 162–164,
    174, 187, 189
Population exchange, 87–90
Prince Sabahaddin, 47, 49–51, 53
Psychological wage, 5, 8, 105

Racial contract, 18, 23
The Racial Contract, 17
Renan, Ernest, 83–84
Rizgarî, 161, 182–183
Roediger, David, 13
Rousseau, Jean-Jacques, 20, 91–93

SACP (South African Communist Party),
    161n15
Sadak, Necmettin, 125
Sartre, Jean-Paul, 167
SBF (Faculty of Political Science), 177–178,
    182–183
Scott, James C., 27
Selim III, 34
Serdar, Ayşe, 136
The Sexual Contract, 24
Sheikh Said Rebellion, 94–97, 157, 165
Sheikh Ubeydullah Rebellion, 43
Smith, Anthony, 91
Social contract, 17–18, 20–21, 23–24, 29,
    32–33, 80, 85, 90n21, 91n25, 92–93, 202
Socialism, 50, 147–148, 159, 162, 177,
    182–183, 202
Soysal, Mümtaz, 169, 185
Steyn, Melissa, 155
Structural racism, 2–4, 7, 17, 96

Tankut, Hasan Reşit, 68
Tanör, Bülent, 35
Tanrıöver, Hamdullah Suphi, 59, 89
Tanzimat Edict, 35–37, 39
Tekinalp, Moiz Kohen, 60, 124
Teşkilat-ı Mahsusa, 63, 69, 76
TİP (Workers' Party of Turkey), 158–159,
    179
TKP (Communist Party of Turkey), 161
Treaty of Berlin, 42–43
Treaty of Lausanne, 79, 85, 87
Treaty of Sèvres, 81
Tunalı Hilmi, 48
Türkdoğan, Orhan, 179

Turkism, 2, 48–51, 59–60, 96, 128, 151, 169,
172, 180, 183
Türköne, Mümtaz'er, 188–189

Unionists, 33, 46, 50–52, 54–55, 57–59,
61–68, 72, 78, 88. *See also* Young Turks;
Committee of Union and Progress
Uşşak, Cemal, 188–189
Uybadin, Cemil, 95

War of Independence, 32, 77–83, 89–90, 94,
100, 172
Weber, Eugen, 204–205
Weber, Max, 99
Whiteness Studies, 4, 12–13, 16–17

Wimmer, Andreas, 203, 207
World War I, 63, 67–68, 74–75, 80, 82
Wright, Richard, 6

Yalçın, Hüseyin Cahit, 77
Yeğen, Mesut, 87, 120n18
Young Ottomans, 39–40, 46
Young Turks, 43, 46–52, 56–57. *See also*
Unionists; Committee of Union and
Progress

Zana, Mehdi, 182
Zarakolu, Ayşe, 192n86
Zarakolu, Ragıp, 192n86
Ziya Pasha, 39

Barış Ünlü is Assistant Professor, General Faculty, in the Department of Sociology at the University of Virginia.

www.ingramcontent.com/pod-product-compliance
Lightning Source LLC
Chambersburg PA
CBHW030647270326
41929CB00007B/246